EXPERT SYSTEMS

EXPERT SYSTEMS

Artificial Intelligence in Business

PAUL HARMON AND DAVID KING

A WILEY PRESS BOOK

JOHN WILEY & SONS, INC.

New York • Chichester • Brisbane • Toronto • Singapore

Publisher: Judy V. Wilson
Editor: Theron Shreve
Managing Editor: Katherine Schowalter
Composition, Design, & Make-Up: Ganis & Harris, Inc.
Illustrations: Don Sherefkin

*Transcripts of the interaction with MYCIN were produced by
the authors using the facilities of SUMEX-AIM. SUMEX-
AIM is the Stanford University Medical EXperimental computer exploring Artificial Intelligence applications in Medicine. The
assistance of Edward H. Shortliffe and Miriam Bischoff is
appreciated.*

Library of Congress Cataloging in Publication Data

Harmon, Paul.
    Expert systems.

    Bibliography: p.
    Includes index.
      1. Expert systems (Computer science) 2. Artificial
intelligence. 3. Business—Data processing. I. King,
David, 1949-   . II. Title.
QA76.9.E96H37 1985   001.53'5   84-27148
ISBN 0-471-81554-3
ISBN 0-471-80824-5 (pbk.)

Printed in the United States of America

85 86 10 9 8 7 6 5 4 3 2 1

To
Denny Brown and Steven Hardy

Photo and Figure Credits

Contents

Foreword

Everyone in business, from trainer to chief executive officer, must daily face problem solving and decision making based on extensive but incomplete, uncertain, and even contradictory data and knowledge. Up until now, the conventional use of the computer has filled rooms with printouts without being of much assistance in these areas. This state of affairs is largely due to a literal-minded approach to the computer.

Well, help is on the way. Paul Harmon and David King have created a fine introduction to the design and use of the expert systems that enlist the computer in a healthy and powerful way to solve the difficult and important problems of business.

"Artificial intelligence" has a forbidding and threatening ring to most of us. The words suggest supplanting, rather than supplementing, and denying, rather than extending, our human capabilities to set goals and directions. But this area of computer science has now fathered the creation of expert systems (also called knowledge systems), and these new systems promise to harvest the remarkable developments of computer science and computers to make all of us more effective.

Furthermore, as this book teaches us, expert systems can be developed that factor experience into decision making in a fashion that is friendly as well as powerful and that gives us comfort and confidence in our actions. A proper expert system can be far more useful and reliable than any expert information source otherwise available to us. Expert systems do not tire or become cranky; they do not bluff but instead tell us the limitation of their knowledge and estimate the uncertainty of their conclusions; they process and distill the experience of many experts and apply it to our problem without bias; they tell us upon our demand what assumptions they are making and

what their line of reasoning is; in short, they add breadth and depth to our reasoning and decision processes.

The authors here introduce us to expert systems over the whole range, from the simpler here-and-now training exercises to prospective systems that will aid the very top levels of a large corporation. They show us how to get started by adopting a limited system for a confined task and observing its costs, its benefits, and how it changes the way we view our tasks and the use of experts. They make a compelling case that the time is ripe to invest in the experience that we shall soon need to move promptly as ever more capable expert systems are developed.

As this development occurs, we shall be applying this experience as we interact with our own experts, with the knowledge engineers who create the expert systems, and with the vendors of tools and systems. This book provides the knowledge that will be indispensable as we decide how and where to start, how to assess the claims and the performance of people and vendors, and how fast to move. There is a great deal of push from the computer scientists, engineers, and ambitious corporations to develop systems rapidly; this book educates us so that we can decide how rapidly to pull expert systems into our businesses.

It is early yet to estimate the magnitude of the contribution expert systems will make to the extension of human capability and to our effectiveness as managers, and it would be more than a little reckless to rank it now along with steam power and electricity. But the contribution will be in that class and will be indeed profound. With the help of this book we can now move into this new world.

Robert L. Sproull

Preface

Suddenly everyone is talking about artificial intelligence and expert systems. Those who come in contact with the basic ideas behind expert systems immediately begin thinking of ways to improve business by applying this new computer technology to solve some of the persistent and difficult problems they face.

We first became excited about expert systems in 1983. One of us is a psychologist and the other a management consultant who specializes in helping corporations solve human performance problems. We've worked on several projects together, and in early 1983 we found ourselves engaged in helping a new expert systems company develop workshops to explain its technology to businesspeople. The more we've learned about expert systems, the more we have become convinced that expert systems will, in fact, change the way businesses operate. Moreover, expert systems will change the way people think about solving a vast array of different problems.

We have consulted with many large corporations and several small businesses. In each case, we worked with a client to help solve some practical business problems. Occasionally, we encountered problems that simply could not be solved with existing technologies. More often, we have faced problems that were so difficult or complex that they could only be partially solved. As we learned about expert systems, we realized that this new technology will make it possible to develop quick, pragmatic solutions to a wide range of problems that currently defy effective solutions.

We have written this book for executives, middle managers, computer systems personnel, and corporate trainers. We are convinced that each of these groups of people needs to know about expert systems. In order to address such a diverse audience, we have included some material that will be of interest to one group and not the other. We have avoided unnecessary computer and business jargon. Where we introduce technical terms we define them with clear, nontechnical examples.

The following suggestions should help you maximize the useful information that you gain from this book.

Everyone should read Chapter 1. It provides a general introduction to the subject and defines key terms.

If you are an executive or a middle-level manager, you should probably skip to Section Four and review how expert systems are likely to be used in the near future. Then, depending on how much depth you want, you can look at Section Three for some ideas on the steps involved in actually developing a system, or at Section Two for information on the costs involved in purchasing system building tools or for examples of systems that have already been built.

If you are involved in computer systems development or implementation, you will probably want to read the chapters in the order in which they are presented. If you already know about the theoretical underpinnings of AI and expert systems, you might skip Section One and only return to it after you have looked at Section Two. Our reference list, explained below, will be especially useful in locating primary sources.

If you are involved in training or are particularly interested in applying expert systems to the practical problems of improving employee productivity, we recommend that you read Chapters 3, 7, 8, 11, and then Section Four. This route through the book emphasizes the development of "small knowledge systems." After taking this path you will probably want to go back and read Section One more carefully, but that is something you can decide a little later.

The book does develop concepts in a systematic manner and thus, if you skip around, you may encounter terms that you don't know. We have included a glossary as Appendix A that should help readers who choose an unconventional route.

To make the book flow as smoothly as possible, we have avoided footnotes and references. Annotated citations are collected in Appendix C. Information about companies is located in Appendix B. We have limited our references to commonly available books or magazine articles. This is consistent with our goal of providing a broad overview of expert systems and their business applications. For readers needing more technical depth, we identify books in our reference list that provide citations to the extensive technical and scholarly literature of artificial intelligence.

Our understanding of applied artificial intelligence has been shaped by a number of people. Our professional and academic interests in cognitive science provided the foundation. Our first professional contact with expert systems occurred when we assisted Teknowledge Inc. with the development of training programs. Many people at Teknowledge have given us advice and shared their ideas with us, and we gratefully acknowledge their influence.

We have talked to many other people—more than we can list—who have helped us to clarify our ideas. A few individuals stand out and we'd like to acknowledge them: Thomas F. Gilbert, Frederick Hayes-Roth, Cliff Hollander, Peter E. Hart, Tom Kehler, Claudia Mazzetti, and Karl M. Wiig.

We also thank James Eilers, who helped prepare the manuscript and graphics for the book, and Theron R. Shreve and the many other helpful people at John Wiley & Sons. Finally, of course, we must express our appreciation to our families for tolerating our obsession with this project.

Paul Harmon
David King

1.

Introduction

This book is about expert systems and how they will change the world of business. In the next 10 years, the concepts and techniques described in this book will revolutionize what we do with computers. Some computers will still process data, crunch numbers, and perform all the tasks we expect computers to handle today. New software and new computers, however, will soon be available.

Since World War II, computer scientists have tried to develop techniques that would allow computers to act more like humans. The entire research effort, including decision-making systems, robotic devices, and various approaches to computer speech, is usually called artificial intelligence (AI). Most AI efforts remain in the research labs. A collection of AI techniques that enables computers to assist people in analyzing problems and making decisions, called knowledge-based expert systems, however, has recently proved its value, and numerous commercial applications are now underway. Expert systems are being developed to assist managers with complex planning and scheduling tasks, diagnose diseases, locate mineral deposits, configure complex computer hardware, and aid mechanics in troubleshooting locomotive problems.

As recently as 1980, expert systems research was still confined to a few university research laboratories. Today, the United States, Japan, England, and the European Economic Community are all in the process of launching major research programs to develop and implement expert systems in the near future. Many Fortune 500 corporations are assembling AI departments, venture capitalists are rushing to invest in entrepreneurial expert systems companies, and expert systems technology is well on its way to commercial success.

Expert systems will change the way businesses operate by altering the way people think about solving problems. This new technology will make it possible to develop quick, pragmatic answers for a wide range of problems that currently defy effective solutions.

Consider, for example, the problem of designing a program to train salespeople to develop highly structured financial proposals when the services and the packaging options are constantly changing. You can teach the general skills, but the specific products and techniques will be out of date before the course is even completed. Imagine, instead, that you could design a workshop that would teach the salespeople the general skills and then teach them to use a personal computer-based program that interacts with the salesperson by asking questions and then recommending appropriate options. It would be as if each salesperson could talk with a senior salesperson who had all the latest information whenever he or she wanted advice. Imagine, further, that the computer program that provided this advice was so modularized and so user-friendly that it could be quickly updated by product specialists rather than computer programmers. Thus, the program would always represent the latest products and packaging strategies. This sort of scenario is on the verge of becoming a reality.

Expert systems technology will also help America solve its productivity problems. It will help businesses reorganize themselves into more efficient and effective organizations. It will do this by helping individuals solve problems more quickly and efficiently than they can today.

Along with expert systems, executives will soon

have powerful computerized workstations that will enable them to handle more information in more complex ways than is now considered possible. Using these workstations, managers will be able to monitor more activities and personnel while simultaneously increasing the quality and quantity of decisions that they make.

Individuals responsible for operating complex equipment such as chemical plants and nuclear reactors will soon be assisted by expert systems that will monitor the equipment, anticipate problems, and make intelligent suggestions to the operators.

Training will also be revolutionized by the introduction of expert systems. Most companies are struggling to teach employees to use new procedures and to understand and explain new products. Skills that are now difficult to teach will become easy once we equip the employees with smart programs that will assist them in performing the tasks. Moreover, the concepts underlying expert systems will change the way we think about the tasks that people perform. In the near future, when analysts study jobs, they will be able to specify exactly what knowledge is and is not necessary to perform the jobs with a precision that is currently impossible.

In short, the whole business environment should become much more rational. More information will be gathered, synthesized, and put into useful form more rapidly than has ever before been possible. Individuals responsible for managing businesses will be in a position to utilize this information. In effect, middle managers of large corporations will be equipped with a staff of 15 to 20 automated experts who will always be available to answer questions and give advice about problems those managers face.

The introduction of expert systems will also prove exciting to experts and professionals. These systems will help experts define problems and determine what knowledge is available to solve problems in ways they have never considered before. As expert systems are built, experts will be freed to focus on the more difficult aspects of their specialty. This, in turn, will result in solutions to new problems, and the range of problems that experts can solve will widen.

ARTIFICIAL INTELLIGENCE

As World War II ended, separate groups of British and American scientists were working to develop what we would now call a computer. Each group wanted to create an electronic machine that could be guided by a stored program of directions and made to carry out complex numerical computations. The principal British scientist, Alan Turing, argued that such a general-purpose machine, once developed, would have many different uses. Reflecting his knowledge of the accomplishments of formal logic in the years before the war, Turing argued that the fundamental instructions given to such a machine ought to be based on logical operators, such as "and," "or," and "not." One could then use such very general operators to assemble the more specialized numerical operators needed for arithmetic calculations. Moreover, programs based on logical operators would be capable of manipulating any type of symbolic material that one might want to work with, including statements in ordinary language.

The American scientists, being more practical, knew that the machine was going to be expensive to build. In addition, they assumed that they would not build very many of them. And since they were confident that they were building a machine that would do only arithmetic calculations, they decided against using logical operators and chose instead to use numerical operators, such as "$+$," "$-$," and "$>$." This decision, which the British subsequently followed as well, resulted in large computers that are essentially very fast calculating machines. In spite of the great proliferation of computers since 1946, this decision always seemed like a reasonable one to most people involved with computers. Until very recently.

In spite of the fact that computers were built as numerical processors, a small group of computer scientists continued to explore the ability of computers to manipulate non-numerical symbols. Simultaneously, psychologists concerned with human problem solving sought to develop computer programs that would simulate human behavior. Over the years, individuals concerned with both symbolic processing and human problem solving have formed that interdisciplinary subfield of computer science called artificial intelligence (AI). AI researchers are concerned with developing computer systems that produce results that we would normally associate with human intelligence.

About 15 years ago a number of corporations thought that some of the research coming out of the AI laboratories would prove useful in business. Several companies set up AI groups to develop practical applications. By and large, these efforts failed because

AI programs were too costly to develop, were too slow, and didn't produce sufficiently practical results. AI programs were simply too complex to run on the computers that existed at the time. However, AI researchers continued to work in the universities and made steady theoretical progress. Meanwhile, the development of microelectronics technology resulted in a new generation of faster, more powerful, and relatively inexpensive computers. Today AI has once again emerged from the laboratories. Existing compu-

Figure 1.1 The evolution of expert systems.

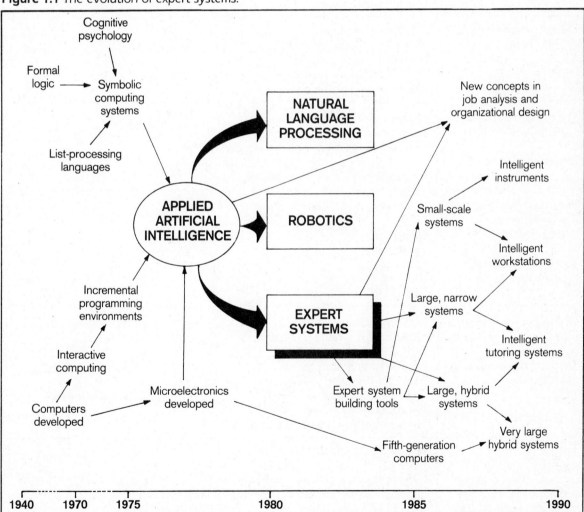

ter hardware, combined with significant theoretical advances in AI, has resulted in a technology whose time has come.

AI can be subdivided into three relatively independent research areas. (See Figure 1.1.) One group of AI researchers is concerned primarily with developing computer programs that can read, speak, or understand language as people use it in everyday conversation. This type of programming is commonly referred to as natural language processing. Another group of AI scientists is concerned with developing smart robots. They are especially concerned with

Table 1.1 An Overview of the Key Events in the History of Artificial Intelligence

Period	Key Events
Pre-World War II roots	Formal logic Cognitive psychology
The postwar years, 1945–1954 *Pre-AI*	Computers developed H. Simon, *Administrative Behavior* N. Wiener, *Cybernetics* A. M. Turing, "Computing Machinery and Intelligence" Macy Conferences on Cybernetics
The formative years, 1955–1960 *The initiation of AI research*	Growing availability of computers Information Processing Language I (IPL-I) The Dartmouth Summer Seminar on AI, 1956 General Problem Solver (GPS) Information processing psychology
The years of development and redirection, 1961–1970 *The search for general problem solvers*	A. Newell and H. Simon, *Human Problem Solving* LISP Heuristics Satisficing Robotics Chess programs DENDRAL (Stanford)
The years of specialization and success, 1971–1980 *The discovery of knowledge- based systems*	MYCIN (Stanford) HEARSAY II (Carnegie-Mellon) MACSYMA (MIT) Knowledge engineering EMYCIN (Stanford) GUIDON (Stanford) PROLOG Herbert Simon—Nobel Prize
The rush to applications, 1981– *International competition and commercial ventures*	PROSPECTOR (SRI) Japan's Fifth-Generation Project E. Feigenbaum and P. McCorduck, *The Fifth Generation* U.S.'s Microelectronics & Computer Technology Corp. (MCC) INTELLECT (A.I.C.) Various corporate and entrepreneurial AI companies

how to develop visual and tactile programs that will allow robots to observe the ongoing changes that take place as they move around in an environment. A third branch of AI research is concerned with developing programs that use symbolic knowledge to simulate the behavior of human experts. Table 1.1 gives a brief overview of the key developments in AI.

KNOWLEDGE-BASED EXPERT SYSTEMS

Professor Edward Feigenbaum of Stanford University, one of the leading researchers in expert systems, has defined an expert system as:

> . . . an intelligent computer program that uses knowledge and inference procedures to solve problems that are difficult enough to require significant human expertise for their solution. Knowledge necessary to perform at such a level, plus the inference procedures used, can be thought of as a model of the expertise of the best practitioners of the field.
>
> The knowledge of an expert system consists of facts and heuristics. The "facts" constitute a body of information that is widely shared, publicly available, and generally agreed upon by experts in a field. The "heuristics" are mostly private, little-discussed rules of good judgment (rules of plausible reasoning, rules of good guessing) that characterize expert-level decision making in the field. The performance level of an expert system is primarily a function of the size and the quality of a knowledge base it possesses.

Feigenbaum calls those who build knowledge-based expert systems "knowledge engineers" and refers to their technology as "knowledge engineering." Early systems were usually called "expert systems," but most knowledge engineers now refer to their systems as "knowledge systems."

The first systems were built by interviewing a recognized human expert and attempting to capture that expert's knowledge, hence the term "expert systems." Recently, however, several systems have been built that contain knowledge of a difficult decision-making situation that is quite useful, but hardly the equivalent of a human expert. To avoid suggesting that all systems built by means of knowledge engineering techniques capture the knowledge of a human expert, "knowledge systems" is rapidly becoming the preferred name. Throughout this book we use "expert systems" and "knowledge systems" as synonyms, but we generally refer to large systems as "expert systems" and smaller systems as "knowledge systems."

AI is a research field concerned primarily with studying problem solving in the abstract. Knowledge engineers, on the other hand, focus on replicating the behavior of a specific expert when he or she is engaged in solving a narrowly defined problem. (See Figure 1.2.) Many regard this shift from the study of generic problem-solving techniques to a focus on building systems that contain large amounts of specific knowledge about a particular problem as the major conceptual breakthrough in AI in the last 15 years.

In subsequent chapters we shall develop each of these concepts in considerable detail. For the moment, it is sufficient to note that AI's contribution to knowledge engineering lies in its insights into how to analyze problems and develop general search strategies to use in solving problems. Knowledge engineers are concerned with identifying the specific knowledge that an expert uses in solving a problem. Initially, the knowledge engineer studies a human expert and determines what facts and rules-of-thumb the expert employs. Then the knowledge engineer determines the inference strategy that the expert uses in an actual problem-solving situation. Finally, the knowledge engineer develops a system that uses similar knowledge and inference strategies to simulate the expert's behavior.

If a program is to function like a human expert, it must be able to do the things that human experts commonly do. For example, experts consult with others to help solve problems. Thus, most knowledge systems ask questions, explain their reasoning if asked, and justify their conclusions. Moreover, they typically do this in language that the user can easily understand. They allow the user to skip questions, and most can function even when the user provides incomplete or uncertain data. In other words, knowledge systems interact with a user in pretty much the same way that a human consultant does.

Figure 1.2 The different concerns of AI and knowledge engineering.

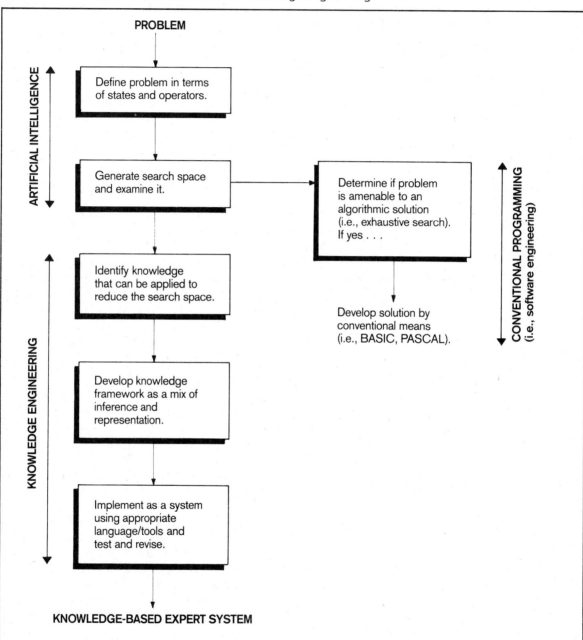

Expert systems are knowledge-intensive computer programs. They contain lots of knowledge about their specialty. They use rules-of-thumb, or *heuristics*, to focus on the key aspects of particular problems and to manipulate symbolic descriptions in order to reason about the knowledge they are given. They often consider a number of competing hypotheses simultaneously, and they frequently make tentative recommendations or assign weights to alternatives. The best expert systems can solve difficult problems, within a very narrow domain, as well as or better than human experts can.

All this is not to suggest that most of today's expert systems are as good as human experts. The technology is new and just beginning to be applied to tough commercial problems. Today's knowledge systems are confined to well-circumscribed tasks. They are not able to reason broadly over a field of expertise. They cannot reason from axioms or general theories. They do not learn and, thus, they are limited to using the specific facts and heuristics that they were "taught" by a human expert. They lack common sense, they cannot reason by analogy, and their performance deteriorates rapidly when problems extend beyond the narrow task they were designed to perform.

It's reasonable, for example, to consider developing a small expert system to assist a manager in the analysis of a specific type of cash flow problem or to help managers decide how to respond to a particular type of employee error. In most companies, these problems are probably sufficiently well-defined and adequately constrained so as to result in a very useful small system. One would not, however, want to try to develop a system to help a manager analyze a potential legal problem. Most legal problems tend to be poorly defined and broad-ranging. Moreover, they typically involve large amounts of common sense and reasoning by analogy—things that existing expert systems are unable to do.

On the other hand, knowledge systems do not display biased judgments, nor do they jump to conclusions and then seek to maintain those conclusions in the face of disconfirming evidence. They do not have "bad days"; they always attend to details, and they always systematically consider all of the possible alternatives. The best of them, equipped with thousands of heuristic rules, are able to perform their specialized tasks better than a human specialist. And, as we shall explain in subsequent chapters, new concepts and techniques that are now being introduced are certain to result in knowledge systems that are more flexible and powerful than those to which we have just alluded.

CONVENTIONAL PROGRAMMING VERSUS KNOWLEDGE ENGINEERING

Conventional programming techniques have been used to create the large data processing systems we commonly associate with computers. These systems are capable of collecting and processing large volumes of data. They process this data by means of complex algorithms. Algorithms are simply step-by-step procedures that guarantee that the right conclusion will be reached when the correct data have been entered. For example, each evening all of the data regarding all of the changes in every account at your local bank are fed into a computer. Then a very complex algorithm works through the data, making additions and subtractions, calculating the proper fees, and finally arriving at the bank's overall balance for the day. The numbers differ each day, but they are always processed in the same way, and they always result in a predetermined conclusion—the bank's overall balance.

Today's large computer systems automate complex and time-consuming clerical tasks that previously would have required hundreds or thousands of clerks. Indeed, prior to 1950, the word "computer" referred to a human who made calculations according to a set procedure. The U.S. Census Bureau, for example, was staffed by a small army of computers who slowly and systematically processed the data that census takers had gathered. The first internally programmed electronic machines designed to do similar tasks were called "electronic computers." Once electronic computers managed to supplant all their human competitors, of course, they acquired the shorter name.

Conventional programs behave in ways that only programmers understand. If a nonprogrammer stopped a program in mid-run and examined the code to determine what was happening, he or she would not be likely to learn anything useful.

Knowledge-based systems are quite different. They are highly interactive. A user can halt the processing at any time and ask why a particular line of questioning is being pursued or how a particular conclusion was reached. In many cases, the systems make recommendations that are neither correct nor incorrect, but only more or less plausible.

Here are other contrasts between an expert system and a conventional program:

- The task performed by an expert system was previously performed by a knowledgeable human specialist.
- Knowledge engineers and experts maintain knowledge systems. Conventional programs are maintained by programmers.
- The knowledge base of an expert system is readable and easy to modify.
- Conventional programs tend to rely on algorithms to provide their overall structure, whereas knowledge systems tend to rely on heuristics for their structure.

Another important difference between conventional programming and symbolic programming can be illustrated by describing how knowledge engineers work. Knowledge engineering focuses on both the development of software for expert systems and on the analysis of ways in which human experts solve problems. Knowledge engineers interact with human experts to help them describe their knowledge and inference strategies in terms that will allow the knowledge to be encoded. Thus, a knowledge engineer combines a large measure of cognitive psychology with symbolic programming techniques to develop expert systems. Table 1.2 contrasts the different emphases of conventional and symbolic programming.

Individuals working on expert systems use highly interactive techniques. They tend to meet frequently with an expert. Instead of trying to pin down the

exact nature of the problem during their first meetings, they seek to get only a first cut at the problem. They implement a prototype system—a small system with just a few facts and rules. Then they use the prototype on some test cases to see how it works. They soon return to the expert to ask more questions, and then implement a second version of the system. Along the way, the expert becomes engaged in the process and begins to develop some of the rules. Frequently the expert becomes an active member of the development team. In other words, developing an expert system is an exploratory process that is done in a series of approximations.

The approach must be flexible and pragmatic, because neither the knowledge engineer nor the expert knows at the beginning of the development effort what the finished knowledge system will look like. Knowledge engineers actively help the experts figure out how they solve problems and convince the experts, through prototype demonstrations, that their knowledge can be represented in a useful way.

Conventional programmers approach their tasks in ways that contrast with knowledge engineers' approach. Conventional programmers begin by working with an expert to develop a design. They specify the design in great detail, and then leave the expert and retreat to their offices to develop a program that will

Table 1.2 The Different Emphases of Conventional and Symbolic Programming

Conventional Programming	Symbolic Programming
Algorithms	Heuristics
Numerically addressed data base	Symbolically structured knowledge base in a global working memory
Oriented toward numerical processing	Oriented toward symbolic processing
Sequential, batch processing	Highly interactive processing
Mid-run explanation impossible	Mid-run explanation easy

implement the design. Programs tend to be very complex, and, thus, the time between when an expert meets with the programmer and when the program is delivered can be quite long. Programmers can spend so much time away from the experts because their initial design dictates the entire programming effort.

We do not want to put too much emphasis on the differences between knowledge engineering and conventional software engineering. As you become more familiar with expert systems, you will realize that, in an important sense, expert systems technology is not revolutionary at all. It is simply an extension of basic computer science principles to new levels of sophistication. Expert systems, after all, often run on the same computers that run programs written in FORTRAN or BASIC. Knowledge systems can be translated into conventional programming languages. Ultimately, the revolutionary ideas about expert systems are primarily new conceptual insights into how people can use computers to help solve problems. Learning about knowledge systems will expand your concept of the possible.

THE EXPERT SYSTEMS MARKET

The market for expert systems is difficult to define. The technology itself is complex, and it is developing quite rapidly. When we first prepared an outline for this book, in mid-1983, for example, we assumed that sophisticated expert systems development tools would not be available for personal computers until about 1986. By the time we completed the book, in late 1984, the first sophisticated expert system building tools for personal computers had just been released.

Figure 1.3 illustrates the speed with which the technology is developing. In this figure you can see how quickly the cost of developing a typical expert system is declining as new software tools are introduced.

Knowledge engineering still has strong roots in academia. At the same time, however, many knowledge engineers are finding jobs in the commercial marketplace. Terminology is inconsistent; everyone seems to have his or her own special terminology. Some entrepreneurs, eager to make a lot of money, are making claims that are totally unjustified. In most cases these claims are not deliberately false, but rather are being made by people who simply do not realize the difference between a product that is viable in the academic world and a system that would be useful in a commercial setting.

We sorted through and summarized the information that businesspeople will need to make reasonable decisions.

Most entrepreneurs working in expert systems realize that the market is going to be defined over the course of the next 10 years as companies introduce products and services, and as customers gain more

Figure 1.3 The declining cost of developing a knowledge system.

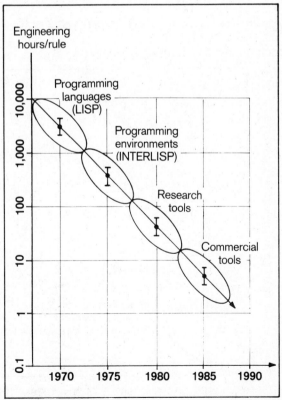

experience. Estimates of the size of the current market range from a few million dollars up to $50 million annually. The estimates vary, depending on what is considered AI or an expert system. The estimate is much larger, for example, if research grants and defense spending are included. Most estimates of the combined size of the AI market in 1990 range from $2 billion to $3 billion.

The impact of expert systems will probably come in at least two waves. (See Figure 1.4.) The first wave is just beginning to swell, and it will crest in the next two to four years. The larger wave is truly just beginning and will probably not crest before about 1992. Two major sets of variables control the rise of these waves. In part they are controlled by the availability of AI and supporting computer technology. The other set of variables involves the ability and willingness of business and industry to incorporate this new technology.

The first and smaller wave will include small knowledge systems that will be used to solve small, specific problems. Some of these systems will be developed by users on personal computers. They will supplant training and other types of on-the-job supervision and enable employees to perform tasks that previously required close supervision or access to knowledgeable senior specialists. Because they can be implemented in existing business environments without major dislocations and offer significant immediate benefits, these systems will be quickly assimilated by business and industry. Other small knowledge systems will be put on microchips and incorporated directly into a wide variety of instruments. In addition, some smart generic software will be marketed to managers, professionals, and home users of personal computers. At the same time, some small natural language interfaces will become popular. The use of these small knowledge systems will, in turn, lead to

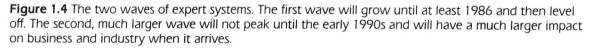

Figure 1.4 The two waves of expert systems. The first wave will grow until at least 1986 and then level off. The second, much larger wave will not peak until the early 1990s and will have a much larger impact on business and industry when it arrives.

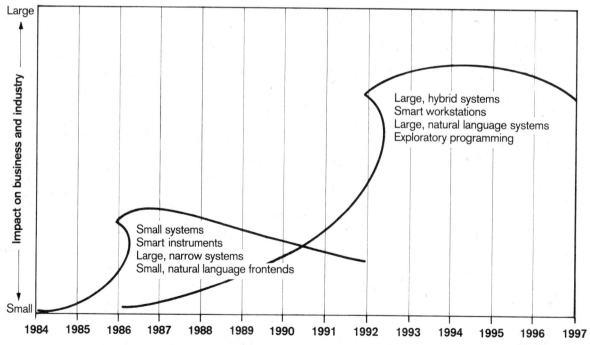

significant changes in the way trainers and managers approach the analysis and design of employee training programs. In addition to these small knowledge systems, a number of large but very narrowly defined expert systems will appear. All of these applications should prove quite popular and useful and will help prepare businesses for the larger systems that will come with the second wave.

The first wave depends on two preconditions. First, people outside the AI community must learn how to use knowledge engineering techniques to solve problems. Second, small knowledge engineering system building tools must become available. Both of these preconditions are rapidly being fulfilled, and thus we expect to see a rapid rise in the number of small knowledge systems being used in the next few years.

The second wave will be building up momentum for several years. The second wave promises to provide large, hybrid expert systems that will truly rival many human experts. These systems, supplemented by much more sophisticated natural language interfaces, will be used throughout business and industry by the late 1990s. At the same time, intelligent workstations that combine a large number of small and large knowledge systems and make them available to managers via desktop terminals will make a large impact on how businesses are organized and run. In addition, by the mid-1990s, AI programming techniques will change the way conventional data processing departments approach complex programming tasks.

The second wave cannot really begin to rise until several preconditions are met. Techniques and tools for the development of large, hybrid systems are only beginning to be developed. Major breakthroughs in machine learning must occur. More knowledge engineers and much friendlier system building tools will need to be developed. Personal workstations will need to become more powerful and much cheaper. Probably the most sophisticated applications will need to wait until new computer hardware that incorporates parallel processing has been developed. Equally important, large corporations will need to experiment and figure out how and where to use the new techniques most effectively. Many Fortune 500 companies are already rushing to set up AI groups and experiment with large-scale knowledge system development. Now is certainly the time to begin, but the wisest must assume that their efforts will be rewarded in the 1990s, not the 1980s.

The distinction between the smaller knowledge systems that will come with the first wave and the larger expert systems that will come with the second wave can be put another way. Large expert systems are programs that cannot be easily built using conventional techniques. The skill and knowledge necessary to build them is just beginning to emerge. The hardware required is still very expensive and major application efforts are still quite risky. Large expert systems have received most of the media's attention, but they will only have a marginal impact on business operations during the next few years.

Many of the techniques that have been created to facilitate the development of large expert systems, however, are ripe for application. These techniques, assembled into "expert system building tools," allow nonprogrammers to build small, powerful systems that can aid in problem analysis and decision making. These small systems will never rival human experts; they emphasize the user-friendly aspects of AI technology rather than trying to model complex human cognitive processes. The widespread use of these small systems will have a major impact on the way companies do business in the next few years.

One might say that large expert systems are like large general ledger programs. Their development requires lots of time and the skills of a team of well-trained systems analysts and programmers. Small knowledge systems, however, are like electronic spreadsheet programs. Middle-level managers will use them to increase the productivity of employees that need assistance in making routine decisions. The "AI market" is already dividing into two parts to reflect these two approaches to commercializing the techniques emerging from the AI laboratories. (See Figure 1.5.)

Throughout this book we shall try to maintain a balance between informing you about the smaller systems you will begin to encounter in the next two

Figure 1.5 Two major trends in AI applications.

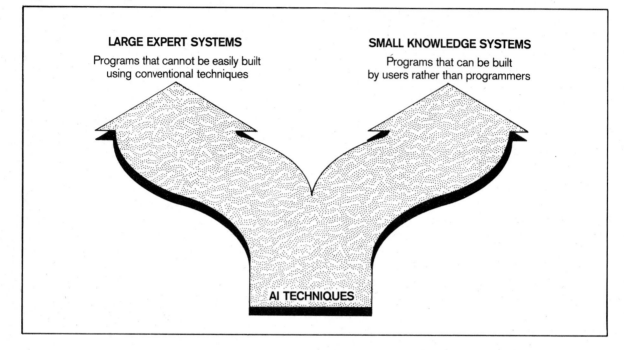

to four years and the larger systems that you will probably not encounter for some eight to ten years but that you should begin to plan for in the remaining years of this decade. We shall also stress that AI, in general, and expert systems, in particular, will be introducing fundamental new concepts that will reorganize the way people think about and use computers. More to the point, expert systems will revolutionize the way we conduct business.

Section One

BASIC CONCEPTS AND TECHNIQUES

2.

MYCIN

In this chapter we describe the performance of a knowledge system called MYCIN. MYCIN was the first large expert system to perform at the level of a human expert and to provide users with an explanation of its reasoning. Most expert systems developed since MYCIN have used MYCIN as a benchmark to define an expert system. Moreover, the techniques developed for MYCIN have become widely available in the various small expert system building tools. In effect, most small systems developed during the next few years will clearly bear the marks of this important pioneering system. We shall not explain how MYCIN works in this chapter. Instead, we shall focus on what MYCIN does.

In three subsequent chapters we shall describe some of the basic concepts and techniques used in the analysis, design, and development of expert systems. Then, in Chapter 6, we shall return to MYCIN and discuss its operation in detail. In effect, this chapter considers the benefits and surface features of MYCIN, whereas Chapter 6 describes its inner workings.

MYCIN was developed at Stanford University in the mid-1970s. It was designed to aid physicians in the diagnosis and treatment of meningitis and bacteremia infections. MYCIN was strictly a research system. AI investigators wanted to advance the state of expert system building by undertaking a hard problem with clear, practical ramifications.

Before the development of MYCIN, AI had often been criticized for solving only "toy problems." Clever solutions to parlor games suggested ways in which the technology might apply more generally, but no one had undertaken a truly hard problem and succeeded. AI might still be in the research laboratories today were it not for the success of the MYCIN project.

MYCIN'S EXPERTISE

MYCIN provides consultative advice about bacteremia (infections that involve bacteria in the blood) and meningitis (infections that involve inflammation of the membranes that envelop the brain and spinal cord). These infectious diseases can be fatal and often show themselves during hospitalization. A patient, for example, might develop such an infection while recovering from heart surgery. The need to act quickly further compounds the problem. The attending physician typically takes samples to determine the identity of the infectious organisms, but positive identification normally takes 24 to 48 hours. In many cases, the physician must begin treatment in the absence of complete lab results. The diagnosis and treatment of these diseases are complex enough that an attending physician will often seek the advice of an expert.

MYCIN is a computer program designed to provide attending physicians with advice comparable to that which they would otherwise get from a consulting physician specializing in bacteremia and meningitis infections. To use MYCIN, the attending physician must sit in front of a computer terminal that is connected to a DEC-20 (one of Digital Equipment Corporation's mainframe computers) where the MYCIN program is stored. When the MYCIN program is evoked, it initiates a dialogue. The physician types answers in response to various questions. Eventually MYCIN provides a diagnosis and a detailed drug therapy recommendation.

MYCIN reasons about data associated with a patient. It considers, for example, laboratory results of body fluid analyses, symptoms that the patient is displaying, and general characteristics of the patient, such as age and sex. MYCIN obtains this information by interrogating the physician. A MYCIN consultation proceeds in two phases. First a diagnosis is made to identify the most likely infectious organisms. Then one or more drugs are prescribed that should control for all of the possible organisms. The antibiotics prescribed must rid the patient of the disease. They must also interact favorably with each other, and be appropriate for the specific patient.

MYCIN may ask for the results of a test that has not yet been completed. In this case the physician must answer UNKNOWN. This is proper because, when diagnosing infections, doctors rarely have the luxury of perusing a complete set of laboratory data. Rather, because early treatment is important, doctors have learned to work from partial information. MYCIN accommodates to this situation by accepting UNKNOWN as a response. Like a human specialist, MYCIN will reason with incomplete information.

In addition to unknown information, there also may be information of which the doctor is uncertain. Ambiguities arise in reading cultures, for example, or in labeling symptoms. To accommodate uncertainty, all information given to MYCIN may be qualified by a certainty factor—a number between -1 and $+1$—that indicates the doctor's degree of confidence in the

answer to a question. Thus, if a doctor is only moderately certain that a particular symptom is present, he or she can respond to a question by typing "YES .4" to indicate a limited confidence in the response.

Doctors, like most consumers of expertise, are often interested in how a conclusion is reached or why information is requested. MYCIN is able to respond to such queries and, within constraints, can explain its reasoning. Users can ask "WHY?" when MYCIN is asking for data, and MYCIN will explain what hypotheses it is considering and how the present question will provide data that will add support or help to rule out that hypothesis. After diagnosis and prescription are complete, the physician can, if desired, trace MYCIN's entire diagnostic trail.

A CONSULTATION WITH MYCIN

Perhaps the best way to grasp the flavor of MYCIN is by looking at a transcript of a consultation. The dialogue between MYCIN and the physician is indented below, with the physician's responses underlined. Our comments are interspersed throughout.

MYCIN begins by asking for four pieces of information about the patient—name, age, sex, and race. All are essential to any diagnosis, so they are asked at the onset of the session.

1) Please enter information about the patient.

Name	Age	Sex	Race
Sally	*42 years*	*Female*	*Caucasian*

The physician enters the information and MYCIN continues.

2) Are there any positive cultures obtained from SALLY?
   No

3) Are there any pending cultures of SALLY?
   Yes

4)   site: date   stain   method of collection:
                        collected: examined?   (urine, sputum only)
     CSF   _3-Jun-75_   _Yes_   _N/A_

5) stain of smear: morph:
   (type NONE if no organism was seen on the smear)
   None

*The second piece of information that MYCIN wants concerns the availability
of cultures with positive readings. Rather than attempting to deduce the results
of tests, MYCIN allows the physician to state what is known. In this case the
physician does not have any positive cultures, and so MYCIN probes further
(question 3), asking whether this patient has pending cultures. The patient
does—and so MYCIN provides headings for the physician, who enters CSF
to indicate that a cerebrospinal fluid culture has been taken but that no
organism has yet been seen. MYCIN is unable to reach conclusions from
laboratory findings, but like the physician, MYCIN continues to ask questions. Eventually MYCIN reaches this:*

13) Has SALLY recently had symptoms of persistent headache or other abnormal
    neurologic symptoms (dizziness, lethargy, etc.)?
    Yes

14) Has SALLY recently had objective evidence of abnormal neurologic signs (nuchal
    rigidity, coma, seizures, etc.) documented by physician observation or examination?
    Yes

The CSF cultures will be considered to be associated with MENINGITIS.

*MYCIN's questions 13 and 14 show a more traditional approach to the
diagnosis by symptoms, and after receiving the answer to question 14,
MYCIN reports its first conclusion: The CSF infection is likely to be
meningitis. MYCIN then begins another line of reasoning aimed at identifying
the particular organisms responsible for the meningitis infection. Further
questions lead to the following:*

34) Is the meningitis a hospital-acquired infection?
    _No_

35) Is SALLY's clinical history consistent with EPIGLOTTITIS?
    _No_

36) Is SALLY's clinical history consistent with OTITIS-MEDIA?
    _No_

37) Has the patient ever been to an area that is endemic for coccidiomycoses?
    Unknown

38) Is SALLY a burn patient?
Why

When asked whether the patient is a burn victim (question 38), the physician responds by typing WHY. MYCIN responds by restating its understanding of "why" in this context, and then explains what the information will be used for. To explain, MYCIN displays the particular heuristic rule it was considering, Rule 578, and MYCIN explains how the requested information would be useful.

[i.e.   WHY is it important to determine whether SALLY has been seriously burned?]

[4.0] This will aid in determining the organisms (other than those seen on cultures or smears) which might be causing the infection.
It has already been established that
[4.1] the infection which requires therapy is meningitis, and
[4.2] organisms were not seen on the stain of the pending csf culture (CULTURE-1), and
[4.3] the type of the infection may be bacterial
Therefore, if
[4.4] SALLY has been seriously burned
then
there is suggestive evidence that Pseudomonas-aeruginosa is one of the organisms (other than those seen on cultures or smears) which might be causing the infection [RULE578]

[back to question 38 . . .]

How 4.3

The physician is curious about how MYCIN was able to conclude that the type of infection is bacterial. "HOW 4.3" is a request to explain how MYCIN established clause [4.3] of the rule it is considering. MYCIN responds with its understanding of the question, and then reports the rules it used in determining this fact. The physician can press for greater detail by asking HOW 4.5 to track down what heuristic Rule 500 is and how it was confirmed. By repeatedly asking HOW, the physician can backtrack right to the beginning of the consultation.

Notice that MYCIN has four rules that support the likelihood that the infection is bacterial, and one rule that suggests (certainty factor of .17) that the infection is not bacterial. MYCIN is considering both possibilities. Momentarily, it is following up on the more probable one.

[i.e. HOW was it established that the type of the infection may be bacterial?]

The following rules concluded about: the likelihood that the type of the infection may be bacterial

	Rule	Yes	No
[4.5]	RULE500	(.4)	
[4.6]	RULE501		(.17)
[4.7]	RULE502	(.1)	
[4.8]	RULE524	(.42)	
[4.9]	RULE504	(.28)	

Thus, it has been established that the type of the infection may be bacterial.

We rejoin MYCIN several questions later as it reports its conclusions about the culprit organisms, and then turns to the final phase of its consultation, the prescription of a set of antibiotics. MYCIN checks for known allergies (question 43), for other characteristics that relate to the use of particular medications, and then for the patient's weight.

My therapy recommendations will be designed to treat for organisms that either are very likely or, although less likely, would have a significant effect on therapy selection if they were present. It is important to cover for the following probable infection(s) and associated organism(s):

INFECTION-1 is MENINGITIS

+ <ITEM-1> MYCOBACTERIUM-TB [from clinical evidence only]
+   . . .   COCCIDIOIDES [from clinical evidence only]
+   . . .   CRYPTOCOCCUS [from clinical evidence only]

43) Does SALLY have a clinically significant allergic reaction to any antimicrobial agent?
No

[Considering ETHAMBUTAL-AND-INH-AND-RIFAMPIN
for use against INFECTION-1 . . .]

44) Is SALLY pregnant or breast feeding?
No

45) Do you have reason to suspect that SALLY may have impaired renal functions?
No

46) SALLY's weight in kilograms (or <number> POUNDS):
51.3

From these 46 questions MYCIN makes a prescription (REC-1), explains its reasoning, and proposes additional tests and procedures.

[REC-1] My preferred therapy recommendation is as follows:
Give the following in combination:

1) ETHAMBUTAL

Dose: 1.28g (13.0 100mg-tablets) q24h PO for 60 days
[calculated on basis of 25 mg/kg]
then 770 mg (7.5 100mg-tablets) q24h PO
[calculated on basis of 15 mg/kg]
[The dose should be modified in renal failure. I can adjust the dose only if a creatinine clearance or a serum creatinine is obtained.]
Comments: Periodic vision screening tests are recommended for optic neuritis.
2) INH
Dose: 513 mg (5.0 100mg-tablets) q24h PO
[calculated on basis of 10 mg/kg]
3) RIFAMPIN
Dose: 600 mg PO q24h
Comments: Administer dose on an empty stomach.

Although I suspect that fungus may be a possible pathogen, in the absence of definitive evidence I will not recommend antifungal therapy at this time. Please obtain samples for fungal, TB, and viral cultures, cytology, VDRL (blood and CSF), crypto-coccal antigen (blood and CSF), viral titers (blood and CSF). An infectious disease consult may be advisable.

MYCIN's explanations, although quite useful, are limited to a review of its reasoning process and a display of its knowledge. MYCIN cannot justify or explain the rules themselves, nor can it define the terms it is using. That is, the physician cannot ask WHY RULE578 or WHAT IS PSEUDOMONAS-AERUGINOSA. Rules contain the knowledge gleaned from an expert.

It is assumed that the terms MYCIN uses and the answers it requests are familiar to the physicians using the program. Knowledge systems like MYCIN must be carefully tailored to match characteristics of their user communities. The knowledge engineers who built MYCIN were responsible for making sure that terms such as "culture," "staining," and "Mycobacterium-TB" would be familiar terms to MYCIN's users.

HOW GOOD AN EXPERT IS MYCIN?

MYCIN has been evaluated in several different ways. Its success with several hundred cases has confirmed its competence in identifying the infectious agents, selecting appropriate doses of effective drugs, and recommending additional diagnostic tests.

In one complex evaluation, eight independent evaluators with special expertise in the management of meningitis compared MYCIN's choice of medicines with the choices prescribed by nine human diagnosticians for 10 difficult cases of meningitis. The task used for this test was the selection of drugs for cases of infectious meningitis before the causitive agent had been identified. In the first phase of the evaluation, MYCIN and faculty members in the Stanford University Medical School's Division of Infectious Diseases each evaluated 10 cases that had been chosen to offer a wide variety of difficult problems. In the second phase, prominent infectious disease specialists assessed each set of cases and reviewed the diagnoses and prescriptions without knowing either the identity of the prescribers or that one was a computer.

Two evaluative criteria were used: First, prescriptions were evaluated to see whether the recommended drugs would be effective against the actual infective agent after it was finally identified. MYCIN and three of the faculty prescribers consistently prescribed therapy that would have been effective in all 10 cases. The second criterion was whether the prescribed drugs adequately covered for other plausible pathogens while avoiding overprescribing. Using this criterion, MYCIN received a higher rating than any of the human prescribers. In this double-blind study, the evaluators rated MYCIN's prescriptions correct in 65 percent of the cases, whereas the ratings for the prescriptions of the human specialists ranged from 42.5 to 62.5 percent.

MYCIN's strength in this test against highly qualified human physicians is based on at least four factors:

1. MYCIN's knowledge base, derived from some of the best human practitioners, is extremely detailed and is as comprehensive as that of most physicians in the domain of meningitis.

2. MYCIN does not overlook anything or forget any details. It considers every possibility. There is a popular saying among doctors that "One has to think of the disease in order to recognize its symptoms." MYCIN considers every possible disease it knows about.

3. The program never jumps to conclusions or fails to ask for key pieces of information. No matter how obvious the disease is, MYCIN methodically checks for all of the details and considers all alternatives.

4. MYCIN is maintained at a major medical center and is, consequently, completely current. Several of its therapy recommendations are based on recent data published in specialized journals. Such information is not in textbooks, and would be known only by specialists who monitor the journals and who remember to incorporate new information into their diagnostic procedure.

The various evaluations that have been undertaken all suggest that MYCIN is as good or better than most very skilled human experts.

The original MYCIN program has been changed a number of times for various research purposes. Unlike traditional computer programs, which are very difficult to modify, MYCIN is easy to change. Each of MYCIN's rules is a separate module. Any particular rule can be removed and the system will still run. Likewise, a rule can be modified or a new rule can be added, and the system will immediately be ready to provide advice. Rules can be changed in minutes using English-like input. Compared with software packages of its size, MYCIN is easy to modify.

The ability to add rules and modify reasoning is a key characteristic of expert systems. This feature is as necessary as the ability of the system to reason with uncertainty or to explain its reasoning. Expert systems are developed and maintained incrementally with the active involvement of one or more experts. To remain current and effective, the programs must be easy for users to update.

SUMMARY

MYCIN represents the first of a new generation of computer programs that reason about the world, explain their reasoning, and provide advice that is comparable to advice provided by human experts. MYCIN's development marks a transition in AI research. MYCIN's success proved that expert systems technology was strong enough to leave the laboratory, with its academic and well-circumscribed problems, and enter commercial environments with their incomplete and uncertain information, skeptical users who demand justifications, and domains where substantial amounts of knowledge are the prerequisite of good judgment.

In this chapter we have focused on how MYCIN appears to a user. In the next three chapters we consider the psychological assumptions underlying MYCIN's design and the architectural principles and techniques used in MYCIN's development. In Chapter 6 we return to MYCIN and explain how it produces the results we have just described.

3.

Human Problem Solving

In this chapter we consider how people solve problems. The themes and concepts introduced in this chapter will recur throughout subsequent chapters, since they form a set of fundamental assumptions that underlie most expert systems development efforts. We shall begin with a description of how people process information. Next, we shall examine problem-solving behavior, a subcategory of information processing. Finally, the nature of human expertise will be discussed. We want to know how some individuals become superb performers and what it means to apply expertise to solve problems. This chapter should also give you new insights into your own thinking and problem-solving behavior.

Human problem solving is used as a model by AI researchers, and most knowledge engineers are well versed in cognitive psychology. Key AI researchers such as Herbert Simon and Alan Newell are respected for their work in both psychology and computer science. (In fact, Simon was awarded a Nobel Prize in Economics for his studies in how business administrators make decisions.) Cognitive psychologists and AI researchers believe that problem solving, along with other varieties of thought, can be understood as *information processing*.

HUMAN INFORMATION PROCESSING

From the information processing perspective, a person's cognitive behavior is best described in the same way that we describe information processing in a computer. This is not to suggest that people *are*

computers. Biological systems are vastly different from existing computer systems, and no one suggests that the precise inner workings are the same. By focusing on the question of how people process information, however, psychologists are able to be more precise about the specific strategies people use to *encode* information, to *store* information, or to *recall* it from memory.

Previous models of cognitive behavior have usually been quantitative. You are probably familiar with tests administered to measure how much someone knows or how well he or she can perform. Differences among people are the focus of such tests. In contrast, cognitive scientists provide qualitative descriptions of the ways in which people are similar. They investigate *how* people think, rather than how *well* people think.

The information processing model of human mental activity consists of three major subsystems, a perceptual system, a cognitive system, and a motor system. Figure 3.1 illustrates the memories and processors included in each subsystem.

Sensory Inputs

External stimuli are the *input* for the human information processing system. These stimuli enter through sensors, such as our eyes and ears. The perceptual subsystem consists of these sensors along with buffer memories that briefly store incoming information (or percepts), while it awaits processing by the cognitive subsystem.

Short-Term Memory

Shortly after sensory information is stored, some of it is transferred by the cognitive processor to a short-term working memory. Not all percepts in the buffer memories are encoded. The senses are constantly placing a huge amount of information in the buffer memories. The cognitive system must manage the selection and encoding process. We ordinarily refer to the process of selecting percepts for storage in working memory as "paying attention."

The cognitive processor, like the central processing unit (CPU) of a computer, cycles periodically as it obtains information from the sensory buffers and transfers it to working memory. These "recognize–act" cycles, which form the basic quantum of cognitive processing, are analogous to the "fetch–execute" cycles of the computer. During each cycle the cognitive processor obtains information from a memory, evaluates the information, and then stores it in another memory. It is estimated that each cognitive processing cycle takes approximately 70 milliseconds.

In the simplest tasks, the cognitive system merely serves as a point for transferring information from sensory inputs to motor outputs. Habitual tasks, such as reaching to turn off a light switch, are like that. The performer needs to coordinate the action, but there is little or no "deep thought." In fact, the "thinking" that occurs during such behavior is impossible to recover. Try to explain to someone how you flip a lever.

More complex tasks involve more information. That, in turn, calls for more elaborate processing. Learning a new programming language, meeting a

Figure 3.1 An overview of the human information processing system.

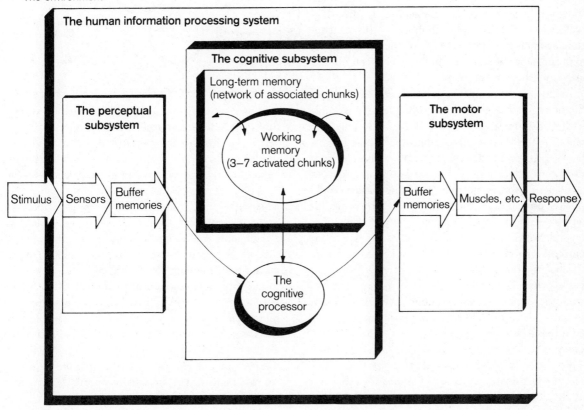

new person and remembering facts about him or her, or solving a quadratic equation are examples of complex tasks. To accomplish these tasks, the cognitive processor will draw on a second memory system, long-term memory.

Long-Term Memory

Long-term memory consists of a large number of stored symbols with a complex indexing system. There are competing hypotheses about what the elementary symbols are and how they arrange themselves. In the simplest memory model, related symbols are associated with one another. In a more elaborate model, symbols are organized into temporal scripts (e.g., we have stored scripts for how to introduce ourselves to strangers, how to shop at stores, etc.). Another view is that memory consists of clusters of symbols called "chunks." A chunk is a symbol associated with a set or pattern of stimuli. Chunks, as shown in Figure 3.2, are hierarchically organized collections of still smaller chunks. In this conception, memory is a vast network of chunks. Learning and remembering occur as linkages between chunks are established and revised.

In studies of human problem solving, Newell and Simon allowed chess masters to observe a chessboard, with a game in progress, for 5–10 seconds. Then the chess masters were asked to duplicate the board. Most could easily and flawlessly set up all of the pieces in their correct locations. For reasons we shall discuss in a moment, we assume that the chess masters could not have memorized the position of each of the 30-odd pieces on a particular board. Instead of focusing on individual pieces, they observed from four to six patterns or sets of pieces. When asked to re-create the board, they began by recalling that a particular pattern had been present, and then they deduced what pieces must have been present. In effect, chess masters learn to "chunk" individual chess pieces together into small patterns. Then they learn to chunk the small patterns into still larger patterns. Thus, when they think about a particular game, they are able to think in terms of the interactions that can or should occur between the four to six patterns that

Figure 3.2 A chunk of the memory network consists of a symbol, such as DOG, and an association of other related symbols that are activated along with DOG when one begins to think about dogs.

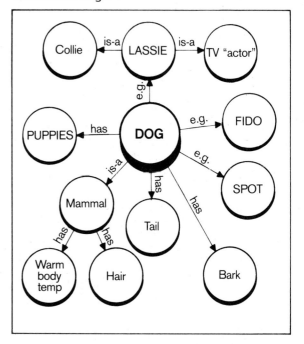

they see. Studies of cognitive performance suggest that most skilled performers, from jugglers and concert musicians to trial lawyers and executives, use a similar approach to organizing the data they must memorize and manipulate during problem solving.

When we are young, we begin to organize our experiences into chunks of information, like our "dog" example in Figure 3.2. As we get older, we cluster more and more information together around successively more abstract concepts. Interestingly, no matter how complex our chunks become, our ability to manipulate chunks seems to stay about the same. A human can maintain from four to seven chunks in his or her short-term memory at the same time. In this case, we are assuming that our thinker is working without books, charts, or notes. By storing some information outside and looking at it while we think, we can increase the amount of information we can manipulate simultaneously.

One way to conceptualize this is to think about a Macintosh computer screen. The Macintosh screen has a number of windows. In one window you might have a memo you are composing. In another window you might have a spreadsheet that you are looking at as you work on the memo. In still another window you might have a memo that you received via electronic mail to which you want to respond. If you think of each window as a chunk, than research suggests that you can deal effectively with only about four or five windows simultaneously. Extending this example slightly, you'll see that each window can be enlarged and parts of the window can be "blown up" to allow you to see additional levels of detail. A chunk is like that; as you focus on it, you can recall more and more of the associated details that help define the chunk.

In early information processing models of memory, separate short-term (working) and long-term memories were identified. Currently, most researchers conceptualize working memory as that small portion of long-term memory that is activated at any particular time, just as the screen display on a Macintosh represents only a small portion of the data that is stored in the various programs and files in the computer. Previously activated chunks become less accessible as activation spreads to new chunks. This is due to the limited resources of the human cognitive processor. The activation model is intuitively appealing because it describes thought as the spreading of activation from one set of chunks to the next.

Long-term memory holds an individual's mass of accumulated knowledge, related in some kind of complex network. There is no known limit to the amount of information that can be stored in long-term memory. The trick, as we all know, is not storing information but maintaining ways to retrieve or remember things.

Time is needed to add new chunks of information to long-term memory. On the average, it takes about 7 seconds per chunk to assure that the fact is properly linked into the long-term memory network. We all recognize this when we adopt different strategies for scanning the local newspaper versus really "paying attention" to new terminology. We attend not simply to a new term but also to other terms we already know that are associated with the new term.

Although storage takes a relatively long period of time, the human information processing system can access long-term memory relatively quickly—once in each 70-millisecond cycle. This asymmetry is of great importance in understanding how people function. Sophisticated performance at a rapid rate is not uncommon among humans, but the rapid storage of new information for long-term use is very rare. Put another way, world-class experts, like the chess masters discussed above, ordinarily emerge after 10 years or more of work in their fields. It simply takes that long to acquire, encode, chunk, and organize experience.

Motor Outputs

To end our journey through the human information processing system, we return to the recognize–act cycle of the cognitive processor. After scanning and searching memories, information is ordinarily sent to the motor system. Motor processors initiate actions of muscles and other internal systems. This, in turn, results in some observable activity.

THE PRODUCTION SYSTEM AS A PROCESSING MODEL

To describe how humans process symbolic information, AI researchers created a "programming language" called a *production system*. Production systems consist of two parts: (1) *production rules*, or *"if–then"* statements, and (2) a *working memory*. Put another way, a production is an instruction for a "recognize–act" processor like the one described above. Production rules (or simply productions) are applied to working memory. If they succeed, then they ordinarily contribute some new information to memory. Here is an example:

> You awaken and look at your calendar watch to note that it is May 15th. "May 15th" goes into working memory, and by activation a production is retrieved: "If it is May 15th, then it is your wife's birthday." A new fact goes into working memory:

"Today is Susan's birthday"; and the process continues when, again by activation, the production, "If it is someone's birthday, then think of a gift," is located. "Gift" is placed in memory, and the cycle continues.

The production system provides an extremely powerful model for human thought because it is discrete, simple, and flexible. Its success in developing programs that model human behavior lead AI researchers to focus their attention on the role that *if–then* rules play in human cognition. Indeed, many expert systems could be described as production systems.

An additional advantage of the production system approach is that it makes cognitive psychology intuitively compatible with the behaviorist theories that were popular in the 1950s and 1960s. Behaviorist theories ignore cognition and focus on external stimuli and overt responses. A cognitive psychologist using a production system model can easily integrate external behavior with internal mental activity. Events in the world produce stimuli that impinge upon us. We sense stimuli and store them in buffers. Some stimuli are transferred to working memory. The transferred stimuli activate the *if* portion of a production rule. The *then* portion of the production then indicates appropriate actions. The actions are implemented by the motor system and are observed as responses.

This very brief overview of the human information processing system provides us with a number of key terms and distinctions that we shall use later when we discuss knowledge engineering in more detail.

PROBLEM SOLVING

Now we want to look at human thought from a different, wider perspective. We shall shift from a microscopic analysis of cognition to a more general description of intelligent, problem-solving behavior.

Problem solving is finding a way to get from some initial situation to a desired goal. A simple example is figuring out how to get from your home to some unfamiliar theater by showtime. Problem solving is a mental activity. It is what we just referred to as "figuring out how."

Problem solving usually means thinking about how to solve problems that you do not know how to solve at the onset. Thus, not all information processing is problem solving. In discussing how the human information processing system works, we said that some incoming stimuli from the perceptual subsystem are passed directly to the motor subsystem for action. These nearly instantaneous responses frequently occur when you perform familiar physical actions. Rapid responses also occur when you answer the question, "What is 10 times 3?", or when you follow well-designed, step-by-step instructions. Highly habituated or carefully structured tasks like these, although they do have a starting point and a goal, are not ordinarily labeled as problem-solving tasks. A well-designed, step-by-step procedure *tells how* to solve a problem, and adults *know how* to multiply.

A Small Problem to Solve

Here is a problem that you probably do not know how to solve. Dig in your pocket for two pairs of coins, for example, two nickels and two dimes. Make a row with a gap in the middle, as shown in Figure 3.3, labeled "Start." The problem is to exchange the position of the nickels and the dimes using two simple moves and following the single rule shown. If you take a few minutes to work on this problem right now, the experience is likely to help you understand the discussion that will follow. You need not solve it, but take a minute or two to work on the "nickel and dime problem" (NDP) before reading on.

Figure 3.3 The "nickel and dime problem" (NDP).

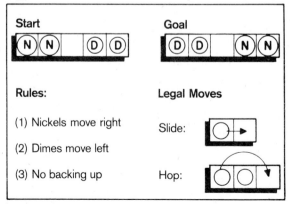

Problem-Solving Strategies

There are common elements in how people approach problem situations like this one. If you approached it as we did, you probably tried a few moves without much planning just to gain familiarity with the problem. It is reasonable to see if the problem is trivial before investing any serious effort in trying to analyze it.

Relaxing a constraint is another common strategy. When we found ourselves at a dead end, we started backing up the coins. We also tried backing up from the goal to see if that was easier, but it turned out to be equally hard. We reasoned that if we could somehow get from beginning to end, then we could polish up the solution and eliminate our illegal moves.

When the problem did not succumb to these approaches, we turned to more tedious and systematic approaches. We set up an informal notation and looked at the results of our first trials. We converted the external, physical stimuli into symbols to make it easier to manipulate the problem, just as we convert images in our buffer memories into symbols when we place them in long-term memory. In effect, when we move from conceptualizing our problem in terms of a picture to thinking about it in symbolic terms, we create a mental model of our problem. Cognitive psychologists refer to this type of model as a *problem space*. A problem space consists of the following:

- Patterns of elements or symbols, each representing a *state* or way that the task situation may occur. Each configuration of coins is a state of the NDP problem. Other problem states might be events, combinations of symptoms, or hierarchical taxonomies of species.
- Links between elements corresponding to the *operations* that can change one state to another. "Hop" and "slide" are the two NDP operators. These are the legal moves that cause one state to change to another. For other problems the links might reflect causal relationships, chemical reactions, or legal actions.

This new terminology allows for a more precise definition of problem solving. Problem solving is *the process of starting in an initial state and searching through a problem space in order to identify the sequence of operations or actions that will lead to a desired goal.*

With this new terminology we can describe some of our earlier attempts to solve the NDP. Figure 3.4 shows how we tried a few moves and got stuck in a state where no legal moves were possible. Then we started over again, got stuck again, and so on. This strategy, called "generate and test," works perfectly well for many ordinary problems. Finding matching socks or locating a book in an unordered stack are problems where it is appropriate to generate a state and then check to see if we have reached our goal. If

Figure 3.4 Some generate-and-test trials for the nickel and dime problem.

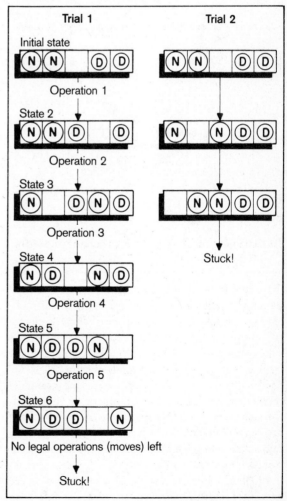

you were lucky, you may even have hit upon the NDP sequence that works.

To be more systematic, we tried expanding our initial state in every possible way. Figure 3.5 shows the problem space after all permissible first moves have been tried. There are four new states. From the initial state, two states are reached by using the "hopping" operator. From these two states there are no further legal moves. Two other states are reached by using the "sliding" operator. These states, in turn, can lead to other legal states.

Figure 3.5 Five states for the nickel and dime problem.

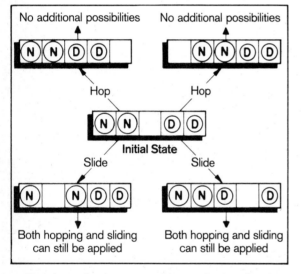

Search is the key to problem solving when we represent problems in this way. For this small problem we can take a direct approach. We can generate the entire problem space by expanding each of the states shown in Figure 3.5 by continuing to apply both operators whenever possible. Figure 3.6 shows the results of such an effort. It is the complete problem space for the NDP problem. If you search through it, you will find that the goal state is at the bottom. By tracing through the map, you can easily find a path that is made up of a set of moves that leads from an initial state to a solution.

Problem solving can sometimes be viewed as the process of searching through legal states of a problem looking for the goal. In a "well-formed problem" we know the initial state, the goal state, and the operators. From these, we can systematically generate all the intermediate states, and hence we can theoretically develop a "map" of the entire problem space.

Ill-Formed Problems

Not all problems are "well formed." Our first example, getting from home to an unfamiliar theater on time, is ill-formed for several reasons:

1. The goal is not stated explicitly. Determining the goal, that is, finding out the address of the theater and the time of the showing, is part of the problem.
2. Problem states are not discrete. It is not obvious what a "move" is or how we can locate and study interim states between being-at-home and being-at-the-theater.
3. Operators are not specified. Common sense and world knowledge suggest that the operators are movements such as riding in cars or buses and walking, but others, such as riding a skateboard, could also be included.
4. The problem space is unbounded. Are we considering theaters anywhere in town, or in the state, or theaters throughout the entire country? If we tried to generate every possible state, the problem space would quickly become unmanageably huge. It is not the vague goal that makes the space unbounded; it is the unbounded nature of the *operators*. The idea of taking all possible first moves, as we did when we solved the NDP problem, just will not work. Moreover, operators that cause discrete moves are vastly easier to model than those that cause continuous motion. (See Figure 3.7.)
5. Time places additional constraints on the problem. Our goal involves not only locating ourselves at the theater, but also doing it before the show starts.

In summary, ill-formed problems like this one lack one or more of the features of well-formed problems. And ill-formed problems are more common than well-formed problems.

Figure 3.6 Complete problem space for the nickel and dime problem.

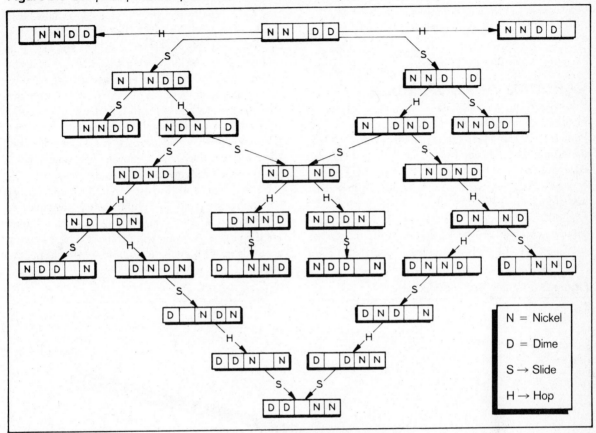

Figure 3.7 An ill-formed problem has an un-bounded search space and thus presents an infinity of "first moves."

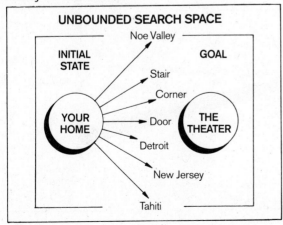

Problem Solving Is Enabled by Knowledge

If problems like planning an evening at the theater are generally harder than the NDP puzzle, how is it that we solve problems like these, and many harder ones, on a daily basis? The reason we can solve such problems so easily is that we have stored experience that we can use to simplify the problem. We know that a quick call to the theater will clarify the goal. If we have the address and the time, we can usually figure out a plan. If not, we can consult other knowledge sources, such as a map or a bus schedule. Many logical options, such as walking to a theater that is 20 miles away, are immediately dismissed without further consideration. We simply know that it is an impractical idea. Hence, the study of complex problem-solving skills quickly becomes a matter of determining what knowledge is needed in order to be able to reduce the huge problem space of an ill-formed problem to a more manageable size.

VARIETIES OF KNOWLEDGE

Knowledge can be classified in a number of ways. Figure 3.8 presents one general classification of knowledge. The level horizontal arrow describes a dimension that indicates how much compiled knowledge an individual has acquired. By compiled knowledge we mean information that is organized, indexed, and stored in such a way that it is easily accessed. Compiled knowledge is readily usable for problem solving. Put another way, compiling is the process of *chunking*. Meaningful portions of knowledge are stored and retrieved as functional units.

The compiling process occurs in two complementary ways. First, topics may be studied formally, as in a school or when we attend lectures and read textbooks. As a result of such study, knowledge is chunked as definitions, axioms, and laws. Successful students emerge from courses in accounting or physics with a firm grasp of the terms, equations, and laws that constitute the formal theories and accepted principles of their disciplines. Typically, however, even though they can describe the knowledge they have learned, they do not know exactly how to apply that knowledge in any practical way.

Earlier, when we discussed the NDP problem, we ended by resorting to combinatorial principles to determine a solution. Principles, laws, and axioms are useful in explaining and justifying why a solution succeeds or fails. But they are often of little help in finding a solution in the first place. General laws

Figure 3.8 Varieties of knowledge.

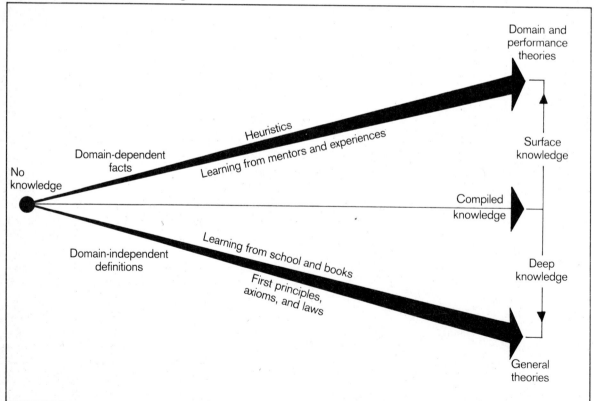

usually fail to indicate exactly how one should proceed when faced with a specific problem. Except in simple cases (like the NDP), formal axioms tend to generate problem spaces that are too large to search.

A second way that knowledge can be compiled is by means of experience or by learning from a mentor. In this case the results are different. Domain-specific facts are learned first. Experience, or a mentor, usually teaches the student to rely on rules-of-thumb to perform tasks or solve problems. Apprentices also acquire competence quickly by learning domain-specific theories. Thus, accountants who learn from a mentor behave *as if* they know accounting theory, even though they may not. Knowledge compiled from experience results in *heuristics*. Heuristics are rules-of-thumb that prune search spaces to a manageable size. They tend to focus attention on a few key patterns. We have seen how a chess master focuses all of his or her attention on a few general patterns. With domain experience, people become competent because they learn to focus quickly on the important facets of a problem, and because they learn the important relationships.

Compiled heuristic knowledge, that is, experience that is well organized and indexed in long-term memory, gives us the edge when we face and solve numerous daily problems. The form of the knowledge is simple, and its power is drawn from all the experience that it summarizes. Knowledge like "Don't walk to cover distances greater than a half-mile" is easily represented as a production rule. As you encode and attend to features of the problem, such productions are recalled and enable you to construct plans and solutions. By this analysis, what makes the NDP hard or easy is your past experience in sliding and hopping coins in a row.

There are many varieties of human problem-solving behavior. One variety occurs when you struggle with a new and relatively unfamiliar problem. With little to go on, you find yourself guessing and experimenting. You use a different approach when you encounter problems that you know a lot about. In that case you systematically gather relevant information, build prototype solutions, ignore lots of irrelevant details, and revise your hypotheses in the light

of constraints. A good theory of problem solving that allows you to reduce your problem to states and operators will usually help. Knowledge about the specific problem domain, including some good heuristics, however, will help a lot more.

THE NATURE OF EXPERTISE

So far, in talking about problem solving, we have focused on two relatively simple problems: solving a puzzle and planning a trip to the theater. Knowledge engineers are concerned primarily with how experts solve problems. The word "expert," of course, can be used in many ways. When we talk about an expert, we mean *an individual who is widely recognized as being able to solve a particular type of problem that most other people cannot solve nearly as efficiently or effectively.*

By insisting on general agreement about who is an expert, we are focusing on performance and thus narrowing our use of the term. We are excluding, for example, individuals sometimes called "experts" in the area of stock market predictions. There is no general agreement among most of the people engaged in stock transactions that any individual knows how to predict stock market behavior with any consistency or accuracy. In contrast, most physicians can agree on a common list of individuals who are experts in radiation therapy, the diagnosis of particular diseases, or in performing specific types of heart surgery. Likewise, in oil exploration, a few individuals are recognized as having expertise in such specialties as diagnosing drilling problems or interpreting geological survey data.

The graphs in Figure 3.9 provide an easy way of visualizing domains in which there is expertise. Results are measured on the vertical axis; the bars represent groups of performers, the top 10 percent, the next 10 percent, etc.

Graph A in Figure 3.9 shows that the best performers are very good, whereas most performers are rather poor. If performance data for a particular task displays this pattern, it indicates that there are experts who perform this task substantially better than most people who attempt it.

It is possible that no one consistently obtains excellent results. Graph B shows the pattern we expect from a task such as stock market analysis. Finally, it may be that just about everyone performs a task very well, as indicated by Graph C in Figure 3.9.

"Expert," as the term is used in knowledge engineering, refers only to the top 10 to 20 percent of the performers in Graph A of Figure 3.9.

Figure 3.9 Finding expertise in a sample of problem solvers.

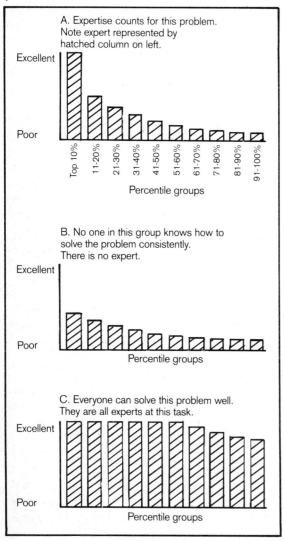

A. Expertise counts for this problem. Note expert represented by hatched column on left.

B. No one in this group knows how to solve the problem consistently. There is no expert.

C. Everyone can solve this problem well. They are all experts at this task.

What Do Experts Know?

Experts perform well because they have a large amount of compiled, domain-specific knowledge stored in long-term memory. It is estimated that a world-class expert, such as a chess grandmaster or a Nobel laureate in Chemistry, has 50,000 to 100,000 chunks of heuristic information about his or her specialty. Each chunk, with all its myriad associations, can be retrieved, examined, and utilized at will. Further, psychologists believe that it takes at least 10 years to acquire 50,000 chunks. This estimate is based on the constraints that our mental "hardware" places on our ability to enter information into long-term memory. Also, a decade seems to fit available biographical data—chess grandmasters, honored scientists, and respected professionals all seem to require at least 10 years of study and practice before they become recognized experts.

Look at Figure 3.10, and recall that compiled knowledge takes two forms: first principles and general theories on the one hand, and heuristics and domain theories on the other. The amount of knowledge an expert requires is such that it is nearly impossible to gain it all from experience. Experience can be too confusing and difficult to organize if one lacks general categories to help classify and index one's experience.

Skilled technicians and master craftspersons sometimes start as apprentices, observe mentors, and become experts within their domain without benefit of formal training. Similarly, some academic specialists, such as logicians or theoretical mathematicians, compile general theories without benefit of experience. Most experts, however, including scientists, physicians, lawyers, composers, accountants, and managers, begin by studying their specialty in school. They acquire a knowledge of the first principles and general theories that are regarded as basic to their profession. Then they begin to practice their profession. If they are lucky, they have a mentor who helps orient them to the specific practices of their profession. In any case, they gain experience, and, in the process, they recompile what they know. They move from a descriptive view of their profession to a procedural view. If they succeed in becoming an expert,

Figure 3.10 General pattern of professional development.

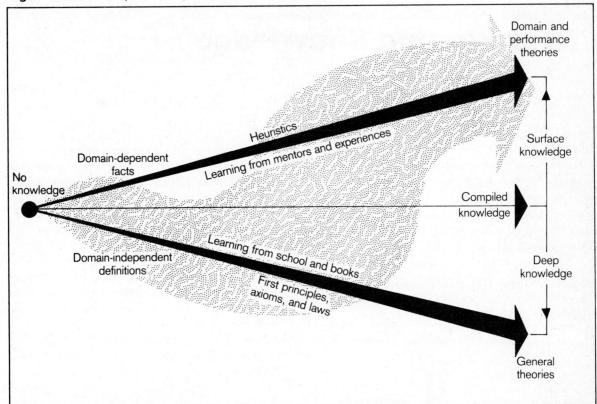

they have rearranged the knowledge in long-term memory so that they can respond to problem situations by using heuristics and specific domain theories. Practicing experts hardly ever explain their recommendations in terms of first principles or general theories. If they encounter unusual or complex problems, however, they will return to first principles to develop an appropriate strategy.

Knowledge engineers refer to the heuristics and domain theories on which experts typically rely as *surface knowledge*. Most expert systems include only surface knowledge, and it normally suffices. The first principles and general theories that an expert will fall back on when faced with a really difficult problem are termed *deep knowledge*. The application of deep knowledge, as we noted earlier, tends to generate unmanageable problem spaces. The use of the heuristics and facts that constitute surface knowledge, on

the other hand, tends to prune a problem space to a manageable size.

SUMMARY

This chapter has provided a brief description of human problem solving from three contrasting perspectives. The chapter began with a microscopic view of the human mind as an information-processing engine. At a higher level of abstraction, we described a formal analysis of how humans seem to approach problems. Finally, we gave a brief summary of how experts solve problems. It turns out that they solve problems the same way we do; they just happen to have compiled a lot of facts and heuristics that allow them swiftly to prune the search spaces presented by the problems in which they specialize.

4.

Representing Knowledge

In the previous chapter we said that human experts solve problems by employing a large number of domain-specific facts and heuristics. In this chapter we want to consider how knowledge engineers analyze the knowledge of an expert and how they represent that knowledge in the software that comprises an expert system.

Figure 4.1 The architecture of a knowledge-based expert system. (The knowledge base is shaded for emphasis.)

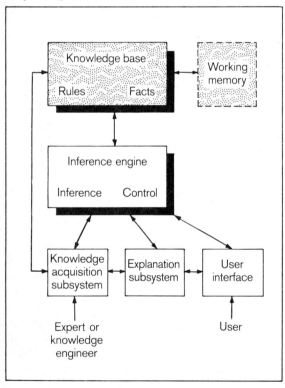

Knowledge base

Rules   Facts

Working memory

Inference engine

Inference   Control

Knowledge acquisition subsystem

Explanation subsystem

User interface

Expert or knowledge engineer

User

Our discussion will focus on one portion of a knowledge system. Figure 4.1 illustrates the architecture of a generic expert system. The system can be divided into two parts. The knowledge base and the working memory constitute one part of the system. The inference engine and all of the subsystems and interfaces constitute the second part.

The knowledge base contains the facts and rules that embody the expert's knowledge. In this chapter we focus on how one can represent facts and rules in a knowledge base. The inference engine contains the inference strategies and controls that an expert uses when he or she manipulates the facts and rules. We consider the design of an inference engine in the next chapter.

The subsystems and interfaces shown in Figure 4.1 vary greatly from system to system, so we shall delay any serious discussion of them until we consider specific tools and systems in Section Two.

AN INFORMAL LOOK AT A KNOWLEDGE BASE

Before a knowledge engineer can begin to think about building a knowledge base, he or she must first acquire and analyze some knowledge. It is typical to talk with an expert and to ask the expert to describe several cases he or she has recently encountered. Here we listen as an expert detective explains how he gathered data on a case:

> "Beyond the obvious facts that Mr. Wilson has at some time done manual labor, that he has been to China, and that he has done a considerable amount of writing lately, I can deduce nothing else. . . ."
> ["But how. . . ."]

"Your hands, my dear sir! Your right hand is quite a size larger than your left. You must have worked with it and the muscles are more developed. . . . The fish you have tattooed immediately above your wrist could only have been done in China. That trick of staining the fishes' scales of a delicate pink is quite peculiar to China. [and] What else can be indicated by that right cuff so very shiny for five inches, and the left one with the smooth patch near the elbow where you rest it upon the desk . . ." (after Sherlock Holmes, *The Red-Headed League*).

When the knowledge of an expert is dissected and examined closely, we often find that it consists of simple ingredients rather than the deep or complex ideas that we might have imagined. Sherlock Holmes has keen observation skills. He pays attention to clothing and its condition. He notices (encodes) ordinary features of Wilson's person—the tattoo and his larger right hand. He links these features to events in Wilson's life with simple relationships. He knows where one must go to acquire certain tattoos, for example, and he makes logical inferences about the plausible causes of unusual wear to clothing.

To create a "detective's knowledge base," we certainly want to include the elements or objects, such as Wilson's coat, to which Holmes attends. In addition, we need a list of characteristics of each of those objects. We need to be able to represent the condition of Wilson's cuffs, for example. Finally, we need some way to link things together. We need to be able to record the fact that "Writers have worn cuffs."

STRATEGIES FOR REPRESENTING KNOWLEDGE

In this chapter we consider five different ways to encode the facts and relationships that constitute knowledge. We shall use Sherlock Holmes's knowledge to illustrate each of five different approaches, which include:

- Semantic networks
- Object–attribute–value triplets
- Rules
- Frames
- Logical expressions

Each method has advantages and disadvantages. At this point we want to provide an overview of each method.

SEMANTIC NETWORKS

The most general representational scheme, and also one of the oldest in AI, is the semantic network (or semantic net). A semantic network is a collection of objects called *nodes*. The nodes are connected together by arcs or *links*. Ordinarily, both the links and the nodes are labeled. Figure 4.2 shows a portion of Holmes's knowledge represented as a semantic network.

There are no absolute constraints as to how nodes and links are named. However, some typical conventions are the following:

1. *Nodes* are used to represent objects and descriptors.
   - *Objects* may be physical objects that can be seen or touched. The coats, hats, and people in the detective's knowledge base are examples of physical objects.
   - *Objects* also may be conceptual entities such as acts, events, or abstract categories. "China" and "2" are nodes in the detective's knowledge base that are conceptual. Places and numbers are more abstract than elbows and sleeves.
   - *Descriptors* provide additional information about objects. "Worn and shiny," for example, stores information about Wilson's coat.
2. *Links* relate objects and descriptors. A link may represent any relationship. Common links include the following:
   - *Is-a* links are often used to represent the class/instance relationship. In our detective's knowledge base, we note that Holmes *is-a* man, for example. That is, Holmes is an instance of the larger class, male. A male, in turn, is an instance of a larger class, persons.
   - A second common relationship is the *has-a* link. *Has-a* links identify nodes that are properties of other nodes. A coat *has-a* sleeve in

Figure 4.2 A detective's knowledge base.

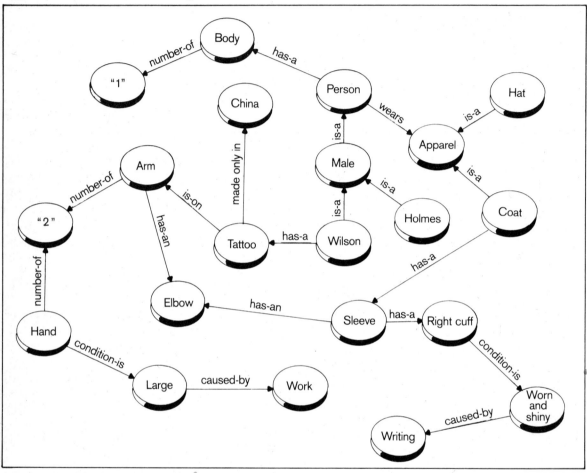

our knowledge base. In contrast to the *is-a* relationship, a sleeve is not an example of a coat. *Has-a* links show part–subpart relationships.

- Some links are definitional. In this knowledge base, the *cover* link between sleeves and arms is a good example of a definitional link, as is the *wear* link between people and clothes.
- Other links capture heuristic knowledge, such as "Work *causes* cuffs to be shiny." Relationships like these enrich the network by providing additional paths.

Flexibility is a major advantage of this representational scheme. New nodes and links can be defined as needed. If we were representing an electrical device, for example, then nodes might be *parts* that are *wired-to* one another. If the network were to describe an institutional hierarchy, then *reports-to* or *supervises* might be the most useful links between people.

Inheritance is another feature of semantic networks. It refers to the ability of one node to "inherit" characteristics of other nodes that are related to it. Property inheritance is one implication of an *is-a* relationship. Property inheritance means that instances of a class are assumed to have all properties of more general classes of which they are members.

Here is how property inheritance works: In our detective's knowledge base, we note that Wilson is a man. Men are persons, persons have bodies, and bodies have arms. This "arm" node is linked as the location of Wilson's tattoo. And, rather than having to create a great number of nodes about Wilson's body structure, we encode a single class, "person," and then reason about Wilson by noting that he is a person. A question such as "Does Wilson have a hand?" is answerable by determining that Wilson is a person and that people have hands. By simply asserting that Holmes is a man, we are able to conclude that he has all the same person features as Wilson.

The benefits of handling redundancy by means of inheritance has a related weakness—the difficulty of handling exceptions. Assume for a moment that Wilson is a one-armed man. We can assert this fact in several ways:

- We can change the enumeration of "arm" from 2 to 1. Of course, that would lead us to believe that Holmes also has one arm.
- We can add a node call "one-armed" and link it to Wilson with an "exception" arc. That represents the exception to the semantic net. Of course it is not clear what implications arise from this exception.
- One problem visible in our example is that one-armed men have but one hand. We can fix that problem by linking the number of hands to the number of arms.

This very small example illustrates that inheritance works very efficiently when there are few exceptions. When exceptions do arise, patches and fixes must be provided. General-purpose exception handling can be quite difficult.

The knowledge representation schema described in this chapter are closely related to AI research in human cognition. Thus, the concepts of semantic nets, links, nodes, and inheritance hierarchies are all related to research into how humans store information.

Figure 4.3 illustrates a semantic net that Collins and Quillian used to study memory. The net is a hierarchy with different attributes associated with different objects. The attributes assigned to the different levels of the hierarchy were derived empirically from laboratory studies. Students were asked questions about different relationships. Thus, for example, a student might be asked: "Is a canary a bird?", "Can a canary sing?", "Can a canary fly?" As obvious as these questions seem, careful studies show that it takes students longer to respond that a canary can fly than it takes them to agree that a canary can sing. Collins and Quillian explain the differences in response time by arguing that people store information at the most abstract level possible. Thus, rather than trying to remember that canaries fly and that robins fly and that sparrows fly, we simply remember that they are all birds and we remember that birds fly and have feathers and lay eggs, etc. Likewise, we store even more general traits, such as eating and breathing, with animals. To determine if a canary can breathe, we first recall that a canary is a bird and then that birds are animals and thus we determine that canaries can breathe.

The only attributes that we store at the lower levels of such a hierarchy are the specific traits associated with the particular species. Thus, we associate song directly with canaries and can recall this fact faster than we can recall that a canary can fly. We also store exceptions with particular species. Thus, if asked if an ostrich can fly, we say "no" because we have stored this specific fact with our concept of ostrich and we do not "move" from ostrich to bird before answering this question. This concept seems to explain test data derived from studies of human subjects, and it has inspired AI researchers to use a similar approach in modeling knowledge representation in some expert systems.

Figure 4.3 The relationship between human recall time and hierarchical storage. Note that recall times increase as the subject must "move up" in the hierarchy to locate values.

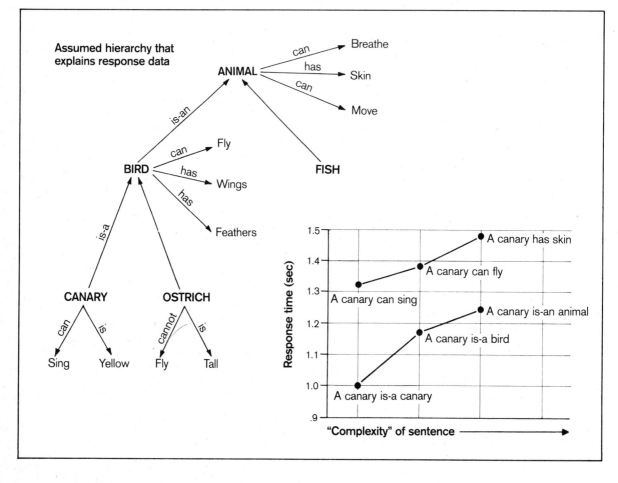

OBJECT–ATTRIBUTE–VALUE TRIPLETS

Another common way to represent factual information is as object–attribute–value (O–A–V) triplets. This representational scheme is used in MYCIN, and so we shall consider it in some detail. In this scheme, objects may be physical entities such as a *door* or a *transistor,* or they may be conceptual entities such as a *logic gate,* a *bank loan,* or a *sales episode.* Attributes are general characteristics or properties associated with objects. Size, shape, and color are typical attributes for physical objects. *Interest rate* is an attribute for a

bank loan, and *setting* might be an attribute for a sales episode. The final member of the triplet is the value of an attribute. The value specifies the specific nature of an attribute in a particular situation. An apple's color may be *red,* for example, or the interest rate for a bank loan may be *12 percent.*

Figure 4.4 shows one of Holmes's facts represented as an object–attribute–value triplet. In this case the object is Wilson's coat. One attribute of the coat is the condition of its cuffs. In our particular examples, the value of "condition of cuffs" is "worn and shiny." Two other objects, Wilson's hands, are shown in

Figure 4.5. Size is an attribute that Holmes identified as important to his reasoning, and we have guessed about some other possible attributes and their values.

Figure 4.4 An object–attribute–value triplet.

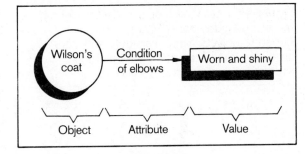

Figure 4.5 Attributes and values of two objects (hands).

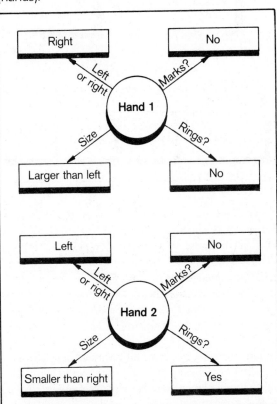

O–A–V and Semantic Networks

Representing knowledge with object–attribute–value triplets is a specialized case of the semantic network approach. Exotic links are banished in favor of just two simple relationships. The object→attribute link is a "has-a" link, and the attribute←value link is an "is-a" link. For example, a bank loan *has a* rate of interest, and 12 percent *is a* rate of interest. Nodes are classified into the three categories: They are either objects, attributes, or values.

Static Knowledge Versus Instances

There is an important distinction between a *static*, unchanging object (with its generic attributes) and a *dynamic instance* of that object that changes from case to case. Our examples so far have been dynamic because they concern Holmes's reasoning about this particular fellow named Wilson. Another time he may be reasoning about Dr. Watson, and Watson's cuffs are likely not to be shiny. If we remove the portions of the object–attribute–value triplet that are specific to this particular case—namely, the values—we are left with a static or generic description of Holmes's knowledge. Figure 4.6 shows the object "coat" with three of its attributes. If a coat appears in Holmes's next case, we expect that he will check to determine new values for the different attributes of a coat.

If you return to Figure 4.1, you will notice that the upper portion of the diagram indicated that the

Figure 4.6 The static portion of an O–A–V triplet.

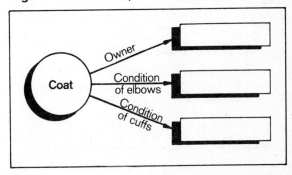

knowledge base is connected to a box labeled "working memory." That box is drawn with dashed lines to indicate that it isn't always there. When an expert system is "between consultations," its *static* knowledge of facts and rules is stored in the knowledge base. When a consultation begins, the system seeks to determine the values of various attributes relative to the particular situation. As values are determined, the system stores this dynamic information in its working memory. The process of determining specific values for the attributes stored in a static knowledge base is often called *instantiation*.

Objects Can Be Related

A second important feature of the O–A–V representation is the manner in which objects are ordered and related to one another. In Figure 4.7 we show a possible ordering of objects for our "detective's knowledge base." Graphs like this are called *trees*. The top object is called the "root" and is used as a starting place for reasoning and for acquiring information. Notice that the objects of the tree are static—this is a possible representation of the objects that Holmes thinks about whenever he meets a new client.

A dynamic form of an object tree is shown in Figure 4.8. In this case objects have instances with values. They are not abstract characteristics; they are Wilson's characteristics. Moreover, objects other

Figure 4.7 Object tree for a detective's knowledge base. (No values have been assigned to any objects or attributes.)

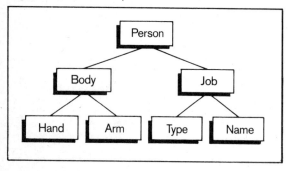

than the root may have multiple instances. In this representation, we do not need to identify two objects, such as "left hand" and "right hand." Instead, we simply provide an object called "hand" with an attribute to store whether it is left or right.

Figure 4.8 *Instantiated object tree for a detective's knowledge base. (Values have been assigned to objects. Moreover, lower objects and attributes have "inherited" the values [Wilson] assigned to higher-level objects.)*

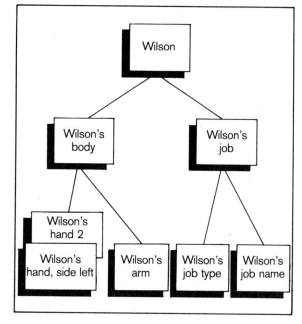

We have not stated exactly what the linkage is between objects. In this example the links could be labeled "subpart," but this is not always the case. Figures 4.9 and 4.10 illustrate two other object trees. If our knowledge base is for appliance troubleshooting, the links may indicate causes or dependencies. Or, if our knowledge base is about career paths in a company, then the links might be labeled "chosen from."

The career path tree also illustrates a new irregularity—trees of objects may be *tangled*. In other words, subordinate objects may be related to more than one higher-level object. This means that the subordinate

Figure 4.9 Appliance fault hierarchy.

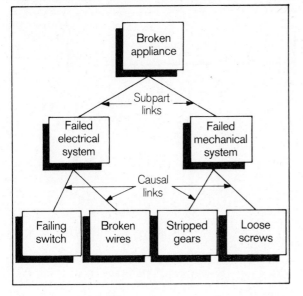

object will inherit properties (or in the case of an organization, assignments or responsibilities) from more than one higher-level object. Tangled trees, like exceptions in an inheritance hierarchy, can be difficult to state unambiguously (just as decision making in a tangled organizational hierarchy can be quite difficult).

Representing Uncertain Facts

A third feature of O–A–V schemes is a procedure for handling uncertainty. It may be that a fact like Wilson's coat sleeves being worn is simply not definite. They are definitely shiny, but only slightly worn. In this case the O–A–V triplets can be modified by a number called a certainty factor. In this case we can say that Wilson's sleeves are worn ".7."

Certainty factors represent the confidence that we have in a piece of evidence. There are a number of different ways of representing certainty factors. Figure

Figure 4.10 Organizational hierarchy.

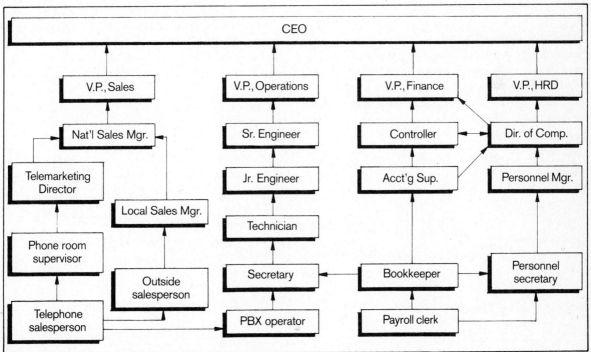

Figure 4.11 Confidence represented by the certainty factors used in MYCIN.

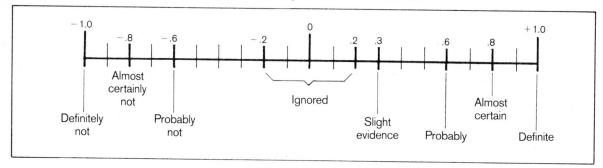

4.11 shows the certainty factors used in MYCIN. The numbers range from −1, indicating definite evidence that a fact is false, to +1, indicating that a fact is definitely true. Certainty factors are not probabilities. They are informal measures of confidence or certainty for a piece of evidence. They represent the degree to which we believe that evidence is, in fact, true. We shall discuss how these weights are used in Chapter 5.

Attribute–Value Pairs

Some systems are built around single objects or, in any case, do not formally represent multiple objects. In such cases the systems represent facts in terms of attribute–value (A–V) pairs rather than triplets. This representation schema works much like an O–A–V schema except that, since it cannot represent multiple objects, it cannot take advantage of inheritance hierarchies.

RULES

Rules are used to represent relationships. Rules can be used with either A–V or O–A–V representations. Since we shall be discussing rules frequently throughout the remainder of the book, it is worth pausing a moment to establish a basic vocabulary. Rules can be simple or quite complex. We have chosen a relatively simple rule from MYCIN to examine. (See box below.)

Each of the four parts of the premise is called an *expression* or an *if clause*. The conclusion below con-

---

Rule:

Premise { If the site of the culture is blood, and
the morphology of the organism is rod, and
the gram stain of the organism is gramneg, and
the patient is a compromised host,

Conclusion { Then there is suggestive evidence (.6) that the identity of the organism is Pseudomonas-aeruginosa.

tains a single expression or *then clause,* although it could just as well contain more than one. The clauses in the premise are connected with the logical operator *and.* They could have been connected by *or* with different results.

We have analyzed the five expressions, the five O–A–V triplets, that comprise the rule in the following table:

	Attribute	Object	Value	(cf)
If	Site	Culture	Blood	—
	Morphology	Organism	Rod	—
	Gram stain	Organism	Gramneg	—
	Compromised	Patient	True	—
Then	Identity	Organism	Pseudomonas-aeruginosa	(.6)

This same rule, written for an A–V system, would simply omit the reference to the object. In addition, the *if clauses* referring to "culture" and "patient" would have to be omitted or rephrased, since the entire rule would implicitly refer to the organism.

In MYCIN, rules link the values for attributes of objects. When a rule is invoked, the system checks to see if the O–A–V values in each of the *if clauses* are true. If any *if clause* is false, the system simply stops processing the rule. If they are all true, then the O–A–V in the *then clause* is assumed to be true. The rule below is one that Holmes could have used to establish how a size difference between Wilson's hands is related to the type of job that Wilson once had:

Premise   If   a person's right hand is larger than his left hand,

Conclusion Then his job type is/has been manual labor.

Uncertain Rules

Just as certainty factors can be attached to facts, they can be attached to rules. If Holmes is only moderately certain that pink tattoos originate only in China, then we can represent that indefinite relationship by attaching a certainty factor as shown in the rule below. Uncertain rules conclude values that are less than definite. Thus the method of handling uncertain facts and relationships is unified.

Premise   If   tattoo is a fish, and
                     the color of the fish's scales is
                     pink,

Conclusion Then origin of tattoo is China. (.7)

"Variable" Rules

Some knowledge systems have rules that incorporate pattern-matching "variables." In such systems, the "variable" rule allows the system to substitute many different facts into the same general format. Consider, for example, the following three rules:

Rule 1: If   the tattoo is of a fish, and
                  the color of the fish's scales is pink,

          Then the origin of the tattoo is China.

Rule 2: If   the tattoo is of a snake, and
                  the color of the snake's scales is
                  blue,

          Then the origin of the tattoo is Hong
                Kong.

Rule 3: If   the tattoo is of a dragon, and
                  the color of the dragon's scales is
                  red,

          Then the origin of the tattoo is Beijeng.

We could represent all three rules by means of a single "variable" rule, as follows:

If   the tattoo is of an X, and the color of the X's
      scales is Y, and origin (X,Y) is Z,

Then the origin of the tattoo is Z.

To make it possible for a system to use such a rule, of course, we would need to add some kind of "look up" table with information like that on the next page:

origin (fish,pink) is China
origin (snake,blue) is Hong Kong
origin (dragon,red) is Beijeng

FRAMES

Frames provide another method for representing facts and relationships. A frame is a description of an object that contains slots for all of the information associated with the object. Slots, like attributes, may store values. Slots may also contain *default values,* pointers to other frames, sets of rules, or procedures by which values may be obtained. The inclusion of these additional features make frames different from O–A–V triplets. From one perspective, frames allow for richer representations of knowledge. From another, they are more complex and more difficult to develop than simpler O–A–V/rule systems.

Figure 4.12 shows a frame of our detective's knowledge base. Wilson's coat is the object, and there are slots for its properties. Notice that some slots allow for default values. The default values in this frame assert that, in lieu of contradictory information, we assume that the coat has two arms, that it is made of wool, and that it has pockets. Default values are quite useful when representing knowledge in domains where exceptions are rare.

A *procedural attachment* is another way that a slot in a frame can be filled. In this case the slot contains instructions for determining an entry. The last two slots in the frame in Figure 4.12 illustrate procedural attachments for determining the size and the style of Wilson's coat. An attachment is a sequence of instructions for computing an entry. The instructions may combine information from other slots (as is the case with style) and from other frames (such as the size procedure).

The inclusion of procedures in frames joins together in a single representational strategy two complementary (and, historically, competing) ways to state and store facts: *procedural* and *declarative* representations.

• A *declarative representation* of a fact is simply an assertion that the fact is true. "April is the fourth

month of the year" is a declarative statement about the position of the month. Along with assertions about the remaining months of the year and an inferencing scheme, a list of dates such as "November 14" and "August 23" could be put in order.

• A *procedural representation* of a fact is a set of instructions that, when carried out, arrive at a result consistent with the fact. We could write a procedure, therefore, that sorts dates into a proper order. The result of the procedure, which is likely to be more efficient than the declarative route, is a list identical to the declarative result. But nowhere in the procedural instructions is there an explicit, inspectable statement that "April is the fourth month of the year."

Thus, declarative and procedural representations are alternative strategies that achieve the same results. (See Figure 4.13.) To the degree that facts are independent and changing, then declarative approaches are more understandable or transparent to readers and more easily maintained due to their modularity. Experts and users usually feel more com-

Figure 4.12 Frame for Wilson's coat.

COAT	
Slots:	**Entries:**
Owner	Wilson
Condition	Rumpled
Condition of cuffs	Worn, shiny
Condition of elbow	Worn, shiny
Number of arms	Default: 2
Fabric	Default: wool
Pockets?	Default: yes
Size:	If needed, find owner's height and weight, and compare to Table X.
Style:	If needed, find out collar:, pockets:, and length:; then look in Table Y.

fortable using a declarative perspective. Procedural representations, on the other hand, are more efficient to use but harder to maintain. The outcome of a procedure is easier to trace, since one can easily examine the flow of instructions. Knowledge engineers are usually more comfortable using a procedural perspective. In principle, any procedural representation can be recast as declarative representation, and vice versa. The two perspectives, considered as two complementary aspects of knowledge, are often referred to as *dual semantics*. (See Figure 4.14.) Frames gain power, generality, and popularity by their ability to integrate both declarative and procedural representations.

Frames can also support pictorial representations of values arranged so that a change in the value results in a change in the pictorial representation or vice versa. Representations of this type are typically called *active values*, and we shall defer further discussion of them until we reach the chapters on tools and systems.

In summary, the key ideas behind a frame system are as follows: Each object consists of a set of slots. Some slots contain properties associated with the

Figure 4.13 *The stress between procedural and descriptive perspectives.*

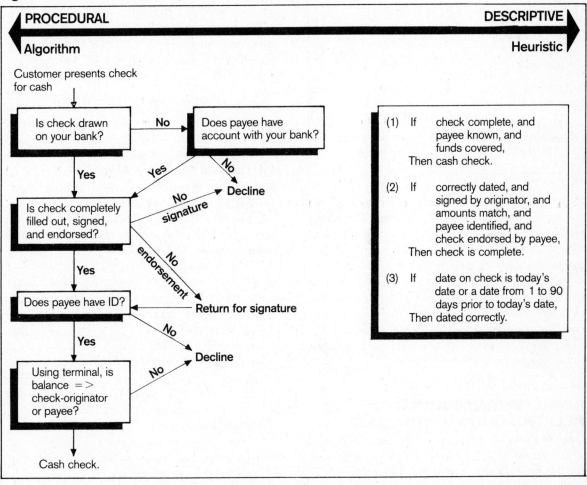

Figure 4.14 Dual semantics—two perspectives on the same knowledge.

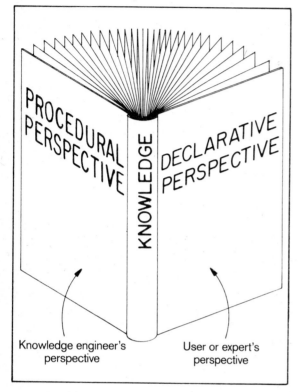

Knowledge engineer's perspective

User or expert's perspective

object of the frame. Other slots may include default values, display instructions, or rule sets. Procedural attachments can be incorporated in what is otherwise a declarative representation. Frames may be linked together to allow for inheritance.

Ultimately, frames, and O–A–V/rule systems, can each be considered as special cases of semantic networks. O–A–Vs and frames can each be viewed as portions of a semantic net, as shown in Figure 4.15. The same facts can be represented in any one of the three systems.

REPRESENTING FACTS AND RELATIONSHIPS USING LOGIC

Logic provides another way to represent knowledge. There are several logical notations. We shall discuss the two most common forms: propositional logic and predicate calculus. We shall then examine how a logical system can be used to represent factual and relational knowledge.

Systems of Logic

Propositional logic is a common logical system. Propositions are statements that are either true or false. Propositions that are linked together with connectives, such as AND, OR, NOT, IMPLIES, and EQUIVALENT, are called compound statements. Propositional logic is concerned with the truthfulness of compound statements. There are rules for propagating the truthfulness of statements, depending on the connectives. For example, if one proposition X is true and another proposition Y is false, then the compound statement "X AND Y" is false, whereas the compound statement "X OR Y" is true. Other rules allow for inferences. If X is known to be true, and if X IMPLIES Y, then we can conclude that Y is true.

Predicate calculus is an extension to propositional logic. The elementary unit in predicate logic is an object. Statements about objects are called predicates. For example, "*is-red*(ball)" is an assertion that says that a ball is red. This assertion is either true or false. Predicates can address more than one object. The statement that "*daughter-of*(Mimi, Susan)" is an example of a two-place predicate. This statement asserts that Mimi is the daughter of Susan. Ordinary connectives can be used to link together predicates into larger expressions. Thus, the statement "*daughter-of*(Mimi, Susan) AND *daughter-of*(Mimi, David)" is an expression that is either true or false, depending on whether Susan and David are, in fact, the parents of a daughter named Mimi.

To assert that Wilson is a man, we can simply say "man(Wilson)." Additional assertions that constitute our detective's knowledge base are shown in Table 4.1. As is typical of logic, facts are numbered to facilitate their use in proofs. Also, as assertions 2 and 3 show, predicates may be nested.

Logical formulations represent knowledge in a different manner than the preceding three approaches. Ordinarily, when we represent facts we do it because

Figure 4.15 Semantic nets, object–attribute–value triplets and frames.

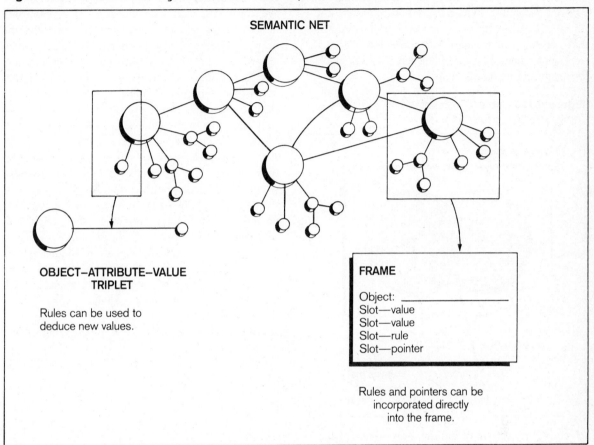

SEMANTIC NET

OBJECT–ATTRIBUTE–VALUE
TRIPLET

Rules can be used to
deduce new values.

FRAME

Object: _____
Slot—value
Slot—value
Slot—rule
Slot—pointer

Rules and pointers can be
incorporated directly
into the frame.

we want to retrieve them directly. They may be the names of semantic network nodes, the values associated with an object and an attribute, or the entries in the slot of a frame. We ordinarily search to locate the needed values.

Table 4.1

1. *man*(Wilson)
2. *condition*(sleeves(coat),worn)
3. *condition*(sleeves(coat),shiny)
4. *mark*(arm,tattoo)
5. *color*(tattoo,pink)
6. . . .

Logic is a bit different. If we assert a fact in predicate calculus, its value must be either *true* or *false*. We cannot ask, "What is the condition of Wilson's coat?" and find out that the sleeves are shiny and worn. We can, however, ask: "Is it true that the condition of the coat's sleeves is worn and shiny?" The answer, in accordance with Table 4.1 (items 2 and 3), is TRUE.

It is difficult graphically to compare a logical approach to the three previous systems we described. One simple way is to display logical statements with Venn diagrams. The overlapping circles identify sets of objects with common characteristics. We use logic to assert facts that are represented graphically by overlapping circles. Then we can ask the system: "Is a particular segment occupied?" and get a "yes" or "no" answer, depending on whether or not the system finds the appropriate segment among the relationships that have been asserted. Figure 4.16 shows how we might represent a small portion of our detective knowledge by means of a Venn diagram.

Figure 4.16 A logical (Venn diagram) view of some detective knowledge.

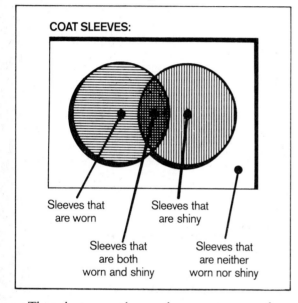

Thus, logic provides another way to assert facts about the world. Facts take the form of logical expressions that consist of predicates and values. Logical expressions that describe knowledge are either true or false. Seeking values in a logic-based system is not as direct as seeking values in the other systems we have discussed. On the other hand, great theoretical elegance can be achieved when logic is used to formalize an appropriate knowledge domain.

SUMMARY

We have described four methods for representing factual knowledge. The most general is the semantic network. Nodes and links of any kind are used to arrange and relate facts. Attribute-value pairs and object–attribute–value triplets are one specialization of a semantic network. Frames are another. The O–A–V triplets are intuitively simpler to use because they carry in them categorizations of knowledge. Most of the knowledge systems built to date use O–A–V triplets and rules to represent the knowledge they contain. Frames are particularly useful for specifying all the important features of an object (its slots), for providing default values, and for attaching procedures with which the values of a slot are obtained. Frame systems are becoming more popular as more complex systems are being built. Predicate logic is a fourth way of representing knowledge. It is more popular in Europe and Japan at the moment, but will undoubtedly become more popular in the United States in the near future, since it is a very powerful approach to building knowledge representations.

5.

Drawing Inferences

In Chapter 4 we considered how an expert's knowledge can be formalized and stored in the knowledge base. In this chapter we consider the strategies used to draw inferences and control the reasoning process. Inference and control strategies guide a knowledge system as it uses the facts and rules stored in its knowledge base, and the information it acquires from the user.

Figure 5.1 provides an overview of the architecture of an expert system. Notice that the inference engine stands between the user and the knowledge base. The inference engine performs two major tasks. First, it examines existing facts and rules, and adds new facts when possible. Second, it decides the order in which inferences are made. In doing so, the inference engine conducts the consultation with the user.

As you begin to read this chapter you may think that you have finally arrived at the heart of an expert system. The representation of facts and rules was not very complicated. You may imagine that it must be that the inference engine is powerful and complex. In fact, this is not the case. Inference engines, like representational schemes, are relatively simple.

This chapter discusses the following topics related to inference and control:

Inference
- *Modus ponens*
- Reasoning about uncertainty
- Resolution

Control
- Backward and forward chaining
- Depth-first versus breadth-first search
- Monotonic versus nonmonotonic reasoning

INFERENCE

Modus ponens
The most common inference strategy used in knowledge systems is the application of a logical rule called *modus ponens*. This rule says, as we all do without

Figure 5.1 The architecture of a knowledge-based expert system. (The inference engine is shaded for emphasis.)

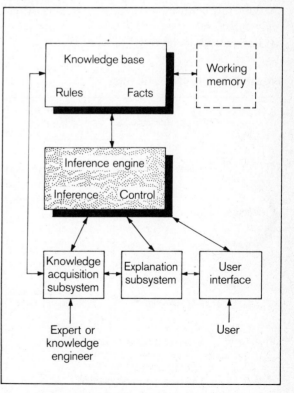

thinking about it, that when A is known to be true and if a rule states, "If A, then B," it is valid to conclude that B is true. Stated differently, when we discover that the premises of a rule are true, we are entitled to believe the conclusions.

Figure 5.2 shows two rules and some facts from the detective's knowledge base. Rules test and conclude values for attributes of objects. Wilson, for example, has an attribute called *hand sizes,* which has the value *different.* Rule 1 states that if a *person's hand sizes* are *different,* then a *person's job type* has been *manual labor.* Because the antecedent of Rule 1 is true, *modus ponens* allows us to conclude that Wilson's job type has been manual labor. If the second rule is tested, it will not succeed. Since Wilson's collar is not a clerical collar, the rule does not support the conclusion that his job is religious.

There are two important implications to be learned from the use of *modus ponens* in knowledge systems. First, the rule is simple, so reasoning based on it is easily understood. Holmes's reasoning, when represented with rules and when *modus ponens* is used, is quite clear and easy to understand.

Figure 5.2 Some facts and rules.

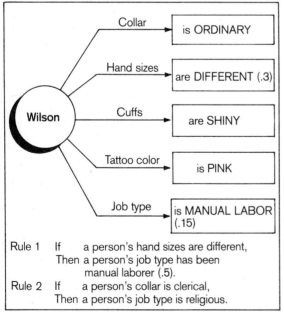

Collar	is ORDINARY
Hand sizes	are DIFFERENT (.3)
Cuffs	are SHINY
Tattoo color	is PINK
Job type	is MANUAL LABOR (.15)

Rule 1   If   a person's hand sizes are different,
         Then a person's job type has been
              manual laborer (.5).
Rule 2   If   a person's collar is clerical,
         Then a person's job type is religious.

A second implication of the singular use of *modus ponens* (and many knowledge systems depend entirely on this rule) is that certain implications that are valid cannot be drawn. For example, another rule of logic states: When B is known to be false, and if there is a rule, "If A, then B," then it is valid to conclude that A is false. This rule, which has the Latin name *modus tollens,* applies to cases like the following:

Rule:

> If   Wilson has a tattoo of a fish with delicate pink scales,
>
> Then   Wilson has been to China.

Given fact: Wilson has *not* been to China.

New fact: Wilson does *not* have the fish tattoo.

This conclusion, as obvious as it seems to us, cannot be reached by most expert systems.

In summary, a common rule for deriving new facts from rules and known facts is *modus ponens.* It is a simple, intuitively appealing way to conduct reasoning. Not all possible valid inferences can be drawn using just this rule.

Reasoning about Uncertainty

In conventional programming we expect that all required information is provided before computation takes place. It makes no sense to try to balance a checkbook with missing numbers. In knowledge programming, this is not necessarily the case. Just as consultants and advisors must typically deal with cases for which some information is missing or unknown, an inference engine must be able to handle incomplete information.

Unknown information is handled by allowing rules to fail when information necessary to evaluate the premises of these rules is simply unavailable. The result, of course, depends on the exact nature of the premise. If clauses in a premise are connected to each other by AND, then all the clauses must be evaluated as true before a rule can succeed. In this case, if the user answers "unknown" to any part of the premise, the rule fails. If, however, the clauses are connected by ORs, then one piece of unknown information need not preclude the rule from succeeding. In this second case, a rule may succeed even though the user answered "unknown" to a question related to one clause in the premise of that rule.

Rules can also be included in a knowledge base to provide knowledge about incomplete information explicitly. Experts are usually familiar with providing advice without complete information. In fact, part of their expertise is knowing when to ignore missing information and when to stop and get it. We can imagine Holmes asking, "Has that revolver been fired lately?" and Dr. Watson answering, "I don't know." At this point, Holmes may ask another question: "Does the barrel smell of sulphur?" Such selective probing is represented by means of a rule like this:

If "Revolver recently fired?" is unknown, and smell of sulphur is strong,

Then "Revolver recently fired?" is "Yes."

It may be unnecessary to probe further. Another rule about revolvers that Holmes might suggest is:

If "Revolver is loaded?" is unknown,

Then "Revolver is loaded?" is "Yes!"

The user of a knowledge system may believe that a fact is true, but not be entirely certain. Most knowledge systems provide for uncertain information. Degree of certainty is represented as a number attached to a fact. In MYCIN, for example, certainty factors range from -1 to $+1$. Rules also have a certainty factor associated with them. The inference engine handles indefinite or uncertain information by propagating certainty factors.

There are three ways that the degrees of certainty are managed in MYCIN:

- Facts may be concluded by more than one rule. A combining function blends the certainty factors.
- Compound premises (those with more than one clause joined by the operators AND or OR) may

test uncertain facts. An uncertain premise leads to an uncertain conclusion.
- Rules themselves may be less than definite.

The same value can be concluded for an attribute more than one time. Several rules can succeed, each one indicating that a value of an attribute is likely, although not definite. The MYCIN inference engine combines these less definite results. For example, the value for Wilson's job type may be concluded as "manual labor" with a confidence of .6 and later concluded again as "manual labor" with a confidence of .5. When the first conclusion is made, "manual labor" is entered into active memory with the confidence .6. Later, when the second conclusion occurs, .6 and .5 are combined as shown in Figure 5.3. There remains a distance of .4 between the original certainty (.6) and a definite conclusion (1.0). This remainder, .4, is multiplied by the certainty for the new fact (.5) to generate an additional increment of .2. The increment factor is added to the original value, resulting in combined .8 confidence in "manual labor." As more positive information emerges, the confidence in a conclusion rises. If a definite conclusion occurs, then the combined certainty becomes definite. Indefinite information, on the other hand, will never accumulate to yield a definite conclusion.

Figure 5.3 A graphic view of the effect of combining two certainty factors. The first conclusion is .6 certain. The second conclusion is .4 certain, which thus pushes the total certainty 40 percent closer to total certainty.

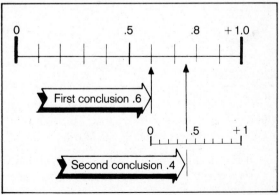

The order in which information is combined does not matter. Combining .6 with .5 is the same as combining .5 with .6.

Premises are evaluated differently depending on the number of clauses and logical connectives they contain. In MYCIN, rules succeed if:

- The premise is a single clause that has a confidence factor (cf) greater than .2, or
- The premise contains clauses connected by ORs, and the maximum cf value for the clauses is greater than .2, or
- The premise contains clauses connected by ANDs, and the minimum cf value for the clauses is greater than .2.

The conclusion reached by a rule is tempered by uncertainty in the premise. Figure 5.4 shows how this works. Holmes has a rule that certain tattoos come only from China. However, when he looks at Wilson's tattoo, he may be only partially convinced (cf = .60) that the tattoo is the special one. This certainty factor is propagated by the rule that concludes Wilson has been to China (.60).

Figure 5.4 A conclusion tempered by the uncertainty of a premise.

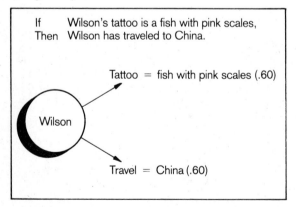

In the MYCIN system, the conclusions of a rule can carry separate certainty factors. The cf attached to the conclusions operates in one of two ways:

- If the premise succeeds with definite certainty, then the value is concluded with its attached cf.

- If the premise succeeds but is less than definite, then the product of the conclusion cf and the premise cf are multiplied to obtain the final conclusion cf. This case is shown in Figure 5.5, and discussed below.

We return now to the detective's knowledge base. If Holmes is somewhat certain (.4) that he sees a man with shiny cuffs, then the rule comes into play (or "fires," as knowledge engineers say). The rule declares a likely but indefinite relationship between shiny cuffs and writing (.7). The premise succeeds because Holmes's certainty is greater than .2. The conclusion is weighted by a certainty factor that is the product of the premise cf and the conclusions cf, or .28.

Figure 5.5 Rules propagate uncertainty.

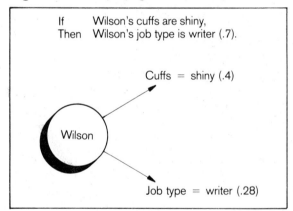

Resolution

Resolution is one way to discover whether a new fact is valid, given a set of logical statements. As we noted earlier, in a logic-based representation we cannot ask: "What is the value of *advice*?" Rather, we can ask: "Is *advice = take a cab* true?"

In order to show an example of resolution, we need to establish two other logical operations. First, it is equivalent to say "If A, then B" or "Not (A) or B." For example, we can say, "If you have an apple, then you have a fruit." Or, equivalently, we can say, "Either you do not have an apple or you have a fruit."

The expressions sound different, but they really are the same.

In logic, the way to prove equivalence is with a *truth table*. If two expressions are equivalent, then the pattern of true and false will be the same as in the truth table. Here is the truth table for the expressions in question:

A	B	Not (A)	If A Then B	Not (A) or B
T	T	F	T	T
T	F	F	F	F
F	T	T	T	T
F	F	T	T	T

The second operation we need for resolution theorem proving is as follows. If we have not(A) or B and A or C, then we can resolve these two clauses to a single one: B or C. A and not(A) cancel when the clauses are combined.

Applying the two operations: (1) The ability to write IF–THEN statements as OR statements, and (2) the ability to combine OR statements, gives us the resolution strategy. Here is how it works with a subset of the information from our theater knowledge base.

Given:
1. If distance > 5 miles,
   Then means = drive.
2. If means = drive,
   Then advice = take a cab.
3. Fact: Distance > 5 miles.

Step 1: Rewrite the IF–THEN statements as OR statements:
1. Not (distance > 5 miles) or means = drive.

2. Not (means = drive) or advice = take a cab.

3. Distance > 5 miles.

Step 2: Assert the negation of the thesis in question, and add it to the list:
4. Not (advice = take a cab).

Step 3: Resolve pairs of facts with the following rule:

Not (X) or Y
Not (Y) or Z
───────────
Not (X) or Z

In our example, we have:
1. Not (distance > 5)
       or   means = drive
   Not (means = drive)
       or advice = take a cab
   ─────────────────────────
   Not (distance > 5)
       or advice = take a cab

2. Not (distance > 5)
       or advice = take a cab
   Distance > 5
   ─────────────────────────
   Advice = take a cab

3. Advice = take a cab
   Not (advice = take a cab)
   ─────────────────────────
   CONTRADICTION!!

Step 4: Accept that the thesis is *true* if a contradiction is encountered when resolving clauses, one of which is the negation of the thesis.

In the example above, this means that we should believe that "advice = take a cab" is correct.

Resolution strategies can be automated. The example we have shown is an example of resolution used with propositional logic. An example using predicate logic would be more complex, but similar. The important point is that logical systems use resolution strategies in place of *modus ponens*.

CONTROL

There are two primary problems addressed by the control portion of the inference engine:

1. A knowledge system must have a way to decide where to start. Rules and facts reside in a static knowledge base. There must be a way for the reasoning process to begin.

2. The inference engine must resolve conflicts that occur when alternative lines of reasoning emerge. It could be, for example, that the system reaches a point at which three or five or more rules are ready to fire. The inference engine must choose which rule to examine next.

Table 5.1 shows some facts and rules about getting to a theater on time. If the distance is greater than 5 miles, for example, then we probably ought to drive to get there. Another rule says that if we need to drive and the location is downtown, then it is better to take a cab. Table 5.1 is a miniature knowledge base that contains knowledge about what action to take to get to a theater.

Table 5.1   Rules about Getting to the Theater

Rule	IF: (Premise)	THEN: (Conclusion)
1	Distance > 5 miles	⟶ Means is "drive"
2	Distance > 1 mile and Time < 15 minutes	⟶ Means is "drive"
3	Distance > 1 mile and Time > 15 minutes	⟶ Means is "walk"
4	Means is "drive" and Location is "downtown"	⟶ Action is "take a cab"
5	Means is "drive" and Location is not "downtown"	⟶ Action is "drive your car"
6	Means is "walk" and Weather is "bad"	⟶ Action is "take a coat and walk"
7	Means is "walk" and Weather is "good"	⟶ Action is "walk"

In an object–attribute–value system, it is common to identify a goal attribute and attempt to discover its value. Attributes in the theater knowledge base rep-resent properties such as the distance and location of the theater, as well as the time available for travel. The purpose of the system is to select one action from four choices. Thus, the goal attribute is *action*.

Rule 4 says, "If the theater location is downtown and the means of travel is driving, then action is, 'Take a cab.'" *Modus ponens* allows us to conclude that we should "Take a cab" if the premise of this rule turns out to be true. The premise of Rule 4 contains attributes for which values are not known. One standard control strategy, called *back-chaining*, identi-fies these new attributes as subgoals. Then other rules are examined that conclude values for this new sub-goal attribute. Back-chaining continues until values are obtained for the subgoal attribute. Results are passed forward, and eventually conclusions are drawn about the original goal.

Here is an example of how back-chaining with a goal attribute works, using the knowledge base about getting to the theater:

1. *Action* is identified as the goal attribute. Rules 4, 5, and 6 conclude about *action*.
2. Rule 4 concludes that *action* is "Take a cab." Its premise is true if *means* is "driving," and so obtaining the value for *means* is the new goal.
3. Rules 1, 2, and 3 conclude about *means*. Rule 1 tests the magnitude of a numerical attribute, *distance*.

Back-chaining must stop at some point. The sys-tem must inquire occasionally in order to obtain information from the user. In the theater knowledge base it makes sense to ask the user, "What is the distance to the theater?" Attributes are ordinarily marked as to whether or not their values should be obtained from rules or by asking.

4. A value for *distance* is obtained by asking. We shall assume that the answer is "2 miles."
5. Two miles is less than 5 miles, and so Rule 1 fails. Finding a value for *means* is the current subgoal. Rule 2 is tried.
6. The first clause of the premise of Rule 2 depends on the value of *distance*. The value is stored in the dynamic knowledge base, and so it can be tested immediately. The first clause is true.

7. The second clause in Rule 2 depends on the value of *time*. A second question is generated. Here we shall assume that the time to get to the theater is 10 minutes. Hence, the second clause is true, and Rule 2's premise succeeds.

8. Rule 2 concludes that *means* has the value *driving*.

Now the inference engine has another choice to make. It could take this single value for *means* and go back to Rule 4. Or it could continue searching for other rules that conclude about *means*. The decision depends on the nature of the attribute under consideration. If the attribute can take on more than one value, then the search for additional rules should continue. In this example, we shall assume that more than one means is possible, and we shall allow the search to continue.

9. Rule 3 is tested but fails due to its second clause. All necessary values are in working memory, so this step takes place "quietly." That is, the user of the system is not queried, because the information is already known.

10. No other rules conclude about the value of *means*. The subgoal is complete, and the inference engine focuses on Rule 4 again.

11. The first clause of Rule 4 succeeds, and the second comes under inspection. *Location* is an attribute determined by asking, and here we shall assume that the answer is "downtown."

12. Rule 4 succeeds, and a value for *action* is entered as a new fact in the dynamic knowledge base. We shall assume that there can be more than one action, so the consultation session continues.

13. Rules 5, 6, and 7 are tested, but each fails due to either the value of location or the value of means.

14. After Rule 7 fails, the consultation is over. *Action* is marked as an attribute to be displayed, so the advice, "Take a cab," is typed on the screen.

Figure 5.6 shows another view of the inference process. Attributes are shown as nodes connected by links. The links refer to rules that first call for values of the attributes. Some expert systems display this inference network dynamically during a consultation. The numbers in circles indicate the order in which events would occur in a MYCIN-type consultation. The sequences do not need to occur in this order. To discuss some alternatives, we shall need to introduce some technical terms.

Backward and Forward Chaining

In the theater example, the inference engine started at the goal and worked "backward" through the subgoals in an effort to choose an answer. MYCIN, and most existing expert systems, use a backward chaining strategy. If the possible outcomes (i.e., the values of the goal attribute) are known, and if they are reasonably small in number, then backward chaining is very efficient. Backward chaining systems are sometimes called goal-directed systems.

In some cases the goal or solution needs to be constructed or assembled. It may be because the number of possible outcomes is large. In such cases, a forward chaining strategy is often used. In a forward chaining system, premises of the rules are examined to see whether or not they are true, given the information on hand. If so, then the conclusions are added to the list of facts known to be true and the system examines the rules again. Forward chaining systems are sometimes called data-driven systems.

Forward chaining systems make clear the distinction between the knowledge base and the working memory. Working memory contains facts that emerge in a consultation. The premises of the rules in the knowledge base are compared to the contents of working memory. When a rule succeeds, its conclusion(s) is placed in the working memory.

Reasoning in a forward chaining system is described as a "recognize–act" cycle. First, the rules that can succeed, given the contents of working memory, are recognized. One rule is selected, and then the action or conclusion is asserted into working memory. Then the system proceeds to the next cycle and checks again to see what rules succeed.

We can illustrate forward chaining with the theater

Figure 5.6 Inference tree for the theater knowledge base. Circled numbers indicate the order in which the knowledge base was searched during a consultation.

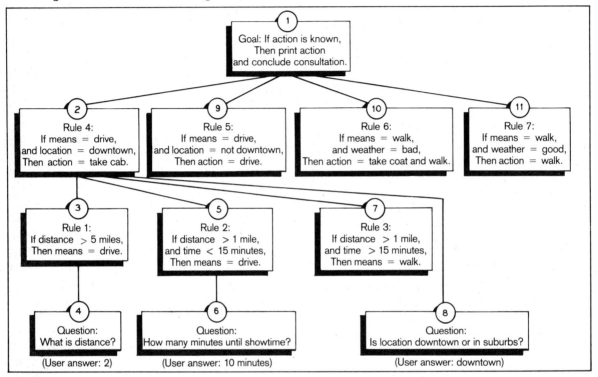

knowledge base. Let's begin by asserting that the theater is located 6 miles away, the weather is bad, the theater's location is downtown, and the film starts in 10 minutes.

1. On the first cycle, Rules 1 and 2 both succeed. One strategy for selecting one of the two rules is to choose on the basis of rule order, so we shall select Rule 1. We act on Rule 1 and assert "means is driving" into working memory.

2. On the second cycle, we recognize that Rules 1, 2, and 4 succeed. Another common strategy for selecting a single rule when several compete is to set aside rules that have already succeeded. Using this strategy in combination with rule order yields Rule 2. Acting on Rule 2, "means is driving," is again asserted to working memory.

3. On the third cycle, Rules 1, 2, and 4 are again

recognized. We toss out 1 and 2 because they have succeeded. Rule 4 remains, and when we act on Rule 4, "action is take a cab" is stored in working memory.

4. On the next cycle, no new rules emerge, so we stop. Alternately, in a forward chaining system we would have rules such as "If action is known, then print action" or "If action is known, then stop."

Conflict resolution schemes for larger systems are more complex than the two simple rules we used here. Control of forward chaining systems is somewhat more complex than that of backward chainers. Our miniature knowledge base, although it is small, shows some of the complexities associated with forward chaining systems.

The shape of the search space determines whether forward or backward chaining is more efficient. Figure

5.7 shows two different search spaces. In column A, there are a number of attributes linked via rules to enumerated sets of solutions. Such a search space might occur in a problem associated with configuring computers. If there are 50 basic configurations, then the task of the knowledge system is to select which of the 50 is the most appropriate configuration for this problem.

Column B represents a problem in which the goal states may not even be known when the system begins to reason. Building plans from the ground up is an example of reasoning where no solution exists until the reasoning process is complete. When there are no goal states, there is no place from which to back-chain. Forward chaining is the only solution. Problems associated with monitoring are often solved with forward chaining inference mechanisms.

Depth-First Versus Breadth-First Search

In addition to distinguishing between backward chaining and forward chaining strategies, we also need to distinguish between depth-first and breadth-first search of a knowledge base. In a depth-first search, the inference engine takes every opportunity to produce a subgoal. From "action," the engine backs up to "means" and then "distance." Searching for detail first is the theme of back-chaining in a depth-first manner. A breadth-first search sweeps across all premises in a rule before digging for greater detail. Breadth-first search will be more efficient if one rule succeeds and the goal attribute's value is obtained.

Most systems employ depth-first search. Digging deeper and deeper into details and following a chain of rules directs the questions that the knowledge

Figure 5.7 *Major categories of search strategies used by inference engines.*

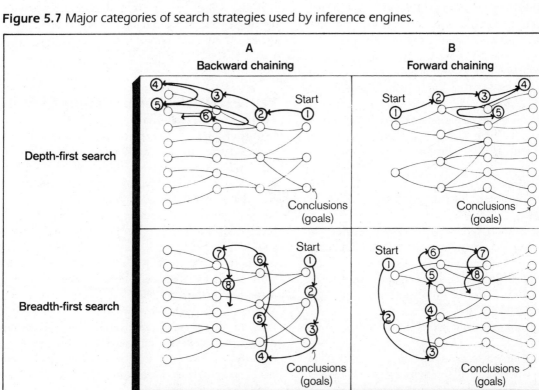

system asks in a meaningful way. The results of a blood test, for example, might indicate a certain disease. A depth-first back-chaining knowledge system asks all the particular questions about a particular blood test at the same time, because it is digging into these details. A breadth-first search across a rule base will often produce questioning that appears to be random as it jumps from one topic to the next: "How is the blood test?", "What is the respiration like?", "How about color and tone?" Random questioning can be disconcerting to users. Depth-first search has the effect of pursuing a particular theme until all information has been obtained, and it seems to be the preferred method in the field.

If one wanted to draw a loose analogy to human problem solvers, one could say that "generalists" use a breadth-first strategy. They begin by inquiring in a general way about aspects of a problem. "Specialists," on the other hand, tend to focus on a specific aspect of the problem and then probe for a lot of details about that aspect. Obviously, each has its place. In the long run, a mixed strategy is probably best.

Figure 5.7 summarizes and defines the basic terms we have introduced thus far, namely, forward and backward chaining, depth-first and breadth-first search. If all states are examined, then search is exhaustive. If search is suspended when a value is obtained, then it is nonexhaustive.

Monotonic Versus Nonmonotonic Reasoning

Another distinction among inference engines is whether they support monotonic or nonmonotonic reasoning. In a monotonic reasoning system, all values concluded for an attribute remain true for the duration of the consultation session. Facts that become true remain true, and the amount of true information in the system grows steadily or *monotonically*.

In a nonmonotonic reasoning system, facts that are true may be retracted. Planning is a good example of a problem type that demands nonmonotonic reasoning. In the early stages of a planning problem, it may make sense to go a certain way. Later, as information

continues to come in, it may turn out that an early decision was wrong. Decisions and their consequences need to be retracted.

Changing the value of a single attribute to retract a conclusion is not difficult. Tracking down all of the implications that are based on that fact is difficult. We can imagine such problems with a theater travel adviser. If we conclude that a cab is the best way to travel, we may also make other assumptions about not needing any parking space, about the capacity of the cab, etc. If later we realize that a cab is not the appropriate means, the inference engine must track down each implication and undo it. The undoing process can be quite expensive and confusing, both computationally and conceptually. Most knowledge systems marketed today support monotonic reasoning, but allow only carefully controlled types of nonmonotonic reasoning.

Active values, which we shall consider when we discuss specific system-building tools, is one way of implementing nonmonotonic reasoning.

THE FUTURE OF REPRESENTATION AND INFERENCE

In this chapter and the preceding chapter we have discussed the common ways of representing knowledge and guiding inference. Although we have not been exhaustive, we have covered most of the strategies that are employed in commercially available systems. There are a number of additional strategies being studied in research laboratories. Some of these additional strategies will become available in commercially viable systems in the next few years, whereas other strategies will need considerable refinement before they are ready to be used in business settings.

Figure 5.8 presents an overview of the current domain of knowledge engineering techniques. The area in the lower left of the figure encloses well-structured problems, which can be analyzed by means of exhaustive search. These are problems that existing, conventional programming languages and techniques can handle. These problems are largely numerical, although word processing and other non-numerical applications occur within that area. The area beyond the well-structured problems represents the types of problems that existing symbolic programming techniques can help solve. The problems in this area are less structured and often involve problem spaces that cannot be exhaustively searched. These problems are largely symbolic in nature. The use of heuristics and large amounts of very specific knowledge can be used to prune these problem spaces and provide workable answers.

The area on the top and right of Figure 5.8 represents problems that cannot currently be represented by either conventional or commercially available AI techniques. The barrier between current and future AI solutions is composed of two very difficult challenges. One challenge is a hardware challenge.

Existing computers cannot process enough knowledge fast enough to allow knowledge engineers to build workable systems to deal with many types of problems. If the amount of knowledge needed to solve a problem is truly massive, we shall have to wait for computers capable of processing large amounts of rules simultaneously. The computers that are currently being designed to handle this type of operation are referred to as *parallel processing systems* or *fifth-generation computers*. It will be several years before such computers become available at commercial prices.

A second challenge to be overcome is a software problem. Current software systems can handle non-monotonic problems only with considerable difficulty. Many significant problems require that the data be constantly reevaluated to take ongoing changes

Figure 5.8 *Problem domain of existing knowledge engineering techniques.*

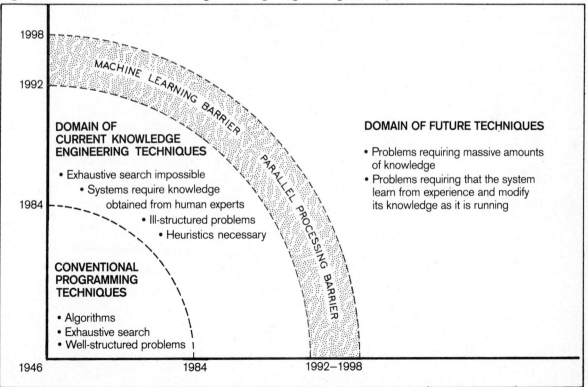

into account. If knowledge systems are to handle such problems, the systems will have to be able to learn from their own experience and constantly update their own knowledge. The various approaches to building systems that can learn from experience are normally spoken of as *machine learning*. There are a number of difficult problems that researchers are only beginning to understand, and it will be several years before systems capable of learning are available. Thus, the twin problems, how to construct machines capable of massive parallel processing and how to design software that can learn from its experience, place an effective limit on the types of knowledge systems that will be developed in the next few years.

SUMMARY

Inference and control mechanisms contained in the inference engine of an expert system direct the system in its use of the facts and rules contained in the knowledge base. In fact, since rule order is impor-

tant, and since the order of clauses within a rule determines which clause is examined in what order, inference and control are actually spread subtly throughout an expert system. The major strategies, however, such as back-chaining and depth-first search, are determined by the inference engine.

As we noted in the beginning, the inference strategies used in the design of expert systems are not very complex. In part, this represents the limits of current technology. More complex strategies will become available in the next few years. In part, however, it represents the fact that in many cases human experts do not use very complex strategies. Instead, they combine simple strategies with massive amounts of very specific knowledge. Well-chosen heuristics allow experts quickly to cut a problem down to a size they can then examine in considerable detail.

In the next chapter, we shall return to MYCIN and see how these simple strategies combine to produce a system capable of holding its own against world-class experts in the diagnosis of meningitis infections.

6.

MYCIN Revisited

In this chapter we return to the MYCIN system to examine it in greater detail. With the basics of representation and inference from the intervening chapters, you should now be able to understand how MYCIN really works. Once again we shall examine the transcript of a MYCIN consultation. This time, however, we shall look deeper into the underlying mechanisms that account for MYCIN's performance.

MYCIN represents 50 man-years of effort. Much of that effort is embedded deep in the software. Our examination of MYCIN will be at a deeper level than our first pass. At the same time, it is important to point out that there is much more to MYCIN than we shall explain here. Our interest is in looking more closely at the way in which MYCIN represents medical facts and draws inferences.

The following interaction with MYCIN was con-ducted on the Stanford University Medical Experimental computer facility (SUMEX-AIM), which is where MYCIN was developed. It is not necessary that you understand either all the medical terminology or all the medical reasoning. MYCIN uses the jargon of medicine, just as a program in credit analysis would use the jargon of the banking world; and neither would be entirely comprehensible to a nonspecialist in the field. The point of reproducing this transcript in so much detail is to show you the general way in which a true expert system functions. The important thing is that you follow the overall use of facts and rules and the way the user can ask questions and probe for additional information. Our comments on the various parts of the consultation should help. The transcript of the actual consultation is indented below, with the responses from the physician underlined.

> @<mycin>mycin

MYCIN is run by an ordinary call to the executive prompt of the DEC computer system, the "@."

> MYCIN 15-May-84 . . .
>
> Hi.
>
> Special options (type ? for help):
> <u>No</u>

Available options include opening a transcript file to record the interaction so that it can be printed, setting different levels of tracing, or requesting that a case be run from MYCIN's case library.

Instructions? (Y or N)
No

24-Jun-84 19:03:51

————PATIENT-1————

This means that an object has been created in the dynamic knowledge base. It is an instance of the static root object—"Patient." As soon as the dynamic object—"Patient-1"—is created, the attributes associated with it are considered. Initially, the values for these attributes are unknown.

1) Patient's name:
David King
2) Age:
34
3) Sex:
Why

[i.e. WHY is it important to determine the sex of PATIENT-1?]

[1.0] The sex of a patient is one of the 4 standard parameters that identify a patient. This may be useful later in the consultation. For example, it is relevant in determining whether an organism is normally found at this site and is relevant in determining PATIENT-1's most recent creatinine clearance (in ml/min).
[back to question 3. . .]
Male

Name, age, sex, and race are necessary attributes for every patient, so values are obtained by asking the user immediately after the object Patient-1 is created in working memory. Also, MYCIN refers to attributes as "parameters," which is the common medical term.

"WHY" is a request for explanation. MYCIN responds by explaining that sex is a standard parameter (necessary attribute) for the patient.

4) Race:
Caucasian
5) Are there any cultures for David King which may be related to the present illness, and from which organisms have been grown successfully in the microbiology laboratory?
Why

[i.e. WHY is it important to determine organisms isolated from PATIENT-1?]

[2.0] This will aid in determining the therapeutic regimen of PATIENT-1.
   If
      [2.1] information has been gathered about organisms isolated from this patient, organisms noted on smears of this patient, negative cultures of this patient, suspected infections without microbiological evidence,

current drugs of this patient and prior drugs of this patient, and
[2.2] an attempt has been made to deduce the organisms which require therapy, and
[2.3] you have given consideration to organisms (other than those seen in cultures or smears) which might be present

then

determine the best therapy recommendation from among the drugs likely to be effective against the significant organisms, or indicate that no therapy is required at this time

[RULE092]

[First, of course, it is necessary to ask about a positive culture.]

[back to question 5. . .]

This time "WHY" generates a more typical MYCIN explanation. Namely, MYCIN is testing the premise of a rule. This rule (Rule 92) controls the inference process. It says that MYCIN should determine all possible diseases before determining what drugs to use to treat them. A positive culture is the first indication that the patient has an infection.

Why

[i.e.   WHY is it important to determine the therapeutic regimen of PATIENT-1?]

[3.0] Deducing the therapeutic regimen of a patient is the goal of an infectious disease consultation.

[back to question 5. . .]

Ask WHY again and MYCIN will explain its reasoning further. The first WHY revealed that MYCIN was examining a rule that concludes about a drug regimen for Patient-1. By asking WHY again, we are asking why MYCIN wants to know about regimen. The answer, that deducing a regimen is the task of MYCIN, reveals the importance of the attribute, regimen. *Regimen is the goal attribute of the MYCIN system.*

   In order to determine the regimen, MYCIN looks for rules that conclude about regimen. Rule 92 was located by MYCIN's back-chaining inference engine. A graphical view of the objects, attributes, and values in working memory is shown in Figure 6.1.

No
6) Are there any pending cultures for David King?
Yes

————CULTURE-1————

Culture is the second of MYCIN's objects (Patient was the first). Culture is linked to Patient. One patient can have many cultures (see Figure 6.2).

7) From what site was the specimen for CULTURE-1 taken?
   CSF
8) Please give the date and time when the pending csf culture (CULTURE-1) was obtained. (mo/da/yr time)
   JUNE/24/84 7:00

Figure 6.1 Beginning of the MYCIN consultation's backward chaining process. Attributes are shown in boxes.

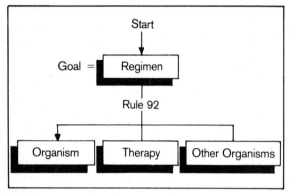

Figure 6.2 Comparison of static and dynamic (or instantiated) objects, attributes, and values.

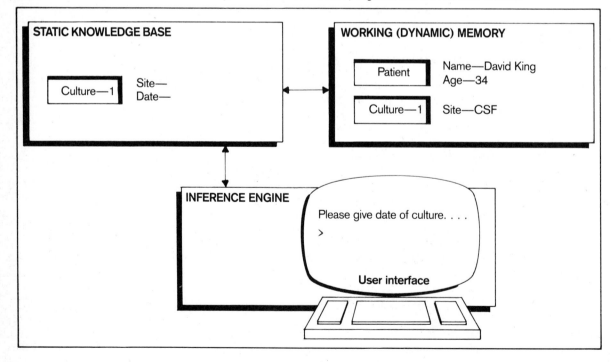

9) Was a smear examined at the time that the specimen for the pending csf culture (CULTURE-1) was obtained?
   Yes

10) Were any organisms seen on the smear of the specimen submitted as pending csf culture (CULTURE-1)?
   No

Indentations reveal which object is under inspection by MYCIN. Here the attention shifts from Culture-1 back to Patient-1.

11) Are there any other pending cultures?
   No

12) Have there been negative (as opposed to pending) cultures obtained from David King which may be relevant to the present illness?
   No

13) Do you suspect David King may have an infection at a site from which you have not obtained culture specimens?
   No

14) Is David King currently receiving therapy with any antimicrobial agent?
   No

15) During the present illness, has David King been treated with an antimicrobial agent which is no longer being administered?
   No

[Considering organisms (other than those isolated from cultures) which might be present. . .]

16) Has David King recently had symptoms of persistent headache or other abnormal neurologic symptoms (dizziness, lethargy, etc.)?
   Yes

17) Has David King recently had objective evidence of abnormal neurologic signs (nuchal rigidity, coma, seizures, etc.) documented by physician observation or examination?
   Yes

The CSF cultures will be considered to be associated with MENINGITIS.

18) Please give the date on which clinical evidence (symptoms, signs, or laboratory tests) of the meningitis first appeared.
   23/JUNE/84 7:00

19) Does David King have an abnormal chest X-ray?
   No

20) Does David King have one or more of the following risk factors for tb: a) positive intermediate strength PPD, b) history of close contact with a person with active tb, c) a household member with a past history of active tb, d) apical scarring on chest xray, e) history of granulomas on biopsy of liver, lymph node, or other organs?
   No

21) Does David King have any cutaneous lesions or rash on physical examination?
   No

22) Does David King have evidence of ocular nerve dysfunction?
Why

[i.e. WHY is it important to determine whether PATIENT-1 has evidence of ocular nerve dysfunction?]

[4.0] This will aid in determining the organisms (other than those seen on cultures or smears) which might be causing the infection.
    It has already been established that
        [4.1] the infection which requires therapy is meningitis
    Therefore, if
        [4.2] David King has evidence of ocular nerve dysfunction
    then
        there is weakly suggestive evidence (.2) that Mycobacterium-tb is one of the organisms (other than those seen on cultures or smears) which might be causing the infection
Author: Yu
        [RULE366]
[back to question 22. . .]

This is one of a few hundred heuristic rules that MYCIN uses to make its decisions. The first clause in the premise of the rule has been tested and the second is under consideration. This rule is refining the general hypothesis that the infection is meningitis to a narrower, more specific hypothesis about a particular organism, mycobacterium-tb. See Figure 6.3 for a pictorial representation.

Figure 6.3 MYCIN searches its tree of inferences.

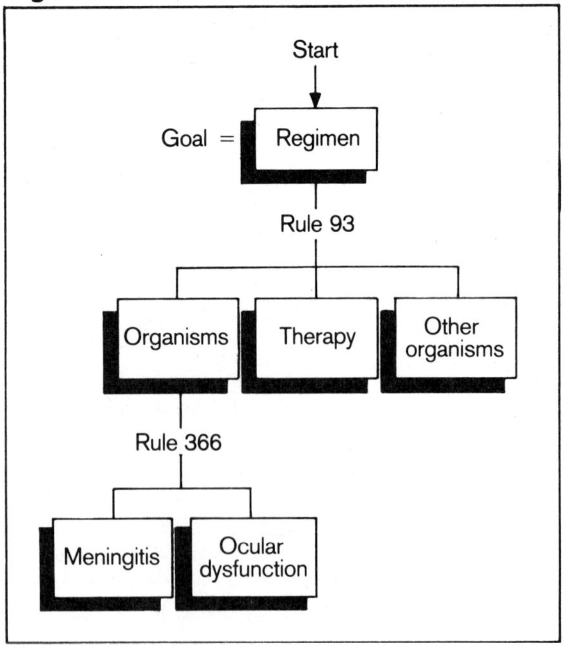

No
23) Is David King a compromised host (e.g. alcoholic, sickle-cell-disease, immunosuppressed)?
Why

[i.e.   WHY is it important to determine whether PATIENT-1 is a compromised host?]

[5.0]   This will aid in determining whether PATIENT-1 is immunosuppressed.
         If
           [5.1] David King is not a compromised host
         then
           it is definite (1.0) that David King is not immunosuppressed
         [ALSO:
           it is definite (1.0) that David King is not an alcoholic
           it is definite (1.0) that David King is not a diabetic
           it is definite (1.0) that David King is not uremic
           it is definite (1.0) that David King does not have sickle-cell-disease]
Author: Yu
         [RULE343]
[back to question 23 . . .]

*Some of MYCIN's rules conclude values for attributes as intermediary steps
toward arriving at a final diagnosis. In this case, MYCIN is asking if the
patient is a compromised host. If not, then values are concluded for several
related attributes.*

No
24) For how many days has David King had abnormal neurologic signs?
1 day
25) For how many days has David King had neurologic symptoms?
1 day
26) Has David King had recent evidence of tender or enlarged salivary glands?
No
27) Has David King been exposed to any contagious disease recently (e.g. meningococ-
cal disease, mumps)?
No
28) What is the protein value (mg/100cc) in the CSF?
280
29) What is the total WBC count of the CSF?
1.9
30) What is the glucose value (milligrams percent) in the CSF?
5
31) What is the simultaneous blood glucose?
Unknown
32) Do you know the results of a recent CBC of David King?
Yes
33) What was David King's peripheral white count (in thousands)?
Unknown

34) Has David King had any injury or insult to, or defect in, the central-nervous-system (excluding neurosurgery)?
_No_

35) Has David King ever undergone any type of surgery?
Why

[i.e.   WHY is it important to determine whether PATIENT-1 has undergone surgery?]

[6.0]   This will aid in determining whether PATIENT-1 has had neurosurgery.
If
    [6.1] David King has not undergone surgery
then
    it is definite (1.0) that David King has not had neurosurgery
[ALSO:
    it is definite (1.0) that David King has not had cardiac surgery
    it is definite (1.0) that David King has not had a splenectomy]
Author: Yu
        [RULE462]
[back to question 35 . . .]

Here is a rule that aims to improve the consultation by screening out unnecessary or foolish questions. The rule asks a general question that is a precondition for other questions. If the patient has had no surgery, then we can be certain that he or she has not had neurosurgery.

Yes
36) Has David King had neurosurgery?
Why

[i.e.   WHY is it important to determine whether PATIENT-1 has had neurosurgery?]

[7.0]   This will aid in determining the organisms (other than those seen on cultures or smears) which might be causing the infection.
It has already been established that
    [7.1] the infection which requires therapy is meningitis, and
    [7.2] organisms were not seen on the stain of the pending csf culture (CULTURE-1), and
    [7.3] the type of the infection is bacterial
Therefore, if
    [7.4] David King has had neurosurgery, and
    [7.5] the time since the neurosurgical operation was performed is less than 2 months, and
    [7.6] the type of neurosurgery is not ventricular-ureteral-shunt
then
    there is evidence that the organisms (other than those seen on cultures or smears) which might be causing the infection is staphylococcus-coag-pos (.75), staphylococcus-coag-neg (.5), e.coli (.4), klebsiella-pneumoniae (.3),

> streptococcus-group-a (.3), or pseudomonas-aeruginosa (.2)
> Author: Yu
> [RULE511]
> [back to question 36 . . .]

In contrast to the control rule above, here is another heuristic rule. Certain surgeries, combined with other patient symptoms, suggest particular infections with varying degrees of certainty. WHY does not answer the question of why this relationship between surgery and infection is true or what the causal explanation for the relationship is.

Notice that the premises in the rule are sorted into two groups: those that have been affirmed and those that are yet to be considered. Clause 7.4, which asks if the patient has had neurosurgery, will be concluded by the current question, question 36.

<u>No</u>
37) Does David King live in a crowded environment?
<u>No</u>
38) Is the meningitis a hospital-acquired infection?
<u>Yes</u>
39) Is David King's clinical history consistent with EPIGLOTTITIS?
<u>No</u>
40) Is David King's clinical history consistent with OTITIS-MEDIA?
<u>No</u>
41) Has David King ever undergone splenectomy?
<u>No</u>
42) Is David King a burn patient?
<u>Yes</u>

> I have found evidence (RULE507) that treatment should cover for Diplococcus-pneumoniae causing meningitis.
> I have found evidence (RULE545) that treatment should cover for E.coli causing meningitis.
> I have found evidence (RULE545 RULE578) that treatment should cover for Pseudomonas-aeruginosa causing meningitis.

The diagnostic portion of the consultation is over. Now MYCIN is attempting to find a set of medications that will kill the invading organisms without harming the patient.

43) Does David King have focal neurological signs?
<u>No</u>

Additional characteristics of the patient are needed when medications are considered. Different questions are asked in different consultation sessions depending on interim results. This question, for example, probably arises from the particular medication under consideration. Had the patient been diagnosed as having a different infection, this medication might never have been considered, and hence this question might never have been asked.

[Determining which drugs are desirable for use against the Diplococcus-pneumoniae . . .]
[Determining which drugs are desirable for use against the E.coli . . .]
[Determining which drugs are desirable for use against the Pseudomonas-aeru-ginosa . . .]

INFECTION-1 is MENINGITIS
+ <ITEM-1> DIPLOCOCCUS-PNEUMONIAE [from clinical evidence only]
+ <ITEM-2> E.COLI [from clinical evidence only]
   <ITEM-3> PSEUDOMONAS-AERUGINOSA [from clinical evidence only]

44) Does David King have a clinically significant allergic reaction to any antimicrobial agent?
   Yes
46) What is the most recent creatinine clearance in ml/min which you feel is a true representation of David King's renal function?
   77
47) David King's weight in kilograms (or <number> POUNDS):
   77
48) David King's height in centimeters (or <number> INCHES):
   Why

[i.e.   WHY is it important to determine the height of PATIENT-1?]

[8.0]   This will aid in determining PATIENT-1's estimated body surface area.
          It has already been established that
             [8.1] the weight of David King is known
          Therefore, if
             [8.2] the height of David King is known
          then
             Use Boyd's algorithm to calculate body surface area from weight and height [Boyd, E. The Growth of the Surface Area of the Human Body, 1935 pp 1-133.]
Author: Wraith
Justification: A comparative evaluation with statistical analysis of the Boyd method with the DuBois formula demonstrated that the Boyd formula is more accurate for abnormal body types. [Sendray J et.al., Determination of human body surface area from height and weight, Applied Physiology, 7(1):1-12, July 1954.]
Literature: Boyd, E. The growth of the surface area of the human body, c. 1935, pp 1-133.
[RULE104]
[back to question 48 . . .

Note that rules contain slots for additional information. This information is most useful to developers and maintainers of the system. It also turns out to be helpful to novices who use MYCIN as a training tool.

70
Estimated body surface area is 1.5 sq. meters.

Dosage adjustments will be based on the calculated creatinine clearance of 88.8 ml/min/1.73 sq. meters (adjusted to average body surface area).
This creatinine clearance is within the normal range for the patient's age group.
Normal doses are recommended.

[REC-1] My preferred therapy recommendation is as follows:
In order to cover for Items <1 2 3>:
Give the following in combination:
1) AMPICILLIN
Dose: 3.85 g (30.8 ml) q4h IV [calculated on basis of 50 mg/kg]

2) GENTAMICIN
Dose: 131 mg (3.2 ml, 80mg/2ml ampule) q8h IV [calculated on basis of 1.7 mg/kg] plus consider giving 5 mg q24h Intrathecal
Comments: Monitor serum concentrations

Since high concentrations of penicillins can inactivate aminoglycosides, do not mix these two antibiotics in the same IV bottle.

MYCIN's final advice is highly specific and complete. It includes extra recommendations about interactions among two of the drugs.

Do you wish to see the next choice therapy?
Yes

MYCIN can look a second time and come up with a second set of medications. This is useful because a physician may want to avoid a drug for some reason. Also, this ability to reconsider and construct a second answer is an indication that MYCIN is meant to consult with but not replace the physician.

Which, if any, of the above drugs do you wish eliminated from consideration?
Ampicillin

[Considering PENICILLIN for use against INFECTION-1 . . .]
[Considering CHLORAMPHENICOL for use against INFECTION-1 . . .]
[Considering GENTAMICIN for use against INFECTION-1 . . .]

[REC-2] Next best therapy recommendation:
In order to cover for Items <2 3>:
Give: GENTAMICIN
Dose: 131 mg (3.2 ml, 80mg/2ml ampule) q8h IV [calculated on basis of 1.7 mg/kg] plus consider giving 5 mg q24h Intrathecal
Comments: Monitor serum concentrations

In order to cover for Item <1>:
Give: PENICILLIN
Dose: 3.9 million units (7.8 ml) q4h IV [calculated on basis of 50000 units/kg]

RECOMMENDATION-2 is substantially inferior to RECOMMENDATION-1 (because it requires more drugs or drugs that are not as good).

Would you like to see details of this comparison?
Yes

Looking at the coverage of the 'most likely' items, we see that:

RECOMMENDATION-1 consists of 2 first choice drugs (AMPICILLIN for ITEM-1 and ITEM-2 and GENTAMICIN for ITEM-2)

RECOMMENDATION-2 consists of 1 first choice drug (PENICILLIN for ITEM-1) and 1 third choice drug (GENTAMICIN for ITEM-2)

ORGANISMS most likely	RECOMMENDATION-1 Drug Choice Ranking	RECOMMENDATION-2 Drug Choice Ranking
ITEM-1	AMPICILLIN—1st	PENICILLIN—1st
ITEM-2	AMPICILLIN-AND-GENTAMICIN—1st	GENTAMICIN—3rd
less likely ITEM-3	GENTAMICIN—2nd	GENTAMICIN—2nd

(The desirability of a drug is defined to be its lowest ranking for the items it covers.)

Do you wish to see the next choice therapy?
No

Do you wish to continue with the regular QA module?
Yes

The QA or Question/Answer module is a system of probes that allows users to inquire about the contents of both the static and dynamic portions of the knowledge base.

Please ask questions now. When you are finished and want to begin a new consultation or sign off the terminal, enter the word STOP.

Type HELP for the list of question options.

PR 578

We can print any or all of the rules in the knowledge base. This is the rule about burn victims.

RULE578

[This rule applies to pending cultures and suspected infections, and is tried in order to find out about the organisms (other than those seen on cultures or smears) which might be causing the infection]

If: 1) The infection which requires therapy is meningitis,
     2) A: A smear of the culture was not examined, or
         B: Organisms were not seen on the stain of the culture,
     3) The type of the infection is bacterial, and
     4) The patient has been seriously burned
Then: There is suggestive evidence (.5) that Pseudomonas-aeruginosa is one of
       the organisms (other than those seen on cultures or smears) which might be
       causing the infection
Author: Yu
What burn

*In fact, if we are curious about rules that use information about whether a
patient is a burn victim, we can ask directly. Rule 578 appears along with two
other rules. The ability to probe the knowledge base selectively is of great
importance to the knowledge engineers who build and modify the system.*

The following rules use:
    whether the patient has been seriously burned

578, 577, 47

The parameters concluded by these rules are:
    the organisms (other than those seen on cultures or smears) which might be
    causing the infection and the identity of the organism
Which of the rules do you wish to see?
577,47

Let's look at the other rules that concern patients who have been burned.

RULE577
[This rule applies to organisms, and is tried in order to find out about the organisms
    (other than those seen on cultures or smears) which might be causing the infec-
    tion]

If: 1) The infection which requires therapy is meningitis,
     2) The stain of the organisms is known,
     3) The morphology of the organism is known, and
     4) The patient has been seriously burned
Then: There is weakly suggestive evidence (.3) that Pseudomonas-aeruginosa is
       one of the organisms (other than those seen on cultures or smears) which might
       be causing the infection
Author: Yu

RULE047
[This rule applies to organisms, and is tried in order to find out about the identity of
    the organism]

If: 1) A: The genus of the organism is not known with certainty, or
         B: The genus of the organism is Pseudomonas,

2) The site of the culture is blood,
3) The stain of the organism is Gramneg,
4) The morphology of the organism is rod, and
5) The patient has been seriously burned
Then: There is weakly suggestive evidence (.4) that the identity of the organism is Pseudomonas-aeruginosa

Figure 6.4 Dynamic information is stored in working memory as MYCIN conducts a consultation.

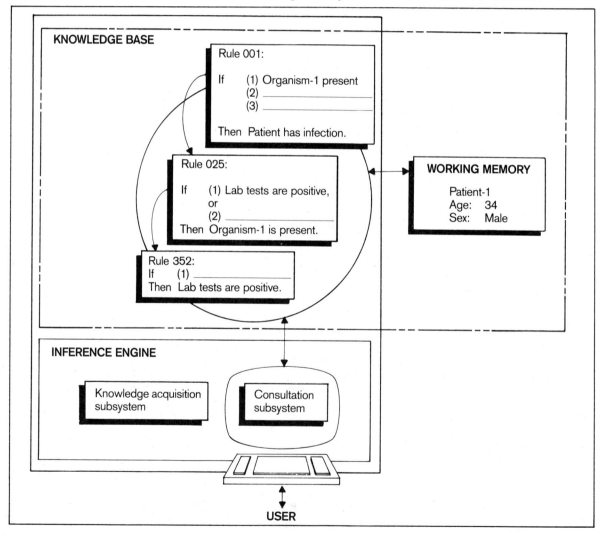

Stop

Do you wish to run another consultation?
No

Thank you.

A graphic overview of the MYCIN consultation is presented in Figure 6.4.

WHERE IS THE EXPERTISE IN MYCIN?

One of the puzzles in learning about knowledge systems is deciding exactly where the expertise lies. The inference schemes are simple. MYCIN back-chains through the knowledge base attempting to apply the *modus ponens* rule. Object–attribute–value triplets are a simple scheme for representing facts about the world, and production rules are very straightforward. So where exactly is the expertise in MYCIN?

The expertise lies in two places: First, although the schemes for representing knowledge are simple, the factoring of the knowledge to fit the O–A–V model is difficult. By analogy, in mathematics it is the formation of the appropriate mathematical model that is crucial to solving many problems. Once the unknowns are isolated and the formulas are selected, then hard problems suddenly look easy. Similarly, MYCIN has a smart set of objects, attributes, and values.

The second source of expertise is found in the wisdom compiled into the heuristic rules. Any one of the rules might be known by a competent physician, or even a novice intern. MYCIN has "on hand" a large set of heuristics. Its simple inference engine applies these rules consistently, methodically, and tirelessly. Such patience led the expert involved in another project to say, "The system behaves as I do on my best days."

Section Two

LANGUAGES, TOOLS, AND SYSTEMS

7.

Languages and Tools

In the preceding chapters we discussed some of the different ways that knowledge engineers have found to represent knowledge and draw inferences. In this chapter we provide an overview of the general characteristics of AI languages and the different tools that are used to develop knowledge systems. In Chapter 8 we survey the commercially available tools.

LEVELS OF SOFTWARE

Figure 7.1 provides an overview of the various levels of software that lie between a human problem situation and computer hardware. At the top of the figure, drawn to resemble the surface of a pond, are the problems that we encounter in our daily existence. We have isolated one portion of that surface and labeled it "Problem Domain." When we encounter a problem that lies within such a domain, all we can observe are the behaviors the expert uses to solve the problem. The expert may ask questions or make measurements, and we can easily notice such activity. What we do not see, however, are the mental models, rules-of-thumb, and cognitive strategies the expert uses when deciding what to do in a particular situation. The expert's knowledge about how to solve problems that fall within a particular problem domain is a cognitive layer that lies below the behavior we observe when the expert is actually working on a problem.

If we decide to build a knowledge system to assist or replace our expert in a particular domain, we must create a software package. It is instructive to consider exactly what levels of software might underlie the knowledge system.

No matter what software we use, ultimately our knowledge system will depend on some computer hardware—the physical machine on which the software is run. Moreover, the hardware will surely carry out its most fundamental actions as a result of commands encoded in binary form. A long series of 0s and 1s will flow into the central processing unit of the computer and direct the computer to make discrete physical responses. This most primitive software level is termed *machine language*.

At a slightly higher level, there will be a software program that will direct the fundamental operations of the computer. The *operating system* handles utility functions and can be written in or compiled to machine language.

Most programming is done in one of a number of *high-level languages*. Well-known high-level languages include BASIC, COBOL, FORTRAN, PASCAL, and C. AI programmers commonly use high-level languages such as LISP and PROLOG. PROLOG contains constructs that make it easy to write programs that manipulate logical expressions, whereas LISP consists of operators that facilitate the creation of programs that manipulate lists. These constructs are useful for developing symbolic computing programs, just as iterative constructs like the "DO WHILE" loops of PASCAL are useful for numerical programming.

Just above the high-level languages are special packages of prewritten code that are typically called *programming environments*. An environment is usually closely associated with a particular high-level language and contains chunks of the code written in that language that are useful for particular programming tasks. By analogy to conventional programming languages such as FORTRAN, environments are "libraries of subroutines" that can be chained together to develop specific applications.

Knowledge engineering *tools* are the fifth level shown in Figure 7.1. Tools are designed to facilitate the rapid development of knowledge systems. Tools also incorporate another aspect of knowledge engineering—specific strategies for representation, inference, and control. They contain elementary constructs for modeling the world that determine the sorts of problems the tool can easily handle. One tool, EMYCIN, "knows" about storing facts as

O–A–V triplets, for example. It also knows how to trace the value of a goal attribute by back-chaining through a network of rules. As a result, system designers have a clear set of constructs on which to map their problems. A tool has fewer applications than the language or environment in which it was written, but it is usually designed to facilitate the rapid development of knowledge systems that address a specific class of problems.

An appropriate analogy is to the tools a repairman uses. Rather than creating a new tool for each new task, the repairman collects a set of tools that have

Figure 7.1 The six levels of software between human problems and computer hardware.

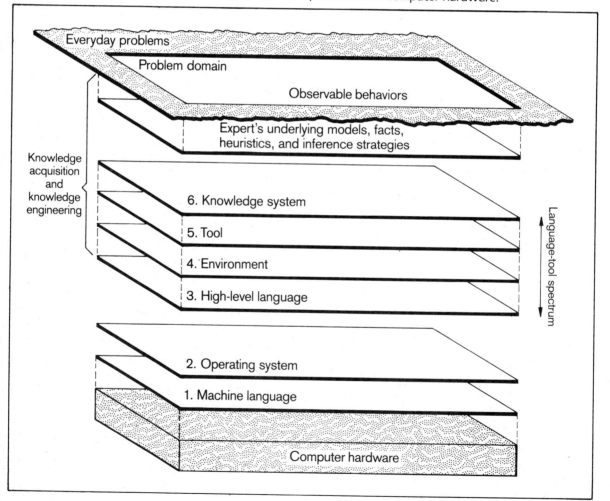

proven useful in past situations. Long screwdrivers take their place along with hammers and pliers in the toolbox. The hammers are useless for removing screws, and the pliers make poor hammers. Each tool is especially designed to perform a specialized task.

Knowledge engineering tools offer two advantages to knowledge system developers:

1. They provide for rapid system development by providing a substantial amount of computer code that would otherwise need to be written, tested, debugged, and maintained.

2. Tools provide specific techniques for handling knowledge representation, inference, and control that help knowledge engineers to model the salient characteristics of a particular class of problems.

When a tool is combined with knowledge in a specific domain, the result is a knowledge-based expert system, which is depicted on level 6 in Figure 7.1. A knowledge system delivers advice similar to that which an expert in a specific problem domain might give.

Figure 7.2 The levels of software between a company cash flow problem and a personal computer.

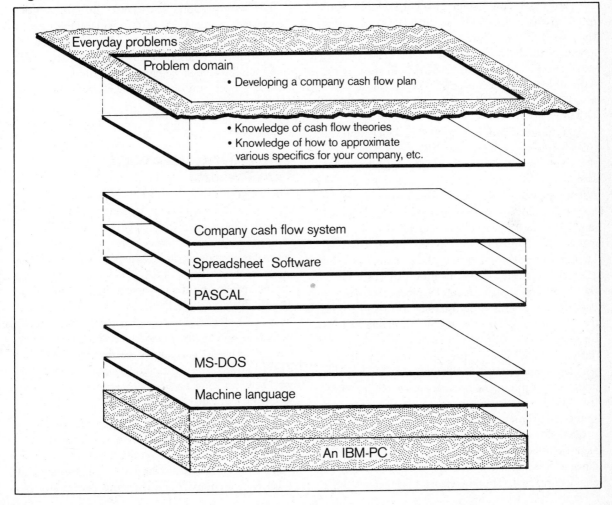

Figure 7.2 applies this analysis of software levels to a conventional problem domain. In this case, we assume that the problem domain involves the development of cash flow plans for a company. The company's manager has an underlying knowledge of cash flow theory in general, as well as specific facts and rules-of-thumb about how to approximate the company's cash flow. Since this is a traditional arithmetic problem, the manager need not consider an expert system. Instead, he or she just acquires an electronic spreadsheet package—VisiCalc, for example. A program like VisiCalc is a *tool*. When the manager enters formulas and data into the program, he or she creates a specific plan for the company. That program is the company's cash flow system. It is not useful to think of an environment in this context, so we have left that level blank. VisiCalc, itself, could be programmed in the high-level language PASCAL. To complete the comparison, PASCAL, in turn, is run with an MS-DOS operating system on, for example, an IBM-PC or any similar computer that can run MS-DOS.

Returning to Figure 7.1, notice the bracket on the right-hand side of the figure. This bracket indicates the levels that are typically involved in an expert system development effort. To create a knowledge system, the knowledge engineer must study a particular problem domain. At first the knowledge engineer may focus on surface behavior, but he or she soon moves on to question the expert in an effort to identify the underlying models, facts, heuristics, and inference strategies that constitute expertise. Once the knowledge engineer understands the general characteristics of the expertise to be incorporated, he or she can consider if a tool is available that is suitable. As we shall continue to stress, there are different kinds of expertise, different consultation paradigms, and, similarly, different tools. Each tool is designed to capture one or a very few types of expertise. It is a waste of time to try to develop an expert system using an unsuitable tool.

Generally, the knowledge engineer finds that the expertise he or she is studying can be effectively modeled by means of one or another knowledge engineering tool. The knowledge engineer proceeds to formalize the expert's knowledge in the syntax of the tool. If there is a good match between the tool and the task, all will go smoothly. If the particular task varies in minor ways from the task the tool is designed to handle, the knowledge engineer may need to "drop down" into the environment that lies below the tool to develop some special routines.

The process the knowledge engineer goes through, studying the expert's behavior, uncovering the expert's underlying knowledge, and selecting and employing a tool to build a knowledge system, is called *knowledge acquisition*. We shall consider knowledge acquisition in more detail when we consider the actual development of expert systems in Chapter 12.

The considerations that lead to the selection of a language, environment, or tool will be the focus of the remainder of this chapter. We shall begin by comparing and contrasting languages, environments, and tools. Although we have described them as three different levels, they can also be conceptualized as a single continuum.

THE LANGUAGE–TOOL CONTINUUM

The language–tool continuum is a simple way of classifying the various AI languages and tools. In general, languages are more flexible and more difficult to use to prototype a new system rapidly. Only well-trained programmers build systems starting with languages such as LISP or PROLOG. Tools are much less flexible. Major knowledge engineering decisions have already been incorporated into the tools. Consequently, if a problem matches the tool, a solution can be developed quickly. Indeed, even nonprogrammers can use well-designed tools to develop small but useful knowledge systems. Environments stand midway between languages and tools in terms of both flexibility and ease of use.

Figure 7.3 indicates where a number of the better-known software packages fall on the language–tool continuum. We have not yet discussed the languages and tools shown on this chart, so it can provide only a general orientation at this point. Later, after we

Figure 7.3 The language-tool continuum.

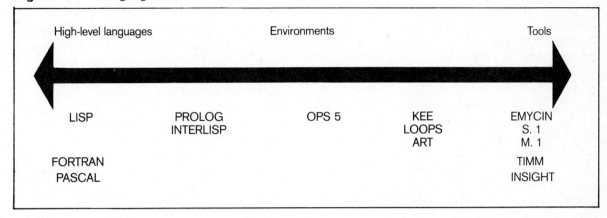

have discussed each of the languages and tools in more detail, you will probably find it useful to return to this chart for another look. Meantime, we can give you a quick overview. LISP is a language. IN-TERLISP is a version of LISP that contains a large number of prepackaged routines; thus, INTERLISP is closer to an environment. PROLOG and OPS5 are also called languages, but some observers would call them tools. They are much less flexible than LISP, but not nearly as constrained or as highly focused as tools such as M.1 or EXPERT. Hence, they are probably best classified as environments. KEE is a tool, but it is a "hybrid tool." It can be used to represent knowledge in several different ways. S.1 is a narrowly focused tool; it is designed to allow its users to develop large diagnostic/prescription consultations rapidly and efficiently. By contrast, KEE is more flexible, and more difficult to use; it is more of an environment and less of a tool than S.1. On the other hand, S.1 can really be used only to build one specific type of knowledge system. If you are faced with a large, classically defined diagnostic/prescription task, however, S.1 is very easy to use to develop that type of knowledge system. If your task requires forward chaining, however, it cannot be represented via S.1.

Figure 7.4 introduces a little more complexity. In reality, there is not only a dimension running from languages to tools, there are other dimensions to consider as well. Languages can either be AI lan-

guages, such as LISP and PROLOG, or they can be conventional languages, such as FORTRAN and PASCAL.

AI languages have built-in features that make it much easier to build expert systems. They are designed to handle symbolic processing, for example. Conventional languages are essentially designed to handle numerical operations. It is much more convenient to program a tool or a knowledge system in an AI language than it is to use a conventional language such as PASCAL or Ada. Some languages naturally lend themselves to certain functions more easily than others; AI languages naturally lend themselves to constructing knowledge systems. By analogy, one can explain most physics concepts using only ordinary language and high school algebra, but it takes a long time and is very tedious. If one really wants to solve physics problems, one naturally wants to use the technical vocabulary of modern physics, including calculus, quantum mechanics, and so forth.

On the other hand, LISP and PROLOG are less well known than FORTRAN and PASCAL. Implementations of FORTRAN and PASCAL are available for almost all computer hardware. Until recently, implementations of LISP and PROLOG were not available for mainframe computers. To make it easy to run tools on a wide variety of existing computers, some tool developers have coded their tools in conventional languages. In the short run, being able to acquire a tool that is written in a conventional language and, hence, will run on an existing mainframe may prove to be a marketing advantage. In the long run, however, as knowledge systems development becomes more established, programmers will want to use tools written in AI languages, just as physicists naturally prefer calculus to algebra when they are trying to explain accelerated motion.

The third dimension in Figure 7.4 indicates that the operating systems that underlie the high-level languages (see Figure 7.1) can also be a major concern. Conventional languages assume conventional operating systems. Thus, if one uses an IBM mainframe and one of the IBM-supported operating systems, one can be confident that one can run FORTRAN or PASCAL on one's computer. Within the field of conventional computing there is currently a lot of interest in UNIX, an operating system devel-

oped at Bell Labs. A system written in a language "running under" UNIX is easier to move from one type of hardware to another. Hence, many companies now prefer to use UNIX instead of an operating system that is closely tied to a particular type of hardware. Most expert system building tools that have been developed in conventional languages have been associated with UNIX operating systems to make it easy to move the system from one hardware configuration to another.

Whether one uses UNIX or one of the less portable operating systems, however, all conventional operating systems, like conventional high-level languages, are ultimately designed to facilitate conventional processing. One reason that AI programs run slowly is related to the inefficient way in which conventional operating systems "translate" LISP into machine language. For years, AI researchers have

Figure 7.4 A multidimensional language-tool spectrum.

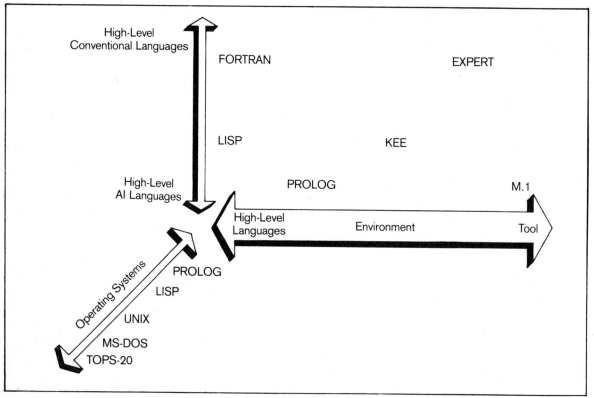

worked to develop hardware that uses LISP as its operating system. Such machines, called "LISP machines," which are just beginning to be marketed, run knowledge systems much faster and more efficiently than conventional hardware using a standard operating system.

The Japanese, when they initially designed their Fifth-Generation program, decided that they wanted to build supercomputers that would use PROLOG as an operating language. Recent reports indicate that the Japanese are currently testing initial versions of personal "PROLOG machines."

We shall consider the virtues of using LISP or PROLOG as an operating system when we discuss these languages in more detail in a subsequent section. Suffice to say that tool designers have to make complex decisions about the languages they use to code their tools. If portability is their primary concern, they will probably choose to translate their tool code into a conventional language that, in turn, will run with a conventional operational system. On the other hand, if they want to develop very complex or sophisticated tools and are focused on the near future, rather than the present, they will probably develop a tool that is coded in LISP or PROLOG and designed to run on a LISP-based or PROLOG-based machine.

AI LANGUAGES AND ENVIRONMENTS

We do not have the space in this book to consider AI languages in any detail. It is worthwhile, however, to describe briefly the two major languages that dominate current work in AI and knowledge engineering.

The LISP Family

Until very recently one could have said that LISP was the only AI language used in the United States. LISP stands for List Processing Language. The language was created by John McCarthy in 1958. Of the major languages still in use, only FORTRAN is older than LISP.

In a 1978 article on LISP, McCarthy describes the key ideas in LISP as follows:

1. Computing with symbolic expressions rather than numbers; that is, bit patterns in a computer's memory and registers can stand for arbitrary symbols, not just those of arithmetic.
2. List processing, that is, representing data as linked-list structures in the machine and as multilevel lists on paper.
3. Control structure based on the composition of functions to form more complex functions.
4. Recursion as a way to describe processes and problems.
5. Representation of LISP programs internally as linked lists and externally as multilevel lists, that is, in the same form as all data are represented.
6. The function EVAL, written in LISP itself, serves as an interpreter for LISP and as a formal definition of the language.

To emphasize what McCarthy says: There is no essential difference between data and programs, hence LISP programs can use other LISP programs as data. LISP is highly recursive, and data and programs are both represented as lists. The lists can be nested, one within another within another, like a Chinese "puzzle box." It doesn't always make for easily read syntax, but it allows for very elegant solutions to complex problems that are very difficult to solve in the various conventional programming languages.

There are only a few basic LISP functions; all other LISP functions are defined in terms of these basic functions. This means that one can easily create new higher-level functions. Hence, one can create a LISP operating system and then work up to whatever higher level one wishes to go. Because of this great flexibility, LISP has never been standardized in the way that languages such as FORTRAN and BASIC have. Instead, a core of basic functions has been used to create a wide variety of LISP dialects.

The ability to change LISP easily leads to an excellent source of programming environments designed to address specific problems. Thus, LISP has mutated into a variety of LISP-based environments, including MacLISP, FranzLISP, and INTERLISP. LISP is also being used to create most of the knowledge system building tools currently being offered for sale.

Recently, there have been several moves to standardize LISP for commercial purposes. A tentative standard, Common LISP, seems to be making headway. Digital Equipment Corporation supports VAX LISP, which is an industrial-strength version of Common LISP designed to run on VAX computers using the VMS operating system. In addition, IBM has recently announced LISP/VM, an industrial-strength LISP that runs under VM/SP on IBM System/370 architecture machines. In addition, a version of Common LISP called Golden Common LISP (GCLISP) has recently become available for IBM PCs with 256K of memory and a PC-DOS 2.0 operating system. Figure 7.5 shows the relationships among some of these LISP languages.

LISP is unique among programming languages in storing its programs as structured data (at least in its uncompiled form). The basic data structures in LISP are the atom, any data object that cannot be further broken down, and the CONS node. Each atom has an associated property list that contains information about the atom, including its name, its value, and any other properties the programmer may desire. A CONS node is a data structure that consists of two fields, each of which contains a pointer to another LISP data object. CONS nodes can be linked together to form data structures of any desired size or complexity.

LISP relies on dynamic allocation of space for data storage. Memory management in LISP is completely automatic, and the programmer does not need to worry about assigning storage space. To change or extend a data structure in a LISP list, for example, one need only change a pointer at a CONS node (see Figure 7.6). In Figure 7.6 one can see that we can add Mimi's name to a list without otherwise changing the program. If we wanted to rearrange a FORTRAN array to insert Mimi's name, we would need to change everything after Susan, which could easily turn out to be a very time-consuming procedure. To make Mimi's name occur in several lists, we would simply point to it from each list in which we wanted to include it. Mimi and her associated property list, however, would occur in memory only once. Ele-

Figure 7.5 The LISP family tree.

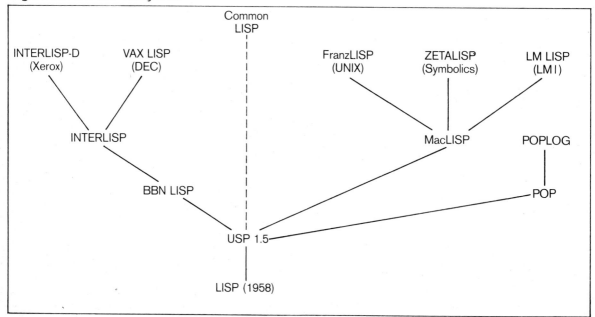

Figure 7.6 Changing a list in LISP simply involves adding a new CONS node and then changing a pointer. This illustrates the modularity of LISP and the ease with which large data structures can be modified.

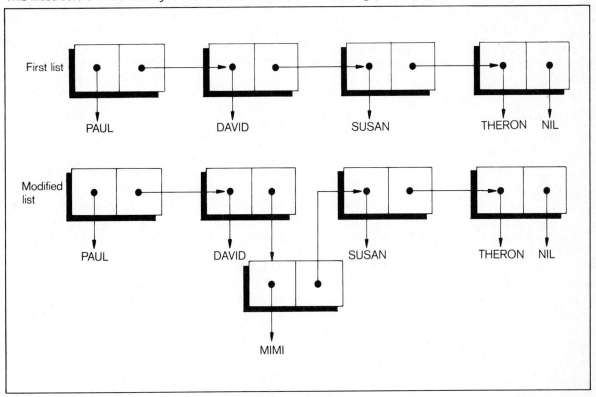

ments of lists need not be adjacent in memory—it's all done with pointers. This not only means that LISP is very modular, it also means that it manages storage space very efficiently and frees the programmer to create complex and flexible programs.

Conventional programming languages normally consist of sequential statements and associated subroutines. LISP consists of a group of modules, each of which specializes at performing a particular task. This makes it easy for programmers to subdivide their efforts into numerous modules, each of which can be handled independently.

Although one can easily carry the analogy too far, it is possible to see the germ of the *if–then* rules that are so popular in expert systems in LISP's CONS nodes. Likewise, it is possible to see the beginnings of frames in the property lists that are attached to atoms (objects). Suffice to say that LISP is a very powerful

language that is popular with programmers who routinely construct very large and complex expert systems.

PROLOG

PROLOG, which stands for PROgramming language for LOGic, was initially developed in 1972 by A. Colmerauer and P. Roussel at the University of Marseilles. PROLOG is a programming language that implements a simplified version of predicate calculus and is thus a true logical language. PROLOG has enjoyed great international popularity. The first efficient PROLOG compiler was developed at the University of Edinburgh. The Hungarian government has encouraged extensive industrial use of the language, and the much-publicized Japanese Fifth-Generation project has adopted PROLOG as the fundamental language for the supercomputers they hope to build.

Like LISP, PROLOG is designed for symbolic rather than simply for numerical computation. PROLOG is very efficient at list processing. Similarly, PROLOG is an interpreted language and thus responds to any query by attempting to return an answer immediately.

To program in PROLOG, one does the following:

1. Specifies some facts about objects and relationships.
2. Specifies rules about objects and relationships.
3. Asks questions about objects and relationships.

Thus, if one entered the following facts:

```
likes(bob, mary).
likes(paul, mary).
likes(mary, bob).
```

and then asked:

```
?-likes(bob, mary).
```

PROLOG would respond by printing:

```
yes
```

In this trivial example, the word "likes" is the *predicate* that indicates that such a relationship exists between one object, *bob,* and a second object, *mary.* The question, in effect, simply asks PROLOG to say whether it can establish the truth of the assertion that "Bob likes Mary." In this case PROLOG says that it can, based on the three facts it has been given.

In a sense, computation in PROLOG is simply controlled logical deduction. One simply states what one knows—the facts—and PROLOG is then prepared to tell whether or not any specific conclusion can be deduced from those facts. In knowledge engineering terms, PROLOG's control structure is logical inference.

PROLOG is the best current implementation of logic programming, although it cannot begin to handle all the deductions that are theoretically possible in predicate calculus. At the same time, PROLOG's syntax is much less complex than most conventional programming languages of comparable power.

A programming language cannot be strictly logical, however, since input and output operations necessarily entail some extralogical procedures. Thus, PROLOG incorporates some basic code that controls the procedural aspects of its operation. The procedural aspects of PROLOG are kept at a minimum, however, and it is possible to conceptualize PROLOG strictly as a logical system.

Indeed, there are two PROLOG programming styles: a *declarative* style and a *procedural* style. In declarative programming, one focuses on telling the system what it should know and relies on the system to handle the procedures. In procedural programming, one considers the specific problem-solving behavior the computer will exhibit. Knowledge engineers who are building new expert systems concern themselves with the procedural aspects of PROLOG. Users, however, need not concern themselves with procedural details and are free simply to assert facts and ask questions. This declarative approach has made PROLOG a very popular language. It is being widely used in European schools in a variety of subjects, and it is becoming increasingly popular in the United States.

In analyzing how the Japanese might benefit from the Fifth-Generation project, even if they fail to meet all of their specific goals, Johan de Kleer, a noted AI researcher, said in 1984:

All the main computer languages (of which Ada is an extreme example) used in the United States are based on the idea that one must specify the task of the computer program by outlining the sequence of steps it takes to achieve the task. PROLOG contains the germ of a great idea. A PROLOG programmer does not specify how the computer is to perform its tasks, but rather a description of the task as a sequence of constraints to be satisfied. Said succinctly: in LISP one must specify the "how" of a computation, while in PROLOG one need only specify the "what"—it's the machine's task to determine the "how". This latter approach is advantageous because it frees the programmer from worrying about the details of algorithms which achieve some task. Instead he need only concern himself with the precise specifications of the task. Admittedly, this takes more computational resources but that is what is becoming cheap. Doubtless, the issue is not PRO-LOG vs. LISP, but rather that a generation of Japanese computer scientists will be educated within a context where their best researchers will be working in terms of specifying computation in terms of "what" not "how". This one idea may justify all the expense of the Fifth Generation and enable the Japanese to leapfrog over American software methodology.

PROLOG is readily available on both large IBM systems and on a wide variety of personal computers. Many suspect that the combination of PROLOG's theoretical elegance and its declarative interpretation will result in its steadily increasing use in the United States.

POPLOG

POPLOG is an increasingly popular programming environment that combines PROLOG, LISP, and POP-11 into a single package that is friendlier and, when compiled, runs faster than PROLOG or LISP. Undoubtedly we shall see a steadily increasing number of programming environments that will attempt to combine the power and utility of symbolic languages like LISP and PROLOG with the popular processing features available in one or another of the widely used conventional programming languages.

KNOWLEDGE ENGINEERING TOOLS

EMYCIN: The First Knowledge Engineering Tool

As they finished their work, the developers of MYCIN realized that there were two distinct parts to their system: (1) the knowledge base, which was specific to the area of medical diagnosis; and (2) the inference engine, which was a general-purpose back-chaining rule evaluator. This distinction led to building an "empty" MYCIN, or EMYCIN—a MYCIN without its knowledge base.

EMYCIN (see Figure 7.7) is a tool for building MYCIN-like consultation systems. EMYCIN expects

Figure 7.7 The architecture of EMYCIN, a typical tool. Note that a tool normally includes an inference engine, knowledge acquisition, explanation, and user interface subsystems. In addition, it includes specific provisions for the creation of a knowledge base.

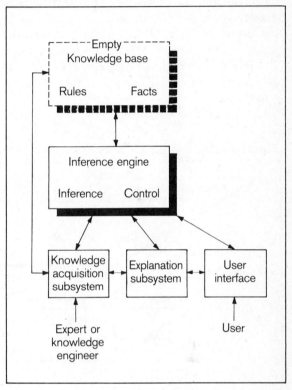

knowledge to be represented as objects, attributes, values, and rules in much the same way that a spreadsheet program expects its data to form rows and columns. EMYCIN contains all the machinery needed to reason over a knowledge base and to conduct consultations with a user. Over the years, editors and debugging aids were added to assist a knowledge engineer in building the system. EMYCIN is a knowledge system without any domain knowledge.

EMYCIN is a tool and not a computing language. It is less general than LISP or INTERLISP, in which it was written. LISP is a general-purpose list processing language, whereas EMYCIN is a special-purpose

O–A–V/rule processor that uses *modus ponens* and backward chaining.

Figure 7.8 uses our software hierarchy to analyze how MYCIN is constructed. In the case of MYCIN, we already know that the problem domain is meningitis and bacteremia diagnosis. MYCIN is an expert system that incorporates the knowledge of meningitis specialists. MYCIN was not developed by means of a tool. Instead, MYCIN was programmed in the INTERLISP environment. The EMYCIN tool was derived from MYCIN only after the system was completed.

To complete our analysis, INTERLISP is an environment programmed in LISP. LISP, in turn, can be implemented with various operating systems, and it can be run on several different computers. In the case of MYCIN, the operating system is TOPS-20, the standard operating system used with DEC 11/20 computers.

Figure 7.9 shows a selection of AI software development projects completed over the past 10 to 15 years. As the figure indicates, EMYCIN is not the only generic tool derived from a specific expert system building project. Just as MYCIN led to EMY-

Figure 7.8 The levels of software between potential meningitis infections and computer hardware.

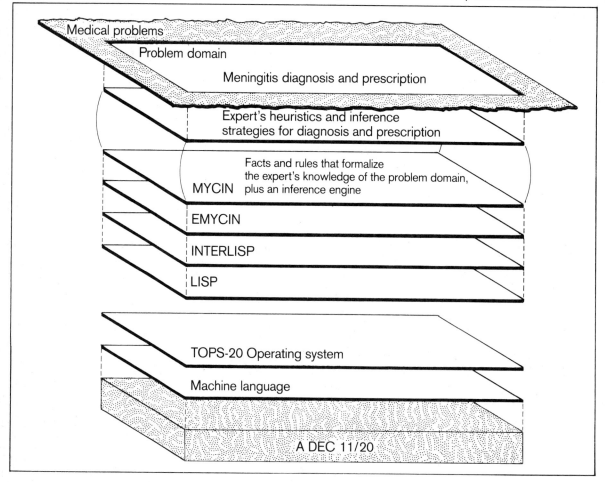

CIN, so the PROSPECTOR expert system led to a tool called KAS (Knowledge Acquisition System), HEARSAY I led to HEARSAY II and AGE, and UNITS led to KEE. Each of these software tools provides a different means for representing and reasoning about knowledge. Each provides power for programmers by creating an environment in which the building blocks for machine problem solving are readily available and well integrated.

Of course, there is variability in what researchers have deemed the important parts of a tool. For example, the ability to explain reasoning is one hallmark of the MYCIN system and the EMYCIN tool. Other tools emphasize other features. Moreover, it is one thing to remove the inference engine from a system and call it a tool, and another matter to expand and develop the user support facilities for a tool that will render it a commercially viable product.

In the next chapter we consider most of the readily available programming environments and tools that can be used to develop knowledge systems. As you will see, different companies have adapted different marketing strategies. Some tools are written in conventional languages to run on standard computers, whereas others are written in AI languages and designed to run on LISP workstations. Likewise, some tools are narrowly focused, whereas others are designed to allow the user to develop systems appropriate to several different consultation paradigms. The knowledge engineering field is new and evolving very rapidly, and the only safe prediction is that a wide variety of languages and tools will be used in the coming years.

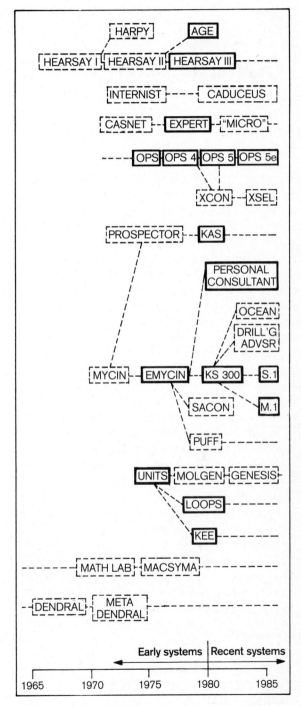

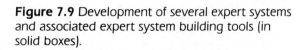

Figure 7.9 Development of several expert systems and associated expert system building tools (in solid boxes).

8.

Commercial Tools

This chapter provides brief descriptions of many of the commercially available knowledge system building tools. The market is developing very rapidly, however, and no compilation would be completely up to date. In addition, we have included a few tools and programming environments offered by universities or research centers. The latter may be of interest to a corporation undertaking the establishment of a full-scale AI research and development center, but should probably be avoided by companies seeking to enter the field in a more modest way.

Some of the vendors whose tools are described are very business-oriented. They have packaged their tools for commercial use and provide support, training, and documentation. Others, while positioning themselves for commercial sales, have not really packaged or supported their tools adequately. By the same token, some vendors go to considerable lengths to explain what sorts of tasks their tools are appropriate for, whereas others claim that their tools can be used for almost any conceivable application. As the competition between enterpreneurial AI companies heats up, the technical specialists are rapidly being replaced by marketing specialists. In all cases, the interested businessperson must inquire, see how the vendor responds, examine the product and available documentation, and then decide. The market for tools is very new, so the buyer must exercise considerable caution.

CATEGORIES OF TOOLS

We have divided the tools we describe into three general categories:

1. *Small system building tools.* Tools that can be run on personal computers. These tools are generally designed to facilitate the development of systems containing less than 400 rules.
2. *Large, narrow system building tools.* Tools that run on LISP machines or larger computers and are designed to build systems that contain 500 to several thousand rules but are constrained to one general consultation paradigm.
3. *Large, hybrid system building tools.* Tools that run on LISP machines or larger computers and are designed to build systems that contain 500 to several thousand rules and can include the features of several different consultation paradigms.

CONSULTATION PARADIGMS

Different types of experts use different approaches to problem solving. Knowledge, for example, can be represented in many different ways. Similarly, there are many different approaches to inference and many different ways to order one's activities.

Cognitive psychologists, AI researchers, and knowledge engineers have hardly begun to identify and formalize the numerous problem-solving strategies that most people use routinely in their daily lives. Table 8.1 provides a list of some of the better-known problem-solving strategies that experts have been known to use.

A *consultation paradigm* is a generic conception of a particular type of problem solving that is common to several different domains. Thus, we refer to one consultation paradigm as the *diagnosis/prescription par-*

adigm. The name derives from medical problems, such as diagnosing meningitis infections and recommending drugs. Many other medical problems also seem to involve a similar approach to problem solving. But problems in various nonmedical situations often seem to require similar expertise—reviewing a set of symptoms, considering various possibilities, and then recommending action(s) based on a qualified estimate of the probable cause(s).

Tools allow knowledge engineers to construct knowledge systems to help users solve problems that can be described in terms of one, or at most a very few consultation paradigms.

Knowledge representation, inference, and control strategies are specific software techniques. In some cases one technique, such as certainty factors, will contribute to a solution for more than one consultation paradigm. On the other hand, some techniques are strongly associated with particular paradigms. In general, specific types of problems imply tools that are built up with a certain set of representation, inference, and control techniques. (See Figure 8.1.) There is not, however, a one-to-one match between software techniques and problems. One programmer may approach a constraint satisfaction problem using a tool based on backward chaining; another knowl-

Figure 8.1 Problems, paradigms, tools, and strategies.

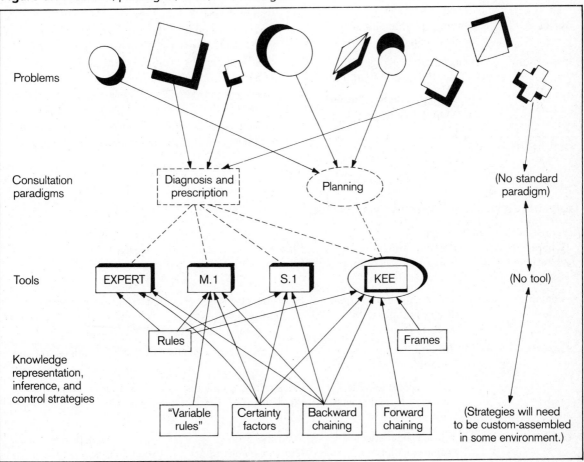

Table 8.1 Generic Types of Problem Solving

Interpretation	Inferring situation descriptions from sensor data
Prediction	Inferring likely consequences of given situations
Diagnosis	Inferring system malfunctions from observables
Design	Configuring objects under constraints
Planning	Designing actions
Monitoring	Comparing observations to plan vulnerabilities
Debugging	Prescribing remedies for malfunctions
Repair	Executing a plan to administer a prescribed remedy
Instruction	Diagnosing, debugging, and repairing student behavior
Control	Interpreting, predicting, repairing, and monitoring system behavior

After Hayes-Roth et al., 1983.

edge engineer, faced with the same problem, might choose a tool that relies on forward chaining. However, few knowledge engineers would probably choose to use a backward chaining tool to tackle a complex planning problem.

In choosing a tool, one wants to be very sure that the specific tool one chooses is appropriate for the type of problem on which one wants to use it. Unfortunately, since knowledge engineers do not understand how to handle most of the problems that human experts routinely solve, and since there are only a few tools available, many types of expert behavior cannot be conveniently encoded with any existing tool. Thus, in most cases, managers who want to employ knowledge engineering techniques have a choice. They can focus on problems that are well understood and ignore those for which there are no tools available at this time. Or they can develop a sophisticated knowledge engineering team and try to build a system by creating a unique set of knowledge representation, inference, and control techniques in some general-purpose AI language or environment such as INTERLISP, PROLOG, or perhaps OPS5. Most companies have decided to focus on solving problems for which there are already established

Table 8.2 Consultation Paradigms (Types of Problem-Solving Behavior)

Consultation Characteristic	Diagnosis/ Prescription	Planning	Design
Alternate names	Structured selection, classification	Constraint satisfaction	Discovery
Example	Diagnosing an infectious disease and prescribing drugs	Planning a project, configuring a computer	Designing an integrated circuit
Input	Conditions, answers to inquiries	Goals, limitations, means	Goals, limitations, means
Knowledge	Expert uses rules-of-thumb and simple calculations	Constraints, templates, heuristics	Constraints, templates, heuristics
Output	Solution heuristics, simple calculations	Planning heuristics, templates, constraints	Discovery heuristics, constraints

tools. Given the large number of available problems with significant paybacks, this is certainly a reasonable strategy. Moreover, even companies that have decided to develop a team capable of creating unique knowledge systems have usually built that team while working on some fairly well-understood problems.

Three of the better-known consultation paradigms are summarized briefly in Table 8.2. Table 8.3 indicates what tools are available if one is faced with one of these more familiar paradigms. And Table 8.4 indicates the knowledge representation, inference, and control strategies embodied in each tool. A comparison of Tables 8.3 and 8.4 will suggest some of the alternative software strategies that have been bundled together to deal with similar consultation paradigms.

COST CONSIDERATIONS

Since companies are rushing to bring out tools without knowing what other tools they will be competing with, the pricing of tools is not yet very rational. There are a number of different costs that someone purchasing these tools must consider, and none of the companies seems really to have spelled out all the costs yet. First, there's the cost of the tool itself. In some cases the tool is implemented in an AI language that must be purchased as a separate software package. If the tool will run only on a LISP workstation such as a Xerox 1100 machine or a Symbolics 3600, you may need to purchase special hardware as well. In some cases the vendor has included the costs of programmer training, maintenance, and some consulting in the price of the software. In others, training is sold separately. Training is a must for the more complex tools, so the cost of training is a major consideration.

If you need only one copy of the tool for research purposes, then the initial costs are all you need to worry about. If you want to use the tool to create knowledge systems that several people can use, however, the cost of making additional copies of the tool plus a knowledge base is significant. These "user

Table 8.3 Consultation Paradigms Typical of Various Tools

| Environment or Tool | Consultation Paradigm* | | |
	Diagnosis/ Prescription	Planning	Design
EMYCIN	●		
ES/P ADVISOR	●		
Expert-Ease	●		
INSIGHT	●		
M.1	●		
Personal Consultant	●		
EXPERT	●		
KES	●		
OPS5	●		●
S.1	●		
TIMM	●		
ART	●		
KEE	●		●
LOOPS	●		

*Filled circle indicates that the tool is good at the consultation.

versions" are sometimes called "runtime copies." They are usually modified systems that allow a user to use the tool to run a specific knowledge base. In addition, they usually allow a user to ask "how" and "why" questions, but they do not allow the user to modify the knowledge base. If you are a company that hopes to develop an expert system and then make copies of it to use in 25 different locations, you will want to know both the price of the initial tool and the cost (or royalties, perhaps) of making 25 duplicate, or runtime, versions. Another possible way to make a knowledge system available to multiple users is via a network. Most vendors would probably charge a royalty for a runtime version that a client planned to make available to a number of users via a network system.

Naturally, anyone hoping to use one of these tools

Table 8.4 The Knowledge, Inference, and Interface Features of Various Tools

Key:
- ● Function present in tool
- ◐ Limited presence of function
- ○ Function could be programmed but is not provided as part of tool

| | Knowledge | | | | | | | | | | Inference | | | |
| | Facts | | | Relationships | | | | Uncertainty | | | Generating New Facts | | | |
	A–V Pairs	O–A–V Triplets	Frames	IF–THEN Rules	"Variable" Rules	"Examples"	Multiple Objs.	Inheritance	Certainty Factors	Probabilities	Recognize–Act Cycle	Modus ponens	Resolution	Decision Tree Algorithm
EMYCIN		●		●			●	◐	●			●		
Small tools														
ES/P ADVISOR	●			●				○	◐				●	
Expert-Ease						●								●
INSIGHT	●	◐		●					●			●		
M.1	●	○		●	●			○	◐	●	○	●		
Personal Consultant		●		●			●	◐	●			●		
SeRIES-PC	◐			●								●		
K:base							●							●
Large, narrow tools														
EXPERT	●			●					●					
KES	●			●			●	●		●				
OPS5*	●	○		●			○				●	●		
S.1		●		●			●	◐	●			●		
TIMM						●			●					●
Large, hybrid tools														
ART	○	○	◐	◐			◐	◐	○	○		○		
KEE	○	○	◐	◐			◐	◐	○	○		○		
LOOPS	○	○	◐	◐			◐	◐	○	○		○		
SRL +	○	○	◐	◐			◐	◐	○	○		○		

*Different versions have different features.

Inference							Interface										
Control Strategies							KE				User			Sources of Data			
Backward Chaining	Forward Chaining	Depth-First Search	Breadth-First Search	Procedural Control	Active Values	Event History	Knowledge Base Editor	Case Facilities	Trace and Probes	Graphic Display (Windows)	Explanations and Justifications	Line-Oriented Display	Prompted-Menu Display	Sensors	Instruments	Data Bases	Other Languages and Procedures
●	◑	●				●	●	●	●		●			○			
●		◑									●		●				●
													●				
●	◑	●	◑						●		●		●			○	
●	◑	●						○	●		●	●		○	○	○	○
●	◑	●			●		●		●		●		●	○	○	○	○
●		●					●		●								
									●								
◑				●					●		●	●				●	●
	●	○	○			●	○		●	○	◑	●					
●		●		●		●		◑		●	●			○	○	○	○
												◑	●				
○	○	○	○	○	○	○		○	○	○	○			○	○	○	○
○	○	○	○	○	○	○	○	○	○	○	○			○	○	○	○
○	○	○	○	○	○	○		○	○	○	○			○	○	○	○
○	○	○	○	○	○	○		○	○	○	○			○	○	○	○

to develop a generic system that can then be resold to a mass market will have an interest in what the vendor would charge if one wanted to make 1,000 or 10,000 copies. In most cases vendors have not yet announced all of these costs, and you will have to negotiate with a vendor to arrive at a workable arrangement.

TRAINING AND USER INTERFACE ISSUES

Training ranges from user manuals to two-week courses with elaborate documentation and extensive hands-on experience. Most of the tools are sufficiently different from anything that conventional programmers are accustomed to that training is vital. A key issue when considering training is to determine exactly who the training is designed for. If you decide to purchase a small tool and hope to train subject matter experts to program the system, you will want to be sure that training is available that will be effective with nonprogrammers. The worst of the training and documentation is very difficult for a non-AI person to comprehend.

Separate from training are the user interface features that make the tool more or less friendly. Some user interface features are designed to help knowledge engineers create the systems in the first place. Other features are designed to help users interact with a knowledge system once it has been built. MYCIN is a reasonably good system as far as interface features go. By examining the MYCIN dialogues in Chapters 2 and 6, you can get a good idea of how the most common features work.

Obviously, if you are building a small system that will be used by clerical personnel to make routine decisions, you do not need a tool that will allow the clerks to examine the system's reasoning in great detail. If you are building a knowledge system for someone who will be explaining recommended services to customers or building a system for use by a technical expert or a professional, you will want to provide the user with means to examine how the system arrived at its conclusions.

EVALUATING KNOWLEDGE ENGINEERING TOOLS

The checklist we used to evaluate tools for this book is reproduced as Table 8.5. Although we were not always able to obtain all the information, we tried to get as much as we could for each tool. The list is divided into eight sections, which are described below.

- *Consultation paradigm.* Some tools are best described as "diagnosis/prescription" problem solvers, whereas others are used primarily to build knowledge systems that solve "planning" problems.
- *Representation, inference, and control.* This refers to the cluster of strategies used for representing facts and relationships, for drawing inferences to obtain new facts, and for controlling the reasoning process when information is incomplete, contradictory, or uncertain.
- *Implementation.* Tools gain some of their power from the software environments in which they run, and from the hardware on which they depend. They also may have limited applications because of their unusual hardware requirements. For example, tools that depend on special LISP machines may provide a superior development environment. At the same time, it is harder to install the resulting system in an IBM mainframe environment.
- *User interface.* Knowledge systems vary in the degree to which they support smooth interaction with users. User interface features include explanation facilities, graphical display of the reasoning process, on-line help systems, etc. A second user interface is the one the system developer uses to build, modify, debug, expand, and evaluate knowledge bases. Tools provide features such as trace facilities, break packages, and graphical views of knowledge base in order to observe and dissect the reasoning process. Other features include case management and batch processing facilities. As the knowledge base is modified and expanded, a library of cases can be run and the results verified to be sure that additions to the

Table 8.5 Checklist for Knowledge Engineering Tools

TOOL: _____
Date introduced: _____ Release: _____
Reviewer: _____ Date of review: _____

MANUFACTURER
    Address: _____
        _____

    Contact person: _____
        _____

    Cost (initial): _____
        _____

(To reproduce knowledge systems): _____

CONSULTATION PARADIGM
(What class of problems is this tool designed to solve?)

_____
_____
_____

REPRESENTATION, INFERENCE, AND
CONTROL STRATEGIES
Knowledge Base Objects:
    Facts: _____
    Rules: _____
    Inheritance and association: _____
    Cf/probabilities: _____
Inference engine:
    Inference strategies: _____
    Control strategies: _____
Methods for incomplete and inexact knowledge:

_____

IMPLEMENTATION
    Base language(s): _____
    Required hardware: _____
    Interface possible:
        Data bases: _____
        Sensors: _____

USER INTERFACE
    Screen: _____
    Explanation facilities: _____
    _____

KE INTERFACE
    Aids for building new KBs: _____
    Editors for modifying KBs: _____
    Debugging aids (tracing, match): _____
    _____

    Graphical support: _____
    _____

    Case library facilities: _____
    _____

APPLICATIONS
    Examples of systems built with tool:
    (1) _____
    _____
    (2) _____
    _____

SUPPORT
    Documentation: _____
    Training courses: _____
    _____

    Support services: _____
    _____

    Consultants: _____
    _____

INFORMATION USED FOR REVIEW:
    Sources (date): _____
    _____

    Trials (cases run): _____
    _____

knowledge base do not change previously correct behavior.

- *Applications.* We note the categories of problems that a tool is designed to solve. We also look for fielded applications—commercial systems in ordinary use—as another indication of the applications of a tool.

- *Support.* This category includes a description of the reference manuals, training courses, and support services that accompany the tool.

We also noted information about the company that sells the tool, its location, and the cost of the tool.

COMMERCIALLY AVAILABLE TOOLS

The accounts that follow are based on information that has appeared in journal articles or has been provided by the companies. In some cases we have first-hand experience with the tools. In most cases, however, we have only read a reference manual, examined brochures, played with a demonstration system on the tool, and talked with the vendor's representatives.

We have attempted to standardize terminology. This is especially true in our description of a product's consultation paradigms and in our description of how each tool handles knowledge representation, inference, and control. In spite of our efforts, descriptions are undoubtedly incomplete, and may even include subtle errors of interpretation. Moreover, several of these tools have been rushed to market and will probably be revised, improved, and expanded even before this book appears.

The tools descriptions that follow are divided into our three general categories: small tools; large, narrow tools; and large, hybrid tools. Within each category, the tools are considered in alphabetical order. Table 8.6, at the end of the chapter, summarizes the information on all the tools.

SMALL SYSTEM BUILDING TOOLS

Small tools are tools designed to run on personal computers. They can be used to build knowledge systems of up to about 400 rules. Some of the small tools are quite trivial, whereas others are as powerful or more powerful than the original EMYCIN tool that underlies MYCIN. Most of the small tools could probably be used by a subject matter expert willing to spend a good deal of time learning about knowledge engineering. In most cases, however, it would be helpful to have a knowledge engineer available to assist your experts.

The pricing of small tools is particularly confusing. Some less powerful products are priced high, while some of the cheaper products are very credible. One thing is certain; powerful, personal computer-based expert system tools will soon be sold for about the price of other sophisticated business software.

ES/P ADVISOR

Overview

ES/P ADVISOR (for Expert System/Prolog) is a tool created by Expert Systems International (England), an established PROLOG vendor. ES/P ADVISOR was released in 1984. It is tailored to facilitate "text animation"— an application in which expertise that is already recorded as instructions, regulations, or procedures can be easily converted to a small expert system. Applications that have been tried in England include small systems that provide users with advice on:

- Government regulations on taxes and social benefits
- Building regulations
- Accounting standards
- Safety standards for industrial equipment
- Complex office procedures
- Assembling complex documents from predefined paragraphs
- Completing complex forms

Knowledge and Inference

ES/P ADVISOR represents facts as attribute–value pairs (called *expressions*). Heuristic knowledge is represented by means of production rules. The tool depends on backward chaining, and control is largely a matter of arranging the knowledge in the order in which the designer wants it to be considered.

The following example illustrates how one would use ES/P ADVISOR to do text animation. The designer of an ADVISOR system begins with a piece of text that describes a complex set of instructions or regulations and separates the actual advice from the conditions that define when the advice is applicable. For example, consider the paragraph which follows, taken from a British Statement of Standard Accounting Practice:

Where the interest of the investing group or company in any company other than a subsidiary is not effectively that of a partner in a joint venture or consortium and the investing group or company holds 20 percent or more of the equity voting rights of that company as an associated company, details of the accounting treatment adopted, and the reason for doing so, should be stated by way of note to the financial statements.

The first section of the text describes the *conditions* under which the advice is applicable, whereas the second portion describes the *advice*. In effect there are four conditions, which could be expressed in the following terms:

If the interest of the investor is not that of a partner in a joint venture or consortium, and

the company is not a subsidiary of the investor, and

the investor holds 20 percent or more of the

equity voting rights of the company, and

the investor does not account for the company as an associated company . . .

We could turn each of these *if* clauses into an attribute–value pair, using ES/P ADVISOR's notation, as follows:

- Not interest = partner, and
- Notsubsidiary, and
- Investor_voting_equity > = 20, and
- Not associated

In other words, we have four attributes—interest, subsidiary, investor_voting_equity, and associated—each of which we need to define.

An ES/P ADVISOR knowledge base is prepared on any standard word processing system (e.g., Word-Star). The text we are examining would be entered as shown below.

```
{ not interest = partner and notsubsidiary and
investor_voting_equity > = 20 and not associated }

'Details of the accounting treatment adopted and the'          &
'reason for so doing, should be stated by way of note to'      &
'the financial statements.'

interest: 'the interest of the investor in the company'
     category
     options
          partner—'A partner in a joint venture or consortium',
          financier—'A pure financial interest',
          other—'Some other form of interest'
     askable using
          'What is the investor's interest in the company?'.

subsidiary:
     fact
     rule false if interest = partner
     askable using
          'Is the company a subsidiary of the investor?'.

investor_voting_equity: 'the percentage of voting equity rights'
     number range 0..100
```

```
        explanation
                'The investing company will normally have a'          &
                'certain amount of voting equity (a measure'          &
                'of its influence on the board).'                     &
                                                                      &
                'The percentage of such equity may differ'           &
                'from the percentage of its financial equity.'
        askable using
                'What percentage of voting equity rights is'          &
                'held by the investing company?'.

    associated: 'the company is an associated company of the investor'
        fact
        rules
            true if  not subsidiary and interest = partner and significant_
                     influence
            true if  long_term_interest and substantial_interest and significant_
                     influence.
```

Note that in the last rule, three new attributes, "long_term interest," "substantial_interest," and "significant_influence," are introduced. Each of these attributes would also need to be defined to complete the knowledge base. Also notice that the knowledge base does two things. It associates advice text with the conditions that make that advice relevant, and it defines the parameters of the problem area in terms of the type of information required (fact, category, or number) and how their values can be obtained. One does not really write rules, one enters A–V pairs and brief commands on how to relate them and allows the tool to handle the information. ES/P ADVISOR does not allow one to assign certainty factors to facts or rules and thus would not be appropriate for problems that involve a lot of heuristic knowledge; but textual instructions, regulations, and procedures rarely involve uncertainties of this kind.

By loading the file created in a word processing system into the ES/P ADVISOR, one creates a system that can run a consultation like that illustrated in Figure 8.2

Figure 8.2 Screen of ES/P ADVISOR.

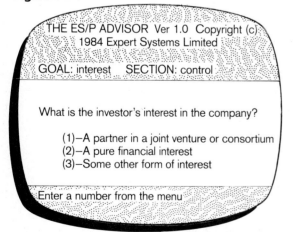

```
THE ES/P ADVISOR  Ver 1.0  Copyright (c)
     1984 Expert Systems Limited

GOAL: interest    SECTION: control


What is the investor's interest in the company?

    (1)–A partner in a joint venture or consortium
    (2)–A pure financial interest
    (3)–Some other form of interest


Enter a number from the menu
```

User/KE Interface

Development of a small knowledge system with a tool like ES/P ADVISOR requires some knowledge of how to analyze text into attributes and values and how to arrange them into rules, but hardly the programming knowledge normally associated with "knowledge engineers." In effect, the user can develop his or her own systems.

The screens illustrated in Figure 8.2 provide a good idea of how a user works with the system. The screen keeps the user aware of what he or she is doing and provides explanations as desired. In addition to "how" and "why" options, ES/P ADVISOR allows the developer to insert paragraphs of text. Then, when the user is running the system and wants a detailed explanation of some concept, he or she can simply type "Explain" and the system will print out the paragraph.

The tool comes on a "locked" floppy disk and is accompanied by a manual that includes a tutorial section that takes you through the construction of an example knowledge base. Sample systems developed on ES/P ADVISOR are also provided.

By stressing that one need not be a knowledge engineer to program ES/P ADVISOR, we do not want to downplay this tool. By separately purchasing ESI's PROLOG-1 software for your personal computer, a comprehensive interface between ES/P ADVISOR and PROLOG is possible. PROLOG is a very powerful logical programming environment, and thus a well-trained knowledge engineer could use the combination to modify and tailor ES/P ADVISOR to suit specialized needs. Thus, it is almost fair to say that ES/P ADVISOR, alone, is a very narrow tool for developing small "text animation" programs, whereas ES/P ADVISOR plus PROLOG is a powerful, hybrid system building tool.

Implementation
This tool runs on an IBM PC with a DOS 2.0 operating system. The tool requires 128K bytes, and a color monitor is recommended.

Purchase
ES/P ADVISOR costs approximately $1,895. Arrangements for reproducing multiple copies of a knowledge system are open to negotiation.

EXPERT-EASE

Overview
Expert-Ease is a very small tool sold by Expert Software International, Ltd. (Scotland). For a brief period this tool was the only "system building" tool available for a personal computer, and it enjoyed a bit of attention for that. The tool is termed a "decision-making spreadsheet," and it is quite good at developing a decision tree that will sort through a number of possible descriptions to determine which one the user actually faces. In effect, however, all of the knowledge entered in Expert-Ease forms one rule. Hence, the knowledge one wants to analyze must be similar in nature.

Knowledge and Inference
Expert-Ease asks the user to create a matrix with all of the possible attributes and the overall generic recommendation for some decision-making process on the top axis. This matrix can be built slowly, since the developer does not need to specify all possible attributes at once. Instead, one describes a single "example" of the decision-making process at a time. Each "example" (or set of values for the attributes listed on the horizontal axis of the matrix) occupies one row of the matrix. Thus, for example, if one were developing a system to determine the postage required for a package, one might start by saying:

If   the *weight* is 1 pound, and
        the *class of service* is to be third class, and
        the *destination* is local,

Then the *postage* will be $1.80.

This rule would appear on the Expert-Ease matrix.

Other "examples" or "rules" could be added as long as they took the same general form. They would have to describe attributes that you would consider in deciding how much postage to put on a package. You could use new attributes—up to 31 different attributes are allowed—but all the examples would have to conclude about "postage," since one Expert-Ease system can draw conclusions about only one type of recommendation. Moreover, since you only have one rule, no matter how many attributes you use to subdivide the decision-making process, you cannot write a rule that will manipulate any of the attributes themselves. Thus, you can't add a rule that tells the system how to determine if a destination is local or not; all you can do is ask the user a question for each attribute. In other words, Expert-Ease is "flat": It is incapable of representing a hierarchy of rules and thus cannot deal with any kind of intermediary results.

The inference and control process is an algorithm that converts all the examples into a decision table and then proceeds to work through the table by asking the user questions that successively divide the options in half. The "intelligence" of Expert-Ease is manifested in its ability to rearrange the attributes in the decision tree in such a way that the questions subdivide the tree in the most efficient way.

User/KE Interface

One does not need to know much about knowledge engineering to use Expert-Ease. The program uses menus to prompt the user through the process of creating and using a system. The problem, of course, is choosing the attributes. Expert-Ease simplifies the task by allowing you to enter as many as you can think of. Then it sorts through them to determine which are necessary when it creates the decision tree.

Implementation

Expert-Ease runs on an IBM PC, a DEC Rainbow, and a Victor 9000. The tool requires 128K bytes of RAM. Expert-Ease requires the UCSD-P Operating System.

Purchase

Expert-Ease sells for $2,000. Arrangements for reproducing copies of a knowledge system for multiple users are open to negotiation.

INSIGHT KNOWLEDGE SYSTEM

Overview

INSIGHT Knowledge System is a product of Level 5 Research. It was introduced in the fall of 1984. This tool is well designed, user-friendly, and very fast. The tool is designed to facilitate the development of 200- to 400-rule systems. It is priced to create a mass market for systems that can be used in a variety of business applications.

Knowledge and Inference

INSIGHT represents facts as attribute–value pairs or as object–attribute–value triplets. The basic units of the system are *if–then* rules and a goal outline. The goal outline allows the system to do simple breadth-first forward chaining. For example, a knowledge base on automotive repair might have the following goal outline:

1. Drive train problems
    1.1 Axle problems
    1.2 Driveshaft problems
    1.3 Transmission problems
2. Electrical problems
    2.1 Ignition problems
    2.2 Light problems
        2.2.1 Headlight problems
        2.2.2 Taillight problems
        2.2.3 Turn signal problems
3. Fuel system problems

The outline is, in effect, a hierarchically organized set of goals that the system can attempt to solve. When an INSIGHT program is run, the user is presented with the top level set of goals, as shown at the top of the next page.

The brackets indicate highlighting. The user moves the cursor to highlight his or her choice and then presses RETURN. If the user cannot choose among the options, he or she can press the F3 key for UNKNOWN. At that point, INSIGHT will consider all rules that apply to any of the goals in the outline.

If the user knows the problem is an "electrical problem," however, he or she can highlight ELEC-

THE AUTOMOTIVE REPAIR GUIDE

CAN YOU NARROW DOWN THE AREA YOU ARE INTERESTED IN?

[DRIVE TRAIN PROBLEMS]

ELECTRICAL PROBLEMS

FUEL SYSTEM PROBLEMS

[ ] [2 RESTART] [3 UNKNOWN] [4 EXPAND] [5 MENU] [6 HELP] [7 EXIT]

TRICAL PROBLEMS and press RETURN. In this case, INSIGHT presents the user with the next level of goals:

IGNITION PROBLEMS
LAMP PROBLEMS

Once again, the user can either narrow the search by indicating the subgoal to focus on or else indicate UNKNOWN and, in effect, direct the system to pursue all rules that pertain to Electrical Problems. INSIGHT's goal outline can accommodate 32 goals at any one level and can handle 48 levels. Thus, the user can easily narrow the search if he or she knows anything about the problem when the consultation begins.

Once the rules are evoked, INSIGHT works as a regular back-chainer. The syntax of a typical rule is as follows:

Rule: to tell if a warm-blooded animal is a mammal
If   the animal has body hair
And   the animal suckles its young,
Then the animal is a mammal
      CONFIDENCE 85
And   the animal lives on the ground,
      CONFIDENCE 65
Else the animal is a bird

INSIGHT rules are given titles (the text after RULE). If a user requests a trace of a session, the titles can be used to make the trace more easily readable. The rules support multiple *if* clauses and multiple conclusions. In the example above, the rule either establishes that the animal is probably a mammal (confidence .85) and also asserts, as a biproduct, that the animal probably lives on land, or the rule asserts that the animal is a bird.

INSIGHT's rule syntax allows the user considerable flexibility. When a user answers a question, the system then asks the user how confident he or she is that the answer is correct. Thus, all rules have two confidence measures, the confidence assigned to the rule, adjusted by the confidence that the user has in his or her answer. The system designer assigns a threshold to a knowledge base and thus controls the total confidence required for rules to succeed.

In choosing the next rule to try, the system selects the *if* clause with the highest confidence. Failing that, the order of the rules determines the sequence.

User/KE Interface
INSIGHT knowledge bases can be developed in any conventional word processing system. Once developed, they are compiled by means of a compiler/ editor that simultaneously compiles and checks the

knowledge base for syntax problems. Once compiled, the programs can be run in the INSIGHT system. The system presents the user with a series of menus. The user makes inputs or selects options via function keys. INSIGHT allows the developer to attach notes and explanations to goals and rules. The user can access this text by pressing a function key.

The ease of development, user-friendly interface, speed, and low cost make INSIGHT Knowledge System an ideal tool for developing small knowledge systems for business applications.

Implementation

INSIGHT is implemented in PASCAL and is available for the IBM PC, the DEC Rainbow, and the Victor 9000.

Purchase

INSIGHT may be purchased from Level 5 Research for $95.

M.1

Overview

M.1 is a product of Teknowledge Inc. It was introduced in June 1984 as a tool to assist knowledge engineers in prototyping knowledge systems. It is intended to be a small and powerful tool for exploring knowledge engineering concepts, for determining the feasibility of a knowledge engineering approach to users' problems, and for fielding small knowledge systems. The typical M.1 application is a 100- to 200-rule system. This strategy of using M.1 as a "get acquainted" tool has influenced the training that accompanies M.1 as well as its price. Teknowledge assumes that only experienced programmers will acquire M.1.

M.1 is designed to function like a friendlier and more efficient version of EMYCIN. Thus, M.1 is designed to aid development of knowledge systems that handle diagnosis/prescription consultations. Be-

fore releasing M.1, Teknowledge used a version of EMYCIN called KS300. M.1 was designed to allow knowledge engineers to develop the same sorts of expert systems that Teknowledge was building with KS300, and thus, although the tool is new, it has been tested against the considerable library of systems that Teknowledge has already developed.

Knowledge and Inference

Facts are represented as attribute–value pairs (attributes are called *expressions*) with accompanying confidence factors. Production rules represent heuristic knowledge. A rule tests the value of an expression and concludes values for another expression. A key feature of M.1 is its support of "variable" rules. This technique makes it very easy to enter a lot of similar rules by writing one generic rule and then entering a lot of information in a manner similar to a "look-up table."

The M.1 inference engine is a simple back-chainer in the tradition of MYCIN. Control is achieved in several ways. First, the order of clauses in a rule influences how back-chaining will proceed. Second, *when-found* rules allow limited forward chaining. The *presupposition* function declares that one expression must be evaluated before it makes sense to explore another. For example, before asking about the details of an event, M.1 can automatically determine whether the event has taken place at all. Uncertain information is marked by confidence factors that range from 0 to 100. M.1 accepts *unknown* as an answer to its questions and continues to reason with available information.

A detailed example of how a small knowledge system can be built using M.1 is provided in Chapter 11.

User/KE Interface

Users interact with M.1 by typing answers to questions posed by the system. There are explanation facilities as well as trace functions for knowledge base debugging. Menus are available that list appropriate responses. M.1 can evaluate and expand abbreviated answers. Figure 8.3 shows a typical M.1 screen.

Figure 8.3 Screen of M.1. This screen illustrates how M.1 appears to a designer. The upper half of the screen is devoted to windows that display the current state of the system's reasoning. The lower half shows the consultation as a user of the completed knowledge system would see it.

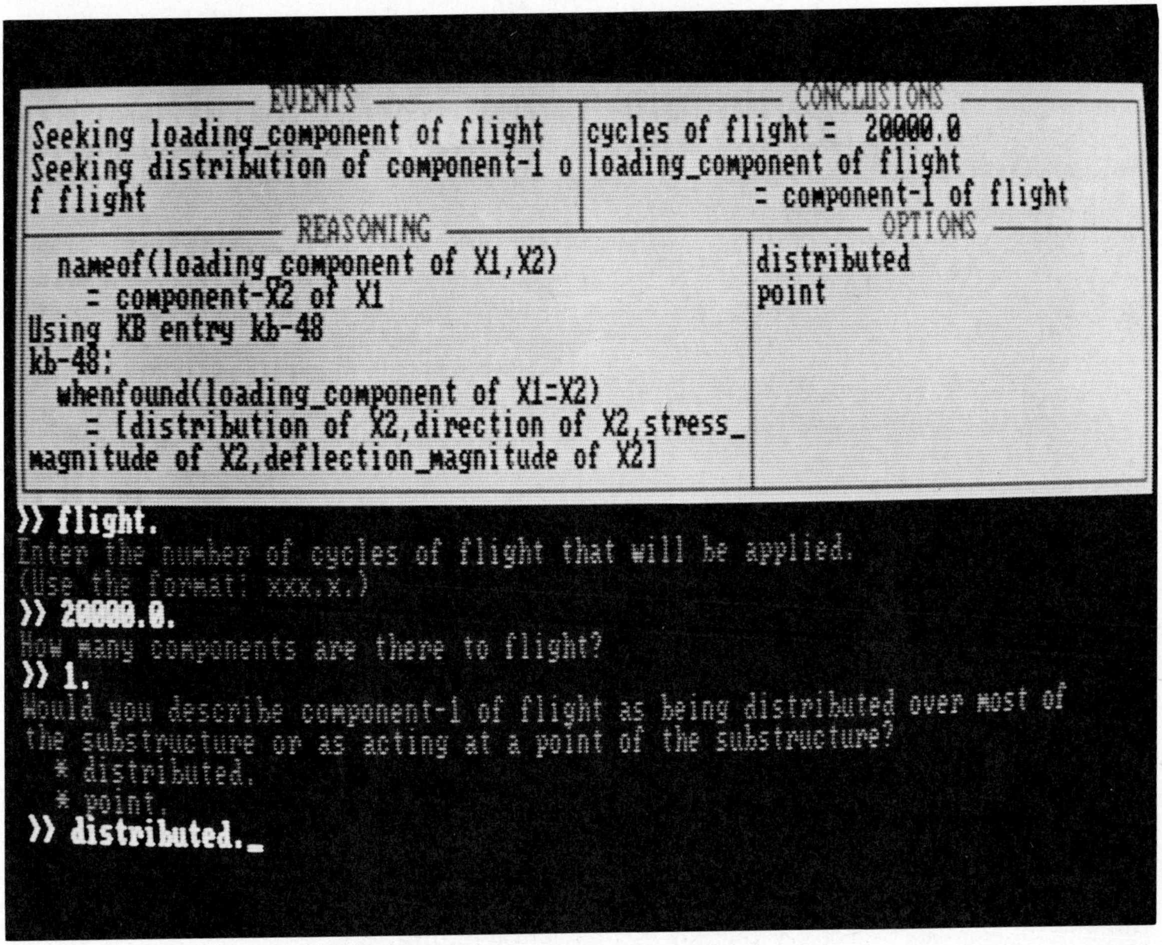

```
━━━━━━━━━━ EVENTS ━━━━━━━━━━━  ━━━━━━━━━━━ CONCLUSIONS ━━━━━━
Seeking loading_component of flight  cycles of flight =  20000.0
Seeking distribution of component-1 o loading_component of flight
f flight                                   = component-1 of flight
━━━━━━━━━━ REASONING ━━━━━━━━━━━          ━━━━━━━━━━━ OPTIONS ━━━━━
  nameof(loading_component of X1,X2)      distributed
      = component-X2 of X1                point
Using KB entry kb-48
kb-48:
   whenfound(loading_component of X1=X2)
      = [distribution of X2,direction of X2,stress_
magnitude of X2,deflection_magnitude of X2]
```

```
>> flight.
Enter the number of cycles of flight that will be applied.
(Use the format: xxx.x.)
>> 20000.0.
How many components are there to flight?
>> 1.
Would you describe component-1 of flight as being distributed over most of
the substructure or as acting at a point of the substructure?
    * distributed.
    * point.
>> distributed._
```

M.1 knowledge bases are assembled outside the tool with the system builder's favorite text editor, for example, WordStar. M.1 provides programming aids for debugging. A *panel* mode, for example, maintains a set of tracing windows where different events are monitored. The system developer can observe what rule is under consideration, what options are open to the user, and what conclusions have been reached. This information is displayed in the top half of the screen while a consultation dialogue takes place in the bottom half.

Implementation

M.1 is implemented in PROLOG and is available for the IBM PC (and XT). A color monitor is recommended.

Purchase

M.1, with its course and documentation, is available from Teknowledge for $12,500. Information is available on request for the production of multiple copies, educational discounts, and the purchase of portions of the M.1 package.

An exploratory version of the M.1 software, M.1a, is priced at $2,000. A one-week training course is offered separately for $2,500.

A reference manual and a library of sample systems accompany the software. User support is available by phone, and a users' group, sponsored by Teknowledge, is being formed.

PERSONAL CONSULTANT

Overview

Personal Consultant is an EMYCIN-like program developed by Texas Instruments to run on its TI Professional and Portable Professional Computers. It was announced in August 1984. No applications have been demonstrated on this system yet, but it is so similar to EMYCIN that one may reasonably assume that any of the smaller applications that have been developed for EMYCIN could be made to run on Personal Consultant.

Knowledge and Inference

Facts are represented as object–attribute–value triplets (using the EMYCIN terminology: contexts–parameters–values) with accompanying confidence factors. Production rules represent heuristic knowledge. Personal Consultant can build systems of up to about 400 rules.

A rule tests the value of an O–A–V fact and concludes about other facts. The Personal Consultant's inference engine is a simple back-chainer. As with EMYCIN, one states a goal attribute and, whenever a consultation system is run, the goal provides the starting point for backward chaining.

Control is governed primarily by the order of clauses in the rules. Uncertain information is marked by confidence factors ranging from 0 to 100. Like all the offspring of EMYCIN, Personal Consultant accepts *unknown* as an answer to its questions and continues to reason with available information.

User/KE Interface

Users interact with Personal Consultant by typing answers to questions posed by the system. There are explanation facilities as well as trace functions for knowledge base debugging. Menus are available that list appropriate responses. The Personal Consultant can evaluate and expand abbreviated answers. The screen with which the user interacts is especially well thought out, and the function keys are used to allow the user to answer "unknown" or to question the system.

Personal Consultant uses questions to prompt the designer to enter the initial information into a knowledge base. The tool provides several programming aids for debugging.

The Personal Consultant can be purchased alone, or it can be purchased with a three-day course accompanied by five days of consulting at some later date. A reference manual and some sample systems accompany the software.

Personal Consultant also allows a knowledge engineer to move from the tool into LISP. Thus, a knowledgeable designer could tailor Personal Consultant in a variety of ways.

Implementation

The recommended configuration for the Personal Consultant is a Texas Instruments Professional Computer with a 10M-byte hard disk, a minimum of 512K bytes of RAM (768K bytes if you really want to do a 400-rule system), and MS-DOS 1.1 or 2.1.

Personal Consultant is implemented in IQLISP. As of late 1984, IQLISP has not released a compiler. Compilers allow one to compact a program after it has been written and thus cause a "compiled" program to run much faster. The existing configuration is quite adequate for the development of an expert system, but if one were planning to create a knowledge system and then make multiple copies for users, one would like to be able to compile the knowledge system before it was reproduced to make it a little faster for users to operate. It is not an easy matter to develop a LISP compiler. If you are considering such an application, you will want to be sure that a compiler is available before settling on this or any other system that depends on an underlying language.

Purchase

Personal Consultant software, with documentation but without training support, sells for $3,000. IQLISP is included in the purchase price. A three-day training course is provided for $1,500.

If you know that you want to make a large number of copies, Texas Instruments offers an arrangement whereby you can pay an initial fee of $25,000 for the right to reproduce 10,000 copies. Each copy that is in fact reproduced costs an additional $25. Thus, if you create an interesting knowledge system and want to make 10,000 runtime copies, it will cost you $275 per copy.

ADDITIONAL SMALL TOOLS

In the following section on large, narrow tools, we describe the two tools, TIMM and KES, that have each announced microcomputer versions. Information about each of these tools is included under the descriptions of their larger parents that follow.

In addition, SRI International (formerly Stanford Research Institute) has announced a tool for a personal computer named SeRIES-PC. This EMYCIN-like tool will be sold only to clients who also purchase consulting services from SRI.

Lehman Brothers (Shearson Lehman/American Express, Inc.), in combination with Gold Hill Computers (the creators of Golden Common LISP) and Symbolics, Inc., has also announced a tool that will run on either an IBM PC, a Symbolics machine, or a combination of the two. This tool, called K:base, is "example-driven," like Expert-Ease and TIMM, and seems to stand somewhere between the two in sophistication.

There is a small expert system building tool called AL/X that is sold by university professors from the University of Edinburgh. AL/X is a diagnosis/prescription system that uses attribute–value pairs, *if–then* rules, forward chaining and Bayesian probabilities. It is loosely modeled on KAS, the tool that SRI used to build PROSPECTOR. The tool is written in PASCAL and runs on an APPLE II. It was originally developed by Donald Michie to help British Petroleum apply AI techniques to an offshore drilling operations problem. It is being used in some universities in the U.S. but is generally hard to locate.

There are no small tools available for the Macintosh yet, but several are said to be in the making. When you consider that the Macintosh was inspired by the AI researchers at Xerox PARC and that most large expert system building tools make extensive use of windows and mice, it's easy to think that small expert system building tools will not really reach maturity until they can take advantage of a Macintosh-like environment. The prospect of a reasonably priced, small expert system building tool with the graphics capabilities of a hybrid tool like KEE, ART, or LOOPS is very exciting.

LARGE, NARROW SYSTEM BUILDING TOOLS

Large, narrow tools are designed to constrain the user to one or a few consultation paradigms. By limiting the tool, the vendor is potentially able to build a much more efficient interface for the knowledge engineer. Narrow tools are limited in the type of problem for which they are useful, but they make up for this by allowing customers with appropriate problems to create large expert systems quickly and effectively.

EXPERT

Overview

EXPERT is a tool for designing and building consultation systems. Its paradigm is the diagnosis/prescription model (which its developers call the classification model). EXPERT was built by Sholom Weiss and Casimir Kulikowski of Rutgers University. These two individuals have used the system to develop several large and small knowledge systems.

The three examples that we outline below are described in detail in a book written by EXPERT's creators, *A Practical Guide to Designing Expert Systems* (1984):

- Serum protein diagnosis program. This knowledge system examines profiles of data from a spectrum analyzer. It classifies the profiles and selects an appropriate diagnosis to display. The system was built with EXPERT and then recoded into assembly language to be stored in a read-only memory (ROM). This ROM is installed in the spectrum analyzer. The instrument plots the profile and prints an interpretation. (See Chapter 10, page 167 for a more detailed description of this system.)
- Another, larger system built with EXPERT is a rheumatic disease consultant.
- EXPERT has been used to develop a log analysis system for oil drilling. The system scans the logs of events that occur while drilling oil wells.

Knowledge and Inference

EXPERT stores facts as attribute–value pairs. Facts are classified in two ways: as *findings* or *hypotheses*.

Findings are observational data coming into the system. Hypotheses are potential solutions, one or more of which will be selected by the system. Relationships and heuristics are stored as production rules grouped in three categories:

- "F–F" rules that link a finding with other findings,
- "F–H" rules that relate findings to hypotheses, and
- "H–H" rules that link one hypothesis with other hypotheses.

In the ordinary course of a consultation, incoming data are interpreted and refined with F–F rules. The consolidated description of the findings are then related to the set of possible solutions with F–H rules. Finally, hypotheses are refined using the H–H rules.

The inference engine for EXPERT is questionnaire-driven. Findings are sought one after another before the system begins to reason. After all information is obtained, rules are fired in the following order: F–F, F–H, and then H–H. Thus, EXPERT is not a back-chainer. Control is established by the order and category of the rules.

The system is able to reason with incomplete and uncertain data. A belief measure ranging from −1 to 1 is associated with facts.

User/KE Interface

The user interface is very simple. Questions are asked, answers are obtained, the reasoning process takes place, and an answer is given. An example of an EXPERT dialogue is reproduced below and indented. The user's responses are all underlined. Comments are interspersed throughout.

Enter Name or ID Number:
Cadillac

Enter Date of Visit:
5/1/82

1. Type of problem:
   1) Car Won't Start

    2) Other Car Problems
Checklist:
1

2. Simple Checks:
    1) Headlights Are Dim
    2) Fuel Filter Clogged
    3) Battery Cables Loose or Corroded
Checklist:
2

3. Starter Data:
    1) No Cranking
    2) Slow Cranking
    3) Normal Cranking
    4) Grinding Noise from Starter
Checklist:
Why

The user wants to know why this question was asked. This question includes several related items about the starter, which are always asked together. The program indicates which item it is most interested in obtaining.

    If: There is a grinding noise from starter
    Then: Conclude starter malfunction (.9).
3. Starter Data:
    1) No Cranking
    2) Slow Cranking
    3) Normal Cranking
    4) Grinding Noise from Starter
Checklist:
Fix 2

The user indicates that he or she wants to change the entry that was made for question 2.

    FIX: Simple Checks
      1) Headlights Are Dim
      2) Fuel Filter Clogged
      3) Battery Cables Loose or Corroded
Checklist:
1,2

3. Starter Data:
    1) No Cranking
    2) Slow Cranking
    3) Normal Cranking
    4) Grinding Noise from Starter

Checklist:
1

4. Gas Gauge Reads EMPTY
   No

5. Odor of Gasoline in Car:
   1) None
   2) Normal
   3) Very Strong
   Choose one:
   2

The system summarizes and reports results.

SUMMARY

Name: Cadillac
Case: 5   Visit: 1   Date: 05/01/82

Type of Problem:
   Car Won't Start

Odor of Gasoline in Car:
   Normal

Simple Checks:
   Headlights Are Dim
   Fuel Filter Clogged

Starter Data:
   No Cranking

The conclusions are printed with associated measures of confidence. These numbers are not probabilities but analogous to them: the closer the number is to 1, the greater the confidence.

INTERPRETIVE ANALYSIS

Diagnostic Status
   1.00   Fuel Filter Clogged
   0.90   Battery Discharged

Treatment Recommendations
   0.80   Replace Gas Filter
   0.80   Change or Replace Battery

From Sholom M. Weiss and Casimir A. Kulikowski, A Practical Guide to Designing Expert Systems. (Totowa, NJ: Rowman & Allanheld, 1984), pp. 77-79.

From the knowledge engineer's perspective, EXPERT is a batch-processing knowledge system tool. There is no interactive editor, nor are there other software aids for building knowledge bases. Trace facilities are available at runtime to assist in debugging.

Statistical functions are available to examine how much a rule improves performance. Modifying a rule changes the system's overall performance on a set of cases. Errors occur in two ways: false-positive diagnoses (cases that EXPERT judges faulty but are not) and false-negative ones (cases where EXPERT fails to locate fault that is present). EXPERT's statistical functions assist the system designer in tuning the performance of the system.

Implementation

EXPERT is written in FORTRAN and is available for a number of different operating systems and many types of hardware. Interfaces to data bases and sensors are supported by FORTRAN.

Purchase

Access to EXPERT is via Rutgers University and is subject to negotiation.

KES—KNOWLEDGE ENGINEERING SYSTEM

Overview

Knowledge Engineering System (KES) is a product of Software Architecture and Engineering (Arlington, Virginia). KES is a family of products that support the development of consultation-style knowledge systems.

KES is suited for diagnosis/prescription problems. We know of no commercial systems built with the tool.

In the summer of 1984, Software A&E announced that Control Data had taken a 20.1 percent equity position in Software A&E (with the option to ac-

quire an additional 10 percent) and that "Control Data and Software A&E will join in developing a new generation Expert System product for release in 1985. Like the current product, this more advanced version of KES will be for use on Control Data computers and those of other manufacturers."

Knowledge and Inference

Facts in KES are represented as attribute–value pairs with associated confidence factors, or probabilities. Attributes and values can be arranged in hierarchies. Relations among facts are represented as production rules, using statistical pattern classification techniques, or with hypothesis test cycles.

- Production rules are ordinary *if–then* statements.
- Statistical pattern classification refers to a Bayesian approach to assessing the likelihood that a fact is true in the light of prior probabilities that it is true.
- The hypothesis test cycle is a strategy for cycling through alternative hypotheses about a problem situation until one is determined with sufficient certainty.

Control is maintained by the inference engine with explicit statements in the knowledge base, called *statements of action*. The commands that a user issues can be stored in the knowledge base and executed during a consultation. For example, one action is declaring a goal attribute. When this occurs the inference engine back-chains through rules in order to obtain a value for the goal. Action statements extend the flexibility of a back-chaining inference engine.

Incomplete or inexact knowledge is represented with probability coefficients or certainty factors (ranging from -1 to 1) attached to the attribute–value pairs.

User/KE Interface

Users communicate with KES through a line-oriented interaction. Multiple-choice questions provide a list of alternatives, and users choose one by number. In this sense the interaction is menu-driven. Explanation facilities are available to define terms, but not to explain reasoning. Probes are available that display portions of the static or dynamic knowledge base.

From the knowledge engineer's perspective, KES is a batch-processing knowledge system. A knowledge base is written with an external editor and stored as a file. Then KES is executed and the knowledge base file is processed. Syntax and other errors appear at runtime. For example, there is an inspector function that locates unlinked or inappropriately linked attributes. Also, during a consultation the knowledge engineer can assert values for attributes and, thus, examine how the system reasons under varying conditions. Neither graphics nor case facilities are mentioned in KES documentation.

Support for KES consists of reference documents and a product support staff. Documents include an end user's manual, a knowledge base author's manual, and a developmental tool user's manual.

Software A&E offers a series of training courses in artificial intelligence and expert systems. The initial courses provide an overview of the technology, whereas the advanced courses show how to apply KES. The courses are as follows:

- Introduction to the Theory of Artificial Intelligence (1 day, $250/person)
- Expert System Development and Knowledge Engineering (1 day, $250/person)
- Introduction to the Knowledge Engineering System (KES) (2 days, $500/person)
- Developing Advanced Expert Systems with KES (5 days, $1,200/person)

Implementation

KES can be purchased in pieces and assembled into various configurations.

KES is implemented in Wisconsin LISP, a dialect of LISP. It is also available written in FranzLISP for the DEC VAX running under the UNIX operating system, for the CDC CYBER running under A-LISP, and for the Apollo workstation running under Portable Standard LISP (PSL).

KES is also implemented in IQLISP for an IBM PC XT with at least 512K of RAM (640K is recommended). In addition, 8087 Math Coprocessor software is required. At the moment there is no IQLISP compiler, so the system runs a bit slowly, but a compiler is promised by late 1984.

Purchase

The total KES Product Group package is $23,000. The package price includes both the development tools and the runtime components. However, the company's description of "runtime" sounds like it limits the use of these components to a single copy. Multiple copies of a runtime knowledge system are negotiable. The individual subsystems can be purchased separately for the following prices:

KES.BAYES (statistical pattern classification subsystem)	$ 3,000
KES.HT (hypothesis and test subsystem)	$12,000
KES.PS (production rule subsystem)	$ 9,000
KES.PS (inspector option)	$ 2,500

Runtime components:

KES.BAYES	$ 2,000
KES.HT	$ 8,000
KES.PS	$ 6,000

The microcomputer-based version of KES costs $4,000 and includes IQLISP. When a compiler becomes available, it will be furnished free of charge. A runtime version is available for $3,000, although the company notes that if the computer on which the runtime version is to be used is part of a network, the cost rises to that of the Total KES Product Group Package ($23,500). The vendor indicates that it will negotiate for the reproduction of multiple copies. In addition, Software A&E offers a temporary license for KES on a mini- but not a microcomputer. The cost for a 90-day license for the Total KES Product Group Package is $2,000.

OPS5

Overview

OPS5 is a production system programming language. It was originally developed at Carnegie-Mellon University as a tool for psychological research aimed at understanding human memory and cognition. (Specifically, OPS5 was developed to test Newell and Simon's hypothesis that *production rules* are sufficient to explain most human cognitive behavior.)

An unsupported version of OPS5 can probably still be obtained from Carnegie-Mellon University, but several companies are now offering supported versions with better interfaces. This entry will consider the original tool, the OPS5e version by Verac, Inc., the OPS5 (for Xerox 1108) by Science Applications Int. Corp., and the OPS5 for VAX offered by Digital Equipment Corp.

It is very hard to classify OPS5. By one analysis, it is a very general programming environment. In the hands of a skilled knowledge engineer, it could easily be considered a hybrid system building tool. On the other hand, it has generally been used as a production rule, forward chaining system; and, thus, we have classified it as a narrowly focused tool that can aid a developer in building rule-based, forward chaining systems.

OPS5 has been used for several major system development efforts, including R-1, later called XCON, XSEL, and PTRANS. (See Chapter 10 for a detailed description of these systems.)

Knowledge and Inference

Facts in OPS5 are represented as objects with attributes and values. Rules or productions are represented as *if–then* statements. That is essentially all there is to the language. Languages, unlike tools, do not have narrow, highly refined, and specific constructs. Rather, languages have a few generic constructs that can be applied in a variety of ways, and OPS5 is no exception.

The inference engine for OPS5 is also very simple. The major event in the inference process is the "recognize–act" cycle. Rules are compared to the elements in working memory until a rule fires and new information is placed in working memory. Then the cycle begins again. There is also a simple conflict resolution scheme, which works as follows. Facts exist in an explicit working memory. When you turn on the program, nothing is in working memory. You begin by asserting facts directly into working memory. After the initial assertions are made, rule sets are tested against working memory. The basic inferencing scheme is forward chaining, and so each *if* clause is checked against working memory. If memory contains an attribute and value recognized by the *if* portion of a rule, then the rule is set to fire. All rules that might fire are collected as a group and then evaluated with a conflict resolution scheme. The essence of the resolution scheme is that rules that have not fired recently are favored over rules that have fired recently. This is accomplished via time tags on facts in working memory. It is possible to see if a rule will conclude into working memory a value that has not been concluded recently. When that is the case, that rule is favored over others. One rule will emerge as the favorite rule, and it will be fired. The actions specified by the rule will be taken. Then the cycle continues and all of the *if* portions of the rule set are once again tested against the contents of working memory.

User/KE Interface

The only knowledge engineering aids built into the original version of OPS5 were a trace function called "Watch" and a "break" package that allowed the programmer to halt processing and inspect working memory at selected points in a consultation. OPS5 might better be termed a language or an environment rather than a tool. It takes a very knowledgeable programmer to use the original version.

Each of the enhanced versions of OPS5 uses graphics and windows to give the developer an overview of the developing knowledge system and hence make development easier.

Implementation

OPS5 was originally implemented in LISP and can be compiled in BLISS to run on the VAX-11/780 computer. Its user interface was basically line-oriented. There were no graphics packages, nor were there any menus that are built into the language.

OPS5 for VAX is sold by Digital Equipment Corp. and is designed to be used on VAX equipment with VMS Version 3.2 or later. A compiler is available, and the system can be used with DEC's window-oriented terminals.

OPS5 is available for the Xerox 1108 and uses the windows provided by the 1108.

OPS5e is an enhanced version of OPS5 designed to run on the Symbolics LISP machines. This tool is implemented in ZetaLISP.

Purchase

An unsupported but inexpensive version of OPS5 can be purchased from Carnegie-Mellon University.

OPS5e designed to run on the Symbolics 3600 machine is available from Verac, Inc. Verac sells an executable version of OPS5e for $3,000, whereas the source code version sells for $10,000.

Figure 8.4 Screen of S.1 showing the beginning of a consultation.

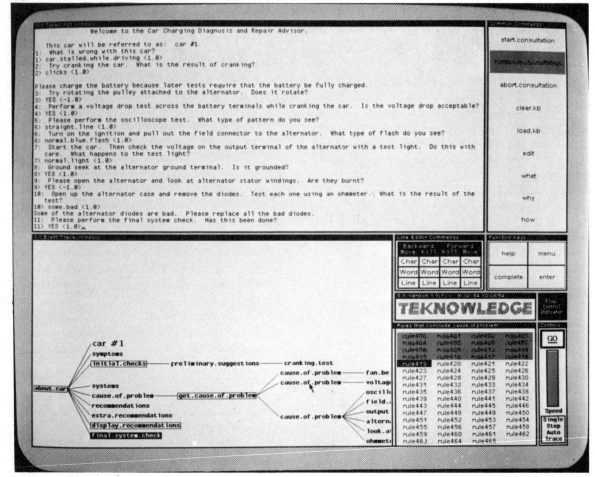

S.1

Overview

S.1 is a knowledge engineering tool offered by Teknowledge Inc. S.1 is an integrated package of software, training, sample knowledge systems, documentation, maintenance, and support. The tool is designed to build knowledge systems that solve diagnosis/prescription problems (which they call *structured selection problems*) that can be organized and classified. Teknowledge has developed a number of commercial systems using KS300, a tool that preceded S.1, and these systems have been tested on S.1 to assure commercial viability.

Knowledge and Inference

Facts in S.1 are stored as object–attribute–value triplets with associated confidence factors. Objects (called *classes*) can be grouped into class types. Members of a class type inherit a set of common attributes. Attributes can be arranged in hierarchies when one property of a class (i.e., an attribute) is a precondition for another. Similarly, value hierarchies declare relationships among values. In these circumscribed ways inheritance and associations among facts are represented in S.1. Figure 8.4 shows the beginning of a consultation with S.1.

Other relationships are represented as production rules. Existential and universal quantifiers may be included in the premises of rules to test whether *any* or *all* of a set of objects have specified properties. Figure 8.5 shows a rule on an S.1 screen.

The S.1 inference engine is a back-chainer. Control of the reasoning process is facilitated by *control blocks* (see Figure 8.6). A control block is an explicit procedural statement of how a consultation is to proceed. Control blocks regulate when classes are instantiated, how the values of attributes are sought, whether default values are assigned, and how results are displayed, for example. Control blocks can contain conditional statements, and so lines of reasoning can be pursued or avoided depending on intermediate results.

The designers of S.1 felt that both declarative and procedural aspects of knowledge belong in a knowledge system. Historically, rule base systems (such as MYCIN) have favored declarative representations. As a result, procedural control was achieved by ordering rules or by writing rules whose only purpose was to affect the order of reasoning. There was no one place in the knowledge base to look for information about control. In S.1 declarative representations remain, and a simple procedural component is added to improve the clarity and maintainability of the inferencing process.

Incomplete and inexact knowledge is handled by

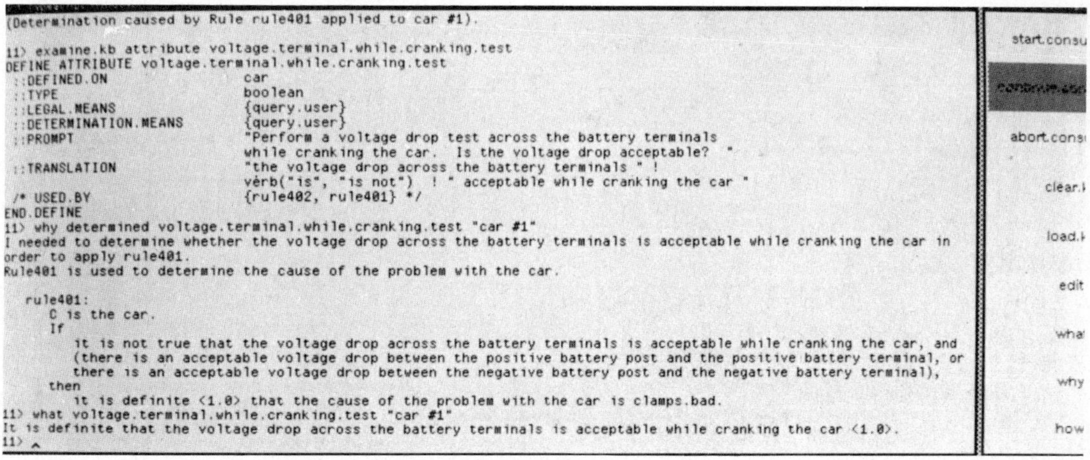

Figure 8.5 Screen of S.1 showing a rule.

```
(Determination caused by Rule rule401 applied to car #1).

1]> examine.kb attribute voltage.terminal.while.cranking.test
DEFINE ATTRIBUTE voltage.terminal.while.cranking.test
  ::DEFINED.ON               car
  ::TYPE                     boolean
  ::LEGAL.MEANS              {query.user}
  ::DETERMINATION.MEANS      {query.user}
  ::PROMPT                   "Perform a voltage drop test across the battery terminals
                             while cranking the car.  Is the voltage drop acceptable? "
  ::TRANSLATION              "the voltage drop across the battery terminals " !
                             verb("is", "is not")  ! " acceptable while cranking the car "
  /* USED.BY                 {rule402, rule401} */
END.DEFINE
1]> why determined voltage.terminal.while.cranking.test "car #1"
I needed to determine whether the voltage drop across the battery terminals is acceptable while cranking the car in
order to apply rule401.
Rule401 is used to determine the cause of the problem with the car.

   rule401:
      C is the car.
      If
         it is not true that the voltage drop across the battery terminals is acceptable while cranking the car, and
         (there is an acceptable voltage drop between the positive battery post and the positive battery terminal, or
         there is an acceptable voltage drop between the negative battery post and the negative battery terminal),
      then
         it is definite <1.0> that the cause of the problem with the car is clamps.bad.
1]> what voltage.terminal.while.cranking.test "car #1"
It is definite that the voltage drop across the battery terminals is acceptable while cranking the car <1.0>.
1]> ^
```

S.1 exactly as in EMYCIN. Namely, there are confidence factors that index the reliability of facts and rules, and these are blended when several conclusions are made about the same attribute's value. *Unknown* is an acceptable answer to any question.

User/KE Interface

Users communicate with S.1 by selecting items from a menu with a mouse, or by entering information with the keyboard. Help and explanation facilities are available. Probes allow users to explore the static and dynamic knowledge base. Graphical displays of the reasoning process are available, depending on the implementation.

S.1 offers tracing and error analysis at runtime for debugging knowledge bases.

Implementation

S.1 is implemented in LISP and is available on Xerox 1100, Symbolics 3600, and VAX computers. Interface to data bases, external functions, or external sensors is available by escaping into LISP.

A reference manual, a user's guide, a library of case studies, and a two-week course accompany the purchase of S.1. There is a product support staff. Additional consulting services are available by contracting with Teknowledge's custom knowledge systems group.

Figure 8.6 Screen of S.1 showing control block information.

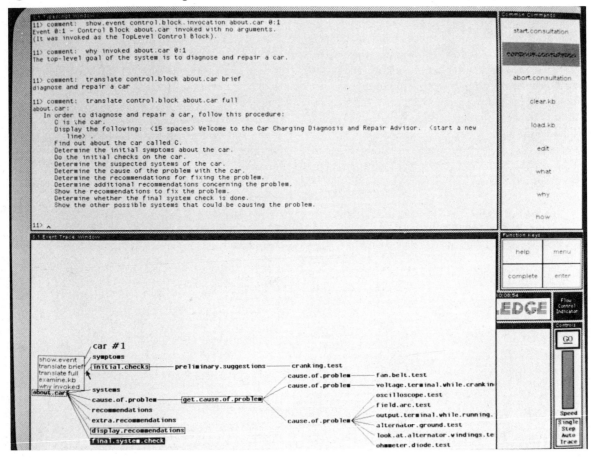

Purchase

S.1 costs $50,000 for the Xerox and Symbolics versions and $80,000 for the VAX version. The price includes a two-week course and extensive documentation for two participants.

TIMM—THE INTELLIGENT MACHINE MODEL

Overview

The Intelligent Machine Model (TIMM) is a knowledge system building tool designed to be used by subject matter experts. TIMM focuses on cases that represent good examples according to the expert. In effect, TIMM works like a more complex version of Expert-Ease. Each set of examples forms a matrix and a matrix is, in effect, a rule. Each rule is created as the expert enters examples. Unlike Expert-Ease, however, TIMM enables several rules to be created and linked together. TIMM's example-oriented knowledge acquisition system makes it especially appropriate for systems builders who want to model their own expertise. Several commercial systems have been built using TIMM.

Knowledge and Inference

Facts in TIMM are represented as attribute–value pairs. Rules are not entered directly but, rather, are built from stylized examples. That is, examples are entered as a set of conditions (attributes) related to a particular outcome or recommendation. TIMM is able to consolidate and generalize rules based on a set of cases. TIMM is capable of storing about 500 rules. It is able to handle problems that require a system to choose among 25 distinct recommendations based on some 50 factors, each of which can have up to 25 different values.

TIMM does not support associations and inheritance relationships, nor are there explicit ways of controlling the flow of a consultation. Inference and control decisions are made by an algorithm that optimizes a path through a decision tree that TIMM creates from the examples and rules it is given.

Inexact and incomplete information is handled in two ways. First, there is a certainty factor between 0 and 100 associated with facts. Second, there is a reliability number, also ranging from 0 to 100, that is associated with each set of examples and their conclusions. Thus, TIMM can report a solution with certainty 50 and reliability 80.

User/KE Interface

In the case of TIMM, the knowledge system designer is a subject matter expert, not a knowledge engineer. Here is how a knowledge system building session proceeds:

- TIMM interrogates the expert about what attributes matter with respect to a particular domain. Ranges of acceptable values are stored.
- TIMM requests the outcome or result for an example in the problem domain. It then probes to see what values are associated with the attributes for that case.
- TIMM generalizes rules and optimizes a decision tree based on the cases generated by the expert.

The text that follows reproduces a screen as it might appear during a consultation with TIMM. The user's responses are underlined.

Name of expert system data file: _Test_

Hello, I'm TIMM. Are you ready to build a new expert system (Y or N)? _Yes_

What would you like to call this new expert system? *Test*

What decision will I be learning how to make? *Decision*
Tell me the possible choices. Enter one per line, and enter a "/" as the last line:
    Yes
    No
    /

Now tell me the name of each factor that influences the decision. Enter one per line, and enter a "/" as the last line:
    Factor one
    Factor two
    /

Are the values of the "FACTOR ONE" numbers (N) or descriptive phrases (P)? *P*
Are these values unordered (U), linearly-ordered (L), or circularly-ordered (C)? *L*
Tell me the possible values. Enter one per line, and enter a "/" as the last line:
    A
    B
    C
    D
    E
    F
    /

Are the values of the factor "FACTOR TWO" numbers (N) or descriptive phrases (P)? *N*
Are these values unordered (U), linearly-ordered (L), or circularly-ordered (C)? *L*
Minimum value = 1
Maximum value = 6

Reprinted by permission of General Research Corporation.

TIMM provides some debugging aids for the system builder. One is an explanation facility, which identifies all rules used in a consultation.

A two-day training course and maintenance is included in the price. Support services, 25 user's manuals, and on-site installation is also provided with each purchase.

Implementation
TIMM is written in FORTRAN. It is available for many mainframe and minicomputers such as IBM, DEC, Prime, and others. General Research has a personal computer-based version of TIMM.

Purchase
TIMM is available from General Research Corporation. Version 2.0, capable of linking together separate knowledge bases, is priced at $39,500. The IBM PC XT version of TIMM costs $9,500. TIMM is also offered via time sharing for a monthly charge of $500 plus computer time.

LARGE, HYBRID SYSTEM BUILDING TOOLS

Large, hybrid tools are tools that lack the narrow focus of the systems we have just discussed. In other words, their designers have not created these tools to build a specific type of knowledge system. Instead, they have created tools that can be used to build other tools that, in turn, will build knowledge systems. When you start working with a hybrid system, you must first decide which techniques or strategies you wish to employ. Do you want to use forward or backward chaining, for example? Once you have made these decisions, you use the hybrid tool to create a narrower tool that you then use to build your knowledge system. You therefore have a lot of flexibility when you use a hybrid tool. The price you pay for that flexibility is considerable, however. You need to know a lot more about knowledge engineering and about symbolic programming to use a hybrid tool effectively. It is a lot easier to make poor decisions or mistakes early on that will result in wasted time and ineffective systems. Hybrid tools are thus more like programming environments than tools.

At the present time, most hybrid systems should probably be considered research tools rather than practical tools that can be used to rapidly prototype an expert system. They are not the ideal tool for a new company just beginning to develop its first system. On the other hand, hybrid tools are undoubtedly the tools of the future. As companies learn more about knowledge engineering and gain experience in developing knowledge systems, they are going to want the flexibility and power these tools offer.

For all of the reasons just mentioned, if you decide to get a hybrid tool right away, and many companies have, you should be sure that the vendor will provide high-quality training, documentation, and consulting support. The learning curve for these tools is very steep, and you will not want to try to negotiate the climb without help.

ART—THE AUTOMATED REASONING TOOL

Overview

The Automated Reasoning Tool (ART) from Inference Corporation is a tool kit for knowledge system development. The kit contains four major components: a *knowledge language* for expressing facts and relationships; a *compiler* for converting the knowledge language into LISP; an *applier*, which is an inference engine; and a *development environment*, which includes debugging aids and trace functions.

ART is a very general tool applicable to many problems. For example, ART supports time tagging within its inheritance functions. This suggests that ART can be used to build systems that reason about time-dependent events. Unfortunately, there are no examples of ART in action in a commercial setting. Examples in the ART materials are about very small, "toy" systems.

Knowledge and Inference

ART provides a number of representations to store and maintain facts. One is the traditional O–A–V triplet. A second means of representation, called a *fact*, is a proposition with a truth value and a scope. Quantifiers (i.e., "There exists at least one . . ." versus "For all . . . ") are supported by ART. Inheritance is represented by logical linkages among objects and facts. Also, attributes and values can be inherited by "parent" objects in a hierarchy. Prototypical classes can be defined with default values that change only if necessary.

The inference engine or knowledge applier is described as being an *opportunistic* reasoner. This means that ART can reason with both forward and backward chaining, or with explicit procedural commands. Rules affect the direction of inference. In this way the inference engine moves opportunistically, depending on the pattern of intermediary results. ART also supports confidence ratings. Like all of the hybrid tools, ART is a very powerful programming environment that can, in the hands of a skilled knowledge engineer, be made to perform in a variety of different ways.

User/KE Interface

ART has a wide variety of interface features, all oriented toward helping the knowledge engineer develop an expert system. The tool is flexible enough that a skilled knowledge engineer can use ART to develop whatever user interface he or she desires. Figure 8.7 reproduces an ART screen showing "browsing viewpoints."

Implementation

ART is written in LISP and runs on LISP machines produced by Xerox and Symbolics.

Purchase

ART is available from Inference Corporation, Los Angeles, California. An initial copy costs $60,000; a second copy can be purchased for $20,000. ART can be leased for $1,000 per month, or for $3,000 per month with an option to buy it at the end of six months.

Figure 8.7 ART screen showing "browsing viewpoints."

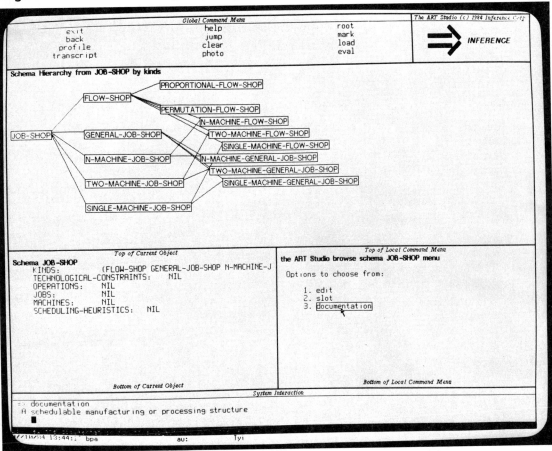

KEE—THE KNOWLEDGE ENGINEERING ENVIRONMENT

Overview

The Knowledge Engineering Environment (KEE) is an integrated package of software tools available from IntelliCorp (formerly IntelliGenetics). IntelliCorp was the first knowledge engineering company, founded in 1980, and its original goal was to market genetic engineering software. In August 1983 Intelli-Corp began selling KEE, a hybrid tool derived from its work with genetic engineering software. KEE is, therefore, a tool that was originally derived from complex analysis and planning applications. An enhanced version of KEE was announced in August 1984.

KEE has been used to build a number of widely used genetic engineering knowledge systems. These systems offer advice about the design of molecular genetics experiments (see Chapter 10). KEE has also been used to develop an integrated interface to a nuclear magnetic resonance spectrometer, an application that demonstrates that KEE can be embedded in laboratory equipment. KEE is popular with several R&D groups that are currently working on prototype applications. Arthur D. Little Co., for example, is working with several of its clients to develop KEE-based planning applications.

Knowledge and Inference

KEE's basic representational paradigm is *frames,* which unify the procedural and declarative expression of knowledge. KEE is an example of object-oriented programming. Facts and rules in KEE are represented as objects or frames that have labeled slots containing either values or means for obtaining values. Slots can contain a number of different entities. A slot may contain a *procedural attachment,* that is, a set of instructions that compute a value for a slot. Similarly, a slot may contain a set of rules that conclude values for other slots in the frame. Procedural knowledge can also be inserted in a slot as a LISP program. A slot may also point to another frame and indicate an inheritance relationship.

Redundant information entry is minimized with inheritance hierarchies. A knowledge engineer can build a knowledge base hierarchy by initially specifying generic objects and their attributes. Then, when specific objects are created, they will automatically inherit attributes of the generic objects in the knowledge base. As a result, the knowledge engineer needs to focus on only a nominal number of unique attributes for each new object.

KEE integrates frame-based and rule-based reasoning techniques to describe structures and behaviors quickly. The frame-based system enables one to include descriptive and procedural knowledge with each object.

KEE allows one to define class member and subclass relationships so that each link type has a uniform semantic interpretation throughout a knowledge base. (In the example shown in Figure 8.8, dashed lines indicate the class member relationships and solid lines indicate subclass relationships.)

Figure 8.9 shows how the rules of a developing knowledge base can be displayed in a lattice format to show interrelationships. Rules currently under consideration are shown in reverse video. The true ($\sqrt{}$) and false ($\times$) states of premises and conclusions already considered are also displayed.

Because user interface commands run as separate processes, the knowledge engineer can change the value of any attribute of any object while the rule system is running. He or she can also browse through and display different objects in the knowledge base. Rules and objects can be easily identified and enhanced to improve the system's performance.

Graphics are linked to the underlying knowledge base to help explain the representation, reasoning, and behavior of a knowledge system. Using KEE's graphics editor menus, the knowledge engineer can design and construct graphic models of physical objects, meters, and gauges, as shown in Figure 8.10.

In the tradition of object-oriented programming, frames (as objects) communicate with one another by sending messages to one another. A message might be a request to display information or to execute a set of rules.

The inferencing scheme for KEE is quite flexible. It can be programmed to behave as a back-chainer or a

Figure 8.8 Screen of KEE showing a frame and an associated hierarchy in overlapping windows.

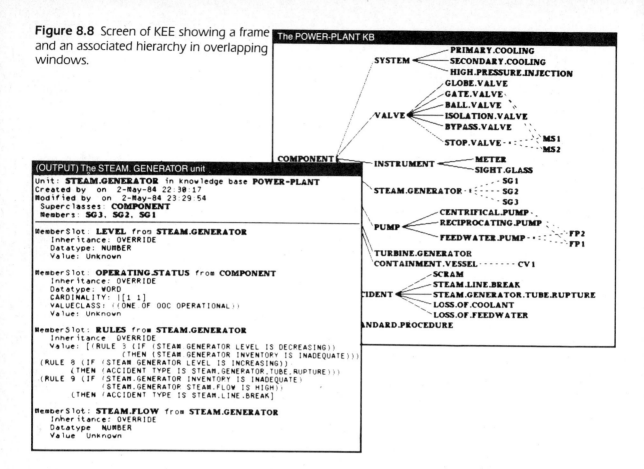

Figure 8.9 Screen of KEE showing how a developer can observe interrelationships among rules.

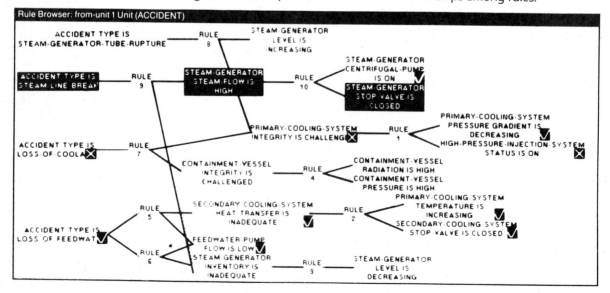

Figure 8.10 Screen of KEE showing some of the graphic devices a developer can obtain and modify for use via "active values."

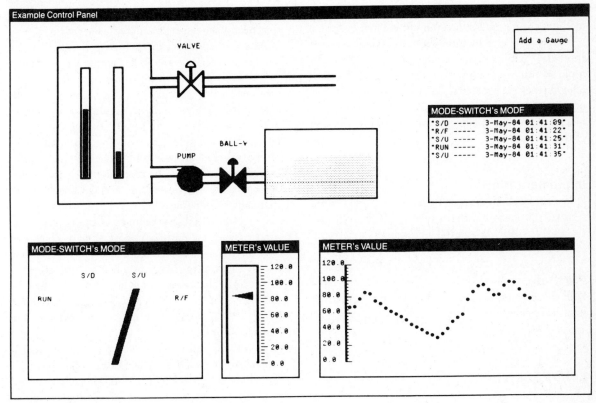

forward-chainer. Values in slots can be manipulated, and results ripple throughout the logical structure of the knowledge base. Such values are called *active values*. Graphical gauges can be attached to active values to monitor their status on the screen.

User/KE Interface

There is no sharp distinction between the consumer and creator of a KEE knowledge base. This is just another way of saying that KEE is a hybrid system that requires considerable sophistication on the part of the knowledge engineer or user. The user interface provides a number of graphics features that aid the knowledge engineer in the development and debug-

ging of a knowledge system. For example, when the knowledge base does not contain information on the state of an attribute, and there are no rules enabling the system to determine values from other knowledge, the system will prompt the user for an answer. The user, in turn, can ask the system why it needs to know, and see the line of reasoning leading to the questions. The line of reasoning for any set of conclusions can be shown graphically, so the user can determine how a conclusion was reached. A graphics display of the decision process adds credibility to decisions that are correct and visibility to decisions that are not.

KEE is a hybrid system and therefore can be extended by the knowledge engineer. Many of KEE's functions are defined by KEE System Knowledge Bases. Thus, the same processes used to build a knowledge system can also be used, for example, to modify existing inheritance rules or create new ones.

KEE is supported by IntelliCorp in several ways. A three-day training course is offered to introduce the tool. A follow-up training program is provided to offer further support after an application project is underway. In addition, on-site consulting by an IntelliCorp knowledge engineer is included with purchase of the tool.

Implementation

KEE is implemented in LISP and is available on the Xerox 1100 machine, the Symbolics 3600 machine, the LMI LAMBDA, and the TI Explorer.

Purchase

KEE can be purchased from IntelliCorp for $60,000. The cost declines rapidly for multiple copies.

LOOPS

Overview

LOOPS is a knowledge engineering environment developed at the Xerox Palo Alto Research Center (Xerox PARC). LOOPS is a software tool that incorporates a variety of different knowledge engineering constructs in one unified package. The constructs include object-oriented programming, the use of active values, a knowledge base management scheme, and a rule package.

Knowledge and Inference

A great number of the features of LOOPS are related to support available in the INTERLISP environment. For example, it is possible to review programs under development in LOOPS with a variety of graphical schemes. These schemes are essentially schemes provided by INTERLISP by means of its windows and break packages. After a rule is fired, it is possible to examine what the rule was, what the effect of its firing was, and to trace down aspects of reasoning that take place during a program's execution.

A second construct incorporated in LOOPS is the idea of an "active value." An active value operates like a probe. By examining an active value, one can see the current status of a variable being reasoned about. By attaching a graphic picture, such as a gauge or thermometer, one can see an analogical representation of a variable that is being reasoned about. Moreover, one can monitor changes in that value as processing continues. By changing an active value, one can cause a series of side effects associated with that value's changing.

Object-oriented programming is an orientation toward viewing the entities in a program as objects (or units or frames) that communicate with each other via messages. Attached to each frame are constructions and declarations that define and elaborate what the frame is about. When a message arrives at a frame, attachments to that frame process the message and carry out its effects.

Procedural and rule-oriented programming is also supported by LOOPS in a conventional way. The unique aspect of having rules and procedures as part of LOOPS comes not from the procedures as such but from how they are integrated with active values and object-oriented programming.

Perhaps LOOPS should be thought of as an environment rather than a tool. In order to build an expert system with LOOPS, one must choose from a variety of different approaches and write a fair amount of code before the system begins to home in on and help to structure the knowledge system. Its utility is primarily as a software engineer's environment, where a variety of useful subroutines have been prepared and are ready to assemble; and that is strikingly different than a tool such as S.1, where a large number of design decisions have already been made and are "hard-wired" into the system.

Figure 8.11 Screen of LOOPS. This screen illustrates the "Truckin" game. Note that active values let participants study gauges as well as rules, etc.

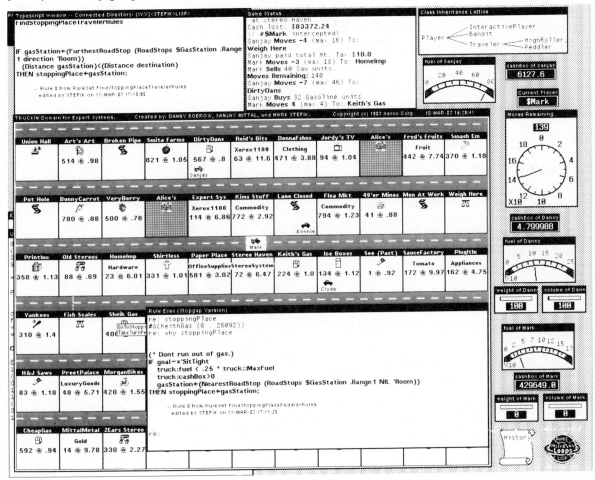

User/KE Interface

Xerox PARC has offered a three-and-a-half day course to teach participants to use LOOPS. The course is built around a game called "Truckin." Each participant develops a program to manage a "truck." Then the various truck programs compete to buy and sell commodities and avoid the hazards of the road in a simulated environment. Figure 8.11 shows a LOOPS screen that displays the "Truckin" game board. Notice the gauges on the screen. These are examples of graphic implementations of active values.

Implementation

LOOPS is implemented in INTERLISP and runs on Xerox 1100 LISP-based personal workstations.

Purchase

LOOPS is available from Xerox for $300 in an unsupported version. Xerox apparently regards LOOPS simply as a research tool and a powerful demonstration of what the 1100 series of LISP workstations can do.

ADDITIONAL LARGE TOOLS

The Carnegie Group, Inc., recently announced SRL+, which they describe as "an integrated knowledge engineering environment." The tool sounds like a very sophisticated frame-based hybrid system, such as KEE or ART. It is implemented in Common LISP to run on VAX and Symbolics machines and in FranzLISP, running under UNIX for the VAX. Price had not been announced as of press time.

SUMMARY

Table 8.6 summarizes the information we have on the various knowledge engineering tools. As we have already noted, our knowledge of these tools is limited and they are changing very rapidly, so all of this information must be regarded as tentative until it is confirmed by the manufacturer.

Table 8.6 Knowledge Engineering Tools

Name	Advice Language/X (AL/X)
Manufacturer	J. Reiter, S. Barth, & A. Paterson University of Edinburgh
Introduced	——
Cost	——
Consultation paradigm	Diagnosis/prescription
Knowledge representation, inference, and control	A–V pairs *If–then* rules Forward chaining Bayesian probability propagation
Implementation	PASCAL Apple II
User/KE interface	Line-oriented Knowledge base created with regular word processing software
Applications	Used by DEC to develop a small classroom assignment program
Support	——

ES/P ADVISOR	Expert/Ease	INSIGHT Knowledge System	M.1
Expert Systems International U.S. Office: 1150 First Ave. King of Prussia, PA 19406 (215) 337-2300	Expert Software International, Ltd. c/o Jeffrey Perrone & Assoc. 3685 17th Street San Francisco, CA 94114 (415) 431-9562	Level 5 Research 4980 S-A1A Melbourne Beach, FL 32951 (305) 676-5810	Teknowledge Inc. 525 University Avenue Palo Alto, CA 94301 (415) 327-6640
1984	1983	1984	1984
$1,895	$2,000	$95	$12,500 (includes all materials) Entry cost is $2,000
Automated text (diagnosis/prescription)	Example-driven	Diagnosis/prescription	Diagnosis/prescription
A–V pairs _If–then_ rules (+/− 400) Backward chaining, depth first Resolution	"Examples" (one rule) Decision tree algorithm	A–V pairs _If–then_ rules (+/− 400) Forward and backward chaining (Goal outline) Certainty factors	A–V pairs _If–then_ rules (+/− 200) variable rules Certainty factors Backward chaining, depth first _Modus ponens_
PROLOG IBM PC (128K)	IBM PC (128K); DEC Rainbow; Victor 9000	PASCAL (includes compiler) IBM PC (128K), DEC Rainbow, Victor 9000	PROLOG IBM PC (192K) Color monitor recommended
Explanation (how, why, explain) Prompted-menu screen Knowledge base created with regular word processing software, then compiled; By purchasing PROLOG separately, a comprehensive interface to PROLOG is possible	Prompted-menu screen	Prompted-menu screen Explanation (how, why, explain) Knowledge base created with regular word processing software and then compiled	Explanation (how and why) Trace (and panels) Knowledge base created with regular word processing software
Small knowledge systems	Small knowledge systems	Small knowledge systems	Demonstration systems
Manual	Manual	Manual	4-day course; Manual; Library of sample systems Phone-in user support

Table 8.6, continued

Name	Personal Consultant	SeRIES-PC	EXPERT
Manufacturer	Texas Instruments P.O. Box 809063 Dallas, TX 75380-9063 1-800-527-3500	SRI International Advanced Computer Science Dept. 333 Ravenswood Ave. Menlo Park, CA 94025 (415) 859-2464	Weiss & Kulikowski Dept. of Computer Sci. Rutgers University New Brunswick, NJ 08903
Introduced	1984	1984	1981
Cost	$3,000	$5,000, but only sold as part of an SRI consulting contract	——
Consultation paradigm	Diagnosis/prescription	Diagnosis/prescription	Diagnosis/prescription
Knowledge representation, inference, and control	O–A–V triplets *If–then* rules ($+/-$ 400) Backward chaining, depth first; Certainty factors Multiple objects	A–V pairs *If–then* rules Backward chaining, depth first *Modus ponens*	A–V pairs *If–then* rules Confidence factors
Implementation	IQLISP (a compiler will be required for speed) TI Professional & Portable Computers	IQLISP IBM PC (384K req., 640K recommended)	FORTRAN Various computers (no personal computer implementations)
User/KE interface	Knowledge base editor Trace and probes Explanation (how and why) Prompted knowledge entry Prompted-menu screen	Explanation (how and why) Knowledge base editor Trace and probes	Line-oriented, question-naire Trace and probes Statistical analysis of performance
Applications	Small knowledge systems	——	Several fielded systems: Serum Protein Diagnosis Program Rheumatic Disease Program Expert Log Analysis System
Support	Manual Workshop and consulting for $1,500 extra	Sold only with consultation	——

Knowledge Engineering System (KES)	OPS5	OPS5e
Software A&E 1500 Wilson Blvd., Suite 800 Arlington, VA 22209 (703) 276-7910	Dept. of Computer Sci. Carnegie-Mellon Univ. Pittsburgh, PA 15213 Other companies offer versions of OPS5 for VAX and the Xerox 1100s	Verac, Inc. 10975 Torreyana Suite 300 San Diego, CA 92121
1983	1980	1983
$23,000 for Product Group Package $4,000 for IBM PC version (includes IQLISP)	——	binary code: $3,000 source code: $10,000
Diagnosis/prescription	Planning and diagnosis/ prescription	Planning and diagnosis/ prescription
A–V pairs; *If–then* rules Multiple objects and inheritance Procedural control (action blocks) Bayesian probabilities	O–A–V triplets *If–then* rules Recognize-act cycle with conflict resolution	O–A–V triplets *If–then* rules Recognize-act cycle with conflict resolution
A-LISP, Wisconsin LISP, and FranzLISP DEC VAX/VMS, VAX/UNIX, CDC CYBER, and APOLLO Xerox 1100s, Symbolics 3600 IBM PC (with IQLISP which is provided)	FranzLISP, MacLISP VAX 11/780	ZetaLISP Symbolics 3600
Line-oriented display Explanation (explain) Trace and probes Hooks to non-KES programs Interface to outside data bases	Line-oriented Break package	Window-based Debugging package
——	Major fielded systems, including XCON, XSEL	——
Manual	Manual	Manual

Table 8.6, continued

Name	S.1	TIMM	Automated Reasoning Tool (ART)
Manufacturer	Teknowledge Inc. 525 University Ave. Palo Alto, CA 94301 (414) 327-6640	General Research Corporation P.O. Box 6770 Santa Barbara, CA 93160 (805) 964-7724	Inference Corporation 5300 West Century Blvd., Fifth Floor Los Angeles, CA 90045 (213) 417-7997
Introduced	1984	1983	1984
Cost	$50,000 for Xerox and Symbolics versions; $80,000 for VAX Includes training	Version 2.0 (supports multiple rules), $39,500 IBM PC XT version, $9,500	$60,000
Consultation paradigm	Diagnosis/prescription	Example-driven	Hybrid tool
Knowledge representation, inference, and control	O–A–V triplets *If-then* rules Multiple objects with inheritance *Modus ponens* Procedural control (Control blocks) Backward chaining, depth first Certainty factors	"Examples" Decision tree algorithm Certainty factors	A "toolkit" for building knowledge systems, consisting of pieces that can be purchased separately; O–A–V, facts (propositions); *If–then* rules; Logical links between objects; Multiple objects and inheritance; "Opportunistic" reasoning; Forward and backward chaining; Certainty factors
Implementation	LISP DEC-VAX 11/750 & 11/780 under VMS, Xerox 1100, Symbolics 3600	FORTRAN IBM, DEC, Prime; IBM PC XT	LISP, ZetaLISP, VAX LISP LMI machines, DEC-VAX
User/KE interface	Explanation (how and why) Graphics display Trace and probes	Line-oriented display Explanation (why)	Powerful graphics interface, windows Many knowledge engineering features
Applications	Several systems under development	Hughes Aircraft: simulation of a helicopter pilot's battle decisions	Several systems under development
Support	2-week course; Manual Sample system library Phone-in user support	Manual	Manual and training available

Knowledge Engineering Environment (KEE)	LOOPS
IntelliCorp 707 Laurel Street Menlo Park, CA 94025 (415) 323-8300	Xerox Palo Alto Research Centers 3333 Coyote Hill Road Palo Alto CA 94304 (415) 494-4000
1983	1983
$60,000 (1st copy), declining to $2,000 for 21st copy Includes training	$300 (not supported)
Hybrid tool	Hybrid tool
Frames with slots Object-oriented programming *If–then* rules Multiple objects and extensive inheritance User-defined inference and control	Frames (objects) with slots Rule sets stored in slots of frames Active values Lattices of objects User-defined inference and control
LISP, Zeta/Common LISP Xerox 1100s, Symbolics 3600, LMI LAMBDA, TI Explorer	INTERLISP Xerox 1100s
Interactive, graphical displays of the knowledge base Gauges and active values for monitoring the behavior of the system	Graphics-supported browsing in the knowledge base Break package allows views of different portions of the knowledge base
Several fielded systems: GENESIS (a pkg. of genetic engineering programs)	Demonstration systems
Product includes 3-day workshop and 10 days of on-site consulting	3 1/2-day workshop ($1,150 plus fees for a prerequisite INTERLISP workshop)

9.

Early Systems

In this chapter we discuss several expert systems. So far our discussion has leaned heavily on analogies and examples drawn from MYCIN, which is probably the best-known system. There are, however, a number of other systems, and many of them take approaches that are quite different from MYCIN. In this chapter we consider some of the more influential expert systems developed prior to 1980.

We have rather arbitrarily divided the systems we discuss into "early systems," which were generally developed prior to 1980, and "recent systems," which include most systems developed since 1980. In the summary at the end of this chapter, we compare and contrast the overall characteristics of early systems. Suffice to say here that early systems were primarily systems developed in universities and were either not designed for commercial use or were designed as timeshared systems that were not intended as profit-making ventures. Recent systems, on the other hand, have been designed largely for commercial applications.

In Chapter 7 we discussed how systems often generate tools with which to build other systems. Figure 7.9 illustrates that process and provides a historical overview of a number of the expert systems considered in this chapter.

In reading about the knowledge systems discussed in this chapter, do not be overly concerned with the details of the knowledge contained in the systems. The systems focus on narrow domains, and their dialogues are addressed to technical specialists. We have reproduced dialogues only to provide a general flavor of expert system dialogues.

The early systems that we consider in this chapter include:

- DENDRAL, an expert system used by chemists
- MACSYMA, a mathematical problem solver used by scientists and engineers
- HEARSAY, a system designed to carry on a conversation
- INTERNIST/CADUCEUS, a medical diagnosis system
- PROSPECTOR, a geological site evaluation system that has already found a major ore deposit
- PUFF, a small knowledge system that aids physicians in interpreting respiratory tests

DENDRAL

DENDRAL is a chemistry expert system designed to examine a spectroscopic analysis of an unknown molecule and predict the molecular structures that could account for that particular analysis. In 1964 Joshua Lederberg, a Nobel Prize-winning chemist, developed the DENDRAL algorithm. This algorithm takes a given set of spectroscopic data and then enumerates all the possible molecular structures that can be predicted from that set of data. The algorithm also allows a chemist to search a spectroscopic analysis for all the possible molecular structures that could explain that particular analysis.

In 1965, Joshua Lederberg, Edward Feigenbaum, and Bruce Buchanan joined together to see if they could develop a system that would use heuristics to produce much the same results that an algorithmic program does, but in a fraction of the time. The heuristic DENDRAL program achieved this objective. It augmented the use of the DENDRAL structure enumeration algorithm and the data from the mass spectrographic analysis of an unknown molecule with a set of rules (heuristics) used by expert chemists to infer constraints on molecular structures from such data. In effect, the expert's heuristics were used to reduce the search space by pruning the solution space generated by the DENDRAL algorithm.

Obtaining heuristic information from expert chemists to formulate rules about how to analyze mass spectrometry data proved to be a long and arduous task. Approximately 15 person-years were consumed in the process of developing heuristic DENDRAL. In the process, however, the field of knowledge engineering was created and named by Dr. Feigenbaum.

DENDRAL was programmed directly in LISP. It takes as its input a histogram giving mass numbers and intensity pairs from a mass spectrometry reading. The program applies heuristics to this input and then develops an initial plan which suggests what molecular structures it could be examining. Then, working within the plan's constraints, the DENDRAL algorithm is used to generate only those structures that do not include components already eliminated by the constraints. Finally, the program simulates the mass spectrometer output of each likely candidate structure. The structures that result in simulated spectra that closely match the initial empirical data are ranked the highest.

An example of one of the production rules used in heuristical DENDRAL appears below.

If   the spectrum for the molecule has two peaks
       at masses X1 and X2 such that
       a. $X1 + X2 = M + 28$, and
       b. $X1 - 28$ is a high peak, and
       c. $X2 - 28$ is a high peak, and
       d. At least one of X1 or X2 is high,

Then   the molecule contains a ketone group.

Since its initial construction, heuristic DENDRAL has been supplemented by additional programs and has even been reformulated entirely into a program called METADENDRAL. The important point for our purposes, however, is that heuristic DENDRAL demonstrated that a computer program could perform on a level equal to experts within a very narrow domain of science. The program's strengths do not lie in knowing more than experts, but in the fact that it is very systematic in its search for all the possible molecular structures. Moreover, it is also systematic in using what it does know to constrain its application of the DENDRAL algorithm.

DENDRAL and its descendants have become standard tools used by chemists to help them determine probable molecular structures. The system is maintained on a Stanford University computer and is available to other chemists through timesharing.

More important, however, the success of DENDRAL convinced many people that expert systems are possible and launched Stanford researchers and colleagues at other universities on a study of the problems of doing knowledge engineering and developing expert systems. DENDRAL was a major impetus that has ultimately resulted in a large number of interesting programs, several of which we shall now discuss.

MACSYMA

MACSYMA is a large, interactive computer system designed to assist mathematicians, scientists, and engineers in solving complex mathematical problems. The design for MACSYMA was originally laid out in 1968 by Carol Engleman, William Martin, and Joel Moses at MIT. MACSYMA has been under continual development since 1969 and now represents about 100 person-years of software design and programming. The resulting system consists of more than 300,000 lines of LISP code and is supported by more than 500 pages of documentation. MACSYMA is used extensively by hundreds of researchers in government laboratories, universities, and private corporations throughout the United States. Some of these users spend a substantial portion of every day logged on this system. MACSYMA currently runs on a Digital Equipment KL-10 computer at MIT and is accessed through the ARPA network, a nationwide timesharing system.

MACSYMA is the most powerful general-purpose

program yet developed to solve algebraic problems with a computer. Input to MACSYMA are formulas and commands, and output are solutions to tough, symbolic problems. Like DENDRAL, MACSYMA was programmed directly in LISP and served the critical role of convincing artificial intelligence researchers that expert systems capable of very high levels of expert performance are possible.

The following examples demonstrate how users interact with MACSYMA. The input lines are underlined and are followed directly by MACSYMA's response. Each of the examples shown below runs in only a few seconds of CPU time.

Example 1: Factorization of a cyclotomic polynomial

$X \wedge 40 - 1;$

$X^{40} - 1$

FACTOR(D1);

$(X - 1)(X + 1)(X^2 + 1)(X^4 + 1)(X^4 - X^3 + X^2 - X + 1)$

$(X^4 + X^3 + X^2 + X + 1)(X^8 - X^6 + X^4 - X^2 + 1)(X^{16} - X^{12} + X^8 - X^4 + 1)$

Example 2: Indefinite integration of a nontabulated function

$(LOG(X) - 1)/(LOG(X) \wedge 2 - X \wedge 2);$

$$\dfrac{LOG(X) - 1}{LOG^2(X) - X^2}$$

INTEGRATE(D3,X);

$$\dfrac{LOG(LOG(X) + X)}{2} - \dfrac{LOG(LOG(X) - X)}{2}$$

Example 3: Taylor (Laurent) series, through the fifth-order term about X = 0

$A * SIN(X \wedge 3) + B * LOG(X \wedge 2 - X + 1)/X \wedge 2;$

$$A\ SIN\ (X^3) + \dfrac{B\ LOG(X^2 - X + 1)}{X^2}$$

TAYLOR (D5,X,0,5);

$$/T/\quad -\dfrac{B}{X} + \dfrac{B}{2} + \dfrac{(2\ B)\ X}{3} + \dfrac{B\ X^2}{4} - \dfrac{(B - 5\ A)\ X^3}{5} - \dfrac{B\ X^4}{3} - \dfrac{B\ X^5}{7} + \cdots$$

Example 4: Solution of an ordinary differential equation

$$(1 - X \wedge 2) * DIFF (Y,X) - 1 + Y * (2 * X - Y) = 0;$$

$$(1 - X^2) \frac{dY}{dX} + (2X - Y) Y - 1 = 0$$

$$ODE(D7,Y,X);$$

$$Y = \frac{X LOG(X + 1) - X LOG(X - 1) - 2 \%C X - 2}{LOG(X + 1) - LOG(X - 1) - 2 \%C}$$

MACSYMA has recently been made available on LISP workstations as a result of a licensing arrangement between MIT and Symbolics, Inc. A very small system that illustrates the MACSYMA approach to algebraic problem solving is the *TK!Solver* package, designed for personal computers.

HEARSAY I AND II

HEARSAY was developed to demonstrate the possibility of a speech-understanding system. In this book we have not spent much time on speech understanding or the problems of natural language. Instead, we focus on expert systems that deal with symbolic knowledge. The HEARSAY architecture, however, has played a very important role in the development of subsequent expert systems, so we shall consider it briefly. HEARSAY I and HEARSAY II were developed at Carnegie-Mellon University in the late 1960s.

Natural language refers to the ordinary spoken language that one naturally uses in conversation. A long-standing goal of artificial intelligence research is to develop computer systems capable of interacting with users by means of natural language. Figure 9.1 provides an overview of the possible approaches to the problem.

One possibility is to limit the computer–user interaction to typed exchanges. One can further limit the typed exchanges by specifying the vocabulary that can be used or by limiting the types of sentence structures one can use. A recently introduced natural language front-end called INTELLECT uses this typed-entry, limited-vocabulary approach. It is designed to help users with data base inquiries.

A more difficult problem is to develop software that can understand spoken input—in other words, the program's input is the speech wave pattern that a user creates as he or she speaks into a microphone. This problem, in turn, can be divided into programming a computer to recognize isolated words or programming a computer to deal with whole sentences—the way we ordinarily talk during a conversation. Considerable progress has been made in programming computers to recognize isolated words, but until the HEARSAY projects, no one had made significant progress in getting computers to deal with sentences, or "connected speech."

Words sounded in the context of sentences are different than words spoken in isolation. Phonemes are left out, and sounds are blended together. In many cases, there are no pauses between words or phrases. The complexity is so great that researchers have come to believe that people understand sentences not only by hearing the sounds but also by

Figure 9.1 Types of natural language problems.

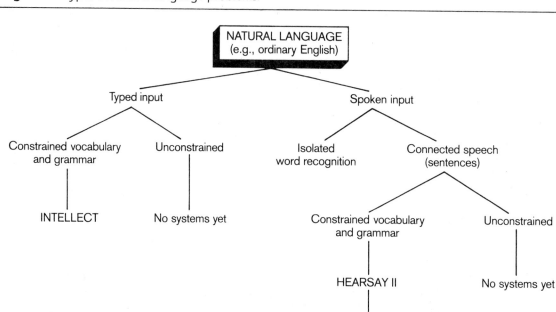

anticipating meaning. We anticipate meaning by following the context of what someone is saying and, thus, expecting that "too," when used in a particular phrase, will mean "also" rather than "toward" or "2." Likewise, we intuitively follow the grammar of someone to whom we are listening and know when a word must be a noun or a verb. Grammatical information is another way we know how to "translate" a spoken sentence into a meaningful piece of communication.

When HEARSAY's developers began, they knew that if they were to succeed, they would have to develop a "speech understanding" system—a system that would not only "listen" for sounds but actively classify possible "words" according to contextual and grammatical rules. Thus, the problem HEARSAY's designers faced was to design a software system capable of organizing and manipulating several very large and diverse bodies of knowledge more or less simultaneously.

Like INTELLECT, HEARSAY II was designed to handle data base queries. HEARSAY takes a speech wave as input and generates as output a set of hypotheses about what was said. It then generates data base queries based on its best guess as to what the speaker intended. The system was programmed in SAIL, and uses a number of independent knowledge sources to analyze different aspects of the speech wave. Each knowledge source contributes its information to the common working memory, referred to as the blackboard. A master control program continually examines the blackboard and decides where to go next. It is as if HEARSAY were made up of several different expert systems, each analyzing a common body of data. Thus, for example, one subsystem uses rules to analyze the initial acoustic signal and to suggest possible segments it finds into the common working memory—the blackboard. Another subsystem examines segments on the blackboard to see if they are recognizable phones. Still another subsystem looks for words—using rules it knows for how sets of phones and syllables are often combined into words. Yet another subsystem analyzes sentences on the blackboard to see if they constitute complete or even approximate matches with the kinds of data base queries it will initiate whenever it finds an appropriate pattern. Figure 9.2 is an outline of how HEARSAY II works.

By the time Carnegie-Mellon finished the HEARSAY II project in 1975, they had developed a system that could deal with a limited amount of spoken grammar and a vocabulary of about 1,000 words. The system correctly interpreted the user's requests about 75 percent of the time and responded (on a very fast computer) in just a few times the time a person would take. This was a major achievement! It demonstrated that a computer could, at least in theory, be pro-

grammed to converse with a user in spoken, natural language.

Since 1975, other connected speech systems have been developed that have gradually improved on HEARSAY II's performance. IBM is currently carrying on state-of-the-art research on connected speech systems, and we can expect continual improvements as larger, faster computers become available in the next 10 years.

More important to our concerns, however, was HEARSAY II's pioneering efforts in software architecture. HEARSAY II demonstrated the clear superiority of symbolic, heuristic methods over statistical methods of dealing with problems involving mean-

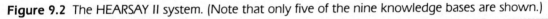

Figure 9.2 The HEARSAY II system. (Note that only five of the nine knowledge bases are shown.)

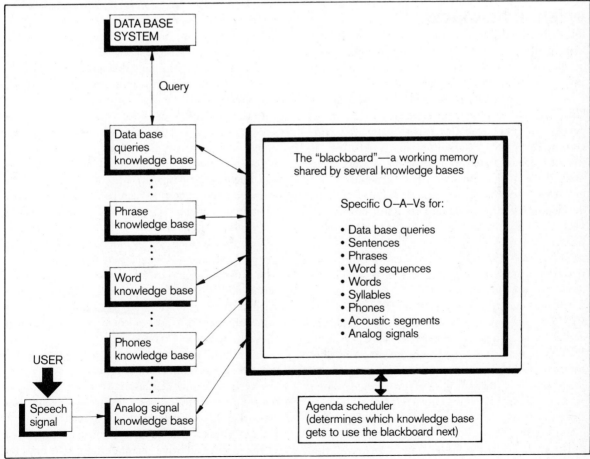

ing. Moreover, it demonstrated how multiple sources of knowledge could be controlled and integrated in order gradually to accumulate a solution to a very complex problem.

HEARSAY II has not only spawned a number of additional speech understanding systems, it has generated several powerful expert system building techniques, including research tools called HEARSAY III and AGE, and it has led to the development of a number of very useful expert systems that take complex auditory or visual signals as their initial data. Most of the latter are being developed for military applications and, hence, will not be discussed in this book.

INTERNIST/CADUCEUS

INTERNIST was begun in the early 1970s. Its domain is the entire field of internal medicine. It was developed by Harry E. Pople, Jr., a computer scientist, and Jack D. Myers, a physician who specializes in internal medicine. These two researchers at the University of Pittsburgh have sought, in effect, to develop the most elaborate expert system yet conceived. INTERNIST is written in INTERLISP. It was first demonstrated in 1974 and has since been used in the analysis of hundreds of difficult clinical problems with notable success. In spite of this, its developers have been working on a still more complex version of the system, which they call CADUCEUS.

The INTERNIST/CADUCEUS effort is in the AI tradition of developing programs that accurately model the way humans actually process information. Thus, the major goal of the INTERNIST/CADUCEUS project has been to model the way clinicians actually do diagnostic reasoning. INTERNIST/CADUCEUS, being concerned with the entire range of internal medicine, must consider not only a very large number of diseases, it must also consider all the possible combinations or interactions among these diseases. Indeed, Dr. Pople has suggested that a conservative estimate of the number of possible combinations is 10 to the 40th power. Obviously, this

number is too great to allow for the individual description of each possible combination in a data base. Therefore, an AI approach, focusing on developing models of the various diseases and then allowing the models to interact, has become the only reasonable approach to this problem.

INTERNIST begins by asking the user to describe the manifestations of the disease. INTERNIST has two different ways of functioning. It conceptualizes the world as a set of manifestations or symptoms, each leading to other manifestations, which lead eventually to a disease. In effect, a causal flow is established that proceeds backward from particular symptoms to other manifestations, ultimately leading to the disease causing the symptoms. Separately, INTERNIST conceptualizes the world by means of a hierarchy, called a nosology by physicians, which describes all of the types of diseases in terms of where they occur within the body. The top link in the hierarchy is "any disease"; the next level down divides diseases among the different body systems. Lower still are branches for diseases of the heart, diseases of the liver, and so forth.

Initial manifestations—for example, pallor and jaundice—lead to other characteristics within the nosological hierarchy. In effect, the logic of the system runs that if the person has pallor, then he or she might have anemia. And if the patient has anemia, certain questions can be asked to determine what kind of anemia is involved. By the same token, pallor also suggests the possibility of fibrotic hepatocellular involvement. This, in turn, suggests other manifestations and diseases the patient might have. The program begins by asking the physician to describe all the manifestations the patient exhibits. Each of these manifestations is examined to determine what sorts of diseases could be associated with that manifestation.

For each disease being considered, there are four general categories of manifestations the system considers. It notes manifestations that are present and consistent with the disease. It checks for manifestations that have not been observed but that must be present if a particular disease is, in fact, present. It checks about still other manifestations that have not been observed but might be associated with the disease. And, finally, it notes those manifestations that are inconsistent with the particular disease. Each disease is scored. A disease receives a positive score for each manifestation that it explains. It receives a negative score for each manifestation it cannot explain. In addition, each disease hypothesis gets a bonus if it is causally linked to some other disease that has already been confirmed.

INTERNIST starts with the highest-scoring disease and investigates it in detail. The investigation seeks to determine whether manifestations that should be present are present. In some cases INTERNIST asks for test results that would confirm the presence or absence of particular symptoms.

Each disease being considered is placed in one of two different groups. Some disease possibilities are, in effect, competing with one another. Thus, if one disease is confirmed, the other possibilities will be eliminated. Other diseases are compatible with confirmation of a particular disease. All diseases that compete with each other are treated as a competing disease set. The system does not try to establish that one disease is the culprit so much as it tries to disqualify unlikely competing diseases from the set, and, thus, choose the disease hypothesis that is more probable than any of the other diseases in the competitive set.

This explanation is simplified in many ways. INTERNIST also establishes other relationships that are superimposed over both of these hierarchies to capture causal, temporal, and other associational patterns among the diseases.

The portion of an INTERNIST dialogue that follows illustrates the way the system appears to the user. The interposed comments help explain what is happening.

INTERNIST-1 consultation   SUMEX-AIM Version

PLEASE ENTER FINDINGS.

After the initial prompt, PLEASE ENTER FINDINGS, the user enters whatever positive findings he or she chooses to divulge. The program prompts with "" to request additional input until the respondent types "GO," after which INTERNIST-1 commences the task-definition procedure. Had the user wanted to enter negative findings during this initial exchange, he or she could have responded "DENY" to the prompt, causing subsequent entries to be interpreted as negative results.*

> *Sex male*
> *Age 26 to 55*
> *Race white*
> *Alcoholism chronic HX*
> *Exposure to rabbits or other small mammals*
> *Fever*
> *Myalgia*
> *Leg <S> weakness bilateral*
> *Leg <S> weakness proximal only*
> *Pressure arterial systolic 90 to 110*
> *Pressure arterial orthostatic hypotension*
> *Tachycardia*
> *Jaundice*

*Anorexia
*Diarrhea acute
*Feces light colored
*Vomiting recent
*Liver enlarged slight
*Skin spider angiomata
*Skin palmar erythema
*Oliguria HX
*Urea nitrogen blood 60 to 100
*Creatinine blood increased
*WBC 14000 to 30000
*Platelets less than 50000

*Go

Manifestations are expressed by means of precise sequences of terms in a controlled vocabulary; there are presently approximately 3,500 vocabulary items that can be used to describe positive and negative findings.

DISREGARDING: EXPOSURE TO RABBITS OR OTHER SMALL MAMMALS, LEG <S> WEAKNESS BILATERAL, LEG <S> WEAKNESS PROXIMAL ONLY, PRESSURE ARTERIAL ORTHOSTATIC HYPOTENSION, CREATININE BLOOD INCREASED, UREA NITROGEN BLOOD 60 TO 100

CONSIDERING: AGE 26 TO 55, SEX MALE, ANOREXIA, MYALGIA, VOMITING RECENT, FECES LIGHT COLORED, FEVER, JAUNDICE, LIVER ENLARGED SLIGHT, SKIN PALMAR ERYTHEMA, SKIN SPIDER ANGIOMATA, WBC 14000 TO 30000, PLATELETS LESS THAN 50000

RULEOUT: HEPATITIS CHRONIC ACTIVE, ALCOHOLIC HEPATITIS, HEPATIC MILIARY TUBERCULOSIS, MICRONODAL CIRRHOSIS <LAENNECS>, HEPATITIS ACUTE VIRTAL

At this point, INTERNIST-1 reports concerning the initial differential diagnosis that will be the focus of problem-solving attention. Three lists are displayed, labeled respectively DISREGARDING, CONSIDERING, and RULEOUT. The CONSIDERING list identifies those positive findings whose differential diagnostic tasks were combined in coming to the differential diagnostic focus, which is described by the RULEOUT list. The DISREGARDING list tells what positive findings are not consistent with the differential diagnosis as formulated and are therefore being disregarded for the moment; they will, however, be attended to in due course. The keyword RULEOUT indicates what strategy INTERNIST-1 is going to pursue relative to this task definition; in this case, as in any case when the different list contains five or more alternatives, the program will try to find questions to ask which, if the response is negative, will serve to downgrade the score of one or more diagnoses on the list. While pursuing a RULEOUT strategy, the program limits the questions to be asked to items of information obtainable via history or physical exam.

Please Enter Findings of JAUNDICE HX
Go

There are two formats used for asking questions. In the preceding line, the user is asked to provide any data that might be available within the specified category of findings. Actually, the respondent is free to enter whatever positive or negative data is desired and is not constrained to the category mentioned in the query. In this case, the user chose to respond GO; this passes the initiative back to the program, which then typically follows up on the general question by asking about the specific finding of that category for which it particularly wants a YES or NO answer.

JAUNDICE INTERMITTENT HX ?
No

If the respondent did not have any information concerning this direction question, he or she could have answered N/A—meaning not available.

Go

WEIGHT LOSS GTR THAN 10 PERCENT ?
No

The program asks a series of questions that have been selected in accordance with its problem-solving strategy, then repeats the scoring and partitioning processes of the task-definition procedure. After repeating this process several times, it arrives at a conclusion.

CONCLUDE: LEPTOSPIROSIS SYSTEMIC

Having concluded leptospirosis, the program now deletes from further consideration those items explained by this diagnosis. If there are significant data remaining to be explained, the task formulation procedure is again invoked to determine the next most compelling differential diagnosis. In the scoring process, any diagnoses that are causally linked to the concluded disease are awarded an extra bonus. This enhances the likelihood of their being noticed by the task formulator, but does not guarantee that they will be considered.

DISREGARDING: CREATININE BLOOD INCREASED, UREA NITROGEN BLOOD 60 TO 100

CONSIDERING: ALCOHOLISM CHRONIC HX, FECES LIGHT COLORED, JAUNDICE, LIVER ENLARGED SLIGHT, SKIN PALMAR ERYTHEMA, SKIN SPIDER ANGIOMATA

RULEOUT: MICRONODAL CIRRHOSIS <LAENNECS>, HEPATIC LEPTOS-PIROSIS, FATTY LIVER SECONDARY, CIRRHOSIS SECONDARY TO CHOLES-TATIC DISEASE, ALCOHOLIC HEPATITIS, MACRONODAL CIRRHOSIS <POSTNECROTIC>, DRUG HYPERSENSITIVITY CHOLESTATIC REACTION

As the signs of acute febrile illness have been accounted for by the conclusion of systemic leptospirosis, the diagnostic task formulated to deal with the liver involvement is now focused primarily on those chronic disorders that commonly cause the type of skin lesions reported in this patient. Note, however, that the possibility of hepatic involvement by leptospirosis—never mentioned in the earlier differential diagnoses dealing with the liver involvement—is now high on the list of alternatives.

LIVER EDGE HARD ?
*N/A

ONSET ABRUPT ?
*Yes

JAUNDICE CHRONIC PERSISTENT HX ?
*No

PLEASE ENTER FINDINGS OF INSPECTION HAND <S> AND FEET

The program continues in this manner through several dozen questions, gradually narrowing in on possible diseases that may afflict the patient.

INTERNIST operates with a very large data base. At the present time some 500 diseases have been included in this data base, and thus it covers some 25 percent of all of internal medicine.

Although INTERNIST was very successful in identifying diseases, it consistently irritated clinicians who used it because if often spent a considerable amount of time considering totally inappropriate diseases. The system eventually dismissed inappropriate options and focused on the right disease, but its initial meandering was very annoying to its users. CADUCEUS is an effort to reformat INTERNIST to eliminate these problems. CADUCEUS uses the same data base, but because some information was unavailable in the INTERNIST data base, it was necessary to totally reconstruct INTERNIST in order to build CADUCEUS. This illustrates the importance of formulating the problem correctly as soon as possible. It also illustrates the fact that, in spite of the best efforts, one often builds a system, realizes that the knowledge representation one has chosen is not the most effective one, and must then drop the initial structure and construct a new one.

CADUCEUS attempts to correct the problems of INTERNIST by beginning with a meta-level analysis of the possibility of different diseases. In effect, CADUCEUS has a very abstract view of how clauses are related to different parts of the disease hierarchy and how these parts, in turn, commonly combine with other diseases. Instead of initially pursuing a particular disease, or a manifestation of a particular disease, CADUCEUS begins by considering, at a very general level, the most likely overall complex of diseases that it might be confronting. It then scores these complexes and checks for overlapping patterns among the complexes. If several of these diseases cluster in a particular part of the disease hierarchy, CADUCEUS begins by considering those diseases that it considers very likely to be among the correct conclusions. This explanation is, of course, a vast simplification of the very elaborate analysis and scoring procedure that CADUCEUS actually uses.

In effect, CADUCEUS works from both the bottom-up and the top-down approach. In examining the initial patient data, the disease manifestation, CADUCEUS starts at the bottom and works up. By obtaining an overview of what particular disease certain sets of manifestations are likely to lead to, CADUCEUS works by a top-down approach.

Doctors Pople and Myers are still working on CADUCEUS. They expect the project to take several more years. CADUCEUS probably represents the most ambitious expert system development effort yet attempted. When it is finally complete, its developers hope to make it available to internists throughout the country on a timeshared basis.

PROSPECTOR

PROSPECTOR has one foot in the world of research and the other in the world of commercial applications. It was developed in the late 1970s at Stanford Research Institute, International (SRI) by a team that included Peter Hart, Richard Duda, R. Reboh, K. Konolige, P. Barrett, and M. Einandi. The development of PROSPECTOR was funded by the U.S. Geological Survey and by the National Science Foundation.

PROSPECTOR is designed to provide consultation to geologists in the early stages of investigating a site for ore-grade deposits. Data are primarily surface geological observations and are assumed to be uncertain and incomplete. The program alerts users to possible interpretations and identifies additional observations that would be valuable to reach a more definite conclusion.

PROSPECTOR is, broadly speaking, a descendant of MYCIN, but it was not developed using the EMYCIN knowledge system building tool. In fact, PROSPECTOR has resulted in a new system building tool. Moreover, PROSPECTOR goes beyond MYCIN in a number of important ways. The knowledge base of PROSPECTOR, for example, is based on a semantic network organized, in turn, around five different models. Each model describes the information and relationships that pertain to a particular

type of mineral deposit. In effect, assertions are nodes in the network. Typical assertions include:

"There is pervasively biotized hornblende."

"There is alternation favorable for the potassic zone of a porphyry copper deposit."

Each assertion is either unknown, true, false, or assumed to be true and assigned some probability. The arcs of the influence networks are inference rules. Each rule specifies how the probability of one assertion will affect the probability of another probability. In effect, PROSPECTOR's inference rules are the same as MYCIN's production rules. Additional inference rules are used to establish assertions and to order search.

The PROSPECTOR team worked with different mineral experts to develop the different models. The assertions and rules used to implement the five models are shown in Table 9.1.

Table 9.1 Five Models Comprising PROSPECTOR (circa 1980)

Model	Number of Assertions	Number of Rules
Koroko-type massive sulfide	39	34
Mississippi Valley-type lead-zinc	28	20
Type-A porphyry copper	187	91
Komatitic nickel sulfide	75	49
Roll-front sandstone uranium	212	133
	541	327

PROSPECTOR is much more flexible than MYCIN when it interfaces with users. To begin with, it employs a constrained natural language interface (LIFER) that allows the user to type sentences just as they would ask questions of a geological consultant. LIFER interprets the sentences for PROSPECTOR. In addition, PROSPECTOR is a "mixed-initiative" system. The user can volunteer information whenever he or she wishes. Thus, one of the major user complaints about MYCIN is eliminated. The user can begin a session by telling PROSPECTOR everything he or she knows. Moreover, the user can stop PROSPECTOR whenever he or she wishes and provide additional information. PROSPECTOR immediately inserts the volunteered data into its inference network and adjusts its strategies and questions accordingly. The basic control strategy, once the user stops volunteering information, is backward chaining.

PROSPECTOR can also accept input in the form of raw data and generate a graphic response. Thus,

the user can enter information about a site and PROSPECTOR can generate a new map showing conclusions about the site. (See Figure 9.3.)

Once the user has volunteered initial data, PROSPECTOR inserts the data into its models and decides which model best explains the given data. Further confirmation of that model then becomes the primary goal of the system, and the system asks the user questions to establish the model that will best explain the data. If subsequent data cause the probabilities to shift, of course, the system changes priorities and seeks to confirm whichever model seems

Figure 9.3 Photograph of a printout made by PROSPECTOR that indicates the site of porphyry molybdenum mineralization that is found in 1978 at Mt. Tolman.

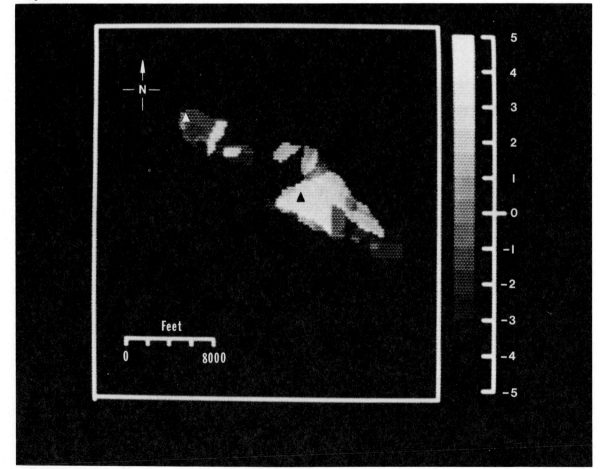

most likely in light of the additional data.

The following edited excerpt from a PROSPEC-
TOR session illustrates many of these ideas. The data
for the run describe a fictitious porphyry copper
deposit that has some, but not all, of the desired
characteristics. We begin at the point where the user
(indicated by underlining) starts volunteering information to the system. Our comments on the dialogue
are inserted throughout.

There is quartz monzonite
Quartz monzonite (5)

There is a cretaceous dike
Cretaceous dike (5)

There is sericite and pyrite
Sericite (5) pyrite (5)

There may be biotite
Biotite (2)

Done

*These simple assertions describe the most prominent rocks, minerals, and
alteration products in the target area. The system indicates its recognition of
each statement by echoing the statement and appending an assigned certainty.
Certainty factors range from −5 (positive that a situation does not hold) to 5
(positive that it does hold). All assertions made by PROSPECTOR have
associated certainty factors. The program now enters the consequent mode of
reasoning.*

Presently, the models in PROSPECTOR and their scores are:
1. Komatiitic nickel sulfide deposit—KNSD (0.0)
2. Type-A porphyry copper deposit—PCDA (0.0) + +current hypothesis + +
3. Kuroko-type massive sulfide—MSD (.001999)
4. Western-states-type sandstone uranium deposit—WSSU (0.0)
5. Mississippi-Valley-type lead/zinc deposit—MVTD (−4.8)
Which of the above would you like to rule out?
None

*The volunteered information was sufficient to rule out one of the models but
was not nearly specific enough to establish any of the others. The choice of the
second model as the current hypothesis was based not on its certainty but on
the number and types of connections between it and the volunteered
statements. To avoid a possibly fruitless investigation of unpromising models,
the system gives the user the opportunity to exclude models of lesser interest.*

In this case, the user allows all of the models to be explored, and the system begins with the current hypothesis.

> I am considering the possibility of a (Type-A porphyry copper deposit—PCDA) in the target area.
>
> The following questions are intended to establish the nature of the petrotectonic setting.
>
> 1—To what degree do you believe that:
> (the target area is a continental margin mobile belt) ?
> *−2*

This is a discouraging answer for the PCDA model, and it removes a context needed for the investigation of other properties of the continental-margin mobile belt.

> The following questions are intended to determine the nature of the regional environment.
>
> 2—To what degree do you believe that:
> (there are granitic intrusives in the region) ?
> *5*
>
> 3—To what degree do you believe that:
> (the region contains an abundance of small stocks) ?
> *−3*
>
> 8—To what degree do you believe that:
> (igneous rocks in the region have porphyritic texture) ?
> *Why*
>
> I am trying to establish whether some of the intrusive rocks in your area have textures suggestive of a hypabyssal to subvolcanic environment. Porphyry textures resulting from the rapid cooling and crystallization of a silicate melt which contains large mineral grains are suggestive of relatively shallow levels of emplacement.

Like MYCIN, PROSPECTOR provides a variety of commands for such things as requesting a summary, changing previous answers, or volunteering additional information. The above response to a WHY command is not automatically generated from the rule but is merely stored text associated with the space.

> 8—To what degree do you believe that:
> (igneous rocks in the region have porphyritic texture) ?
> *5*
>
> My certainty in (the texture and morphology of the intrusive system suggest a subvolcanic (hypabyssal) regional environment) is now: 4.924

Do you want to pursue this further?
<u>No</u>

At this point the system notes that the certainty for the hypothesis about a hypabyssal environment is above 4.5, and it also notes that if the remaining rules are answered in the most unfavorable way possible, the certainty could not fall below 4.5. To save time, it lets the user decide whether or not to continue working on this subgoal.

The questioning then continues until it becomes necessary to consider properties that vary within the target area. Thus, for the first time it becomes necessary to be able to use the rules more than once, and a communication convention must be established to distinguish different spatial locations.

Porphyry copper deposits are often composed of characteristic zones of alteration and mineralization. (In some cases these can be looked upon as different stages superimposed upon one another.) I shall call the most prominent such zone Zone 1. Even though you may have already identified this zone as, say, the propylitic zone or the sericitic zone, I need to consider other possibilities as well. Thus, the following questions are intended to determine the possibilities of Zone 1.

25—To what degree do you believe that:
(there are fresh-looking feldspars in Zone 1) ?
<u>−5</u>

Questioning continues in this manner. Eventually, PROSPECTOR establishes that two zones exist in the region of interest and, after examining each in detail, it concludes that their geologic makeup supports the hypothesis that Type-A porphyry copper exists in the region.

On a scale from −5 to 5, my certainty that (there are alteration zones that are favorable for a Type-A porphyry copper deposit) is now 4.833

There are two favorable factors; in order of importance:
   2.3.1: 1. there is a sericitic zone in Zone 1 (4.834)
           + + establishes 2.3.1 + +
   2.3.1: 2. there is a potassic zone in Zone 2 (4.499)

There are many factors that would have been unfavorable had favorable factors existed to override them; in order of importance:

   2.3.1: 3. there is a barren-core zone in Zone 1 (−5.0)
   2.3.1: 4. there is a potassic zone in Zone 1 (−5.0)
   2.3.1: 5. there is a propylitic zone in Zone 1 (−5.0)
   2.3.1: 6. there is a sericitic zone in Zone 2 (−5.0)
   2.3.1: 7. there is a propylitic zone in Zone 2 (−4.989)
   2.3.1: 8. there is a barren-core zone in Zone 2 (−4.495)

For which of the above do you wish to see additional information?

Reproduced by permission from Avron Barr and Edward A. Feigenbaum, eds. The Handbook of Artificial Intelligence, *vol. 2, Los Altos, CA: William Kaufmann, Inc., 1982, pp. 155-158.*

In 1980, as a test, PROSPECTOR was given geological, geophysical, and geochemical information supplied by a group that had terminated exploration of a site at Mt. Tolman in Washington in 1978. PROSPECTOR analyzed that data and suggested that a previously unexplored portion of the site probably contained an ore-grade porphyry molybdenum deposit. Subsequent exploratory drilling has confirmed the deposit and, thus, PROSPECTOR has become the first knowledge-based system to achieve a major commercial success. Indeed, the weakest part of PROSPECTOR's performance was its failure to recognize the full extent of the deposit it identified.

PROSPECTOR's five models represent only a fraction of the knowledge that would be required of a comprehensive consultant system for exploratory geology. SRI continues to develop and study PROSPECTOR, but there are no plans to market the system. The principal scientists who developed PROSPECTOR and KAS, the expert system building tool derived from PROSPECTOR, have left SRI to form a private company (Syntelligence). Thus, PROSPECTOR, like MYCIN, has never become an operational system. Its innovations and successes, however, have inspired a large number of knowledge engineers, and there are a number of commercial systems under development that rely on one or more of the features first developed and tested during the PROSPECTOR project.

PUFF

PUFF was built in 1979 using EMYCIN. It was created to demonstrate the practicality of using EMYCIN to prototype additional systems rapidly.

PUFF is designed to interpret measurements from respiratory tests administered to patients in a pulmonary (lung) function (PF) laboratory. PF tests are used to measure the volume of the lungs, the ability of the lungs to get oxygen into the blood and carbon dioxide out. A pulmonary physiologist normally interprets these measurements to determine the presence and severity of lung disease in the patient. PUFF is designed to interpret a set of pulmonary function test results and to produce a written statement that

includes a set of interpretations and a diagnosis for the patient. Figure 9.4 shows a screen of PUFF.

PUFF is designed to interface directly with the pulmonary test instruments used in the laboratory. Thus, PUFF does not ask questions of the physician, but instead interrogates the physiological instruments and uses their output as the source of information of its analysis. In choosing the pulmonary function problem, the Stanford researchers chose a classic expert systems problem. It is a hard task that falls within a narrow domain. The biomedical researchers who worked at the PF lab had not previously known how to automate the procedure. The data that drive the system are available from a machine in a single laboratory. The clinical staff at that laboratory was already familiar with computers, and was supportive, and there was a willing expert available at the Pacific Medical Center in San Francisco to work with the development team. Using EMYCIN, the Stanford researchers were able to develop a prototype in a few months.

PUFF was developed on a DEC KL-10 at the Stanford University SUMEX-AIM computer facility. The initial EMYCIN version of PUFF was a goal-directed, backward chaining system that used production rules. It had 64 production rules that were used to interpret the PF test data.

A typical rule is as follows:

If   (1) A: The mmf/mmf-predicted ratio is between 35 and 45, and
           B: The fvc/fvc-predicted ratio is greater than 80, or
       (2) A: The mmf/mmf-predicted ratio is between 25 and 35, and
           B: The fvc/fvc-predicted ratio is less than 80,

Then   (1) There is suggestive evidence (.8) that the degree of obstructive airways disease as indicated by the MMF is moderate, and
           (2) It is definite (1.0) that the following is one of the findings about the diagnosis of obstructive airways disease: Reduced mid-expiratory flow indicates moderate airway obstruction.

The system was tested in several different ways. For example, PUFF was given 144 cases to analyze. PUFF's recommendations were compared with those of two pulmonary physiologists. PUFF agreed with the two pulmonary physiologists about 93 percent of the time. After the researchers were satisfied that PUFF was complete, a second version of PUFF was written in BASIC to run on a PDP-11 at the Pacific Medical Center's laboratory. The BASIC version of PUFF has some 400 production rules.

PUFF, in its BASIC/PDP-11 version, became operational in 1979. It is used routinely for about 10

Figure 9.4 Screen of PUFF analysis of a patient. Note the conclusions on the bottom.

```
     PRESBYTERIAN HOSPITAL OF PMC
      CLAY AND BUCHANAN, BOX 7999
      SAN FRANCISCO, CA. 94120
       PULMONARY FUNCTION LAB

     WT 40.8 KG, HT 161 CM, AGE 69  SEX F
     REFERRAL DX-
     ************************************************TEST DATE 05/13/80
                                 PREDICTED            POST DILATION
                                 (+/-SD)   OBSER(%PRED)  OBSER(%PRED)
     INSPIR VITAL CAP (IVC) L    2.7        2.3  ( 86)   2.4  ( 90)
     RESIDUAL VOL     (RV)  L    2.0        3.8  (188)   3.0  (148)
     TOTAL LUNG CAP   (TLC) L    4.7        6.1  (130)   5.4  (115)
     RV/TLC                 %    43.        62.          56.

     FORCED EXPIR VOL (FEV1) L   2.2        1.5  ( 68)   1.6  ( 73)
     FORCED VITAL CAP (FVC)  L   2.7        2.3  ( 86)   2.4  ( 90)
     FEV1/FVC                %   73.        65.          67.
     PEAK EXPIR FLOW  (PEF)  L/S 7.1        1.8  ( 25)   1.9  ( 26)
     FORCED EXP FLOW 25-75% L/S  1.8        0.7  ( 39)   0.7  ( 39)
     AIRWAY RESIST(RAW) (TLC= 6.1) 0.0(0.0) 1.5          2.2

     DF CAP-HGB=14.5    (TLC= 4.8) 24.      17.4 ( 72) ( 74%IF TLC = 4.7)
     ****************************************************************

     INTERPRETATION: ELEVATED LUNG VOLUMES INDICATE OVERINFLATION.  IN ADDITION, THE
     RV/TLC RATIO IS INCREASED, SUGGESTING A MODERATELY SEVERE DEGREE OF AIR TRAPPING.
     THE FORCED VITAL CAPACITY IS NORMAL.  THE FEV1/FVC RATIO AND MID-EXPIRATORY FLOW
     ARE REDUCED AND THE AIRWAY RESISTANCE IS INCREASED, SUGGESTING MODERATELY SEVERE
     AIRWAY OBSTRUCTION.  FOLLOWING BRONCHODILATION, THE EXPIRED FLOWS SHOW MODERATE
     IMPROVEMENT.   HOWEVER,  THE  RESISTANCE  DID  NOT  IMPROVE.   THE  LOW  DIFFUSING
     CAPACITY INDICATES A LOSS OF ALVEOLAR CAPILLARY SURFACE, WHICH IS MILD.

     CONCLUSIONS: THE LOW DIFFUSING CAPACITY, IN COMBINATION WITH OBSTRUCTION AND A
     HIGH TOTAL LUNG CAPACITY IS CONSISTENT WITH A DIAGNOSIS OF EMPHYSEMA.  ALTHOUGH
     BRONCHODILATORS WERE ONLY SLIGHTLY USEFUL IN THIS ONE CASE, PROLONGED USE MAY
     PROVE TO BE BENEFICIAL TO THE PATIENT.

     PULMONARY FUNCTION DIAGNOSIS:
     1.  MODERATELY SEVERE OBSTRUCTIVE AIRWAYS DISEASE.
          EMPHYSEMATOUS TYPE.
```

patients per day. It has interpreted results in more than 4,000 cases. Approximately 85 percent of the reports generated are accepted without modification. When modifications are made, they are usually simply notes suggesting that the patient's physician compare this interpretation with the results of previous visits. PUFF was not designed to represent knowledge about multiple visits, so this kind of statement must always be added.

PUFF has some significant limitations. It cannot, for example, recognize that a particular case fits a typical pattern or that a particular case varies from a typical pattern in some important way. These are features that physicians routinely look for.

Moreover, the BASIC version cannot offer explanations, nor can it alter the order in which it processes information. And, of course, it would be difficult to alter the BASIC version to incorporate new information.

The EMYCIN version of PUFF is more flexible, can provide explanations, and can be modified easily. The availability of EMYCIN-PUFF guarantees that the system can be rapidly altered and then recoded into BASIC, should that be necessary.

The Stanford researchers who developed PUFF regard it as proof that EMYCIN can be used to rapidly prototype other expert systems. Otherwise, however, they have not given PUFF the attention it probably deserves. PUFF is not a system that has great expertise. Rather, it is a small-scale system that is able routinely and quickly to solve small but otherwise difficult tasks. In effect, PUFF is an intelligent decision aid that allows physicians to be more productive by letting them avoid routine but complex data analysis and report writing.

This brief survey of some early knowledge systems shows that knowledge systems come in a variety of different configurations. Moreover, they range in size from a truly huge system like CADUCEUS to a small system like PUFF. Table 9.2 summarizes the main features of the systems we have discussed. In the next chapter we examine more recent offspring of these early knowledge systems.

Table 9.2 Overview of Selected Early Knowledge Systems

System:	DENDRAL
Developer:	Stanford
Purpose (domain): general area of application and reason for building the system	Organic chemistry—mass spectrometry. Use inductive inference and the "scientific method" in a real scientific environment.
Task: specific task the system is to accomplish	Identify chemical compounds from mass spectra data.
Input: data needed to accomplish task and method for acquiring it	Histogram giving mass number/intensity pairs.
Output: results produced by the system	Description of the structure of the compound.
Architecture: conceptual model used to structure the system	Plan–generate–test with constrained heuristic search.
Tools: software environment in which the system is developed and implemented	None—programmed in LISP.
Results: performance of the system, current status, evaluation, etc.	"Discovery" of knowledge engineering. Large number of chemical publications.

MACSYMA	HEARSAY II	INTERNIST/CADU-CEUS	PROSPECTOR
MIT	Carnegie-Mellon University	University of Pittsburgh	SRI International
Higher-performance symbolic mathematics engine for algebra, calculus, differential equations, etc.	Speech understanding, for simple data base query.	Diagnostic aid for *all* of internal medicine.	Exploratory geology.
Assist user by carrying out complex symbolic manipulation, e.g., interacting symbolic functions.	Long list of design criteria about vocabulary size, complexity of grammar, etc. Generate a "correct" entry.	Medical diagnosis.	Evaluate geological sites.
Formulas and commands interactively.	Speech wave.	Answers to questions posed by the system.	Geological survey data.
Solutions to tough symbolic problems.	Ordered list of hypotheses of what was said, plus data base query based on best guess.	Ordered set of diagnoses.	Maps and site evaluations.
Brute force.	Opportunistic, agenda-based reasoning, using "blackboard" to record hypotheses from multiple independent knowledge sources.	——	Rule-like semantic net with uncertainty.
None—programmed in LISP.	None—programmed in SAIL.	None—programmed in LISP.	None—programmed in LISP. Knowledge Acquisition System (KAS) grew from this project.
Widely used, powerful system.	Successfully accomplished goals of the 5-year research project.	Not yet complete.	In a "blind" test, the program identified a previously unexplored site that could be quite productive.

Table 9.2, continued

System:	PUFF	MYCIN
Developer:	Stanford University	Stanford University
Purpose (domain): general area of application and reason for building the system	Diagnosis of obstructive airway diseases (OAD) using MYCIN's inference engine and a new knowledge base.	Medical diagnosis program for bacteremia and meningitis infections.
Task: specific task the system is to accomplish	Take data from instruments and query, and diagnose the type and severity of OAD.	Interview physician in order to make diagnoses and therapy recommendations.
Input: data needed to accomplish task and method for acquiring it	Instruments.	Answers to questions posed by the system.
Output: results produced by the system	Written report for attending physician to review and annotate.	Ordered set of diagnoses and therapy recommendations.
Architecture: conceptual model used to structure the system	Rule-based, exhaustive backward chaining with uncertainty.	Rule-based, exhaustive backward chaining with uncertainty.
Tools: software environment in which the system is developed and implemented	EMYCIN.	None—programmed in LISP. EMYCIN grew from this project.
Results: performance of the system, current status, evaluation, etc.	Report is correct without annotation 85% of time. A 55-rule system is in daily use, on a microcomputer coded in BASIC.	Not in general use. Interesting validation studies. Ground-breaking work in diagnostic consultation systems.

10.

Recent Systems

Systems built since 1980 are mostly commercial systems. As such, they provide a better idea of the kinds of systems we can expect to see in the next few years. Since most recent systems have been developed by or for private companies, however, less information is available. Moreover, since there are now many companies in the early stages of knowledge system development efforts, this chapter surveys only a limited sample of recent expert systems. We have tried to select systems that illustrate different approaches to expert systems design and development, or that illustrate problems companies have encountered in undertaking knowledge system development projects.

The systems we consider in this chapter include:

- XCON (R1) and XSEL, knowledge systems that help configure computer systems
- GENESIS, a package of knowledge systems that help molecular geneticists plan DNA experiments
- DELTA/CATS-1, an expert system that aids locomotive maintenance personnel
- DRILLING ADVISOR, an expert system that helps oil rig supervisors to solve problems
- A microprocessor-based electrophoresis interpreter, a knowledge system that has been reduced to a chip and incorporated in a piece of laboratory equipment

Table 10.2 at the end of this chapter summarizes information about the systems discussed in this chapter.

XCON (R1), XSEL

XCON, which was originally called R1, is an operational expert system that routinely configures Digital Equipment Corporation's (DEC) VAX-11/780 computer systems. XCON's input is a customer's order, and its output is a set of diagrams displaying the spatial relationships among the components on an order. These diagrams are used by the technicians who physically assemble the system.

DEC does not market preconfigured systems; instead, it offers a customer a wide selection of components to choose from. In 1979, for example, some 420 components were associated with a VAX-11/780. In effect, most of the systems DEC sells are one-of-a-kind systems.

DEC had made several unsuccessful efforts to develop a conventional program that would configure computers. The major problem was not so much that the knowledge was ill-structured but rather that it kept changing so rapidly. In late 1978 the company began a discussion with John McDermott of the Computer Science Department of Carnegie-Mellon University about the possibility of developing a knowledge-based system that would solve the configuration problem. In the course of the next two years McDermott and a number of colleagues from both Carnegie-Mellon University and DEC developed and implemented XCON. The development process is shown in Figure 10.1

In general, we shall not describe the development of other recent systems in as much detail as we shall for XCON. John McDermott has documented the process in considerable detail, however, and it is such a good example of the procedures and problems a company encounters when it undertakes the development of a knowledge system that it is worth a detailed discussion.

The first stage in the development of XCON involved creating a general design and then building

Figure 10.1 Overview of the development of DEC's XCON (R1).

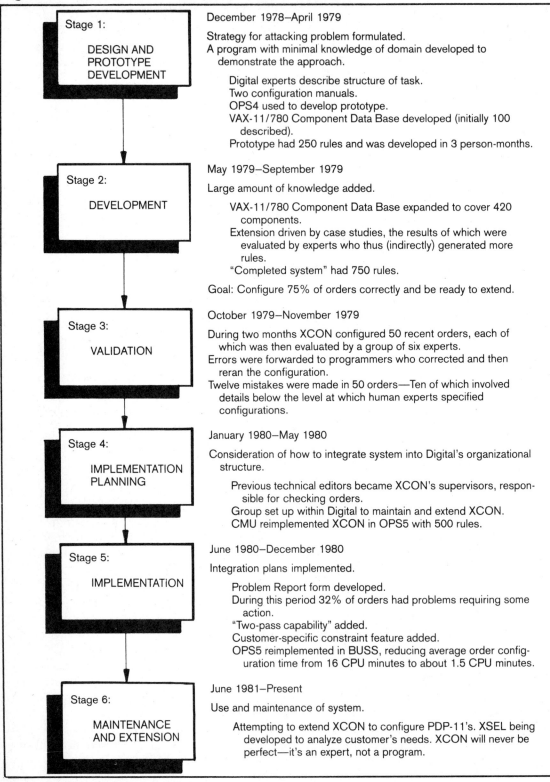

Stage 1:

DESIGN AND PROTOTYPE DEVELOPMENT

December 1978–April 1979

Strategy for attacking problem formulated.
A program with minimal knowledge of domain developed to demonstrate the approach.

> Digital experts describe structure of task.
> Two configuration manuals.
> OPS4 used to develop prototype.
> VAX-11/780 Component Data Base developed (initially 100 described).
> Prototype had 250 rules and was developed in 3 person-months.

Stage 2:

DEVELOPMENT

May 1979–September 1979

Large amount of knowledge added.

> VAX-11/780 Component Data Base expanded to cover 420 components.
> Extension driven by case studies, the results of which were evaluated by experts who thus (indirectly) generated more rules.
> "Completed system" had 750 rules.

Goal: Configure 75% of orders correctly and be ready to extend.

Stage 3:

VALIDATION

October 1979–November 1979

During two months XCON configured 50 recent orders, each of which was then evaluated by a group of six experts.
Errors were forwarded to programmers who corrected and then reran the configuration.
Twelve mistakes were made in 50 orders—Ten of which involved details below the level at which human experts specified configurations.

Stage 4:

IMPLEMENTATION PLANNING

January 1980–May 1980

Consideration of how to integrate system into Digital's organizational structure.

> Previous technical editors became XCON's supervisors, responsible for checking orders.
> Group set up within Digital to maintain and extend XCON.
> CMU reimplemented XCON in OPS5 with 500 rules.

Stage 5:

IMPLEMENTATION

June 1980–December 1980

Integration plans implemented.

> Problem Report form developed.
> During this period 32% of orders had problems requiring some action.
> "Two-pass capability" added.
> Customer-specific constraint feature added.
> OPS5 reimplemented in BUSS, reducing average order configuration time from 16 CPU minutes to about 1.5 CPU minutes.

Stage 6:

MAINTENANCE AND EXTENSION

June 1981–Present

Use and maintenance of system.

> Attempting to extend XCON to configure PDP-11's. XSEL being developed to analyze customer's needs. XCON will never be perfect—it's an expert, not a program.

a prototype system that would demonstrate the effectiveness of a knowledge system approach to DEC's configuration problem. Many DEC managers were skeptical about the possibility of developing a knowledge-based system that could solve their problem. Luckily, John McDermott and Carnegie-Mellon University were able to support the development of a prototype with academic funding. It was also convenient that OPS4 (the precursor to the OPS5 system building tool described in Chapter 8) was already in existence and well understood by the Carnegie-Mellon staff. McDermott determined that DEC's configuration problem was a type of problem that could be appropriately modeled with OPS4.

McDermott began the project by meeting with DEC configuration experts to discuss the procedures they followed when they configured a VAX-11/780. After satisfying himself that he had a good overview of the task, McDermott took two DEC configuration manuals and retired to Carnegie-Mellon University to study them in detail. Using this input, he developed a prototype system in about three person-months. The prototype had approximately 250 rules. When it was demonstrated in April 1979, it was able to satisfy all the basic configuration problems it was given. The people involved in the project were satisfied, and it was decided that they should proceed to the next phase. DEC was now willing to fund the development of a larger version of the system.

McDermott notes in passing that they almost decided to focus their initial effort on developing a prototype of a PDP-11 configuration system rather than focusing on the VAX-11/780. Their actual choice was extremely fortuitous, since the PDP-11 is a much larger system with many more components. Moreover, the constraints that apply to a configuration of a VAX-11 are much less ambiguous than those that apply to the PDP-11 system. In retrospect, conservatism paid off since, in effect, the VAX-11 task was the perfect size. McDermott suggests that if the PDP-11 system had been chosen, the project would probably have been slightly beyond the capability of the OPS4 system and the whole effort might have resulted in failure.

Between May and September 1979, McDermott

and his colleagues at Carnegie-Mellon University expanded their initial prototype system from 250 rules to some 750 rules. At the same time a component data base, which was being developed by DEC personnel, was expanded from an initial 200 components to cover all 420 components that could be involved in a VAX-11/780 configuration. The expert system consulted this data base whenever it needed a description of a VAX component.

McDermott describes how they developed the system from 250 to 750 rules. It was a classic case of how extensions can be driven by case studies. In fact, an expert sat down and a case was given to the computer, which produced recommendations. The expert was then asked to evaluate the recommendation and, if necessary, to suggest why it was inappropriate. As the expert and the knowledge engineer talked over the particular configuration, rules were directly or indirectly generated that assured that in the future that particular configuration would be correct and that also assured that similar configurations would be correct. The goal for Stage 2 was a system that would configure correctly 75 percent of the orders it was given, and that would be designed so it could easily be extended to accommodate additional cases. This goal was achieved in September 1979; and, thus, the original XCON was developed in just under one person-year.

The third stage was the validation of XCON. This was accomplished in October and November of 1979. During these two months, XCON configured the 50 most recent orders that had been received. Each of the configurations it produced was then evaluated by a group of six experts. Some of the errors discovered were the result of inadequate descriptions of the components in the data base. These were forwarded to DEC programmers to correct. Twelve of the mistakes resulted from errors in the knowledge base, and these were forwarded to McDermott. Significantly, 10 of these mistakes involved problems with specifications at a level of detail below that which human experts normally configure systems. Thus, in effect, by attempting to provide detail that human experts do not normally provide, XCON designers had made some minor errors. All of these problems were corrected, and DEC was satisfied with the validation test, and decided to move ahead with implementing the system through the company.

Stage 4 consisted of a five-month hiatus in which DEC began to plan how it would actually fit XCON into its organization structure. Two functions were important. The first was how the system was to be controlled and monitored. It was determined that the technical editor who had previously been supervisor for all of the editors checking orders would now become, in effect, supervisor for XCON. XCON's configuration orders would be given to this person, who would then approve them and send them out. The second problem involved determining how XCON was to be maintained and extended. To accomplish this, DEC established an internal team of knowledge engineers who were assigned the task of maintaining XCON on a day-by-day basis and developing extensions to it.

While DEC was working through the problems of developing an organization structure to maintain XCON, the Carnegie-Mellon team reconfigured OPS4 into the system building tool now known as OPS5. Because of new efficiencies achieved in the OPS5 design, the total number of rules used by the system was reduced from 750 rules to something under 500 rules. Moreover, in reimplementing XCON on OPS5, McDermott realized that the task was not so much a generate-and-test task, as originally supposed, but was, in fact, a matching task that required only a little backtracking. This reconceptualization of the task allowed the designers to change the way the rules were written, and they could thus reduce the total number of rules.

Stage 5 occurred between June and December 1980. During this period the organizational changes that DEC had decided on were implemented. A problem report form was developed to assure that all errors resulting from the use of XCON were reported, investigated, and corrected. During this period 32 percent of the orders had problems that required action. This failure rate bothered some people at DEC. Since the computer had done so well on standard problems, they were unprepared for the fact that the system would make mistakes when it tried to deal with the more specialized cases.

During this same period DEC and Carnegie-Mellon each added some additional features to the system. For example, features were added to allow customers to set specific constraints on the space in which the hardware was to be installed. Certain components were dictated or eliminated on the basis of the customer's constraints. This, and other additions, had not been anticipated at all in the initial design, yet they were added to the XCON system without any significant change in either the architecture of the system or the existing rules. In other words, modifying XCON was largely a matter of adding additional rules to expand the system's capabilities in a systematic manner.

During this same period OPS5 was reimplemented in BLISS, a variation on LISP designed to be compiled into very efficient code. The average time for order configuration at the beginning of the implementation phase had been approximately 15 CPU minutes. Changing OPS5 to a BLISS-based system reduced the average order configuration time to its current 1.5 CPU minutes.

The final stage in the development and implementation of XCON began in June 1981 when the system was put into place in all manufacturing facilities of DEC, and it has been in use and been maintained since that time. The group within DEC is now fully responsible for the system and has provided additional rules to improve its function and operation and its effectiveness in configuring more difficult cases. At the same time, the group has continued to update the data base that describes the components of a VAX-11/780, and has continued to be satisfied with the system. DEC has started to extend the system in two different ways. It is working to extend the system so that it will be able to configure PDP-11s.

At the same time, DEC launched a new effort to develop a front-end for XCON to help salespeople in the field. XSEL will take the customer's original specifications and suggest what additional components may be needed to satisfy the customer's needs. This allows a salesperson to configure and price a customer's initial order more accurately. After XSEL, the salesperson, and the customer have agreed on the overall order, XSEL passes the order on to XCON, which actually configures the order.

By using XCON, DEC has considerably reduced the population of technical editors employed in configuration. The editors that continue to work on configuration problems now focus almost entirely on the various specialized problems that XCON still cannot solve. Thus, the human experts have become more expert in very specialized problems. And, as the human experts learn new heuristics for solving more specialized problems, the resident knowledge engineers working at DEC incorporate the new rules into XCON to make it more effective.

The development of XCON and XSEL illustrates a number of themes that run through the development of all recent expert systems. First, the system was not developed from scratch, but by means of an expert system building tool, OPS4/5. This tool allowed the developers to create the initial prototype of 250 rules in three person-months and to develop the entire first version of the system with some 750 rules in a little under one person-year. Throughout the development and implementation period, however, components of the system and things the system was expected to do were continually changing, and, thus, additional rules were constantly required.

This development process also illustrates the concept of exploratory programming. The initial system was built quite rapidly. It was then expanded and tested while being used on the job. Several changes were made without starting over from scratch. Even today, the system continues to be improved and maintained by the addition of rules.

One unique feature of XCON is that, unlike most other recent expert systems, it does not use probabilities or certainty factors. A component is either included or omitted.

The success of XCON has fostered the creation of a very enthusiastic AI group at DEC that is seeking to develop knowledge systems for a number of additional applications. In addition, DEC's success has encouraged a number of other computer companies to develop computer configuration systems.

GENESIS

Two different MOLGEN programs were developed at Stanford University in the late 1970s. Each program was a variation on an expert system to help a molecular geneticist design complex experiments to determine the nature of a particular DNA molecule. The core of both MOLGEN programs was an expert system building tool called UNITS. UNITS uses a constrained natural language interface whose vocabulary is familiar to molecular biologists. (MOLGEN stands for *mo*lecular *gen*etics.) The earlier MOLGEN system, developed by Mark Stefik, emphasized the creation of abstract plans for genetic experiments. (The modification of UNITS that resulted from Stefik's further research became Xerox's LOOPS.) The second MOLGEN program, developed by Peter Friedland, focused on determining which of several skeletal plans would be most appropriate to a user's needs. Friedland's MOLGEN program also helps users implement the details of a particular plan once it has been selected. In effect, the program uses skeletal plans that have proven useful for closely related problems and thus the user can avoid reinventing general strategies. Friedland's work on MOLGEN led to the development of GENESIS, a collection of commercial systems sold by IntelliCorp. (In addition, further work on UNITS resulted in KEE, which IntelliCorp also sells.)

The specific problem treated by both MOLGEN programs is the analysis of the structure of a DNA molecule. A DNA molecule is a long chain of four different bases: adenine, cytosine, guanine, and thymine. These four bases can be arranged in an almost infinite variety of ways. It is of critical importance to those working in molecular genetics to be able to figure out the specific order of the bases in particular DNA molecules. There are a number of different techniques that can be used to determine the molecular sequence in a DNA molecule. One common type of experiment involves labeling one end of a DNA chain with a radioactive element. Enzymes are then used to "cut" the chain by dissolving a particular base. The remaining initial piece of the chain, identified by the radioactive label, can then be measured to determine its length. By repeatedly cutting a chain with different enzymes, each eliminating a different base, one can ultimately figure out the exact sequence of bases in a particular strand of DNA. Obviously, this type of experiment can be very complex. It requires extremely careful planning so as not to waste time and money.

In 1981 some of the Stanford professors who had been involved in the MOLGEN project established IntelliGenetics (now IntelliCorp). IntelliCorp modified Friedland's original MOLGEN software to create a set of new expert systems useful in the commercial environment. The resulting GENESIS package (Genetic Engineering Scientific Software) currently includes seven different expert systems:

- **SEQ,** a nucleic acid sequence analysis, comparison, and manipulation tool
- **GEL,** for the management of large-scale DNA sequencing projects
- **SIZER,** a tool for use in calculating fragment length
- **MAP,** which determines restriction maps from enzymatic digests
- **PEP,** a tool for polypeptide analysis, comparison, and manipulation
- **GENED,** which facilitates the simplified entry of nucleic and amino acid sequences
- **QUEST,** a data base search, location, and retrieval system

As of July 1983 more than 500 scientists were using IntelliCorp's GENESIS programs in their ongoing research.

When a molecular researcher wants to use the GENESIS package, he or she sits down at a terminal, connects with one of the large data bases established by the National Institutes of Health, and then calls up one of these GENESIS programs.

Data from those data bases or from current research can then be manipulated by one or some combination of the GENESIS programs. Initially, IntelliCorp offered the GENESIS programs on timesharing. The client connects with a DEC-20 computer, located in either Los Angeles or Paris, and accesses the GENESIS programs and data bases as needed. IntelliCorp has since expanded its capacity, and it now licenses

the package if the client has a DEC or VAX computer, an IBM 370 series computer with a VM-CMS operating system, or a 370-compatible.

Recently, IntelliCorp has begun offering the GENESIS package on a genetic engineering workstation called BION. This LISP workstation is a high-performance, graphics-oriented computer that comes in several configurations. In general, the workstation provides 2 megabytes of main memory and can be supported by up to 84 megabytes of hard disk. There is a bit-mapped screen, and a mouse can be used to move the cursor quickly from window to window. The system is UNIX-based, and it is able to compile FORTRAN, PASCAL, and C and allow the user to use a broad range of additional programs. Figure 10.2 shows two BION workstation screens.

The BION workstation represents a prototype of the sort of workstations that we expect will be built in the next few years. The workstation allows the user to draw on a number of different knowledge systems to solve a particular class of problem while working at a conveniently arranged terminal.

DELTA/CATS-1

DELTA (Diesel-Electric Locomotive Troubleshooting Aid) or CATS-1 (Computer Aided Troubleshooting System-1) are used interchangeably to describe an expert system developed by the General Electric Company in Schenectady, New York. The system is designed to help railroad maintenance personnel maintain GE's diesel-electric locomotives.

Prior to the development of DELTA/CATS-1, there were two methods GE employed to solve problems with their diesel-electric locomotives. Either they would fly a maintenance expert to the location of the engine, or they would transport the faulty locomotive to a maintenance yard where an expert was available. The expert in most of these cases was David Smith, Senior Field Service Engineer. He has been with General Electric for more than 40 years and is the acknowledged expert on the maintenance of diesel-electric locomotives. The project to develop

Figure 10.2 Two BION workstation screens.

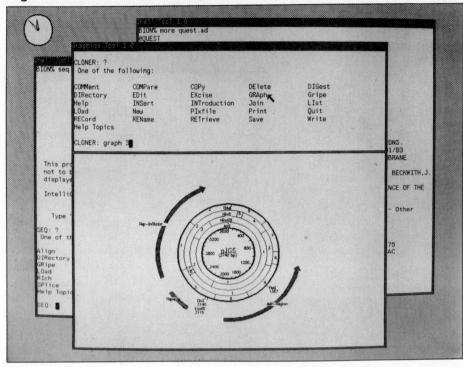

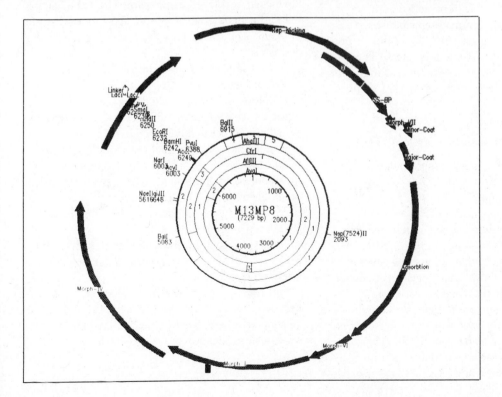

DELTA/CATS-1 was initiated in 1981 with the clear intention of capturing David Smith's knowledge in a system that would allow GE to deliver that knowledge to less expert personnel at the various railroad yards around the country. General Electric set up a team of knowledge engineers in the General Electric Research and Development Center in Schenectady. The DELTA team members worked with David Smith, developed a laboratory prototype by 1982, and began testing the field prototype in 1983. The number of rules added at each phase in the development of the DELTA system, shown in Table 10.1, provides an interesting metric of the overall effort.

The DELTA system uses a hybrid forward/backward chaining inference strategy. This strategy, together with troubleshooting rules, is used to isolate faults and to generate inquiries. In addition, there is a help system that uses a forward-chainer together with a rule-based engine taxonomy to respond to user requests for information, such as the location and identification of individual locomotive components, replacement parts classification, and description of repair procedures. When a maintenance person first sits down at a CATS-1 terminal, he or she is presented with a menu of possible fault areas. The user selects a particular fault area. The system then proceeds with a detailed series of questions. For example:

"Is the fuel filter clogged?"

"Are you able to raise fuel pressure to 40 PSI?"

"If engine-set-idle and fuel-pressure-below-normal and fuel-pressure-O.K.,
Then fuel-system is faulty."

The basic expert system has been interfaced with a device that allows the system to print out diagrams and a videodisk player that allows the system to display diagrams to show where particular components are located on the locomotive. Moreover, if requested, the system can initiate the display of training film sequences that will show the user exactly how to make a particular repair. Thus, the expert system helps the maintenance person figure out what the problem is and, if necessary, switches

Table 10.1 Rules Added to DELTA during Each Phase of the Project

Number of Rules	Year	Project Phase
45	1981	Feasibility demonstration
350	1982	Laboratory prototype
530	1983	Field prototype (handles 50% of problems)
1,200	1984	Production prototype (handles 80% of problems)

over to the video system to show the user how to make the checks or measurements that will generate the information DELTA needs to make a diagnosis. Then, once the problem is isolated, DELTA, if requested, will actually show a step-by-step procedure for fixing the problem. It is interesting to note in this case that the expert system is, in effect, serving as an interface for a large number of training films that have been developed in the past. The system simply helps the maintenance person figure out what the problem is and then provides a training film if it is desired.

The overall architecture of the DELTA system is shown in Figure 10.3.

Hardware used in the field prototype version of the DELTA system includes a PDP-11/23, a 10-megabyte Winchester disk, an industrial microcomputer BT100 terminal, and a Selanar graphics board. In addition, a SONY laser videodisk player and a color monitor are incorporated in the system. The expert system was originally developed in LISP, but was then converted to FORTH, a portable language that is easily adaptable to any microprocessor.

According to GE, the FORTH implementation has proved to be easily transportable and maintains a fast execution speed.

DELTA/CATS-1 is currently being tested in the field (see Figure 10.4), while at the same time the development team is adding additional rules to create a full-scale production prototype system.

Figure 10.3 *The overall architecture of the DELTA/CATS-1 system.*

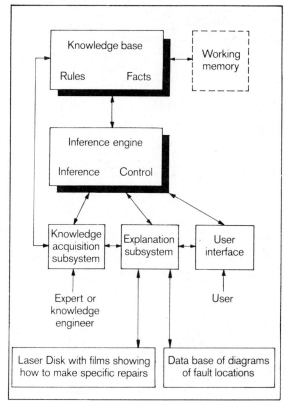

Teknowledge and Elf agreed to develop a prototype system to solve one specific problem—down-hole sticking—which occurs when the rotary and vertical motion of the drill is impeded.

DRILLING ADVISOR was developed by means of a tool called KS300, an EMYCIN-like tool. Thus, DRILLING ADVISOR is a backward chaining, production rule system, like MYCIN, that takes full advantage of EMYCIN's user-friendly interface and knowledge acquisition facilities.

By using KS300, Teknowledge was able to develop the initial problem assessment and design in a little under three months and was able to develop a prototype of the drilling advisor sticking system in a little under nine months.

DRILLING ADVISOR has been implemented on two different systems. It can be run on either a DEC 20 or a Xerox 1100 machine. Figure 10.5 shows the

Figure 10.4 *DELTA system being tested in a locomotive repair shop.*

DRILLING ADVISOR

DRILLING ADVISOR is a prototype knowledge system developed for the French oil company Societe Nationale Elf–Aquitaine (ELF) by Teknowledge Inc. The system is designed to assist oil rig supervisors in resolving and subsequently avoiding problem situations. The oil rig supervisor is familiar with the technology, equipment, and procedures involved in the drilling process, but occasionally requires assistance when special problems occur. Normally, an expert is flown to the rig site when such problems occur. Since it is not unusual for drilling-related expenses to exceed $100,000 per day or for shutdowns related to special problems to last for several weeks until an expert can be brought to the site, the savings that an on-rig knowledge system could effect are considerable.

Figure 10.5 A screen of DRILLING ADVISOR running on a Xerox 1100 machine.

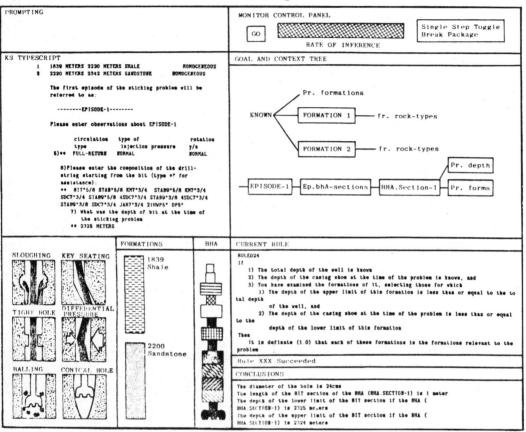

screen the user would see when running the DRILL-
ING ADVISOR on the Xerox workstation.

The following transcript illustrates the DRILLING
ADVISOR's interaction with a drilling supervisor
and the nature of the advice provided. The data,
except the name of the oil well, are drawn from an

actual field case. All depths and diameters given are
in meters and inches, respectively, unless otherwise
indicated. The dialogue is indented, with the user's
responses underlined. Our comments are interpo-
lated.

———WELL-1———
(1) What is the name of WELL-1?
    XBS-15D

DRILLING ADVISOR *now asks the user to enter information about the*
formations.

| (3) | upper
limit
2220 | lower
limit
1839 | main
rock
Shale | homogeneous/
interbedded
Homogeneous |

User types H then <ESC> to get HOMOGENEOUS.
  DRILLING ADVISOR corrects a user mistake.

(5) Lower limit (1839) should be larger than upper limit (2220)—they will be inter-changed.

2220   2342   Sand   Shale
= SANDSTONE
SHALE assumed as secondary rock-type here.
————PROBLEM-1————

| (7) | problem
type
Sticking | prior
action
Repair | total
depth
2342 | casing
depth
1839 |

————EPISODE-1————

| (8) | circulation
type
Full-return | injection
pressure
Normal | rotation
(y/n)
N |

(9) Please enter the composition of the drill-string starting from the bit

(type *? for assistance):
BIT9"5/8STAB9"5/8KM7"3/4SDC7"3/4STAB9"5/84SDC7"3/4
STA9"5/84SDC7"3/4STAB9"5/8SDC7"3/4JAR7"3/4 21HWP5"
DP5"

Notice in Figure 10.5 how the system represents this information visually to allow easy confirmation and recall.
  The system has focused on a specific episode and notes that the bottom hole assembly (BHA) is comprised of a bit, stabilizers, two types of drill collars, a jarring element, heavyweight drill pipe, and ordinary drill pipe.

(10) What is the depth of bit?
  2325

DRILLING ADVISOR begins to consider sticking by differential pressure. In order to do this, it must determine whether a potentially sticking element came into motionless contact with the side wall of an open-hole formation whose fluid specific gravity exceeds the mud specific gravity.

(11) Was the BHA motionless when sticking occurred?
  Y

(12) What is the depth of the freepoint?
      Unk

*The user apparently has not run the freepoint measurement. The DRILL-
ING ADVISOR proceeds without it.*

(13) What is the specific gravity of the mud?
      ??

User wants to know the range of permissible values.

Expecting a positive number between .2 and 3
1.24

(14) What is the fluid specific gravity of the SANDSTONE formation interbedded with
      SHALE between 2220 meters and 2342 meters?
      1

The CAUSE of sticking in EPISODE-1 is:
      DIFFERENTIAL-PRESSURE (.3).

*The .3 is a calculated measure of the system's certainty in this conclusion. In
this case the evidence for differential pressure is weak.*

The REASON that DIFFERENTIAL-PRESSURE was concluded as the cause of
sticking in EPISODE-1 is:

The BHA was motionless at the time that sticking occurred. There is one or
more potentially sticking BHA element in contact with a permeable formation.
The total calculated sticking force is 30 tons.

(17)   What is the filtrate of the mud?
          5.1 cc

(18)   What is the type of mud?
          Sea-water

(19)   In which direction can the current jar operate?
          Both-directions

The possible CURATIVE TREATMENTS for EPISODE-1 are:

Circulate at a normal flow rate to homogenize the mud.
During circulation, consider changing the mud parameters as follows:
    Decrease the filtrater.
    Add lubricant products.
Apply both upward and downward force to the drill string, while trying to regain
rotation.

Jar both upward and downward, using the current jar.
Consider pumping a lubricant and surfactant slug.
(The slug may require 2-3 days to become effective.)
Run a freepoint measurement to determine the back-off depth, then back-off and insert an up/down fishing jar.
If none of these methods free the drill string, consider setting a cement plug and side-tracking.

These curative treatment items are ordered roughly in terms of increasing difficulty and cost.

The possible PREVENTIVE TREATMENTS for EPISODE-1 (assuming the drill string has been freed) are:

During the next trip down, circulate at the bottom of the well, slowly increasing the mud injection pressure until the desired flow rate is reached. Change the mud characteristics as stated above in the curative treatment recommendations.

Change the BHA composition: Incorporate a safety joint, for future backoffs. Consider inserting stabilizers above and below each K-monel, in order to reduce the chance of future differential-pressure problems. When drilling is resumed, maintain a normal flow.

Reproduced by permission of Teknowledge Inc.

The object hierarchy that structures DRILLING ADVISOR's backward chaining analysis of the sticking problem is shown in Figure 10.6.

Currently the knowledge base of DRILLING ADVISOR consists of some 250 rules. Approximately 175 of those rules are used in diagnosis, and the other 75 rules are used in prescribing treatment. Results to date are very encouraging. The system has successfully handled a number of difficult cases that were not included in the set used during its development. Current plans call for extending the capabilities of DRILLING ADVISOR and for integrating it into the actual drilling environment.

A MICROPROCESSOR-BASED ELECTROPHORESIS INTERPRETER

In 1980 Sholom M. Weiss and Casimir A. Kulikowski of the Computer Science Department of Rutgers University, and Robert S. Galen of the Pathology Department of Columbia University, collaborated to develop an electrophoresis interpreter. This system was designed to take data from a scanning densitometer, a widely used laboratory instrument that does a serum protein electrophoresis analysis.

This system was developed using EXPERT, a system building tool that Weiss and Kulikowski have previously used to build expert systems for medical consultation. EXPERT is primarily an event-driven system, rather than a goal-driven system like EMYCIN, but it uses backward chaining and production rules. Using EXPERT, Weiss and Kulikowski were able to assemble an electrophoresis interpreter in six months, relying on one principal expert and several additional consultants. The initial model they developed had 10 production rules, each leading to a single conclusion. The final version has 82 production rules

Figure 10.6 *The object hierarchy of the DRILLING ADVISOR system.*

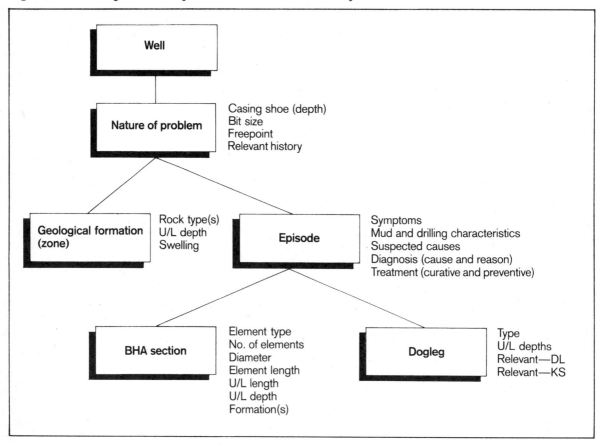

leading to 38 different conclusions. Although the system is not designed to cover all possible cases that a scanning densitometer can encounter, it covers all common cases.

In a test, the system was given 256 cases covering a very wide range of situations. The system's analyses were considered 100-percent acceptable.

Once Weiss and Kulikowski were satisfied with the electrophoresis interpreter as it functioned in the EXPERT environment, they used EXPERT to translate the program into a microprocessor assembly language program. An instrument manufacturer then interfaced the interpretive program to an existing program that prints out instrument readings. In effect, an instrument that had previously simply

printed out data now prints out not only raw data but also an interpretive analysis (see Figure 10.7). Thus, the electrophoresis interpreter has been incorporated in a medical instrument that has been sold since 1981.

To an observer, the compiled microprocessor version looks just as if it had been either coded directly in assembly language or compiled from some traditional algorithmic language. There is, however, a fundamental difference. Using EXPERT, the authors were able to produce a prototype version of the system very quickly. They were then able to test it numerous times and rapidly expand the system until it was able to satisfy all their performance criteria. Moreover, since the initial version still exists as a knowledge system, it will be easy to modify it or include additional information as new laboratory data become available or as clinical field tests indicate that changes are appropriate. A new microprocessor version could be rapidly generated from the modified EXPERT version.

A considerable effort would be involved if one tried to recode directly on the microprocessor, or if one tried to recode a traditional algorithmic version of the system. The elaborate testing and revision that

went into the development of the model could only have been accomplished on an expert system building tool. Moreover, the modular nature of the "expert" version incorporates a wealth of data that allows researchers to see exactly how the program is making its judgments. Thus, researchers can work with the "expert" version of the system to satisfy themselves of the logic of the system before using the embedded version.

Weiss and Kulikowski argue that by incorporating

Figure 10.7 Interpretive output from Helena Laboratories Electrophoretic Interpreter. Note that the knowledge system included on a microchip in this instrument has added the interpretive analysis on the bottom of the printout.

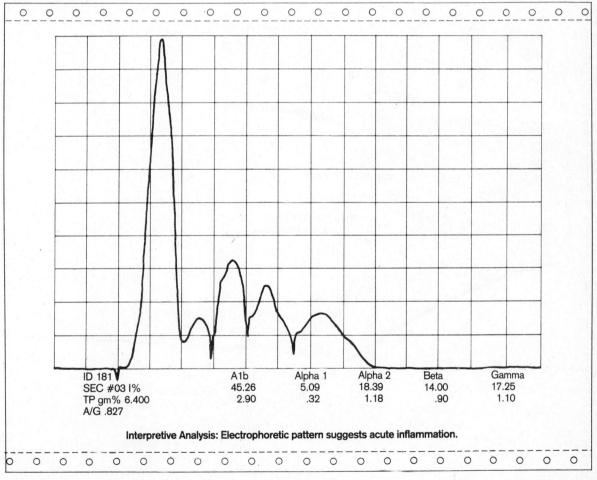

	A1b	Alpha 1	Alpha 2	Beta	Gamma
ID 181	45.26	5.09	18.39	14.00	17.25
SEC #03 l%	2.90	.32	1.18	.90	1.10
TP gm% 6.400					
A/G .827					

Interpretive Analysis: Electrophoretic pattern suggests acute inflammation.

this small knowledge system directly into the instrument, they have made it much more acceptable to the medical community. Physicians and researchers already routinely accept printouts from medical instruments that are microprocessor-controlled. Thus, in many cases, making an instrument more effective simply involves adding an interpretive module to an existing instrument.

It is easy to imagine that if PUFF had been developed with an instrument maker, rather than in cooperation with a particular medical center, it might also have been reduced to a microchip and incorporated directly into a pulmonary function instrument.

SUMMARY

In this chapter we have reviewed a number of the best-known expert systems, as well as a few less well-known systems that illustrate important trends. In discussing these systems we have tried to illustrate a number of general principles in the context of specific systems development efforts. Table 10.2 summarizes information about the systems we have discussed.

Stepping back a bit, we can describe several broad trends in expert system development. As a general rule, earlier systems were programmed in LISP. They were built on mainframes, usually DEC systems, simply because these were readily available at univer-

Figure 10.8 Broad trends in applications illustrated by existing knowledge systems.

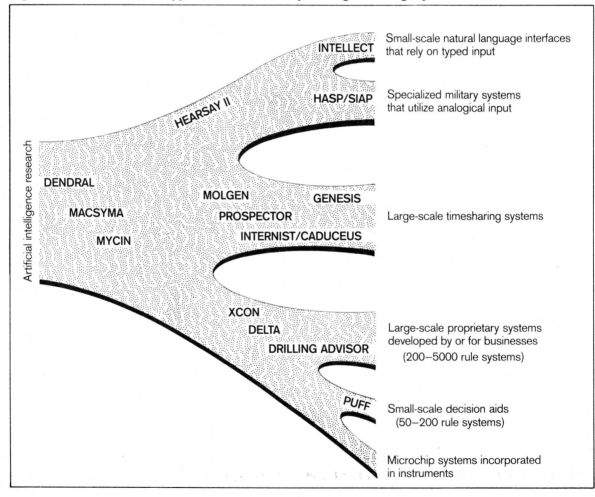

sities. Early systems tried to solve problems that university researchers hoped would prove the power of the expert systems approach.

Recent systems, on the other hand, have tended to focus on more practical or commercial goals. They have, generally, been built by means of the expert system building tools that were extracted from the earlier systems. Thus, recent systems have been developed faster and, generally, more efficiently, since knowledge engineers have begun to formalize the steps that make for the efficient development of a new system.

Looking at the current applications (see Figure 10.8), however, there is no overall trend. There is still strong momentum toward the development of large-scale systems designed to be used on a timesharing basis. Some of these systems are university-based, like CADUCEUS, but others, like the GENESIS system leased by IntelliCorp, are clearly commercial systems designed to assist specific user communities.

Many knowledge systems, such as GENESIS and PROSPECTOR, incorporate constrained, typed-input natural language systems; and at least a few constrained data base inquiry systems, such as IN-TELLECT, are being offered to a broad range of users. Even constrained speech input, however, is still a long way from practical application. Other analog signal processing systems, derived from research in speech understanding, are being developed, primarily for specialized military applications.

Large-scale proprietary business systems is a very active area. Several companies have set up groups to develop expert systems internally. Simultaneously, several companies have been founded to undertake the custom development of expert systems for business clients. Most of these companies are also developing and selling expert system building tools.

A smaller, but rapidly expanding trend is toward the development of small-scale knowledge-based systems. These systems range from 50 to 200 rules and are not so much concerned with capturing expertise as with solving small, but difficult and bothersome problems. At least one of these small systems has been put on a microprocessor and incorporated into an instrument.

We consider the future implications of each of these trends in subsequent chapters.

Table 10.2 Overview of Selected Recent Knowledge Systems

System:	XCON (R1), XSEL	GENESIS
Developer:	Carnegie-Mellon University and Digital Equipment Corp.	IntelliCorp
Purpose (domain): general area of application and reason for building the system	Configure computer hardware.	A package of genetic engineering systems that assist molecular researchers; data base search, analysis, and planning.
Task: specific task the system is to accomplish	Configure VAX computing systems by projecting the need for subassemblies given a high-level description of the system.	Designs molecular genetics experiments and procedures.
Input: data needed to accomplish task and method for acquiring it	Description of a VAX system.	Interacts with user to locate and analyze data and to develop plans.
Output: results produced by the system	Listing of parts, accessories, and a plan for assembly.	Genetic maps, information, and plan sequences displayed on a bit-mapped graphics screen.
Architecture: conceptual model used to structure the system	Forward-chained, rule-based, match–act cycle with almost no backtracking.	Frame-based, forward and backward chaining, with active values displayed as graphics on a bit-mapped screen.
Tools: software environment in which the system is developed and implemented	OPS5, a production system tool.	Initially written in UNITS but transferred to KEE.
Results: performance of the system, current status, evaluation, etc.	In use by DEC and performing better than previous (human) systems. Similar applications now under development.	Currently used by more than 500 research scientists.

DELTA/CATS-1	DRILLING ADVISOR	A microprocessor-based electro-phoresis interpreter
General Electric	Teknowledge Inc. and Elf–Aquitaine	Rutgers University and Helena Laboratories
Diesel-Electric Locomotive Troubleshooting Aid (DELTA).	Advise oil drilling crews about problems.	Annotate analogue output from an instrument.
Assist maintenance personnel in diagnosing and repairing a variety of diesel-electric locomotive faults.	Diagnose drilling problems, initially problems with drills sticking in the well.	Analyzes results of a serum protein electrophoresis analysis.
Answers to interrogation of user. System supports user by providing CAD graphics and videodisk sequences to explain how to locate and examine locomotive components.	Answers to interrogation of user about the characteristics of the well.	Data from a scanning densitometer.
Specific repair instructions, including graphics support as necessary.	Diagnosis of the reason for sticking, prescription for repair, and recommendations for avoiding a repeat of the event.	Interpretive analysis printed on graphic that comes out of scanning densitometer.
	Rule-based, exhaustive backward chaining with uncertainty.	An event-driven system that uses production rules with backward chaining.
Initially written in LISP, but converted to FORTH for portability.	Initially written in KS300. Reimplemented in S1.	Developed with EXPERT.
Acceptance by maintenance workers has been enthusiastic.	Core system design complete; enhancement and integration stage under negotiation.	Currently on a microchip incorporated in a scanning densitometer sold by Helena Laboratories.

Section Three

DEVELOPING EXPERT SYSTEMS

11.

Building a Small Knowledge System

In this chapter we are going to "walk through" the actual development of a small knowledge system, to see what the process of building such a system really involves.

THE ROLE OF SMALL SYSTEMS

Before actually beginning to analyze a knowledge domain and design a system, we should briefly reconsider some of the points that we have made in this book. First, we have been using "expert systems" and "knowledge systems" as synonyms. The term expert system was coined when AI researchers began to develop the first large systems. DENDRAL and MY-CIN really were intended to function like the human experts they were modeled after, and thus "expert systems" seemed to describe the systems rather accurately. As knowledge engineers have begun to explore the commercial market for "expert systems," they have realized that one can build small, useful systems that are not, in fact, modeled on human experts.

One can build a small system, for example, that will help a clerk to classify insurance applications. The knowledge contained in the small system would not normally be said to be the knowledge of an expert. In this case, it might be knowledge possessed by several major insurance application examiners. One could put new examiners through a training program to teach them what they need to know to evaluate applications. In addition, one could provide the new examiners with procedures manuals and evaluation checklists. Or one could develop a small knowledge-based system that would aid the new ex-

aminer to evaluate the application. In effect, new examiners could turn to the knowledge system when they might otherwise leaf through a procedures manual or ask questions of a senior application examiner.

The insurance application evaluation system we have just described is a knowledge system. It contains a knowledge base and can be most efficiently developed by means of symbolic programming techniques. Since several systems currently being developed by knowledge engineers are similar to what we have just described, knowledge engineers have taken to calling the systems they develop "knowledge systems" to avoid the implication that their systems always capture the knowledge of human experts. Thus, we shall now introduce a more refined use of our terminology. When referring to large systems, we shall use the terms "expert system" and "knowledge system" as synonyms. In referring to small systems that may be very useful but clearly do not contain the knowledge or skill of a true human expert, we shall consistently use the term "knowledge system."

Several knowledge engineering companies are currently introducing small knowledge system building tools. These companies are motivated by different business strategies. Some realize that these tools will be used to build small systems to function as performance aids, and they are tailoring their training and support to facilitate that use.

Other companies expect that independent software designers will use small system building tools to develop generic knowledge systems. Still other companies expect their tools to be used only by individuals who want to learn about knowledge engineering. These companies expect that their clients will experiment with the small tools and then acquire larger tools once they begin to tackle "serious" problems. Companies who think of their tools as "beginners' packages" tend to tailor their training and support for advanced programmers who will eventually use large tools rather than providing training to help people who will use the small tools to solve more mundane problems.

Our own view is that small knowledge system building tools can and will be used by middle managers and training developers to solve a vast array of small, irksome problems. The individuals using these tools will not be "knowledge engineers" but will, instead, be people who are close to the problems. Senior application examiners will develop small knowledge systems that will provide assistance to new clerical personnel. Moreover, these same individuals and their managers will also maintain and update the systems. This perception of the usefulness of small knowledge system building tools depends on the user interface provided by the tools. The idea that senior application evaluators can suddenly become "programmers" will become a reality only if the tools are truly easy to use. The burden of this chapter is to allow you to judge this matter for yourself. In the discussion that follows, we have omitted nothing. We have included all of the fine points and details to illustrate that although the "programming" process is not absolutely natural, it is nonetheless simple enough that most technically oriented managers and technicians could use it to develop a knowledge system to help people perform complex tasks better than they do now.

BUILDING A SMALL SYSTEM

In the pages that follow we shall walk through the process of developing a small consulting system to advise users on what media to consider when they undertake to develop a training program. This is not a very complex task. We chose it for two reasons. We wanted the task to be simple enough that the reader can quickly grasp the knowledge that must be encoded to develop the system. At the same time, we wanted a task that one might actually encounter in a business environment. Most large corporations have training departments with responsibility for developing training programs. On several occasions the authors of this book have spent time discussing the issues involved in media selection with training developers and managers. We have already considered developing a software package to help training designers make the decisions that typically must be made when designing a new program. The selection of media is only one of those decisions, and it is usually subsidiary to other considerations. Thus, the MEDIA ADVISOR that we will build in the following pages is not really a stand-alone knowledge system; it is just a fragment of a larger TRAINING ADVISOR knowledge system. Nonetheless, it illustrates just how one can go about capturing knowledge and preparing a small knowledge system.

To develop a small knowledge system, one must go through six steps:

1. Select a tool and implicitly commit yourself to a particular consultation paradigm.
2. Identify a problem and then analyze the knowledge to be included in the system.
3. Design the system. Initially this involves describing the system on paper. It typically involves making flow diagrams and matrices and drafting a few rules.
4. Develop a prototype of the system using the tool. This involves actually creating the knowledge base and testing it by running a number of consultations.
5. Expand, test, and revise the system until it does what you want it to do.
6. Maintain and update the system as needed.

We shall consider each of these steps in turn.

Step 1. *Select a tool and implicitly commit yourself to a particular consultation paradigm.*

Specific tools are designed to facilitate the development of particular consultation paradigms. Interestingly, when one is developing a small system, one is less constrained by the consultation paradigm of a tool than one is when using a large tool. This occurs because large tools incorporate special features that make it easy to manipulate data in certain ways while making it harder to do other things. Small tools, because they are simpler, don't have as many constraints. If you wanted to use a small tool to build a 1,000-rule system, you would soon find yourself overwhelmed and want some of the convenience features that are provided by large tools. As long as you want to develop systems with only 75 to 200 rules, however, you can probably handle the complexity with ease. Still, you must respect the overall consultation paradigm the tool is designed to handle.

There are several small tools now on the market, and there will undoubtedly be several more by the time this book appears in print. These systems differ in price and in user-friendliness. At the moment, most of the tools are designed to handle the most common consultation paradigm—diagnosis and prescription. Thus, we shall assume that we are acquiring a tool designed to prototype diagnosis/prescription consultations. This strongly suggests that the tool will represent knowledge by means of *if–then* rules and facts and that it will incorporate a backward chaining inference strategy.

The tool we shall use in this example will be M.1, a small tool sold by Teknowledge Inc. M.1 is expensive, but it is very well designed and very easy to use. We are not endorsing M.1 for small systems development. We are, however, familiar with it and find it very convenient to use. M.1 is designed to prototype diagnosis/prescription consultations (Teknowledge calls them "structured selection problems"). Moreover, M.1 uses rules and backward chaining. Thus, M.1 is typical of the sort of tool that most companies will probably use to develop small systems during the next few years.

Once we have decided to use M.1 and, therefore, implicitly decided to constrain our search for an appropriate problem to the diagnosis/prescription paradigm, we must look for a problem with the following characteristics:

- It should normally take about 30 minutes to solve the problem. If it takes more, there is probably too much knowledge being used to capture effectively with this tool.

- The problem should not involve an examination of diagrams or any physical contact. M.1 has no way to accept visual inputs. The problem should be one that could normally be solved during a phone conversation.
- The problem should normally be solved by someone who uses rules and, at most, a few simple calculations. If the solution to the problem requires a lot of mathematics, you should use a more traditional programming system, such as an electronic spreadsheet program.
- The prescription that ultimately solves the problem should be chosen from a few dozen possibilities. If the problem involves choosing among 100 different prescriptions, there are probably other tools that could handle the problem better.

These criteria rule out lots of possible problems, but once you begin to consider the various problems you would like to develop a system to help people solve, you will realize that a very large number of problems still fall into the diagnosis/prescription category.

Our MEDIA ADVISOR problem certainly does. When a designer or a committee is considering how to deliver a training program, they normally discuss the matter with a consultant for about 20 minutes. It isn't a problem that takes hours to analyze. Moreover, the media expert uses rules-of-thumb when he or she provides advice. There may be a little calculation about the comparative costs of various media, but the problem is solved mainly in verbal rather than mathematical terms. Finally, the medium recommended is usually one of about a dozen options. There simply are not hundreds of different recommendations one can make.

A media consultant usually talks with a client for perhaps 10 to 20 minutes. During that time the consultant asks the client to describe the type of training program desired, any cost or implementation constraints, and any emotional responses the client has to one or another medium. Then the consultant recommends one of at most about a half-dozen ways in which the goal could be accomplished. Obviously, if the client decides to use videotape, there can be a lengthy discussion about what type of videotape to buy, what type of videoplayers to invest in, or where to have lab work done; but these are supplementary to the basic decision of what generic type of media presentation will be most effective for a particular training program.

In essence, advising a client regarding the selection of training media involves discussing the symptoms of the training problem, considering how those symptoms relate to media characteristics, and then prescribing one or a few media to handle the problem. This is a reasonable description of a diagnosis/prescription consultation, and thus M.1 should be able to help us develop a knowledge system that can help users solve the problem on their own.

Step 2. *Identify a problem and then analyze the knowledge to be included in the system.*

We have already described media selection in general. A good way to be sure we understand the way we expect our consultation to flow is to prepare a very general consultation flow diagram like the one depicted in Figure 11.1.

To prepare to develop a knowledge system, however, we shall have to discuss the problem in more detail. Normally we would meet with an expert and work out the key attributes of media selection during the course of several interviews. We are going to skip the knowledge acquisition phase by relying on a published analysis of media selection. The specific approach to selecting instructional media that we are going to use was first described in 1969 by Donald T. Tosti and John R. Ball ("A Behavioral Approach to Instructional Design and Media Selection"). The Tosti–Ball model is based on research that indicates that training is most effective when the trainees practice performing, in class, the same task they will later be expected to perform on the job. Assume, for example, that you wanted to teach clerks to read insurance applications, note specific signs, and then prepare memos approving or disapproving the applications. The ideal training program to prepare clerks to do such a task would present the trainees with applications and ask them to evaluate the applications and prepare memos documenting their conclusions. Depending on the complexity of the task, one

might begin with a lecture on the hows and whys of the task. One would probably begin with some simple applications and then work up to harder cases. Moreover, one would probably provide some examples, perhaps a checklist to guide the clerk in his or her initial evaluations, and so forth. The important thing, from a media selection perspective, is that you want to use media that provide the trainees with the opportunity to read real applications, do evaluations, and record the results in the same way the trainees will do once they complete the course.

Some media can be rejected out of hand. For example, this course should not be offered on videocassette. A videocassette presentation might be used

Figure 11.1 Training media consultation flow.

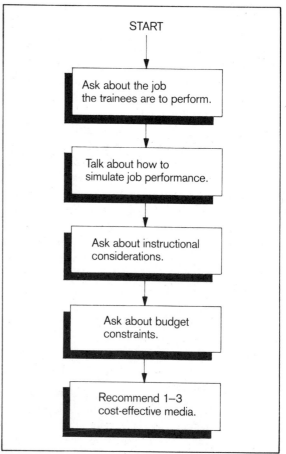

to kick off the program, but one would not want simply to show the trainees a picture of an application and then let them watch someone else completing the application. It would be acceptable as an introduction, but ultimately it would be a poor substitute for having the trainees examine actual applications and prepare memos. Numerous studies and common sense strongly suggest that the trainees won't be ready to do the job until they have actually practiced doing the task.

Consider a slightly different training task. In this case the job requires clerks to study incoming applications on a computer terminal. The clerk checks the screen for key information, types some notes at the bottom of the screen, and then touches one of several keys to route the application to its next destination. Imagine that we wanted to select media for a training program to new clerks being assigned to this job. Ideally, we would like to present the applications to be evaluated on a computer screen and ask the trainee to use the terminal keyboard to enter notations and then forward the application. It is possible that the client could not provide terminals for the trainees. We might decide that we could simulate the task using paper and pencil, but if we did that, we could be sure the trainees would still have to learn to use the computer terminals when they arrived on the job.

Similarly, imagine trying to teach salespeople to interact with customers. Having the salesperson type responses to questions asked by a computer is simply not a good simulation of a human interaction with a customer. There is no reason to expect that the salesperson will learn very much from a human interaction skills program presented by such inappropriate media.

The Tosti–Ball model suggests several criteria to use in choosing appropriate media. We have modified the original model somewhat, but it is essentially the same. The model considers three job or task considerations and three instructional considerations. Different options are considered under each consideration.

The task considerations and associated options are as follows:

The stimulus situation. What is the trainee presented with on the job? In the case of a clerk examining paper applications, the stimulus situation is a paper application. In the case of a clerk evaluating applications on a terminal, the stimulus situation is a screen with application data on it.

The options include:

1.1. An environmental situation—real physical objects either alone or in some combination. A machine to be repaired or a table to be set are both examples of environmental situations.

1.2. A pictorial situation—real or visual aspects of objects. Pictures and illustrations are both examples of pictorial stimuli.

1.3. A symbolic situation—all abstract symbols except the verbal symbols included under 1.4. Symbols range from graphics to schematics and from numerals to equations.

1.4. A verbal situation—spoken words or written verbal symbols and syntax constitute a verbal situation.

The stimulus duration. How long does the stimulus situation remain in front of the performer? In both clerical situations the applications will remain in place as long as the clerk wants them to. The salesperson, however, must respond to the customer as the customer speaks. If a customer asks a question and the salesperson sits and thinks about what to answer, the sales call will probably be a failure.

The options, in this case, form a continuum that we divide roughly into two possibilities:

2.1. Brief duration—the stimulus is available to the performer for only a brief period.

2.2. Persistent—the stimulus is available as long as the performer wants it.

The appropriate response. How must the performer respond to the stimulus situation? In the case of the clerk who processes paper applications, the appropriate response is to write or type a brief memo. In the case of the clerk using a computer terminal, the appropriate response is made by means of the terminal keyboard.

The options include:

3.1. Covert response—a response that cannot be observed, including listening, reading, observing, meditating, imagining, thinking, etc.

3.2. Selective response—the selection between alternatives, as in multiple choice, or the pairing of alternatives, as in matching.

3.3. Constructed response—writing, drawing, or typing.

3.4. Vocal responses—saying something. Vocal is also a constructed response, but it is of sufficient importance to justify a separate listing.

3.5. Motor response—all nonvocal activities that employ the striated muscles but are not included under constructed response.

3.6. Affective response—emotional response defined primarily in terms of the smooth muscles but often inferred from certain subcategories of vocal, selective, and motor responses.

The instructional considerations are more a matter of opinion and include the following.

Instructional feedback. Do you want to tell the trainees when they are correct or incorrect? Some instructional media allow you to provide feedback after each trainee response. Other media make it nearly impossible to give any feedback at all. As a general rule, if the task is very simple and the steps very small, you can structure the instruction so that the trainee will always be doing the right thing and hence you can avoid feedback problems. If the task is complex and there are lots of opportunities for the trainee to make errors that compound as the task progresses, then feedback is a good idea. You would rather not have a student work for an hour doing a complex evaluation and then find out that he or she misunderstood the problem in the first few minutes.

The options, in this case, form a continuum that we divide into two possibilities:

4.1. Yes—the performer is provided feedback immediately after he or she makes a response.

4.2. No—many programs ask the trainees to make responses and simply do not tell the trainees whether their responses are correct or incorrect.

Presentation modification. How often do you want to modify the presentation to accommodate the pace at which the trainee is progressing? Most college lecture courses are planned in advance, and the lectures are given as planned. If the students fail to learn much, the professor may change the lectures in the subsequent semester, but this is rarely done on a lecture-by-lecture basis. Some computer-based math drill programs require that the student answer five problems of a particular type correctly before being allowed to proceed to new subject matter. In effect, the presentation is constantly responsive to what the student is doing. Many training programs have tests at the end of a module. The trainee must complete the test to be allowed to go on to the next module. Imagine, for example, that our application clerk has to learn how to evaluate three different types of applications and can progress from practicing one type of evaluation to the next only when he or she has demonstrated mastery of the first type.

The options, in this case, form a continuum that we divide roughly into four possibilities:

5.1. Per response—each time the trainee makes a response, the instructional system considers what material should be presented next.

5.2. Per module—the instructional system reconsiders the presentation sequence at the end of each chapter, or unit, or module of material.

5.3. Per course—the instructional system reconsiders the presentation at the end of each course.

5.4. None—the instructional sequence is fixed and the trainee can either move from one unit to the next or drop out. The system, in effect, ignores the success or failure of the students going through it.

Training budget. Finally, there is always a budget. Some media are expensive to develop and present. Video presentations, for example, can cost hundreds of dollars a minute to develop. Other media, such as pencil-and-paper exercises or role-play exercises, can be developed for relatively little money. At some point a media advisor must always consider the maximum amount the client can afford to spend on the training program. The choice of ideal simulations must be adjusted accordingly.

This option is also a continuum. In a later version of this knowledge system we divide this category into dollar amounts and ask users to specify if they are prepared to develop the training themselves or want simply to purchase an "off-the-shelf" program. In the first version, however, we simply use rough options:

6.1. Small budget—up to about $10,000.
6.2. Medium budget—up to about $50,000.
6.3. Large budget—over $50,000.

The Tosti–Ball model says that one should determine values for each of the six variables we have described and then choose from among available media those that can deliver the desired training. If we were to state this as a general rule, it would be:

If   (1) stimulus situation is_____, and
        (2) stimulus duration is _____, and
        (3) appropriate response is _____, and
        (4) instructional feedback is _____, and
        (5) presentation modification is _____, and
        (6) training budget is _____,

Then   recommended media are _____ or _____.

Our next problem is filling in those blanks.

Step 3. *Design the system. Initially this involves describing the system on paper. It typically involves making flow diagrams and matrices and drafting a few rules.*

In the case of most simple knowledge bases, this stage of the effort blends from analysis into design and is most easily done by means of a matrix that lists conditions along the top and recommendations on the side. The matrix in Table 11.1 (on page 184) indicates which conditions lead to the recommendation of which media.

Obviously, we could consider other media as well. We could also add several more popular hybrid media combinations. To keep our example from getting too tedious, we have arbitrarily limited our possible recommendations to 10. (In our expanded version of this program, we have included about 35 possible recommendations. In our first prototype, however, we had only five recommendations on our matrix. It is best to develop a small version first to be sure it works and then add more depth later.)

Notice that we could describe Table 11.1 in the language of knowledge engineering by saying that the recommendations are values, the six considerations are six attributes of each rule, and the options in the cells of the matrix are the values associated with the six *if* clauses of the rules.

M.1 requires a goal so it will know what it is trying to do. In the case of our MEDIA ADVISOR, we might establish the following goal:

goal = media-to-consider.

In effect, we are telling M.1 that we want it to try to determine a value for media-to-consider and then tell us what that value is. Once we have completed Table 11.1, we have completed our analysis of the knowledge to be incorporated in our media advisor system.

In this case our first rule might be

if   stimulus-situation = verbal and
       stimulus-duration = persistent and
       appropriate-response = covert and
       instructional-feedback = no and
       presentation-modification = none and
       training-budget = small
then media-to-consider = book.

To illustrate just how friendly knowledge building tools can be, we can build our first MEDIA ADVISOR system using just our goal and the one rule we have just written. To "enter" our knowledge base, we fire up our IBM PC and turn on our word processing system. It could be any one of the common systems; ours happens to be WordStar. So we call WordStar and create a file, which we call MEDIADV. Then we enter our goal and our one rule in the file. We type them exactly as they appear above. It is not exactly

Table 11.1 Matrix Analysis of Training Media Advice

	IF: Task Simulation Consideration			Instructional Considerations			THEN:
	Stimulus Situation	Stimulus Duration	Appropriate Response	Instructional Feedback	Presentation Modification	Training Budget	
OPTIONS	Environmental Pictorial Symbolic Verbal	Brief ↕ Persistent	Covert Selective Constructed Vocal Motor Affective	Yes ↕ No	Per response | Per module | Per course | None	Small | Medium | Large	RECOMMENDATIONS:
	Verbal	Persistent	Covert	No	None	Small	1. Book
	Verbal	Persistent	Selective Constructed	Yes	Per response Per module	Small	2. Self-study Workbook
	Verbal	Brief	Covert	No	Per course	Medium	3. Lecture—no other media
	Verbal Symbolic Pictorial	Brief	Covert	No	Per course	Medium	4. Lecture with slides
	Verbal Pictorial	Brief	Covert	No	Per module	Medium	5. Videocassette
	Verbal	Brief	Vocal Affective	Yes	Per module	Small Medium	6. Role-play exercise Verbal feedback
	Verbal	Brief	Vocal Affective	Yes	Per module	Medium Large	7. Role-play exercise Video feedback
	Environmental	Persistent	Motor	No	Per module Per course	Large	8. Lab/workshop
	Verbal	Brief	Covert	No	None	Small	9. Audio cassette
	Symbolic Verbal	Brief	(All)	Yes	Per response	Medium Large	10. Human tutor

"ordinary language," since we can't use capitals and must put hyphens between terms, etc.; but it is certainly readable enough that you can understand exactly what knowledge the rule entails.

Once we have entered our goal and one rule, we close the file and move to M.1. We call up the M.1 program and tell it to copy and load our WordStar file MEDIADV. Then we begin a consultation by typing "go."

M.1 begins by checking the goal. It then moves to its active memory to see if it has concluded a value for "media-to-consider." It hasn't, since it has just begun, so it moves on and looks to see if it has any rules that will conclude "media-to-consider." It finds our one rule, and then begins to check the *if* clauses to see if the rule is valid in this case. The first *if* clause says that "stimulus-situation = verbal." M.1 goes back to its working memory to see if it can establish that fact. Once again it fails to find any data in its working memory. Once again it looks for rules that conclude a value for stimulus-situation. Obviously it finds no additional rules, so it looks for questions it could ask to obtain a value for stimulus-situation. We haven't entered any questions, so M.1 won't find any, but M.1 has the ability to generate its own questions. Thus, it prints out the following on our screen:

what is the value of:stimulus-situation?

We can answer with any value we want. If we type "verbal," M.1 will enter that fact in its working memory. It will then decide that the first *if* clause of the rule it is examining is correct and move on to the second *if* clause. By repeating the process, M.1 will soon generate another question for us:

what is the value of:stimulus-duration?

If we answer this and each subsequent question with the correct value, M.1 will eventually conclude that the media-to-consider = book. If we answer with any values other than the ones given in the rule, M.1 will conclude that our rule does not apply. It will look for other rules that would allow it to conclude media-to-consider and, finding none, will print out:

media-to-consider was sought, but no value was concluded.

In one sense this has all been a trivial exercise, but in another sense this is an amazing demonstration of a very powerful programming system. It would require a great deal of skill in any conventional programming language to develop a system that did what we just got M.1 to do. A conventional programmer could easily program a system to literally run the interaction we just observed, but he or she would be hard-pressed to write a system that would allow us to enter any rule we wanted and then have the system ask questions and reach appropriate conclusions. We did not need to concern ourselves with any procedural aspects of programming. We simply used an ordinary word processing system to create a file that contained facts we wanted M.1 to know. Then we transferred that file to M.1 and, instantly, we had a program that

was capable of asking us questions and reaching conclusions. In effect, by using M.1, anyone can begin to "program" useful systems that previously required learning the complex syntax of a programming language!

Returning to our MEDIADV project, we could begin generating 10 rules, one for each line on the matrix on Table 11.1. We can also do some other things to make MEDIADV a little friendlier. For example, a user might not know the exact terms that the Tosti–Ball model uses to classify stimulus situations. To give the user more options, we could write some rules that would allow the user to respond more freely. Thus, we might write the following rules:

```
if     situation = physical-model or
       situation = structure or
       situation = object or
       situation = machine or
       situation = tool or
       situation = environmental
then   stimulus-situation = environmental.

if     situation = picture or
       situation = photograph or
       situation = diagram or
       situation = illustration or
       situation = view or
       situation = pictorial
then   stimulus-situation = pictorial.

if     situation = graphics or
       situation = schematics or
       situation = numbers or
       situation = formulas or
       situation = symbolic
then   stimulus-situation = symbolic.

if     situation = listening or
       situation = conversation or
       situation = dialogue or
       situation = reading or
       situation = textual materials or
       situation = verbal
then   stimulus-situation = verbal.
```

The effect of these rules and a similar set we can create for "appropriate-response" is that the user can answer using any of the terms we have listed and M.1 will realize which of the four stimulus-situations the user means.

Another way we can make our system a little friendlier is to specify the questions to be asked. This avoids accepting M.1's terse, automatically generated questions. To specify a question for the first rule above, which concluded that stimulus-situation was environmental, we would type the following:

question(situation) = 'When the student completes the training program and returns to the job, what sort of situation will initiate the performance that this training program is designed to teach?'.

This question assures that when M.1 attempts to determine the situation, it will print out the question in quotes rather than generating its own question.

At the same time as we specify the question to be asked, we can also specify what answers M.1 will accept. Otherwise, the user may respond in a way that we have not considered and it will not fit into any of our rules. Thus:

legalvals(situation) = [physical-model, structure, object, machine, tool, environmental, picture, photograph, diagram, illustration, view, pictorial, graphics, schematics, numbers, formulas, symbolic, listening, conversation, dialogue, reading, textual-materials, verbal].

To complete our program we need to write all of the rules we have discussed, questions and legalvals for each attribute that the user will be asked about, and we need to enter one more statement in the knowledge base:

multivalued(media-to-consider).

This statement tells M.1 that we want it to find all of the possible values it can for media-to-consider. If we omitted this statement, M.1 would stop searching once it found a single value for media-to-consider and might suggest only one medium.

Table 11.2 shows the entire MEDIADV knowledge base that we initially developed.

Table 11.2 The Knowledge Base of MEDIADV

goal = media-to-consider.

rule1:   if   situation = physical-model or
                    situation = structure or
                    situation = object or
                    situation = machine or
                    situation = tool or
                    situation = environmental
            then   stimulus-situation = environmental.

rule2:   if   situation = picture or
                    situation = photograph or
                    situation = diagram or
                    situation = illustration or
                    situation = view or
                    situation = pictorial
            then   stimulus-situation = pictorial.

rule3:   if   situation = graphics or
              situation = schematics or
              situation = numbers or
              situation = formulas or
              situation = symbolic
          then   stimulus-situation = symbolic.

rule4:   if   situation = listening or
              situation = conversation or
              situation = dialogue or
              situation = reading or
              situation = textual-materials or
              situation = verbal
          then   stimulus-situation = verbal.

rule5:   if   response = listening or
              response = reading or
              response = observing or
              response = meditating or
              response = imagining or
              response = thinking or
              response = covert
          then   appropriate-response = covert.

rule6:   if   response = multiple-choice or
              response = matching or
              response = selective
          then   appropriate-response = selective.

rule7:   if   response = writing or
              response = drawing or
              response = typing
          then   appropriate-response = constructed.

rule8:   if   response = saying-something or
              response = talking or
              response = speaking or
              response = singing or
              response = vocal
          then   appropriate-response = vocal.

rule9:   if   response = building or
              response = assembling or
              response = moving or
              response = constructing or
              response = arranging or
              response = dancing or
              response = motor-activity
          then   appropriate-response = motor.

rule10: if   response = emoting or
            response = sympathizing or
            response = empathizing or
            response = feeling or
            response = showing-affect
        then appropriate-response = affective.

rule11: if   stimulus-situation = verbal
            and stimulus-duration = persistent
            and appropriate-response = covert
            and instructional-feedback = no
            and presentation-modification = none
            and training-budget = small
            or training-budget = medium
        then media-to-consider = book.

rule12: if   stimulus-situation = verbal
            and stimulus-duration = persistent
            and appropriate-response = selective
            or appropriate-response = constructed
            and instructional-feedback = yes
            and presentation-modification = per-response
            or presentation-modification = per-module
            and training-budget = small
            or training-budget = medium
            or training-budget = large
        then media-to-consider = self-study-workbook.

rule13: if   stimulus-situation = verbal
            and stimulus-duration = brief
            and appropriate-response = covert
            and instructional-feedback = no
            and presentation-modification = per-course
            and training-budget = small
            or training-budget = medium
        then media-to-consider = lecture.

rule14: if   stimulus-situation = verbal
            or stimulus-situation = symbolic
            or stimulus-situation = pictorial
            and stimulus-duration = brief
            and appropriate-response = covert
            and instructional-feedback = no
            and presentation-modification = per-course
            and training-budget = medium
        then media-to-consider = lecture-with-slides.

rule15: if   stimulus-situation = verbal
            or stimulus-situation = pictorial

              and stimulus-duration = brief
              and appropriate-response = covert
              and instructional-feedback = no
              and presentation-modification = per-module
              and training-budget = medium
              or training-budget = large
        then media-to-consider = videocassette.

rule16: if   stimulus-situation = verbal
              and stimulus-duration = brief
              and appropriate-response = vocal
              or appropriate-response = affective
              and instructional-feedback = yes
              and presentation-modification = per-module
              and training-budget = small
              or training-budget = medium
        then media-to-consider = role-play-with-verbal-feedback.

rule17: if   stimulus-situation = verbal
              and stimulus-duration = brief
              and appropriate-response = vocal
              or appropriate-response = affective
              and instructional-feedback = yes
              and presentation-modification = per-module
              and training-budget = medium
              or training-budget = large
        then media-to-consider = role-play-with-video-feedback.

rule18: if   stimulus-situation = environmental
              and stimulus-duration = persistent
              and appropriate-response = motor
              and instructional-feedback = no
              and presentation-modification = per-module
              or presentation-modification = per-course
              and training-budget = large
        then media-to-consider = lab/workshop.

rule19: if   stimulus-situation = verbal
              and stimulus-duration = brief
              and appropriate-response = covert
              and instructional-feedback = no
              and presentation-modification = none
              and training-budget = small
        then media-to-consider = audio-cassette.

rule20: if   stimulus-situation = symbolic
              or stimulus-situation = verbal
              and stimulus-duration = brief
              and appropriate-response = covert

```
          or  appropriate-response  =  verbal
          or  appropriate-response  =  affective
          and  instructional-feedback  =  yes
          and  presentation-modification  =  per-response
          and  training-budget  =  medium
          or  training-budget  =  large
    then   media-to-consider  =  human-tutor.
```

multivalued(media-to-consider).

question(situation) = 'When the student completes the training program and returns to the job, what sort of situation will initiate the performance that this training program is designed to teach?'.

legalvals(situation) = [physical-model, structure, object, machine, tool, environmental, picture, photograph, diagram, illustration, view, pictorial, graphics, schematics, numbers, formulas, symbolic, listening, conversation, dialogue, reading, textual-materials, computer-program, verbal, listening, reading, observing, meditating, imagining, thinking, covert].

question(stimulus-duration) = 'When the student completes the training program and returns to the job, how would you describe the length of time that he or she will normally be allowed to interact with the job situation before taking action?'.

legalvals(stimulus-duration) = [brief, persistent].

question(response) = 'When the student completes the training program and returns to the job, in what way will he or she normally be expected to act or respond on the job?'.

legalvals(response) = [listening, reading, observing, meditating, imagining, thinking, covert, multiple-choice, matching, selective, writing, drawing, typing, saying-something, talking, speaking, singing, vocal, building, assembling, moving, constructing, arranging, dancing, motor-activity, emoting, sympathizing, empathizing, feeling, showing-affect.]

question(instructional-feedback) = 'Do you want to provide the student with feedback after he or she responds to a question?'.

legalvals(instructional-feedback) = [yes, no].

question(presentation-modification) = 'How frequently will you want to review the student's progress and make decisions about what training to present next?'.

legalvals(presentation-modification) = [per-response, per-module, per-course, none].

question(training-budget) = 'Do you have a large, medium, or a small amount of money to spend on the development of this training program?'.

legalvals(training-budget) = [large, medium, small].

If we were approaching this problem for the first time, we might also find it useful to develop a tree diagram that would map the way the consultation would run. A diagram for the MEDIADV program is pictured in Figure 11.2. Notice that the top node in Figure 11.2 is media-to-consider. When MEDIADV is activated, it will always begin by seeking to determine a value for this root node or goal.

Step 4. *Develop a prototype of the system using the tool. This involves actually creating the knowledge base and testing it by running a number of consultations.*

At this point we can develop a prototype knowledge system. We enter the knowledge base that appears in Table 11.2 in a file in our word processing system—this file will be our knowledge base. Next, we put the M.1 disk into our computer and load our knowledge base. Then we run several consultations. We answer the questions in different ways to see how the system will respond. The transcript that follows is a result of exactly that procedure. In the transcript, all user responses are underlined. Notice that on one occasion we ask the adviser WHY it was asking us a particular question. It responds by telling us the rule it is trying to confirm and then repeats the question. At another point we use "options" to determine what responses the advisor will accept, and it responds by telling us all of the legalvals that it will accept in response to the question.

Figure 11.2 Tree diagram for MEDIADV. For all questions to be generated by Rule 11, as shown below, the user would need to answer in a way that confirms Rule 11. If the user answers in some other way, the questions will be generated by an attempt to confirm one of the subsequent rules.

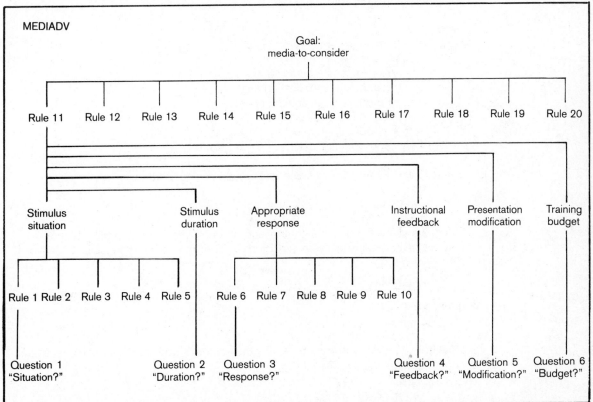

M.1 > *Load MEDIADV.*

M.1 > *Go.*

When the student completes the training program and returns to the job, what sort of situation will initiate the performance that this training program is designed to teach?
>> *Conversation.*

When the student completes the training program and returns to the job, how would you describe the length of time that he or she will normally be allowed to interact with the job situation before taking action?
>> *Brief.*

When the student completes the training program and returns to the job, in what way will he or she normally be expected to act or respond on the job?
>> *Why.*

Your answer to this question will help determine whether the following rule is applicable in this consultation.

rule5:
    if   response = listening or
             response = reading or
             response = observing or
             response = meditating or
             response = imagining or
             response = thinking or
             response = covert
    then   appropriate-response = covert.

The following knowledge base entries are also being used:

    rule13

When the student completes the training program and returns to the job, in what way will he or she normally be expected to act or respond on the job?
>> *Thinking.*

Do you want to provide the student with feedback after he or she responds to a question?
>> *No.*

How frequently will you want to review the student's progress and make decisions about what training to present next?
>> *Options.*

Your response must be chosen from among:
per-response, per-module, per-course, none

How frequently will you want to review the student's progress and make decisions about what training to present next?
>> *Per-course*.

Do you have a large, medium, or small amount of money to spend on the development of this training program?
>> *Medium.*

media-to-consider = lecture-with-slides (100%) because
                            rule 14
media-to-consider = lecture (100%) because rule 13

Step 5. *Expand, test, and revise the system until it does what you want it to do.*

As noted earlier we have expanded the knowledge base shown in Table 11.2 to include some 35 recommendations. We have also used a number of advanced features available in M.1 to make the program much friendlier. M.1 has a way to remove hyphens from rules, for example, so that the rules read a little easier. It also has a way to modify the system so that a user can volunteer information without having to wait for questions. This would be particularly useful if you knew that the same people were going to be using the system frequently. Users could begin by telling the ADVISOR what they knew about the problem and then the system would ask only for any information that had not been provided. If the user provided all the necessary information, the system wouldn't ask any questions, it would simply print out its recommendations.

Similarly, M.1 has a feature that allows the designer to include textual information. Thus, in our advanced MEDIADV we ask the user if he or she wants an explanation of either the Tosti–Ball model or any of the options. If the user requests an explanation, the system will print out a several-paragraph explanation.

Still another feature allows us to ask the user if he

or she is happy with the recommendation. If the user says that he or she isn't happy, then we ask the user to review each of the options chosen and to indicate which might be changed. Additional recommendations are generated in response to the user's new choices.

In our advanced advisor we also use certainty factors to qualify our recommendations. In the initial version illustrated here we ignore certainty factors. M.1 simply assigns a certainty (cf) of 100 to everything.

We have not illustrated these, or other features, because they would overly extend this chapter. Suffice to say that while some of these additional features are slightly more complex than the entries we have illustrated, they are still quite easy to conceptualize and enter.

The other aspect of expanding and testing involves watching users work with the system on the job. If we asked some training developers to use MEDIADV, for example, we might quickly discover that they wanted to use words other than the options provided. Modifying the system to accommodate them would be as simple as going to our word processing file and adding *if* clauses to appropriate rules. Thus, if users want to describe a certain stimulus situation as "talking," we might modify one of our situation rules by adding "talking," thus:

```
if     situation = talking or
       situation = listening or
       situation = conversation or
       situation = dialogue or
       situation = reading or
       situation = textual-materials
       situation = verbal
then   stimulus-situation = verbal.
```

We can literally change the MEDIADV program in just the time that it takes to type in one line in the knowledge base.

Moreover, we can easily add and subtract rules to see how that changes the advice the system gives. It is easy to imagine that a senior insurance application evaluator might take several months to perfect his or her system. Every time a junior clerk came to the senior advisor with a question that APPLICATION EVALUATOR couldn't handle, the senior evaluator would not only provide the answer, he or she would make a note to add or adjust some rule in the APPLICATION EVALUATOR knowledge base.

Step 6. *Maintain and update the system as needed.*

The final step is really just an extension of Step 5. Someone must take the responsibility for maintaining the knowledge base. In the course of time rules change, new application forms are introduced, etc. Someone must change the rules to accommodate the external changes that occur. Such changes are easy to make and can be made by someone familiar with the project in a natural and easy way. One senior insurance application advisor could become the keeper of APPLICATION EVALUATOR.

SUMMARY

We said at the beginning of this chapter that we wanted to show that small knowledge system building tools can be used by nonprogrammers to develop commercially useful small systems. Our example, though simple, is certainly not trivial, and it does show just how easy it is to convert a small body of knowledge into a small knowledge system.

The development of the MEDIADV system, even allowing for a week's time to learn about M.1, would not take two weeks. By the time you added the refinements we mentioned above, you might have spent at most a month on the project.

If you have employees who need occasional assistance that must be provided by means of training, procedures manuals, or senior employees, you have problems that might be solved by using a small knowledge system. Moreover, when an employee looks up a problem in a procedures manual, he or she may waste a lot of time or find the wrong solution. When the employee turns on a computer and asks an ADVISOR, he or she is asked only the questions appropriate to the problem at hand and is then given the correct recommendation.

Because small knowledge systems can be created and maintained by the people who actually use them, and because such systems allow individuals with little training to make decisions they could not otherwise make, we think that small knowledge systems will show up in a great many business operations in the very near future. Moreover, we think their appearance will be welcomed in the same way that managers have welcomed electronic spreadsheet programs. Individuals throughout large organizations will begin to document the knowledge that is actually used to get the job done. They will provide for vastly improved decision making and productivity in hundreds of small ways, and the result will be a revolution in the way businesspeople think about knowledge, training, documentation, and procedural flows.

12.

How Large Knowledge Systems Are Developed

In Chapter 11 we saw how a small knowledge system could be developed. We focused on the analysis of a very small amount of knowledge and on the coding effort required to convince readers that small systems can be developed by users. In this chapter we turn our attention to the process involved in developing a large expert system. We shall not focus on the knowledge that goes into the system or on how that knowledge is encoded. Instead, we shall discuss the major steps necessary to plan and develop a large expert system.

Unlike the development effort we described in Chapter 11, a large expert system can be developed only by a team of people trained in knowledge engineering. In this chapter we assume that the group undertaking the development effort has already chosen an expert system building tool. Moreover, we assume that the tool that has been selected is a narrowly focused tool designed to build production rule systems (e.g., Teknowledge's S.1 or Verac's OPS5e). Thus, we shall be able to focus on how one develops a knowledge system without having to be concerned with how to develop a system building tool. We shall not consider how frames, rule interpreters, or graphical displays are implemented. By choosing to describe the development of an expert system by means of a narrow tool, we are eliminating many complexities. This is a practical perspective, since most commercial systems have been developed using just such an approach.

We shall not dwell on the managerial aspects of project development for two reasons. First, they vary considerably. If a company is going to develop a large

expert system using its internal resources, for example, it already has project management procedures. If an outside contractor is going to develop the expert system, the contractor and the client will need to negotiate an appropriate management arrangement. Second, large-scale knowledge system efforts demand the same level and quality of attention that is paid to any other large software development project, and software project management procedures have been well described elsewhere.

The main focus of this chapter is on the *process* that occurs when a team develops a large expert system. We shall discuss the questions that must be considered at each step along the way, the decisions to be made, and the general activities that must occur.

KNOWLEDGE ENGINEERING

Knowledge engineers acquire knowledge from a human expert and then embed it in an expert system. They are specialists in getting the information from the expert, prototyping an expert system that contains the knowledge, and then working with the expert to improve the system. Figure 12.1 summarizes the roles of a knowledge engineer.

Compared with a conventional software engineer, who also interviews experts and designs and implements a system, knowledge engineers spend much more time with the experts. They are much more concerned with the thought processes of the expert. Moreover, they expect to continue to interact with

Figure 12.1 *The roles of the knowledge engineer.*

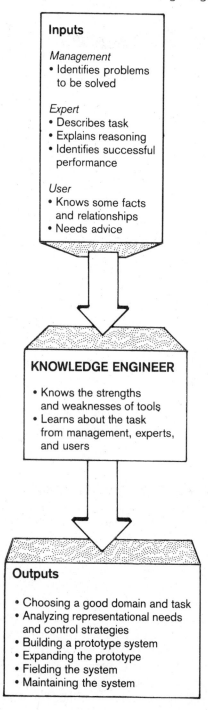

the expert until they can turn over completion of the system development effort to the expert.

Depending on the size of the project or the company, there may, of course, be more than one knowledge engineer. For example, a senior knowledge engineer may have overall management and design responsibilities, while other knowledge engineers are concerned with day-to-day meetings with the expert and still other, more junior engineers are responsible primarily for actually entering code into a machine. We shall speak of a single knowledge engineer, assuming for the sake of simplicity that one individual will perform all the knowledge engineering roles.

Many of the early expert systems were developed "from scratch" using either LISP or some programming environment such as INTERLISP. Now, and in the future, however, most expert systems will be developed by means of knowledge engineering tools designed specifically for the rapid development of expert systems. In this chapter we assume that this tool-mediated strategy is followed and that our knowledge engineer is well versed in the various expert system building tools now becoming available. We shall focus on knowledge system development, the process in which a knowledge engineer and an expert work together to identify and refine a body of knowledge to solve a particular problem.

KNOWLEDGE SYSTEM DEVELOPMENT

Knowledge systems are developed in six more or less independent phases (see Figure 12.2):

Phase I.   Selection of an appropriate problem
Phase II.   Development of a prototype system
Phase III. Development of a complete expert system
Phase IV.   Evaluation of the system
Phase V.   Integration of the system
Phase VI.   Maintenance of the system

This sequence is, of course, not entirely fixed. In fact, later developments may yield insights that affect previous decisions, and some previous work may be revised. Similarly, the sharp conceptual boundaries suggested here may be blurred if additional evaluation suggests modifications after the system has been installed. A sequence of phases and activities is provided only to give you an overview of how an ideal project might proceed. Each step will be discussed in more detail below.

Figure 12.2 Development of a knowledge system.

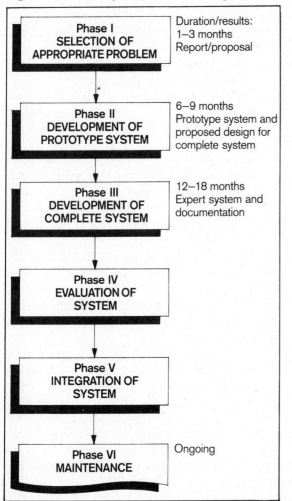

PHASE I: SELECTION OF AN APPROPRIATE PROBLEM

Selection of an appropriate problem includes a number of activities that precede the actual decision to begin development of a specific expert system. It includes the following activities:

- Identifying a problem domain and a specific task
- Finding an expert willing to contribute expertise
- Identifying a tentative approach to the problem
- Analyzing the costs and benefits of the effort
- Preparing a specific development plan

Identifying a Problem Domain and a Specific Task

Choosing the right problem is perhaps the most critical part of the entire development effort. The technology is still quite limited. If an inappropriate problem is chosen, one may quickly find the entire effort bogged down in design problems that no one knows how to solve. Likewise, an inappropriate problem may result in an expert system that costs much more than it saves. Worse, a system may be developed that works, but is unacceptable to users. Even if development is to occur internally, this phase is an especially appropriate time to obtain external advice to assure that one's initial knowledge engineering project is well selected and technically feasible.

As we have suggested elsewhere, the near future will probably witness the development of a few large expert systems designed to solve major problems and many small knowledge systems designed to solve troublesome minor problems. Large-scale systems, because of the very large initial development costs, must necessarily focus on problems that are carefully selected to assure a large and rapid payback for their developers. Developers of large-scale systems will, of course, be concerned to choose problems that are amenable to existing tools, but they will also be vitally concerned with the economics of automating a particular type of expertise.

Small-scale systems, on the other hand, can be developed to demonstrate the application of knowledge engineering and the usefulness of tools. Wise developers will choose small tasks that are particularly onerous, but quickly amenable to solution by means of a particular tool. Thus, projects for small-scale systems will be selected primarily on the basis of whether or not they can be solved quickly by means of a particular tool. Many companies will probably choose to undertake small systems problems, using a particular tool, to experiment with knowledge systems before they undertake the development of a larger system.

The selection of an appropriate domain and task begins with a review of the likely domains in which an expert system might be utilized. If the knowledge needed to perform a task is stable, numerical, and can be easily aggregated, then conventional, algorithmic computer programs will probably be the best way to solve problems in that domain. Knowledge systems do not supplant the need for relational data bases, statistical and spreadsheet software, or general ledger systems. If, however, task performance depends on knowledge that is subjective, changing, symbolic, or partly judgmental, the domain may very well be a good candidate for an expert system embodying a heuristic approach. Some small systems will be developed to solve problems that are amenable to conventional techniques simply because the users need the systems quickly and decide that they can develop workable solutions by themselves using small knowledge system building tools rather than waiting for their data processing groups to help them with their problem.

Some clues to watch for when looking for places in an organization where knowledge systems may be helpful include:

- A few key individuals are in short supply. They spend a substantial amount of time helping others.
- Performance of a small task requires a large team of people because no one person knows enough.
- Performance is degraded because a task demands a thorough analysis of a complex set of conditions and the typical performer never seems to remember everything.
- There is a large discrepancy between the best and the worst performers.

- Corporate goals are compromised as a result of scarce human resources.
- Competitors appear to have an advantage because they can perform the task consistently better.

Each clue is an indicator that knowledge is scarce and that the wider distribution of knowledge would have value. Expert systems distribute knowledge.

You are likely to think of many applications where a wider distribution of knowledge could be useful. The following guidelines help identify the subgroups of tasks that expert systems currently perform proficiently. Appropriate tasks:

- Focus on a narrow specialty.
- Do not depend heavily on background knowledge or common sense.
- Do not require sensory discriminations. Symbols, not signals, are required.
- Are neither too easy nor too difficult for a human expert. The problem ought to take a human expert somewhere from three hours to three weeks to solve.
- Are defined as clearly as possible. The context in which the task is performed is described, and the user of the system is identified.
- Have outcomes that can be evaluated. That is, the relative success of the system's performance can be assessed.

Currently, commercial expert systems are most successful when they process *symbolic* information in relatively *narrow* domains. Like human experts, these systems do not excel on tasks that are poorly defined. Nor do they work well when outcomes cannot be evaluated.

Once a domain and a task are identified, the scope is narrowed down further. It is useful to ask: Exactly what kinds of recommendations will the system make—and to whom? Specific goals for the programming efforts must be identified. Some possible goals include formalizing an otherwise informal set of practices, developing a system that will allow the user to distribute scarce expertise, helping experts solve problems better, or automating the routine aspects of an expert's job.

Finding an Expert Willing to Contribute Expertise

As we noted earlier, expert systems are developed by taking the specific knowledge of an established expert and putting it into a system. Small systems (and some very large systems) may incorporate the knowledge of more than one expert, but most expert systems reflect the knowledge and strategies of a single individual. Hence, finding the right expert is a key step in building an expert system.

The Multiple Expert Problem

Some system building tools accept inputs from multiple experts, but, in general, most large-scale system development efforts have had difficulty incorporating the knowledge of more than one major expert. Figure 12.3 illustrates a tangled hierarchy that a zoologist might draw. At the top level, the really broad terms—"mammal," "bird," "fish"—seem clear and unambiguous. Likewise, the specific animals on the bottom are easy to identify. The middle terms, however, are a different matter. Early zoologists wrote

Figure 12.3 A tangled hierarchy. Zoologists usually agree when they identify species. Moreover, they generally agree on the class to which each species belongs. Different zoologists, however, depending on their specialty, would focus on different characteristics. A typical zoologist would emphasize that most mammals are characterized by fur, live births, and "warm" blood. A specialist in bats would mention that some mammals fly, whereas a specialist of the platypus would note that some mammals lay eggs. Experts start to disagree when they focus on the characteristics of special cases.

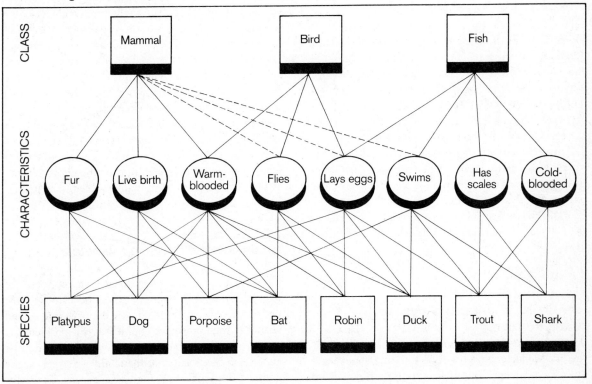

definitions of the major categories of animals that had to be revised when new animals were discovered that had some of the characteristics of one category and some of another. Indeed, within specialized domains, zoologists still argue about whether a particular species should be considered in one class or another. Experts, precisely because they are experts, have learned to make very fine discriminations. The characteristics they choose to emphasize depend on their past experiences and their specific goals. Although two experts working in the same specialty usually agree on the ultimate prescription—the top level of the hierarchy—they commonly prefer to set the problem up in slightly different ways and to search the problem space in a slightly different manner. In other words, they emphasize a slightly different set of characteristics on the second and third levels of the hierarchy. This sort of subtlety is irrelevant when you

are constructing a small knowledge system because the knowledge is usually not that complex and in any case not very voluminous. When a knowledge engineer is preparing to develop a system that may take months and involve many hundreds of rules, however, the initial choice of objects and attributes is very important. If two or three experts start arguing about exactly how to define their terms, the project is in trouble. Hence, with rare exceptions, most projects utilize only one major expert to set up the basic knowledge base and then ask other experts to refine that base. Systems such as HEARSAY and PROSPECTOR (see Chapters 9 and 10) get around the "multiple expert problem" by having several different knowledge bases, and hence several different experts, each focusing on only one aspect of the overall problem.

One knowledge engineer we know says that "the expert you want is the one the company would least like to give you. It's the person the company can least afford to do without." Throughout prototyping and the later expansion of the system, the knowledge engineer and the expert will be working together. The knowledge engineer helps the expert structure knowledge, and identify and formalize the important concepts and rules used to solve problems.

Thus, the expert should feel comfortable in explaining the nature of his or her expertise. In initial interviews both the knowledge engineer and the expert will decide if they can interact successfully. Both parties will probably be working together for at least a year, so it is important that they establish a comfortable rapport.

Identifying a Tentative Approach to the Problem

As the expert describes how the task is performed, the knowledge engineer will be thinking about various expert system development tools with which he

or she is acquainted. The knowledge engineer characterizes the expertise in terms of a few broad kinds of knowledge representations and inference strategies that have been encountered when developing expert systems. In this manner the knowledge engineer begins to formulate an opinion about the likelihood that a particular type of expertise can be captured with an existing tool. If it sounds as if a new tool will be required to create an expert system incorporating a particular type of expertise, the conscientious knowledge engineer will probably recommend against the project. However, a great many problems are amenable to the generic tools currently available.

Analyzing the Costs and Benefits of the Effort

Once a task has been identified as appropriate for expert system development, costs and benefits must be considered. Costs include the expert's time as well as that of the knowledge engineer. If the problem is a major one, both the knowledge engineer and the expert can be expected to spend at least a year on the effort. Additional costs include acquiring a computing environment that will be expensive in terms of both hardware and software.

Balanced against the costs are the benefits of the knowledge system. Those benefits may include reduced costs, increased productivity, enhanced products or services, or even the development of new products and services. The relative costs and benefits of any particular system determine how long it will take for the system to pay back the development expense. As of 1984, most companies that develop large expert systems are choosing reasonably costly projects with very large benefits, and, consequently, with very short payback times. We can expect a trend toward less expensive projects with slightly longer payback times as expert system development tools are refined. Table 12.1 shows some of the resources required for various levels of expert systems development.

Preparing a Specific Development Plan

Once the knowledge engineer is convinced that:

- A specific task can be performed by an expert system,
- It can be built with an existing tool,
- An appropriate expert is available,
- The proposed performance criteria are reasonable, and
- The cost and payback time are acceptable to the client,

then the knowledge engineer is ready to prepare a specific plan to guide the subsequent development effort. The plan should give the rationale of the system and specify the steps to be taken in the development process, the costs involved, and the results to be expected.

PHASE II: DEVELOPMENT OF A PROTOTYPE SYSTEM

Work on the expert system begins in earnest as the knowledge engineer and the expert work together to create a prototype system. The prototype system is a small version of an expert system designed to test assumptions about how to encode the facts, relationships, and inference strategies of the expert. It also provides the knowledge engineer with an opportunity to engage the expert actively in the process of expert system development and, hence, to gain the expert's commitment to expend the considerable effort involved in developing a full-scale system.

The development of a prototype system includes the following activities:

- Learning about the domain and the task
- Specifying performance criteria
- Selecting an expert system building tool
- Developing an initial implementation
- Testing the implementation with case studies
- Developing a detailed design for a complete expert system

Table 12.1 Resources Required to Develop Knowledge-Based Expert Systems

Considerations:	Type of System		
	Small	Large	Very Large
Rules	50–350	500–3,000	10,000
Tool available	Probably	Probably	Maybe
Person-years to develop	$1/4$–$1/2$	1–2	3–5
Project cost	$40,000–$60,000	$500,000–$1 million	$2–$5 million

Note: included in costs: design, development, knowledge engineers, computing, overhead; excluded from costs: company expert, travel, fielding, transition.

Learning about the Domain and the Task

This phase begins with the knowledge engineer making an intensive effort to learn all he or she can about the domain and the task of the expert. Usually the knowledge engineer reviews documents and reads books to become familiar with the problem domain before beginning an extensive interaction with the expert. Once the knowledge engineer feels able to talk with the expert, he or she initiates a dialogue to define the task more precisely. At the same time, the knowledge engineer attempts to teach the expert to formulate his or her judgments in terms of heuristics and to elucidate his or her inference strategies.

The knowledge engineer usually asks the expert to identify four or five typical cases that the expert has solved. The expert assembles all the documentation associated with those cases. The knowledge engineer listens while the expert describes how he or she approached each case and provides a step-by-step protocol for developing a solution to each particular problem. The knowledge engineer will ask the expert to "think out loud" and to explain the reasoning processes behind each decision. In addition, the knowledge engineer may ask the expert to justify the reasoning that he or she used when dealing with particular problems.

When possible, the reasoning processes the expert uses will be reformulated into rules-of-thumb. This helps the knowledge engineer to clarify the expert's analytic activity. It also initiates the process of teaching the expert to formulate his or her thoughts into *if–then* rules. The examination of the expert's problem-solving procedure and the heuristics will lead the knowledge engineer to identify the facts and relationships that are particularly important to the expert's reasoning.

As the knowledge engineer learns about the expert's problem-solving strategies and heuristics, he or she will be thinking about how similar heuristics and strategies have been incorporated in other expert systems. The knowledge engineer will ask questions in order to classify the knowledge structures and the inference strategies into one of several broad categories that are well recognized by knowledge engineers.

Among the questions the knowledge engineer will ask are the following:

- Is knowledge sparse and insufficient or plentiful and redundant?
- Is there uncertainty attached to the facts and rules?
- Does interpretation depend on the occurrence of events over time?
- How is task information acquired or elicited?
- What classes or questions need to be asked to obtain the knowledge?
- Are facts reliable, accurate, precise (hard)? Or are they unreliable, inaccurate, or imprecise (soft)?
- Is knowledge consistent and complete for the problems to be solved?

Specifying Performance Criteria

In the process of determining exactly what the expert does, the knowledge engineer will begin to refine the performance criterion by which the prototype system is to be judged. The performance criterion should be specified in unequivocal terms. Perhaps the system will be expected to reach the same conclusions that the expert reached on five specific cases. Or perhaps the system will be expected to reach the same conclusions as five experts on five as-yet-unspecified cases, under the typical conditions that the experts experience. Whatever the criterion, it must be specified so that a test can be conducted that will prove the knowledge engineer has successfully completed his or her work.

At the same time, formulating a specific performance criterion will focus the knowledge engineer's attention on the precise nature of the initial conditions and the final output that the system will be expected to produce.

Selecting an Expert System Building Tool

As the knowledge engineer comes to understand the overall knowledge structure possessed by the expert and the inference strategies employed to manipulate the knowledge, he or she will decide which existing expert system tools will be used to develop a prototype system. The most important result of the prototyping exercise is ultimately a test of the adequacy of the chosen tool.

Developing an Initial Implementation

After choosing a tool, the knowledge engineer begins to develop a prototype version of the expert system as soon as the first case study is reasonably well understood. Subsequent cases are then tested, and as each case is run, the knowledge engineer and the expert observe the reasoning of the system. They discuss why rules are or are not working as expected. Consequently, the knowledge base is revised in accordance with their refined understanding of the knowledge, heuristics, and inference strategies.

Often the knowledge engineer will select a tool that matches the problem, and the prototype will be satisfactory, at least on the general level. The purpose of prototyping, however, is not to arrive at a final configuration for the expert system, but simply to establish that a tool, a representation of the expert's knowledge, and a strategy for drawing inferences are adequate to a task.

Testing the Implementation with Case Studies

Once the knowledge engineer has built a prototype, the knowledge engineer and the expert work together to see how the prototype functions on a variety of case studies. These tests serve two functions. They allow the knowledge engineer to determine whether the formalisms used in representing the expert's knowledge are adequate to the tasks posed by the cases. They also allow the expert to see how an expert system uses the information being provided. By taking an active part in testing the system, the expert usually becomes even more committed to the knowledge acquisition process. This is particularly critical, because in the next phase of the development the expert will be asked to interact with the system to tune its performance.

Developing a Detailed Design for a Complete Expert System

When the prototype is functioning satisfactorily, the expert and the knowledge engineer are in a good position to assess what will be involved in developing a full-scale system. If the original choice of objects and attributes is awkward, it must be modified. Estimates can be made about the total number of heuristic rules needed to create a complete expert system. Performance criteria can be stated with greater precision. All of this information, along with a plan, schedule, and budget, is included in a design document that will guide the development of the complete system.

PHASE III: DEVELOPMENT OF A COMPLETE EXPERT SYSTEM

After everyone is satisfied that the prototype system can perform as desired, and that the design for the complete system will result in an expert system that will meet the specified performance criterion, the knowledge engineer and the expert are ready to begin expansion of the prototype into a complete system. The development of a complete expert system includes the following activities:

- Implementing the core structure of the complete system
- Expanding the knowledge base
- Tailoring the user interface
- Monitoring the system's performance

Implementing the Core Structure of the Complete System

An adage popular among knowledge engineers is that it is usually best to throw away the prototype. Knowledge engineering tools support rapid prototyping with a low investment of time. Thus, at this stage it is common to rethink the basic design of the knowledge base. By this we do not mean that one abandons a particular tool. We mean that the exact list of *objects* and *attributes* to be included in the system will probably change somewhat. Hierarchical relationships may need to be rearranged. The exact way in which inference is handled in the heuristics may be modified as the expert and the knowledge engineer realize how the expert's knowledge and problem-solving strategies can be best represented.

Serious problems during the prototype phase may indicate that a different tool is needed. If so, the prototype phase must be repeated. Ordinarily, however, the prototype succeeds, but the initial representation of the rules and facts needs to be altered.

Consider an example. Imagine that we developed a prototype FACTORY MAINTENANCE ADVISOR structured around one central object: the manufacturing plant. Assume that the plant has several conveyor belts and several large compressor units of different types, each of which need to be maintained. In the initial prototype, the knowledge engineer and the expert may underestimate the advantages of keeping general information about the conveyors and the compressors on "intermediate objects" and instead try to make both the conveyors and the com-

pressors into attributes of the factory. As they work with the problem, however, the knowledge engineer and the expert may discover that the conveyors and compressors also need to be represented as objects. Figure 12.4 shows how an initial prototype design might be modified to more comfortably represent the importance of the conveyor belts.

As a result of prototyping, the knowledge engineer is in a good position to establish a basic framework for the complete expert system.

Expanding the Knowledge Base

The main work of the third phase is the addition of a very large number of additional heuristics. These heuristics typically increase the "depth" of the system by providing more rules for handling subtler aspects of particular cases. At the same time, the expert and the knowledge engineer may decide to increase the breadth of the system by incorporating rules that handle additional subproblems or additional aspects of the expert's task.

Figure 12.4 Prototype testing often reveals needed changes in the overall representation of objects and the hierarchical relationships among objects.

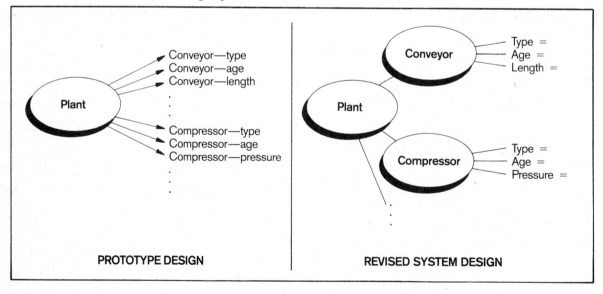

Tailoring the User Interface

Once the basic structure of the expert system is established, the knowledge engineer attends to the development and tailoring of the interface with which the system will actually deliver information to the user. Considerable attention is given to introducing phrases and explanations that will make it easy for the user to follow the logic of the system. The system should make it easy and natural for a user to inquire about any details he or she may desire. Graphic representations may be particularly helpful. Likewise, displays that allow the user to follow the system's reasoning process may be a key to "selling" the system to users.

Monitoring the System's Performance

A good tool provides a knowledge engineering interface that allows the expert to run cases to inspect the system's reasoning. The interface allows the expert to walk through a case asking why particular rules were fired or not fired, and thereby identifying those points in which additional, specific knowledge is needed to allow the system to reach the appropriate conclusion. By this point in the process, most experts have learned enough about the entry of rules that they can enter new rules into the system themselves. Thus, this is the beginning of the process during which the knowledge engineer begins to transfer the "ownership" and "control" of system to the expert to polish, elaborate, and ultimately maintain without the support of the knowledge engineer.

PHASE IV: EVALUATION OF THE SYSTEM

When the expert and the knowledge engineer are satisfied that the expert system is complete, the system should be tested against the performance criteria that were agreed upon at the conclusion of the prototyping phase. This is also the time when other experts are invited to try the system, and to present it with new cases.

PHASE V: INTEGRATION OF THE SYSTEM

The next phase in the expert system development process involves integrating the expert system into the work environment in which it will operate and providing training for those who will maintain the system.

By *integration* we mean all of those procedures necessary to make a new expert system work with existing systems within a company. We do not mean making signficant changes in the expert system. If, after the expert system is put in use, it is determined that major changes are necessary, then one must simply go back to the prototyping or development phase and make those changes. Such changes invariably involve a knowledge engineer or someone else who can change the code of the system. By integration we mean developing linkages between the expert system and the environment in which it operates.

The integration of an expert system is usually undertaken by the expert and systems personnel associated with the users of the system.

Activities during this phase might include:

- Arranging for technology transfer
- Interfacing the system with other data bases, instruments, or other hardware to enhance the speed or friendliness of the system

Arranging for Technology Transfer

When the expert system is ready, the knowledge engineer must assure that the experts, users, and systems personnel know how to use and maintain the system. Once the knowledge engineer has accomplished this transfer of information and technological know-how, he or she is ready to withdraw from the project, leaving the system in the hands of its users.

Every company environment will offer a different challenge to those who have the responsibility for preparing company personnel to accept and use an expert system. Experience to date seems to indicate the experts are quick to accept the system once they are convinced that the system will give useful advice. Convincing experts of the system's usefulness involves having each company expert present cases to the system and then see how the system performs. A critical aspect of acceptance is positioning the system as an aid to free experts from onerous tasks rather than a way of replacing experts.

Convincing nonexpert personnel to accept the system involves all of the problems and challenges associated with introducing any new system into a company environment. Success depends on careful planning, lots of communication, appropriate opportunities for all affected parties to talk about the change, and support once the system is in place.

Interfacing the System with Other Data Bases, Instruments, or Other Hardware

Other goals of an integration effort involve interfacing an expert system with existing data bases and other company systems. An expert system may need to acquire information from instruments or other hardware that will provide input to the system. Still other goals include enhancing time-dependent factors in the system to make the system run more quickly or more efficiently, enhancing the physical characteristics of the hardware if the system is to run in an unusual environment.

PUFF, the small pulmonary diagnosis system used at the Pacific Medical Center in San Francisco, is a nice example of a system that has been well integrated into its environment. After PUFF was completed and everyone was satisfied that it performed as it should, the system was recoded from LISP to BASIC. Once PUFF had been recoded, it was transferred to a PDP-11 computer that was already being used at the hospital. This computer, in turn, was connected to the pulmonary measurement instrument. Thus, as it now stands, a patient breathes into a pulmonary machine, the data from the pulmonary machine are fed directly into the minicomputer, and then PUFF processes the raw data and prints out a recommendation for the physician. The physician is not required to interact with PUFF at all. The system is fully integrated into its environment; it is simply an intelligent extension of the pulmonary machine that the doctors have been using for years.

Another system that has been integrated into its environment is General Electric's CATS-1 expert system for diagnosing diesel locomotive malfunctions. This system was initially developed in LISP and then translated into FORTH so that it could be run more efficiently in various locomotive shops. A repairman can interact with the system to determine probable causes of diesel malfunctions. The system is integrated with a videodisk and a video terminal to provide visual explanations for the repairman about particular checks he might need to make. In addition, if the operator is not sure how to fix a problem, the system will locate training materials that have been previously developed by the company and show them on the video terminal. Thus, the repairman can use the expert system to diagnose a problem, to verify the exact test procedure that he should use, to obtain a video display that explains how to make a test, or to obtain instruction related to the problem he is diagnosing.

PHASE VI: MAINTENANCE OF THE SYSTEM

When a system is translated into a language such as BASIC to facilitate speed and portability, the flexibility of the system is sacrificed. This is acceptable if the system has captured all of the knowledge in the task domain and if the knowledge is not going to change in the foreseeable future. If, however, an expert system has been designed precisely because the task domain is changing, the system may remain in its development environment to allow for ongoing maintenance activity.

A good example of an expert system that has been implemented in this manner is XCON, the expert system that Digital Equipment Corporation uses to configure new VAX computers. One of the key problems DEC faced was the continuing changes necessitated by new equipment releases, new specifications, etc. Thus, DEC keeps XCON in the OPS5 environment. There is an expert whose job involves adding new information and modifying rules in XCON's knowledge base to keep it current. The highly modularized nature of rule-based systems makes the weekly modification of XCON feasible and assures DEC that XCON's recommendations are always current.

In summary, the keys to building large knowledge systems are the knowledge engineer(s) and the choice of an appropriate problem. The knowledge engineer must understand how to work with one or more experts to identify and then formalize their knowledge and their inference strategies. The knowledge engineer must also understand the tools and programming environments available in order to select the right match between the knowledge and the implementation tool. In addition, the knowledge engineer must have the social skills to obtain the active support of the expert and ultimately of the users of the system. In most cases the task is more than one person can handle, and a team of knowledge engineers must be assembled. In addition, since few knowledge engineers have the breadth of experience to determine what problems a company should address first or the organizational insight to understand the politics of orchestrating a major organization transition, skillful project managers and outside consultants will be necessary for most companies attempting to develop their first large expert system. We hope that the knowledge engineering heuristics we have summarized in this chapter will help as well.

Section Four

THE EXPERT SYSTEMS MARKET

13.

The Market for Knowledge Engineering

In this chapter we consider how the market for knowledge engineering and knowledge systems products is likely to develop during the next five years. We present a broad overview of the sorts of problems and needs that will probably create the market and then discuss the sorts of companies that will seek to satisfy those needs. In Chapter 14 we speculate on some of the specific types of systems that will probably be developed in the next five years.

WHAT NEEDS WILL DRIVE THE KNOWLEDGE ENGINEERING MARKET?

At the moment there is no well-defined market for the products of knowledge engineering. Everyone senses, however, that there must be a market, simply because knowledge is so fundamental to modern societies. In an important sense, knowledge engineering is simply a natural extension of the already rapidly expanding demand for computer systems. All of the factors that have created a demand for larger and better computer systems can be extended to justify the development of computer systems that can process symbolic information. It is almost as if all of the problems and needs of modern society have combined to demand that knowledge engineering be created and implemented as soon as possible.

Some of the broad needs for the products of knowledge engineering can be summed up under the following headings:

- There is a need for new approaches to business organization and productivity.
- There is a need for expertise.
- There is a need for knowledge.
- There is a need for competence.
- There is a need for smart automated equipment.

The Need for New Approaches and Productivity

We can hardly read the newspapers or watch television without being told of the increased competition that our companies face from companies in other countries. We must increase our productivity or watch jobs migrate overseas. At the same time we must create new products to expand our trade. Moreover, competition among domestic companies is rapidly increasing. There are some 12,000 banks and savings and loan companies in the United States today. As government deregulation proceeds, these institutions are being forced to compete in ways they never have before. No one who has studied the financial services market expects all of those institutions to be around in five years. Several have failed in the last few years, and many more have merged. At the moment, executives of financial institutions are desperately searching for new ways to organize their companies, for new services to provide, and for new ways to reduce their operating costs. In all of these efforts the computer is playing a major role, and everyone expects it to play an even larger role in the next five years. The same story, with slight variations, could be told regarding our transportation industries, our heavy manufacturing industries, our auto manufacturers, and, ironically, our computer industries. There is a great need to reconceptualize how businesses can be organized to increase their productivity.

The Need for Expertise

One of the dominant trends in modern societies has been toward specialization. This trend has been just as pronounced in the professions and technical specialties as it has been in production operations. We don't go to physicians anymore, we go to clinics where several specialists take turns examining us. Moreover, if we really have a difficult problem, an outside specialist will probably be called in to consult with the clinic's resident specialist. For several years now, knowledge in most scientific areas has been growing exponentially. It takes from 10 to 15 years for an individual to master a specialty. Really good experts are in short supply in almost all areas. In most complex office or production operations, managers are quick to identify the one or two employees who really know how to do the job. They are the ones to whom everyone else turns when something goes wrong or when something really unusual occurs. As problems become increasingly complex, almost everyone would like to have more access to experts. There is a great demand for the advice of experts.

The Need for Knowledge

Leaving aside the desirability of having an expert available, decision making is becoming more complex all the time. Most managers wish they could have more information before they have to make an important decision. Indeed, most of us wish we could have more information before deciding on such increasingly complex things as what telephone system to use or what personal computer to purchase. We really don't want information, however, we want knowledge. We want information organized in a useful way. We don't want to have to wade through volumes of statistics, we want to be able to see at a glance what the critical components of the decision-making process are and know how to go about determining how our situation is affected by those components. It's not exactly expert knowledge we want, but it is certainly knowledge.

The Need for Competence

Products have become more numerous and more complex. All businesses are faced with the problem of training people to explain their products and options to customers. In addition, businesses have problems finding people to service or repair products. Complex products imply complex procedures. It isn't easy to remember to consistently check all of the components all of the time. Finding people who are sufficiently vigilant and consistently attentive is very hard. At the same time that the need for people to perform such tasks has multiplied, the overall education and entry-level skills of new workers have declined. Finding competent employees is difficult; providing consistently competent service is a real challenge.

The Need for Smart Automated Equipment

We increasingly share our environment with a host of machines, ranging from instruments and household appliances to computers, automated bank tellers, airplanes, and huge integrated systems such as power plants and chemical factories. At one extreme, we would like the small machines with which we share our homes and offices to be more friendly and less obtrusive. At the other extreme, we are increasingly concerned about our ability to monitor and control the complex machinery on which we increasingly depend. We would like to build smarter machines that would be easier and safer to use. We are already putting computer chips into our machines; what we need now is to be able to program those chips to make our machines perform in more intelligent ways.

HOW WILL THE KNOWLEDGE ENGINEERING MARKET BE ORGANIZED?

Given needs as broad as those we have described, it is hard to predict the specific ways in which knowledge engineering companies will organize to service such a potentially vast market. At the moment a three-tiered market, as shown in Figure 13.1, seems to be emerging. At the bottom are companies preparing to create and sell knowledge engineering hardware and software. Currently most of these companies are small entrepreneurial companies comprised of knowledge engineers who have left the universities in hopes of making their fortunes. A few large corporations are actively involved, however, and many more are waiting and watching on the sidelines. So far, companies developing LISP workstations and other knowledge engineering hardware are generally not developing knowledge system building software and vice versa, but that could change quite quickly as the early companies expand or consolidate.

On the second tier, the market is composed of a number of firms engaged in developing knowledge systems or consulting with others who are developing such systems. There are several small companies engaged in custom development work, and soon there will undoubtedly be a lot more. Some of these companies have identified specific "vertical" markets, such as financial services or nuclear power, whereas others are willing to consult or develop systems for any client who wants their services. Similarly, some of these companies are interested in developing and then marketing proprietary generic products, whereas others are quite willing to tailor systems for any client who will fund the development of a system. There are also a number of large corporations that have created

Figure 13.1 The knowledge engineer marketplace.

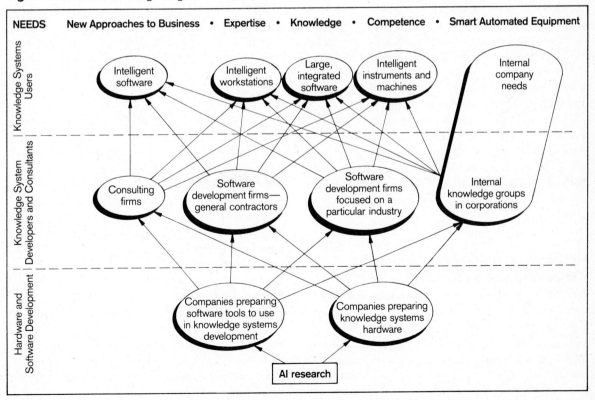

internal knowledge engineering groups. Predictably, many Fortune 1000 companies will soon join this group. Some of these large companies may develop systems for sale outside the company, but most are currently concentrating on developing proprietary knowledge systems to solve pressing internal problems.

At the third level we find companies and individuals who will sell knowledge systems to consumers, probably incorporated in a product. These companies may or may not stress the fact that their products incorporate artificial intelligence. Some companies will sell software packages to businesses or individuals. Such software will generally be marketed as software currently is; the stress will be on the benefits to be derived from the use of the software, not on the techniques used to make the software work. Some companies will specialize in combining hardware and software together into intelligent workstations. Others will specialize in integrating a large number of knowledge systems to control a complex operation such as a chemical plant or a nuclear reactor. Many existing manufacturing companies, ranging from auto manufacturers to scientific instrument manufacturers, will simply incorporate chips that contain knowledge systems into their existing line of products and stress that their products now offer new benefits.

Of course, some companies are already engaged in several of the marketing niches we just described; and as the market develops, a number of other specialties will undoubtedly develop. A few of the larger and more successful companies will gather several niches together to form larger, broad-based service companies.

HOW WILL BUSINESSES USE KNOWLEDGE SYSTEMS?

Another way to think about the knowledge engineering market is to ask how businesses will use knowledge engineering in the next five years. This is asking, in effect, what businesses will constitute the market for knowledge systems. A number of different ways of classifying the corporate need for knowledge

engineering have been proposed. Some have suggested that heavy manufacturing industries, faced with a desperate need to increase productivity, will invest heavily in knowledge systems. Others have argued that knowledge systems will be deployed more rapidly in the highly competitive service industries, such as banks and insurance companies, that depend on delivering complex advice to their clients. The market for knowledge systems is so new, however, and pressing needs seem to exist in so many industries, that it does not seem useful to focus on the particular industries that are most likely to deploy knowledge systems. Instead, we find it more useful to focus on those functions common to all companies that will be improved by means of knowledge systems. Table 13.1 provides an overview of the functional domains common to all companies and suggests some of the problems that will yield to knowledge engineering solutions in the next few years.

We have argued that knowledge systems are not so much a special type of system as a convenient approach to solving problems that are essentially symbolic in nature. Within the limits of the knowledge engineering approach, there are a number of different strategies one can use. These strategies represent extensions of existing computer strategies. When we consider the sort of problems that will yield to knowledge engineering solutions, we are, in effect, asking where difficult problems exist that are not currently being solved by means of existing software. Obviously, the best candidates will be problems that require a large amount of symbolic knowledge for their solution. We shall also focus on problems that currently require experts who use heuristics to generate several alternative solutions.

Senior Managers

Many of the problems facing senior managers are strong candidates for the application of knowledge engineering. A number of Fortune 500 corporations are already investing in development of knowledge-based systems to assist their executive officers. Sev-

Table 13.1 Overview of Knowledge Problems Common to Most Companies or Professionals

Domain	Problems

Senior management:
   Executive officers
   Senior managers
   Strategic planners
   Senior Staff
     Consultants
	Need to reduce organizational complexity
	Need to monitor an increasing volume of information
	Need to access experts and consultants for specific advice

Operations:
   Manufacturing services,
     complex equipment
     operation
   Energy exploration
   Quality control
   Inventory control
	Need to improve coordination of organization, scheduling, and management
	Need for overview of complex systems for rapid decision making
	Need to monitor/control complex equipment
	Need to anticipate results of complex, dynamic interactions

Support services:
   Public relations
   Legal
   Personnel and training
   Data processing services
   Building and maintenance
   Research and development
	Need to train/retrain lots of people to handle complex jobs
	Need to communicate new, complex procedures
	Need to examine/explain policy decisions/options
	Need to control/reduce costs of computer software development and maintenance

Finance:
   Portfolio managers
   Accounting
   Financial managers
   Auditing
   Controlling
	Need for overview of complex existing systems
	Need for smart, goal-directed financial planning tools

Marketing:
   Sales
   Advertising
   Marketing research
   Customer service
   Ordering
	Need for expert assistance in examining marketing questions
	Need for sales assistance programs that provide product knowledge and help configure proposals/packages

Office automation:
   Word processing
   Data management
	Need to increase productivity in handling, filing, communicating, retrieving, and distributing information in offices

Professional services:
   Management consulting
   Lawyers
   Physicians
   Accountants
	Need to monitor an increasing volume of information
	Need to access other experts and consultants for advice
	Need to submit "smart reports"
	Need to prototype and simulate knowledge systems rapidly without having to know about traditional computing

eral of these companies feel a strong need to reduce organizational complexity and to increase productivity. In many cases they also feel a seemingly contradictory need to increase the decision-making power of managers close to the action while simultaneously increasing the centralized control and monitoring abilities of senior corporate officers.

Many American companies are attempting to reduce their layers of middle managers. But this, in turn, means that some middle managers are being asked to be responsible for overseeing and controlling a vastly increased number of activities and subordinates. Expert systems will probably be developed to assist middle managers who are being asked to monitor a large and rapidly increasing volume of information. The systems will help gather and rearrange the information. Moreover, they will provide managers with tools that will help them explore the implications of various fast-breaking developments. Such managerial systems, probably packaged into managerial workstations, may begin to appear in large corporations within the next five years.

Over the past three decades, American approaches to management have emphasized gathering and processing more and more information in an effort to make more rational decisions. As more information is gathered more rapidly, however, managers are increasingly overwhelmed as they try to make sense of all the information available. In one sense the introduction of knowledge systems will probably accelerate this trend. More information will be assembled even faster. Knowledge systems, however, will be smart enough actually to help the manager digest the information. Systems will be developed that can sort through correspondence to identify significant issues. Other knowledge systems will automatically set up files, develop indexing systems, and perform a wide range of analysis and abstracting activities that will allow a manager to stay on top of more information in less time.

Senior managers also consume a lot of expert advice. They turn to consultants for specialized advice on many aspects of corporate management. In the near future, knowledge systems will provide senior managers with instant access to specialized, care-fully tailored advice in areas such as accounting, finance, strategic technology assessment, management technology, and government regulations.

The systems we have mentioned so far will probably run on large mainframes or on sophisticated personal workstations. We also expect that a large amount of software will be developed to run on the small personal computers that middle managers are now installing in their offices. There will undoubtedly be generic software on the order of VisiCalc or Lotus 1-2-3 that will help managers do projections and analyze problems. This new intelligent software, however, will be concerned with symbolic problem solving rather than numerical projections. One can easily imagine programs that help managers make personnel decisions, plan new product introductions, design training programs, or schedule complex productions runs.

In brief, managerial jobs are going to get more complex as corporations seek to make managers more effective and more productive. Simultaneously, however, managers are going to be provided with a wide range of smart programs that they will be able to consult for advice in handling problems that they can now solve only after consulting with peers or experts. They are also going to be supported by an array of smart information processing and summarizing systems that will allow them to digest more information more effectively. These smart management support systems will not come into being overnight, but they will certainly begin to appear in the next two or three years, and they will proliferate in the early 1990s.

Operations

The various operational groups within corporations, including manufacturing departments, service groups of various kinds, groups involved in the management of complex equipment or field operations (e.g., groups involved in exploring for minerals or resources) will be prime targets for early knowledge systems development efforts. A number of recent studies have indicated that the amount of increased productivity that can be obtained by changing work procedures or introducing robots in large production operations is really quite limited. These studies suggest that the only way American corporations will be able significantly to increase productivity will be by improving the overall coordination of their production, scheduling, and management systems. One example of such an improvement might be a "just-in-time" inventory delivery system. Such a system assumes that the organization that is manufacturing inventory items will be able to manufacture and deliver them to the plant where they are needed just as they are required by the production line. This approach eliminates the space and capital that would otherwise be tied up in a standing inventory. Just-in-time inventory management is used by several Japanese corporations with notable success, and is currently being implemented by American automobile manufacturers. The problem with the approach, of course, lies in coordinating the production and delivery of inventory with the operation of a large production line operation. A temporary slowdown in production must result in a quick reduction in a variety of inventory deliveries or chaos will result. This sort of coordination is exactly the type of problem that American companies will face as they seek to increase productivity in the remaining years of this decade.

Most large manufacturing operations are already supported by large computer systems of various kinds. One of the recurring problems these organizations face is training individuals to utilize the capacity of their existing systems. Many of the systems are so complex and offer so many options that users are literally overwhelmed with options and do not know how to use the system to obtain the results they want. Knowledge systems will help alleviate this type of problem by serving as "front-ends" to "stand between" the user and the larger computer package. The knowledge system will ask the user questions in ordinary language. The user will describe the problem as he or she understands it. The knowledge system will suggest how an individual should use or program the large, traditional computer package to solve the problem. See Figure 13.2 for an example of how a knowledge system can benefit a factory manager.

Knowledge systems will also be used to monitor and control complex equipment. In this case, the expert system will be replacing or assisting the expert operator or engineer who currently operates some complex system. IBM, for example, has developed an expert system called YES/MVS. Typically, control of a large computer system rests in the hands of a few operators who must not only monitor routine activities, such as mounting tapes, but must also tune the computer's operating system to assure that the computer's activities are running smoothly. MVS is the most widely used IBM mainframe operating system. During a peak period, MVS sometimes initiates some 100 operations per minute. When a potential problem is encountered, the operator must initiate queries and/or commands to diagnose the problem and initiate corrective action. YES/MVS monitors a number of functions and thereby frees computer operators to perform other tasks.

One of the six tasks that YES/MVS handles, for example, is control of the Job Entry System (JES) queue space. All batch jobs run under the MVS operating system are stored in a specific storage area, the JES queue space, before, during, and after execution. Before the creation of YES/MVS, an operator needed constantly to monitor the remaining available queue space. If the JES queue space is exhausted, the system will shut down. One of the six goals of the YES/MVS system is to keep 50 percent of a computer's JES queue space available at all times. The YES/MVS system constantly monitors an MVS system whenever it is running. When the level of remaining queue space becomes critically low, YES/MVS initiates actions to free additional space. It may force the printing of jobs that have finished execution, dump large print jobs to tape storage, or even order the system to refuse to accept any new jobs from other systems.

By the way of additional examples, several knowledge engineering groups are currently working on knowledge systems designed to monitor and control nuclear reactors. These systems will serve as assistants to the existing operators and will always be ready to provide suggestions regarding the operation of the plant. Systems to provide ongoing monitoring and control of large chemical plant operations are also being developed, and it is likely that most corporations will begin to develop or seek to acquire systems to monitor and control very complex operations within the next five to ten years.

Finally, as the pace of technological change increases and as organizations attempt to gain efficiency through the coordination of many different complex and dynamic operations, there will be a growing need for techniques that will facilitate the investigation of potential problems that might arise during previously untried interactions between various systems. Knowledge systems will probably be used to rapidly prototype complex simulations that will allow designers to explore more complicated interactions before attempting to integrate a new, complex operation.

Figure 13.2 This screen from a demonstration system developed by IntelliCorp with KEE illustrates how a factory manager can easily monitor a production operation. Inset gauges indicate the productivity of various conveyors. Using a "mouse," the manager can quickly change icons to ask "what if" questions and study alternative options.

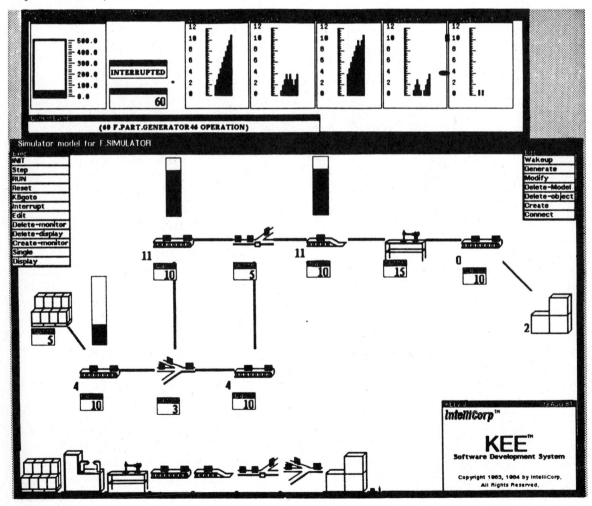

Support Services

We use "support services" to encompass a large variety of groups within an organization. They range from the legal department, public relations, and training and personnel services to computer services, construction, and building and maintenance operations. Research and development may also be included in this category. Knowledge systems will undoubtedly cause changes in each of these groups by providing expert advice for managers and staff professionals.

Knowledge engineering will have a major impact in the area of computer services, although there is considerable debate about what the exact nature of the impact will be. Some expect that existing data processing departments will use knowledge engineering techniques to solve new problems and to increase overall efficiency. Others think that existing computer operations will resist change and that the major effect of knowledge engineering will be to empower users to solve their own problems, just as personal computers and popular generic software have. In keeping with the overall outlook of this book, we believe that both things will occur.

Large-scale expert systems will aid data processing departments in tackling large problems. Exploratory programming techniques will be used to facilitate the rapid development of prototypes of new computer systems. This will allow programmers to check quickly how a new program might work. In addition, programming workstations equipped with various knowledge-based tools will significantly reduce the amount of time and effort that programmers will need to put into creating and maintaining conventional programs. Most companies face rapidly rising computer programming costs. They are stymied by the fact that about 75 percent of their programming budget is spent to maintain and update existing programs. Expert systems that provide automatic programming capabilities will increase the productivity of computer programmers. Automatic programming workstations will allow programmers rapidly to revise or update programs. They will facilitate the development of new programs. The military, for example, has recently contracted with a knowledge engineering firm

to develop a workstation to assist programmers in the use of Ada, the military's new standard programming language.

Existing programming shops are not going to change their practices overnight; the effect of knowledge engineering on the actual operation of data processing personnel will probably be a slow, evolutionary affair. On the other hand, we expect that managers will be much quicker to use small knowledge system building tools to solve numerous problems. They will use such tools to develop programs to run on personal computers. Moreover, since they will be able to maintain the programs they develop much more easily, many line operators will take responsibility for their own programming. In the long run, many functions that are currently controlled by data processing departments will become the concerns of line management, and many conventional programming functions will disappear.

Knowledge systems will also have a major impact on training and on the daily performance of numerous jobs. Most corporations need to train or retrain large numbers of people to handle complex new jobs. In addition, rapid changes in technologies and procedures mean that most companies also face constant need to document and communicate new procedures to personnel. In the next few years, the effectiveness and efficiency of these efforts will be significantly improved by the introduction of knowledge systems.

One can easily imagine that most of the procedures manuals now issued to employees will be replaced in the course of the next five to ten years by small- to medium-sized knowledge systems. Instead of looking up a problem in a manual, the employee will simply access the company mainframe or put a floppy disk in a personal computer and be interrogated by the system. The system will gather the information it needs and then suggest the exact procedure to use in dealing with the problem. The modularity of knowledge systems assures that a "smart procedures manual" can be quickly modified and updated as procedures change.

During the last few years, training developers have learned to make a sharp distinction between knowledge a performer needs to memorize and knowledge a person can access by means of a job aid or decision aid (see Table 13.2). It turns out to be relatively inexpensive to provide job aids. Teaching someone to memorize procedures, on the other hand, is both expensive and time-consuming. At the moment, the major limitation to the use of job aids is the amount and complexity of information that one can reasonably include on a job aid. Knowledge systems will allow training developers to replace most memorization with smart job aids.

Table 13.2 Performance Situations Requiring Job or Performance Aids

IF	THEN
Response speed is more important than accuracy	Memorize the response
The task is performed frequently	(e.g. through instruction or CAI)
Small errors won't have large consequences	
Reading instructions would interfere with performance	
Job prestige requires a memorized response	
IF	THEN
Response speed isn't as important as accuracy (small errors have large consequences)	Use job aids
Tasks are performed infrequently	
Reading instructions won't interfere with performance	
The task involves a complex decision-making process	

Using a knowledge system to construct a smart job aid or decision support system should not be confused with using computers for computer-aided instruction. Computer-aided instruction (CAI), in essence, is aimed at helping an individual memorize information that will be needed to perform a job. The performer studies CAI to learn how to perform the job. One uses a knowledge system while one is actually in the process of performing a job. The performer does not *learn* from the computer, he or she *consults* with the computer. The computer serves in place of the supervisor the individual would otherwise consult. The computer asks questions, processes information, and then suggests appropriate responses. In short, small knowledge systems that help employees make decisions will become commonplace. They will significantly decrease training costs while simultaneously improving the quality of employee decisions and actions.

Another area in which knowledge systems will be used is personnel relations. Here, again, the systems will serve as a specialized type of job aid or decision support system. The systems will help managers make decisions that involve people. Thus, for example, one can imagine a system that has all of the personnel policies and government regulations in it. A manager could "discuss" his or her particular case with a "Personnel Advisor." The system would ask appropriate questions and then prescribe an action that conforms with both company policies and legal requirements. There would rarely be a simple answer, so the "Personnel Advisor" would probably suggest several courses of action, rating each as to its overall likelihood of success and acceptability.

Finance

Expert systems will also be used in financial management and accounting sections. In these departments, expert systems will initially be used to provide advice that decision makers would otherwise seek from a human consultant. A portfolio management system, for instance, might present a controller with the insights of a number of experts on a particular set of portfolio management problems. Likewise, a knowledge-based system might interact directly with a company's computer to analyze its software accounting system. Thus, instead of using an outside computer auditing expert, the accounting group would simply have its "Computer Auditing Program" interrogate its computer program and provide a description of exactly how the company's accounting program handles various accounting functions.

Marketing

Marketing, sales, advertising, and market research will undoubtedly find many uses for knowledge systems. Marketing and market research are constantly asking "what if" questions as they seek to explore various options. Expert systems will allow marketing planners to explore their positioning options in much the same way that a VisiCalc program allows accountants to explore financial "what if" questions.

The ability to prototype models of new products rapidly will also be of great use to marketing people. It will allow them, for example, to program a system with the features and benefits of a new product. Then the system will help them anticipate the questions that customers will probably ask.

Knowledge systems will also provide product knowledge information and assistance in the configuration or packaging of complex products. In effect, DEC's XSEL program is already performing this service for DEC's computer sales force. Future expert systems will help bank loan officers analyze what bank services might be appropriate for a particular client and suggest how the bank might package a collection of services to provide the client with the best possible service while simultaneously assuring that the bank would earn an appropriate profit.

Knowledge systems will allow new salespeople to provide customers with the answers and recommendations that only today's best-trained and most experienced salespeople can provide.

Office Automation

Computers are already driving the office automation revolution. Most executives recognize that their companies need to increase productivity in the handling, filing, retrieving, and distribution of information. The immediate impact of knowledge systems in this area will probably take the form of software that will help managers deal more quickly with communications, sort information, and identify needed infor-

mation. Systems such as IBM's Epistle system will help organize a manager's correspondence.

The major impact of knowledge systems in offices, however, will probably occur only after versatile spoken natural language interfaces are developed. This probably will not happen in the next five years. In the early 1990s, however, "intelligent typewriters" that type as a manager speaks into a microphone will become a reality. Likewise, workstations will be developed that can perform numerous intelligent functions in response to spoken orders.

Professionals

Expert systems will also affect the way professionals perform. Professionals have all the problems that executives have. They often need to consult with more specialized experts. They need help in staying abreast of a rapidly increasing technical literature. And they need to maintain a large number of professional contacts.

Knowledge systems will assist professionals by providing expert advice in various specialized areas. Karl Wiig, Director of Arthur D. Little's Artificial Intelligence Program, argues that knowledge systems will allow professionals to deliver "smart reports" to their clients. Thus, for example, a marketing consultant might develop a study of the marketing potential for a product and deliver both a written report and a floppy disk. The disk would contain a knowledge system that includes all the rules and assumptions the consultant made during the study. The client would be able to put the floppy disk into a personal computer and review the assumptions. Thus, the client could ask "how" and "why" questions to see exactly how the consultant arrived at his or her conclusions. The client could easily change some of the assumptions to explore how various alternatives would affect the outcome of the study. Thus, consultants would not only provide clients with recommendations, they would provide the client with a whole context or environment in which to think about a problem.

Professionals themselves, of course, are experts. Some professionals will undoubtedly become interested in developing knowledge systems that will package their expertise for others. In some cases, professionals will work with knowledge engineers to develop large, sophisticated expert systems that will be sold to specific clients. Others will develop smaller, more generic software that will be sold to a broad market.

In the process of trying to develop a knowledge system, an expert is forced to think about what he or she does in a particularly rigorous way. Even when the system development process fails, experts usually come away from the process feeling that they understand what they know and what they do not know much more clearly than they did when they started. Thus, the use of a knowledge system to prototype a consultation forces the expert to explore his or her own knowledge and to learn just what facts, rules, and inference strategies are really necessary to reach a desired recommendation. In the 1990s we expect that experts and professionals will routinely use knowledge system building tools to refine and improve their own expertise. Professional schools will probably use knowledge systems to train new students, and accomplished professionals will probably vie to add rules to the more prestigious systems, just as professionals are now honored to author a chapter in a prestigious handbook.

The Home Market
By the late 1980s, knowledge systems will undoubtedly be popular in the home computing market. Knowledge systems can be packaged into small generic software programs. Thus, just as individuals can now use a conventionally programmed system to provide budgeting projections, they will be able to buy expert systems that will give them much more sophisticated advice about cash management, nutrition, or emergency first aid.

In addition, some individuals will use knowledge system techniques to develop intelligent games that can keep track of what individual players are doing and change the game in challenging ways. The ability of expert systems to create and synthesize will probably also be used to develop software that will allow personal computers to generate stories, or to

animate sequences. In short, intelligent software will increasingly allow people to create individualized entertainment simply by prompting a knowledge system to elaborate on the initial ideas the user provides.

As one can readily see by reviewing the various uses we have suggested for expert systems, we do not believe that expert systems will be limited to any particular group of users. To date, most knowledge systems have been designed for experts. MYCIN, for example, uses technical language that only a practicing physician would understand. In this sense, MYCIN is an expert system designed to be used by another expert. Expert systems can just as easily be developed to help novices or ordinary practitioners. We expect that interfaces will be developed to allow different individuals to deal with knowledge systems. Designers will simply have to identify the individuals who will use the systems and write the rules and questions and design the graphics to assure that they will communicate with targeted users.

THE MACROENVIRONMENT
In the previous section, we discussed some of the problems faced by large companies that knowledge systems can help solve. The creation and utilization of all of the products we have described depends on a large number of political and economic considerations that are quite outside the realm of technological possibilities or business needs. Many of today's knowledge systems companies are small, entrepreneurial companies. Thus, they depend on an environment in which interest rates are not excessive, money is available for investment, and there is a positive attitude about the near future. Likewise, large corporations must be confident and willing to invest in new technology if their current interest in expert systems is to flourish. A recession in the next few years would probably delay many of our projections. By the same token, continued rapid economic recovery through 1985–1986 should accelerate the pattern that we have projected. No one can foresee all the political and macroeconomic events that will

shape the remainder of the 1980s. No matter what happens, however, knowledge systems will continue to be developed and improved. It is really just a matter of how quickly they will find their way into widespread use.

There are some large-scale efforts underway that should encourage the overall development of expert systems, no matter what happens to the domestic economy. The best-known large-scale undertaking in the support of expert systems technology is Japan's Fifth-Generation computer project, announced by the Japanese government in 1981. The effort is supported partially by the Japanese government and partially by private Japanese companies (see Figure 13.3). The Japanese have budgeted some $500 million to be spent on this project between 1982 and 1991. They anticipate that from 1982 to the end of 1984 they will be doing exploratory research. From 1985 to the end of 1988 they will be doing prototype development, and, beginning in 1989, they will undertake significant commercialization efforts. The two major software goals of the Fifth-Generation project are VLSI design tools and automatic program-

ming. These are ambitious goals, which may or may not be accomplished. The fact that the Japanese government and a number of major Japanese corporations are willing to put a significant amount of money and effort into the development of the hardware and the software to support these goals, however, will constitute a major driving force that will encourage the development of expert systems.

In response to the Japanese effort, IBM has set up several groups to investigate the potential of knowledge systems technology. Moreover, IBM's major competitors have created and funded a joint research company called Microelectronics Computer Technology Corporation (MCC). MCC intends to undertake basic research in hardware and software development and will thus more or less compete with both IBM and Japan's Fifth-Generation project. MCC's results, in turn, will be used by a number of Fortune 500 computer companies and will thus serve to drive knowledge systems development in many corporations during the next six to ten years.

The European Common Market countries have also set up a program, called ESPRIT (European

Figure 13.3 Japan's Fifth-Generation computer project.

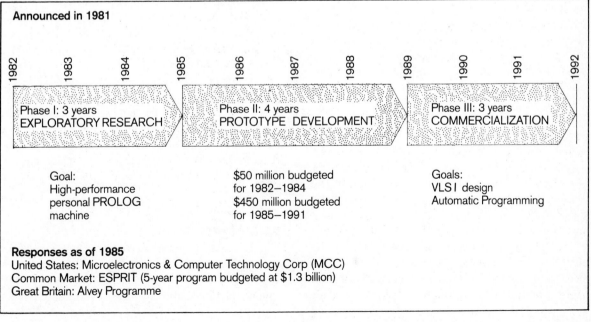

Strategic Program for Research and Development in Information Technology). This five-year research and development effort is budgeted at $1.3 billion. It is designed to compete with both the United States and Japan. ESPRIT will undertake several new computer hardware and software research projects, including a major effort in knowledge systems development. Independently, Great Britain has established the Alvey Programme to stimulate and coordinate the development of advanced information technology. One of Alvey's goals is the development of intelligent knowledge-based systems.

In addition to these large-scale research and development programs, several agencies of the U.S. government are heavily involved in artificial intelligence and expert systems. The Defense Department's DARPA (Defense Advanced Research Project Agency) has recently announced a Strategic Computing program on which it proposes to spend some $600 million over the next five years. In fiscal 1984 they allocated $50 million, the majority to be spent on three different projects. Two of these projects involve robotics. The third project involves developing a "smart procedures manual" to be used with the Army's new M-1 tank. This smart procedures manual is, in effect, a knowledge system that will replace the 61,000-page procedures manual that currently accompanies the tank. It will interrogate tank operators and repair personnel to diagnose problems and prescribe repair procedures. Several other Defense agencies are also budgeting money for expert systems research.

A number of other government agencies are also very interested in artificial intelligence. The National Institutes of Health, for example, have been supporting research in expert systems for medicine for some time. The NIH recently announced the BIONET project, designed to provide networking capabilities for people involved in research in molecular genetics. A contract for $5.6 million was given to IntelliCorp to create and run BIONET over the next five years. Likewise, Arthur D. Little, Inc., has been consulting with the Environmental Protection Agency regarding the possibility of developing expert systems to provide assistance in certain types of environmental crises.

CAPITALIZATION OF AI

It is very difficult to determine just what amount of money is currently being spent on AI research, in general, or on expert systems in particular. Nor is it easy to project how much money will be spent in the near future. In July 1984, *Business Week* suggested that venture capitalists have injected more than $100 million into some 40 small companies involved in various efforts to commercialize AI. The same article noted that more than 30 of the largest U.S. corporations now have hefty research efforts underway, and that new companies are joining in every day. General Motors, for example, recently spent $3 million for a 13-percent equity protection in one start-up company. Another study suggested that expert systems companies earned from $2 to $5 million in 1983, and estimated that their revenues would reach $30 to $40 million by 1987. A recent report by Digital Equipment Corporation estimated that $150 million was being spent on AI research and development in 1984, and that $2.5 billion would be spent for AI technology and expert systems by 1990. DEC noted that of that $2.5 billion, only 5 percent would be for research; most would be for specific applications. DEC's report also estimated that 50 of the Fortune 500 companies currently have some sort of AI development group. They further estimated that within 10 years, more than 80 percent of the Fortune 500 companies would be actively engaged in AI. These figures are only guesses, but everyone seems to agree that AI and expert systems will be major growth industries through the 1980s and 1990s.

SUMMARY

The commercialization of AI technology is moving very fast. The introduction of several sophisticated IBM PC-based expert system building tools in the summer of 1984 came as a surprise to most observers who had assumed, only months earlier, that an expert system building tool operating on an IBM PC was at least three or four years off. The introduction of PC-based tools will significantly expand the number of individuals and companies who can begin to experiment with expert systems. As new people learn what these systems can do, this, in turn, will accelerate the demand for still more sophisticated expert system building tools. Moreover, the existence of PC-based system building tools will facilitate the development of smart generic software. This, in turn, will introduce managers at all levels to the possibility of using knowledge-based decision support systems to perform a wide variety of jobs. It will also result in a demand for additional, large-scale expert systems to solve a variety of business problems.

The estimates we have made in this chapter are conservative. The expansion of the technology in the next five years will be explosive. By 1990, expert systems will be in general use in a large number of companies, and, in the early 1990s, most large- and middle-sized companies will find it necessary to acquire and use knowledge-based systems simply to remain competitive.

14.
Knowledge Systems in the Next Five Years

This chapter considers the types of knowledge systems that will probably become commercially available in the next five years. To simplify what could otherwise be a very confusing survey, we divide knowledge systems into three generic types. We also subdivide the market and then speculate about how the two may interact.

TYPES OF COMPANIES

In the last chapter we argued that knowledge is so important that it makes more sense to focus on how divisions within companies can use knowledge systems rather than on the types of companies that may use expert systems. In this chapter we continue that approach by dividing companies into three broad generic types according to their response to new technologies. We call our three generic types *cutting-edge companies*, *advanced companies*, and *normal companies*. Obviously, companies may fall into different categories depending on the technology being considered. Moreover, some companies pursue the newest technologies as a matter of strategy. Others, generally in high-tech markets, pursue the newest technologies simply because they must to survive. Likewise, most companies are "normal" simply because their margins are narrow and their current procedures are producing results; thus, they pursue new technologies only when they must. We are not suggesting that it is good or bad to be a cutting-edge or a normal company; that depends entirely on the situation of the specific company. We use this dichotomy only to suggest how quickly expert systems technology will move from the research labs of large, high-tech companies into the ordinary offices and factories of the great majority of normal companies.

When we use the term *cutting-edge companies*, we are referring to companies that are willing to investigate a new technology as soon as it leaves the university laboratories. Cutting-edge companies understand that in acquiring a new technology as soon as it is introduced, they run considerable risks. They know they will have to invest considerable amounts of money and professional expertise in the development of the technology. In fact, they expect that they will have to develop major parts of the technology for themselves.

Cutting-edge companies are already developing expert systems. Most of them have already set up AI groups and are well along with the development of several prototype systems.

Advanced companies are not interested in adapting a technology until it has proven itself. They are not willing to try a completely new technology. They do not want to have to develop the technology. They are, however, very eager to acquire a new technology as soon as it begins to show promise. These companies want to stay ahead of other companies; but they do not want or cannot afford to expose themselves to the high risks involved in investigating a technology that is still in the research stage.

Advanced companies are just now beginning to pay attention to AI. Some have begun to move quickly to determine which expert systems techniques are sufficiently developed that they can begin to apply them to their needs.

We call our third type of companies *normal companies*. We imply no disrespect; the great majority of companies are "normal" and wisely so. Most companies are organized to do what they do well, are making a reasonable profit, and will want to invest in a new technology only when it shows itself to be a necessity. Normal companies will adopt a new technology when they have to. By the time these companies adopt a technology, their competitors are also acquiring it and they move because they realize that they will soon be at a competitive disadvantage if they do not. These companies are not currently considering the use of expert systems. Most will not invest in large expert systems until the early 1990s, when they will buy ready-to-use software packages. They will probably begin to acquire some small knowledge systems in the next five years, however.

To understand this three-tiered distinction better, consider office automation. Fifteen years ago, a few cutting-edge companies were experimenting with ways to automate their offices. They were building experimental systems, buying hardware, developing some of their own software, and assembling their own systems. Some of these companies developed valuable office automation techniques. Several took a significant lead in office automation and are now selling that technology to others. Some spent a lot of money and did not get too much in the way of practical results. About eight years ago, advanced companies realized that office automation equipment and the associated technologies had reached the point at which they should invest. These companies moved quickly to set up automation systems that have proven themselves quite useful. Over the last several years, most Fortune 500 companies have committed themselves to office automation. Office automation has now proven itself. Large corporations are using it so effectively that all large- and most medium-sized companies are now being forced to move into office automation. If they do not, their costs and inefficiencies will increasingly place them at a competitive disadvantage. In other words, normal companies are now moving into office automation. Those who cannot afford to automate will be among the companies that fail during the late 1980s.

TYPES OF SYSTEMS

In Chapter 8, when we discussed commercially available system building tools, we divided the tools into three general types: (1) small tools, (2) large, narrow tools, and (3) large, hybrid tools. In this chapter we shall extend this analysis to the knowledge systems themselves, whether built with tools or from scratch. In addition to these three generic types of systems, we shall also discuss workstations, which cluster several knowledge systems together in a personal computer, and nonsystems applications of knowledge engineering concepts. Figure 14.1 shows a continuum that extends from large-scale systems on the left through small-scale systems into applications that derive their techniques from the knowledge engineering effort without necessarily resulting in knowledge systems. Packaging strategies, some tools, and some typical systems are indicated to explain the range better.

LARGE, HYBRID SYSTEMS

At the left end of the continuum in Figure 14.1 are the large, hybrid systems. In general, these systems will be built by means of hybrid system building tools such as KEE or ART, though many will be built in environments such as INTERLISP and PROLOG. These systems will incorporate a number of knowledge representation and inference strategies. The ideal tool for building such a system will allow the designer to simulate almost any kind of consultation situation. Such a tool, for example, might allow one to do forward or backward chaining and to represent a knowledge base as either frames or production rules. The tool would also probably support some type of blackboard architecture and, thus, permit several knowledge bases to cooperate in analyzing a specific

Figure 14.1 A range of expert systems applications to expect in the 1980s.

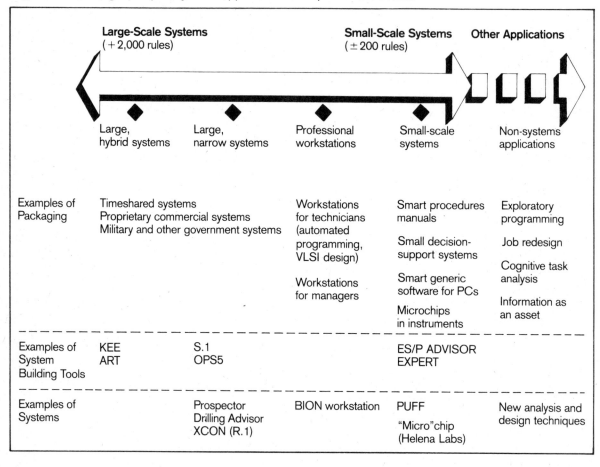

	Large-Scale Systems (+2,000 rules)		Small-Scale Systems (±200 rules)	Other Applications
	Large, hybrid systems	Large, narrow systems	Professional workstations	Small-scale systems	Non-systems applications
Examples of Packaging	Timeshared systems Proprietary commercial systems Military and other government systems		Workstations for technicians (automated programming, VLSI design) Workstations for managers	Smart procedures manuals Small decision-support systems Smart generic software for PCs Microchips in instruments	Exploratory programming Job redesign Cognitive task analysis Information as an asset
Examples of System Building Tools	KEE ART	S.1 OPS5		ES/P ADVISOR EXPERT	
Examples of Systems		Prospector Drilling Advisor XCON (R.1)	BION workstation	PUFF "Micro"chip (Helena Labs)	New analysis and design techniques

case. It would also allow the designer to create an elaborate graphics interface with dynamic representations. It would, in short, be a tool one could confidently reach for, no matter what sort of knowledge engineering problem one faced. It would be a tool that large corporations or government agencies could use to build a new system in an area with a great deal of complexity. These sorts of systems are difficult to build; they are mostly in the research stage at this time. Prototype tools of this sort are available today. IntelliCorp's KEE system and Inference Corporation's ART are both examples of tools designed to build large, hybrid systems. Each of these tools approximates the ideal, but neither of them can do all that a

commercially viable, large-scale hybrid tool will be able to do in a few years.

Figure 14.2 illustrates our estimate of the rate of market penetration that large, hybrid systems will achieve in the next 10 years. The horizontal axis indicates time. On the vertical axis we have indicated the type of company that will probably be using most of the large, hybrid systems during any given period of time. Thus, one can see by looking at Figure 14.2 that only cutting-edge companies are experimenting with large, hybrid systems at this time. Moreover, we expect that this will continue to be the case until very late in the 1980s, when we expect that some advanced companies will begin to develop large, hybrid systems. We do not expect to see large, hybrid systems in use in normal companies until about 1995.

At the moment, and probably well into the foreseeable future, the use of large, hybrid system building tools implies the availability of knowledge engineers with considerable knowledge of the language in which the tool is built. In the case of KEE or ART, this implies a knowledge of INTERLISP. The limited number of senior knowledge engineers, in itself, is sufficient reason to assume that this type of system will be limited to cutting-edge companies for the next several years.

LARGE, NARROW SYSTEMS

When we speak of large, narrow systems, we are speaking of expert systems that have been built using tools that facilitate the use of one or a few specific consultation paradigms. EMYCIN is a good example of a narrow system building tool. It allows its user to build backward-chaining production rule systems. Narrow system building tools are specialized to make it easy to build large, narrow systems. The tool creates a sophisticated programming environment for the development of a system based on a specific paradigm. The knowledge engineer who uses such a system may need some background in LISP, but he or she need not know anywhere near as much as a knowledge engineer who is trying to use a large-scale, hybrid systems building tool. Moreover, at least in the case of tools designed to assist designers in the development of systems built around the diagnosis/prescription paradigm, there have been enough other expert systems built with tools utilizing a similar approach that a large research literature on the use of such tools already exists. New knowledge engineers or programmers without extensive knowledge engineering experience should be able to come up to speed on such tools in a short time.

Figure 14.3 indicates the market penetration pattern we expect for large, narrow knowledge systems. These systems are already in use in cutting-edge companies and are currently being studied by advanced companies. As additional tools become available for other specialized uses, and as the tools become more user-friendly, we expect to see a number of large, narrow systems in advanced companies. We expect that large, narrow systems will be in general use in normal companies by the mid-1990s.

Figure 14.2 Projected market impact of large-scale, hybrid expert systems and tools. The band indicates "where the action will be" during the next 10 years.

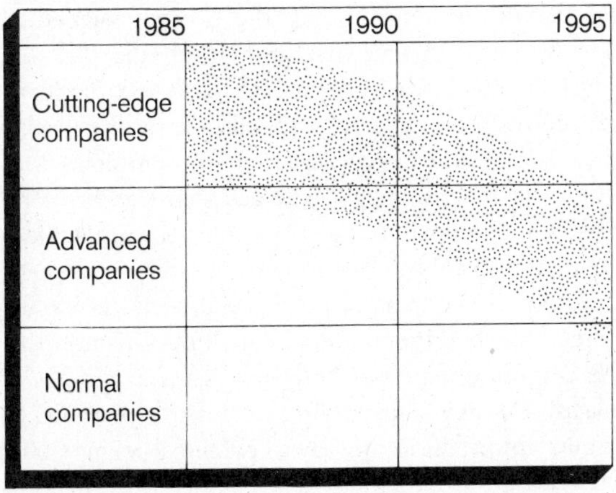

Figure 14.3 Projected market impact of large-scale, narrow expert systems and tools.

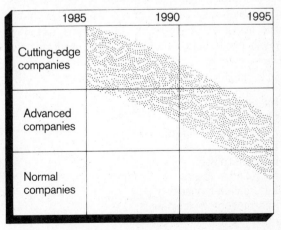

PROFESSIONAL WORKSTATIONS

In the middle range of the continuum on Figure 14.1 are professional workstations. When we speak of a professional workstation, we are referring to a personal computer available to a manager or technician who will use that computer to do a considerable portion of his or her work. There are some professional workstations already in place; for example, large banks have operation centers where each individual in the center sits at a console with one or more computers and is able to track prices of monies or stocks, volumes of funds the bank has to trade, or other data the bank wants to monitor. The individual at the console is able to conduct trading operations using information available at the workstation. These existing workstations use traditional computer systems and are largely oriented toward numerical operations. The workstations of the future will enable senior executives and department managers to control their operations in a similar manner.

Imagine this scene from the future. Susan King, the manager of a major chemical plant, comes to work one day in the spring of 1989. Susan's office looks like a typical office, except that her desk has an intelligent workstation. This workstation looks like a large IBM Personal Computer. The screen is about 16 inches by 16 inches, and there is a "mouse" that Susan uses to move the cursor around the screen. In other words, the workstation looks a lot like the Xerox Star system; its software, however, is a lot more sophisticated. Susan gets her first cup of coffee, sits down, and turns on her workstation. She moves the mouse to an agenda graphic, and a "window" opens on her screen that displays the chief functions for which she is responsible. The following list of items might appear on her screen:

Master schedule
Ceremonial tasks
Public relations tasks
Leadership tasks
Outside liaison
Negotiation tasks
Information monitoring
Information dissemination
Planning/controlling changes

Resource allocation
Disturbances/problems

This list provides Susan with an overview of the different responsibilities she has. Under each item on this list, Susan has stored information relating to that function. Likewise, under each item, there are knowledge systems available to advise her on any special problems she may encounter. Susan moves the mouse quickly and opens her "Master schedule" window to see what her schedule looks like. She can choose to view her schedule for the day, the week, the month, or the next six months. She can also choose to look at titles or expand specific titles to show more detail. Susan skims through her schedule to see what needs to be accomplished today. Her highest priority is to oversee the installation of the new chemical processing unit in factory 6. She moves the cursor to "Information monitoring." In this window she finds that the installation schedule is behind in two particulars. An expert monitoring system has been set to gather data automatically from the company's mainframe and to prepare a report for her each morning. By moving the mouse and opening another window, Susan obtains a general map of the installation, which shows the areas that are complete and those that are being worked on at the moment. Another move of the cursor opens a window that allows Susan to check the PERT chart illustrating the sequence of events that must take place during the next two days if the installation is to stay on schedule. Susan quickly identifies the people assigned to each of the particulars that are behind schedule, and sends an electronic message to each asking for a personal report. She asks specifically if the Friday goals can be met, and points out the problems that will result from slippage. Satisfied that she has done what she can until she gets the reports, Susan slides the mouse to another section of the screen and opens a window on competitors. This file has an expert system attached that automatically not only monitors the corporate data base, but also scans a number of magazines, newspapers, and technical journals to obtain information on rival chemical companies. This scanning operation is constantly feeding new information about both technology and competition into Susan's file. Susan notes that her file already contains information about Company X's decision to construct a new plant in a nearby state. She had just heard that information during a telephone conversation she had yesterday and wanted to be sure the data was on-line.

Susan has an expert system on Strategic Assessment that allows her to evaluate the likely impact of this new plant. She asks the system to examine the economic impact the opening of this plant is likely to have on her projections for the unit she has under construction. If her Advisor suggests that the competitor's new plant will have a significant impact on her projections, she will transfer that information to her Budgeting and Financial Planning Advisor and then examine the financial implications in a great deal of detail. If necessary, she may contact other managers within the company to decide if this move by the competition calls for a change in their plans.

The problem of skimming technical literature, which occupies so much of the time of so many managers today, has been largely automated for Susan. She needs only to skim titles to decide what amount of detail she needs.

Susan's workstation also contains a series of files on correspondence. Unlike a correspondence file organized by date or some topic, Susan's correspondence file is constantly reindexing and cross-referencing itself. Thus, Susan can pick a particular topic and quickly find out what correspondence has been sent or received, who sent or received it, what messages were sent or received by way of the computer network, who has sent memos to whom, what general company policies have been issued on the subject, etc. She can quickly review any particular area of interest and delve into whatever amount of detail she needs.

Susan also has a number of generic decision support systems available to her. Thus, for example, if she notices that she is having a problem with construction personnel on weekends, she can consult her Personnel Advisor. This knowledge system begins by asking her to describe the problem she seems to be having with the construction project personnel. The system, as expert systems will, asks her questions about the specific manifestations of the problem, and then proceeds to ask her about other variables that might influence her decision. The system applies various rules and procedures established by the personnel department; labor union contracts; local, state, and federal legislation; and so forth. The Personnel Advisor helps Susan explore the options she really has. Some of these options are obvious, but several are quite creative options that reflect the best ideas of current management theorists and psychologists. The Personnel Advisor suggests that Susan consult with the Coaching Advisor. This program helps Susan plan a meeting with the individuals involved in the problem. It offers suggestions about how to deal with each individual in the light of recent developments and past history.

All of this is not to suggest that the manager of the near future will no longer leave her office and talk to other people. Human contact will be more important than ever because, although there will be fewer people working on particular projects, it will be very important for each individual to be attuned to others' goals, aims, and feelings about the projects. Since each individual will be able to act so quickly, it will be very important that they share common goals.

Electronic mail services and bulletin board networking will allow people to stay in contact on the intellectual level, but interpersonal contact will also be important and will be structured by people skilled in facilitating meetings and team building. The manager of the future, with a workstation like the one we have described, will have the power of a manager of today who has a large, trained staff of several dozen assistants, all constantly available to help with any problem that may arise. Using such workstations, individual managers will be able to gather and evaluate vast amounts of information. They will be able to make better decisions and will be able to promulgate those decisions much more quickly.

The availability and use of such workstations depend on creating a number of small knowledge systems and then making them all work together. The overall operating system of a professional workstation will necessarily be a hybrid system, and so in Figure

14.1 we indicate that KEE is a type of tool that one would consider if one were trying to design such a workstation. The BION workstation, developed by IntelliCorp, is, in a sense, a prototype of the sort of workstation that we are referring to. Arthur D. Little is already working with several clients to develop workstations using the KEE system.

Significant penetration of intelligent professional workstations into the business environment will depend on the availability of high-quality knowledge systems that can be assembled into a full workstation configuration. Depending on the job, the expert systems in the workstation may be very large. Susan, our hypothetical chemical plant manager, for example, would need a large expert system to simulate the operation of her plant. Many expert systems that will go into workstations, however, will be smaller systems designed to handle more specialized functions, such as correspondence, personnel matters, and memo writing. We expect that workstation penetration will match or lag slightly behind the penetration of large, narrow systems.

SMALL, SPECIALIZED SYSTEMS

When we speak of small systems, we refer to expert systems with from 100 to 500 rules. Such systems can be run on personal computers and might be called intelligent decision aids. They are knowledge-based systems designed to help individuals deal with small but nasty problems. In some cases, these problems require knowledge engineering techniques because they are not easily amenable to traditional solutions. In other cases, the problems are simply ones that users understand and want to solve. Users may not understand the traditional programming techniques that would be required to solve these problems, but they will be able to turn to knowledge-based approaches simply because of the user-friendly interface and the rapid prototyping features that are available.

Figure 14.4 indicates that we expect that small systems will be developed by most advanced companies during the coming years, and that by 1990 these systems will be in daily use by normal com-

panies. One use of small systems that will be widespread, for example, will be intelligent procedures manuals.

Consider this scenario: A bank will send wire telegrams for its customers. Most customers do not know about this service and rarely use it. The large, downtown banks have people familiar with the bank's telegraph operations, because large businesses tend to send large numbers of telegrams. Such individuals can help customers fill out the proper forms necessary to send telegrams. If you walk into a suburban branch and ask to send a telegram, however, no one in the branch is likely to be familiar with the procedure for sending a telegram. Usually, the senior operations person in the branch will go and get a three-ring binder—a manual on how to send telegrams—and will leaf through the manual while talking to you. Normally, the person will find the right section and follow the directions that tell how to fill out the necessary form. People in training and instructional design have spent quite a bit of time developing manuals of this kind, and they are reasonably easy to use; but, at the same time, if the individual is not familiar with telegrams and there is a customer standing there waiting, it takes a long while for the bank employee to figure out exactly what needs to be done. It is not an efficient operation. The information in the telegram manual is essentially procedural infor-

Figure 14.4 Projected market impact of small, specialized knowledge systems and tools.

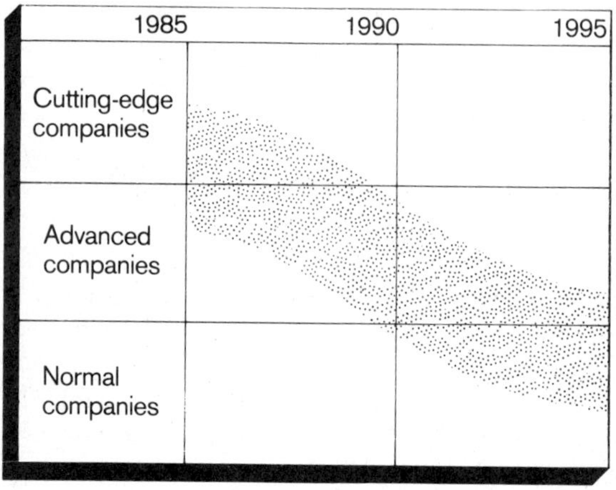

mation. There are, however, a number of heuristics involved. People have to make decisions about whether they want to pay for the telegram out of one or another account, or by cash, etc. In other words, a consultation takes place between the bank employee and the customer about exactly how to handle the particular telegram. Now imagine that, instead of taking a manual off the shelf, the bank employee can simply take out a floppy disk, insert it into a personal computer, and let the TELEGRAM ADVISOR ask a series of questions about the transaction and then present a screen with the telegram form the employee needs to complete. The Advisor will have already completed most of the form, leaving only a few items for the employee to fill in. The operation will be much faster, errors will be significantly reduced, and the hassle involved in sending telegrams will be minimized. Such a small, knowledge-based system could be rapidly prototyped and tested. Further, such a system would be easy and cheap to update. Many organizations are under pressure to increase productivity and, like the bank, hope to use fewer people while offering more services. The key to doing this, from a training perspective, is the ability to teach employees about more products and train them to be able to analyze more problems and explain more services. Realistically, what we need to do is to think about how we can provide intelligent job aids so that employees can ask the right questions and reach the right conclusions without having to memorize a vast amount of new information. Thus, our hypothetical bank employee might have two dozen floppy disks, each concerned with a different specialized service offered by the bank. None of these services might be required very often, so the employee need not be up to date on all the details; but the floppy disk, the advisor program for the particular service, can quickly ask the right questions and prompt the employee through the task.

SMART GENERIC SOFTWARE

Smart generic software is another potential application of small, specialized systems. Both depend on the availability of expert system building tools that can run on commonly available personal computers. We expect that there will be some lag in the development of smart generic hardware, simply because software developers will have to figure out exactly how to use expert system building tools to solve problems that are currently thought to be unsolvable by generic hardware. The process, however, has already begun. The idea of smart generic software exists in a program like VisiCalc, and what we are talking about here is simply extending the concept into symbolic areas; thus, we expect in the very near future to see software vendors offering generic programs to solve tax problems, correspondence problems, and other problems of middle managers. The key to smart generic software is to think of it not as teaching or education in any sense, but rather as a job aid.

SYSTEMS IN HARDWARE

A number of large corporations are exploring the idea of making hardware more intelligent. At least one of these companies has explained the motivation by saying that although people do not always feel comfortable asking a computer for advice, they expect complex laboratory or technical equipment to make suggestions or draw conclusions; and making the conclusions or suggestions drawn by such instruments a little smarter is quite acceptable. Thus, in the example of the electrophoresis interpreter we discussed in Chapter 10, the printout from the laboratory instrument looked pretty much the way it had before a small, smart microchip had been added, and the only real addition was that the system would print out one of a very few lines of advice about what a particular graph probably indicated. The user of this instrument found the new version of the analysis instrument simply a little more useful, because it provided prompts or suggestions about how to analyze particular readings. It is easy to imagine a great many "smart" instruments, especially for the military or other individuals who must respond very rapidly to certain sorts of cues. The builders of these instruments will want to develop very small—50-, 100-,

200-rule—systems that they can rapidly prototype with a small tool, and then reduce the prototype to a microchip and simply insert it in all of the instruments of a particular line. We expect that the rapid development of such a microchip market will constitute a major application of expert system technology by 1990.

OTHER APPLICATIONS

Finally, on the right-hand side of Figure 14.1, we indicate that there will be a number of other applications that will result from a knowledge of expert systems techniques that may not be embedded in knowledge systems, as such. One of the examples we give is exploratory programming. We expect that the techniques originally developed in the expert systems field will be incorporated into other programming environments and languages and that people developing more traditional programs will change their styles to be more exploratory, developing their programs in phases to allow themselves the use of various expert system techniques.

Expert systems can also be used to assist planners in making decisions. Consider this scenario of a senior management meeting to be held in the early 1990s. Senior executives have been convened to discuss an important matter of policy. The meeting begins with the vice-president for finance reviewing five recent cases and concluding: "We need some new guidelines that will tell our credit people what to do in such cases." A senior credit officer, representing a committee that has considered the matter, suggests four rules that she thinks will pretty well handle the problems they are encountering. The senior executives have used an expert system to help them before, and they have a general idea of the way *if–then* rules work, so the senior credit officer has almost unconsciously stated her suggested rules in that format. "That sounds like a pretty comprehensive solution to me," the CEO notes, and asks an administrative assistant to enter the four suggested rules into the company's credit policy system and run the first case. The senior credit officer restates the rules, one at a time, and the assistant types them in at a terminal connected to the company's main computer. The policy system has a limited natural language facility, so the assistant does not need to worry about format or syntax. He just types the rules exactly the way the senior credit officer states them, knowing the computer will reformat the sentences into the correct *if–then* format. Then the assistant enters the first case, which involves extending short-term credit to a small vendor in France. The credit policy system is asked to evaluate the case. Within seconds, a policy recommendation appears on the large, flat computer screen on the wall of the conference room. That seems straightforward, the CEO says, and suggests they try the second case.

Not everyone is happy with the second recommendation. The administrative assistant steps the policy system backward through its reasoning process until they find that the fourth new rule is interacting in an unexpected way with a long-standing rule regarding short-term credits. The senior credit officer acknowledges the problem. Her committee, after all, had run through a similar exercise with the policy system and had encountered this same possible difficulty. She suggests that the older rule needs to be changed in the light of the new developments. This is set aside for the moment and the remaining cases are reviewed, each without complications. The CEO summarizes by asking the senior credit officer to run the last 30 credit cases during the coming week and see how they work if the older rule is modified.

Then, if the committee still wants to support the four new rules and to recommend a modification in the older short-term credit rule, they can do so at next week's meeting. The officers are satisfied that their company will soon have a new policy guideline to deal with these new credit situations and move on to the second topic on their agenda.

This imaginary scenario suggests how an expert system, combined with a user-friendly knowledge acquisition interface, can quickly assimilate new rules and then run cases to see how those rules will interact with each other as well as with previously entered rules. It is really just a matter of quickly developing a new prototype system during a meeting and allowing all present to observe the new system's output. In effect, managers can instantly observe the implications of altering a policy and decide if they really want to make that change. This sort of thing could not occur in a corporation whose officers were unfamiliar with or unaccepting of a computer-based corporate policy system, thus it must wait until various aspects of a corporation's knowledge assets are put into one or more corporate knowledge bases.

A nonsystems change that may occur in accounting would place the value of corporate knowledge on the balance sheet. At the moment, since knowledge resides in the heads of various experts, it is intangible. In the near future, however, after expert systems have been developed that reliably capture and maintain valuable corporate expertise, accountants may decide that the value of that knowledge can be quantified and reported to investors.

Another example of noncomputer applications will probably occur in training. Many of the psychological or cognitive concepts underlying expert systems and knowledge engineering will prove broadly beneficial to a number of professional disciplines. Individuals concerned with analyzing what jobs need to be done or what requirements should be sought when looking for applicants for particular jobs will increasingly resort to knowledge engineering concepts to analyze the required knowledge base and the inference strategy being used by employees and to develop various techniques to determine which individuals have those skills or to develop courses to teach those skills.

The nonsystems changes we have discussed vary so greatly that it is not possible to provide an overall projection of their penetration. Suffice to say that changes in training and job analysis techniques will occur at about the same rate as the acceptance of small systems, whereas changes in programming techniques and management technologies will occur more slowly, say at about the rate that large, hybrid systems become accepted.

We consider specific applications of knowledge engineering to training in the next chapter.

15.

Expert Systems for Training

We have already suggested several ways in which knowledge systems will be used. From the beginning, AI researchers have experimented with educational applications. In this chapter we consider some of the ways in which expert systems may be used in training. When we discussed how experts solve problems in Chapter 3, one of the concepts we introduced was the distinction between knowledge compiled from experience and knowledge compiled from school learning. We observed that people use knowledge from school, and from books, to develop abstract theories. Such theories can be applied to a large number of different situations, but they rarely provide specific direction in a particular situation. On the

Figure 15.1 Varieties of knowledge and their relationships to instructional strategies.

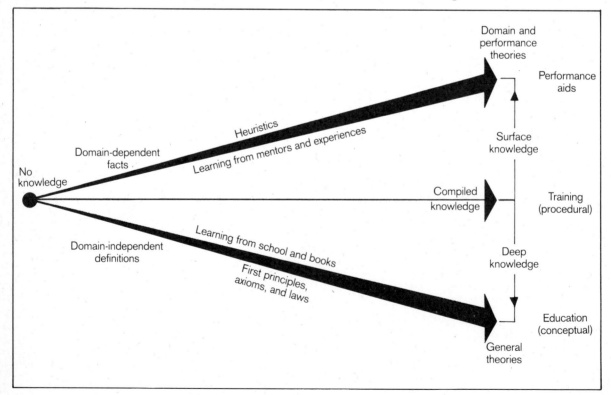

other hand, what people learn from mentors and from experience with a particular problem is domain-dependent facts and heuristics that they gradually compile into domain-theories that tell them how to perform in a specific situation. We refer to the domain-dependent knowledge that one acquires from experience and from mentors as "surface knowledge," and call the knowledge one acquires from books and school "deep knowledge" (see Figure 15.1).

EDUCATION VERSUS TRAINING

In the past 20 years, experts working in the areas of training and instructional design have identified three different approaches to instruction. One way to change performance is to provide conceptual principles that will allow a person to think in abstract terms. This is generally referred to as *education;* it puts emphasis on abstract or general theories. A company adopts this strategy when it sends a promising manager back to school to get an MBA.

A middle course is to provide some theoretical information but to provide it in the context of carrying out a particular procedure or accomplishing a specific goal. This sort of instruction is usually termed *training.* A bank adopts this course when it sends all its new officers through a Loan Analysis Workshop.

The third approach is to provide a minimal amount of training and to put most of the emphasis on providing a *job aid* or *performance aid*—a checklist, a handbook, a pocket calculator, or any device that allows the person to come up with the right answer without knowing a great deal about the subject.

A more rigorous distinction can be drawn between *education* and *training* if one emphasizes what the student will do when he or she completes the instruction. If, after completing a course, the student is expected actually to perform a job, then the performance on the job becomes the criterion by which one can judge the effectiveness of the instruction. In this case, one is dealing with a training problem. Thus, if a student completes a course in how to use algebra to set up a lathe and then, when she has completed the training, she is presented with a lathe in a shop and

she uses algebra to do the calculation and set up the lathe correctly, one can say that the training was effective. On the other hand, if the student completes a course in algebra and the only consequence is an additional course in some other type of math, then one is dealing with education. In other words, it is not the emphasis on concepts or procedures, as such, that makes the difference. It is the ultimate objective of the instruction that is important. Education teaches what it teaches more or less for its own sake. Training prepares the student to perform a specific job in a particular setting. After completing the training program, a student either can or cannot perform some task. There are no such rigorous criteria for successful educational programs, because after completing an education course, the student usually just goes on to take more education.

Still another way of talking about instruction is to say that we can divide all instructional efforts into those that focus primarily on memorization and those that focus primarily on prompting performance. A focus on memorization means that the student should be able to respond to a situation without looking in a book or using a calculator or any other sort of job aid. You want the student to know how to do the task from memory, exactly as one tests students at the end of most college courses. Most education and a large amount of training still focuses on having the student memorize information. If you are asked for your home phone number, you probably have it memorized and simply give the number without thinking about it at all. On the other hand, if you are asked for the phone number of your local civic center, you probably will not know it. You will know, however, that you can look it up in a telephone directory. A telephone directory is a performance aid. We have all memorized a little bit of information, namely, that phone numbers are available in the phone directory and that they are indexed alphabetically. Beyond that, however, we simply depend on a directory to provide us with the information when we need it.

In thinking about the various types of instructional software that are currently on the market, it helps to use some of these instructional heuristics to subdivide the software into some basic categories. Figure 15.2

shows one way in which the whole field of instructional software can be divided. Along the horizontal axis we have divided software into software that helps people memorize things and software that simply aids performance. We have then subdivided memorization into software aimed primarily at helping someone memorize facts or conceptual material and software aimed primarily at teaching someone to perform some specific procedure.

On the vertical axis we have identified three general techniques or approaches that one might use to present information. The first is conceptual or algorithmic software. This is software that pretty much "walks" the student through a sequence. It is sometimes referred to as "drill and practice." Most of the "educational" software currently being marketed to schools and corporate training departments falls into this category. The software is like an automated book: It presents text, asks for responses, and then

provides some sort of confirmation. One might say that a software package that provides drill and practice in math is an extreme example of educational software. On the other hand, an "authoring" software package that allows a teacher to develop "drill and practice" exercises in math, like those being offered today by a number of companies, would be classified as a performance aid. A teacher would buy an authoring package with the intention of using that package as an aid in developing other software to provide educational experiences for students. The authoring software is a performance aid in the sense that it prompts the teacher to enter information and then prompts him or her to choose how the student should respond, and so forth.

The middle row in Figure 15.2 is labeled "Simulations and projections." There are a number of systems now on the market that rely on projecting data or providing some sort of simulation with which the

Figure 15.2 The varieties of instructional software.

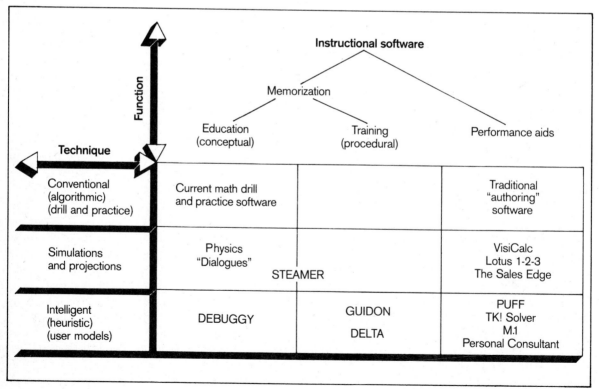

Technique \ Function	Education (conceptual)	Training (procedural)	Performance aids
Conventional (algorithmic) (drill and practice)	Current math drill and practice software		Traditional "authoring" software
Simulations and projections	Physics "Dialogues"	STEAMER	VisiCalc Lotus 1-2-3 The Sales Edge
Intelligent (heuristic) (user models)	DEBUGGY	GUIDON DELTA	PUFF TK! Solver M.1 Personal Consultant

student can interact. An example of educational software that uses simulations is a series of physics programs from the Educational Technology Center at the University of California at Irvine (Arons, 1984). These programs consist of "dialogues" in which the student is asked questions and then provided with diagrams or some other sort of model that responds to the student's inputs. The student is able to observe in a simulated situation what will happen if different strategies are adapted. This material seeks to teach concepts by allowing the student to gain experience in a series of simulated situations. If one moves to the performance-aid side of the chart, one might think of VisiCalc and Lotus 1-2-3. The VisiCalc program is a performance aid. It does not have a specific outcome; it simply presents users with a matrix and allows them to fill in their own numbers and then allows them to make projections.

The last row on the vertical axis of Figure 15.2 deals with intelligent or heuristic techniques. It is this category of software that knowledge systems have begun to impact now and will increasingly impact between now and 1990.

In keeping with this analysis, it is obvious that most small knowledge systems will fall into the category of performance aids. We have listed two or three examples of expert systems in that category. Likewise, knowledge system building tools are also performance aids. Like VisiCalc and Lotus 1-2-3, knowledge system building tools allow individuals to build knowledge systems without knowing as much as they would otherwise need to know to build them from scratch. Our focus in this chapter, however, is not so much on expert systems or on expert system building tools as it is on the spin-offs of knowledge engineering that have been aimed specifically at training or education. We shall consider a few of the better-known examples in a little more detail.

STEAMER

STEAMER is an advanced computer-assisted instructional system being built by the Navy Research Personnel Development Center in San Diego in cooper-

ation with Bolt, Beranek, and Newman, Inc., of Cambridge, Massachusetts. STEAMER is designed to teach Naval officers about the problems of running a steam propulsion plant like those that power many naval ships. Propulsion engineering was chosen by the Naval Personnel Research and Development Center because it was judged to be the greatest single training problem they face, largely because of the complexity of the systems. The steam plant constitutes approximately a third of the space on a typical ship, consists of thousands of complex components, and can be operated only by a team of highly trained individuals. The officer is responsible for the activities of the various members of the team and for the overall management of the system. No officer can possibly memorize all of the procedures involved. Nor can an officer learn to anticipate all the consequences that would follow if different procedures were attempted during various potential emergency situations. The object of the training provided by STEAMER is partly procedural, but it is mostly conceptual. The Navy team that developed STEAMER wanted a system that would give the student an overall conception—a cognitive model—of what was happening in the steam plant, so that the student would have a good feeling for what was happening in the plant at any time. Moreover, they wanted to train the student to anticipate the consequences of various procedures.

The essential idea for STEAMER was to take a full-scale mathematical simulation model that was developed and is used at the Officers' School in Newport, Rhode Island, to modify that model, and to use it as the basis for a graphic model that could be presented to students on a tabletop computer. STEAMER actually uses two tabletop computers. One of the computers shows a diagram of the steam plant. The other terminal presents information about the plant and provides an intelligent tutoring system that supervises the student's interaction with the program. The graphics presentation model was built using a lot of the graphics techniques available in INTERLISP. When the student first looks at a diagram of the steam plant, he sees a very high-level overview that shows him all the major parts of the steam plant—some 20 components—and the flows between them. Each of the 20 components really represents an entire subsystem. The student can access any subsystem by pointing at the subsystem with a mouse and giving a command, "Expand." The overall diagram is then replaced by a diagram of the subsystem. Proceeding in this way, the student can go to whatever depth he wants, right down to the smallest component. Figure 15.3 shows STEAMER in use.

STEAMER displays the diagram of the propulsion system in color to facilitate showing flows and conditions in the various units of the plant. The student can change conditions in almost any area of the plant by opening or closing valves, raising temperatures, and so forth. The various gauges that an officer would normally be able to monitor are all pictured on the second terminal, along with the tutorial information. As the student makes changes in the plant, he can see those changes take place throughout the system. At the same time he can see how the gauges are affected. The system also has a replay facility; the student can store an interaction with the system and review it at a later date. He can see what happened when a particular order was given, try something different at some point, and watch what happens when the new decision is implemented.

The key conception underlying the development of STEAMER is that it is an interactive, inspectable simulation. In part, the effectiveness of this simulation depends on the existence of a mathematical model of the steam propulsion plant, but equally it depends on the graphics package that is part of INTERLISP. There is a sense in which STEAMER is properly termed a simulation and projection technique. But it is an intelligent technique in the broader sense that the simulation is not simply a model that allows the student to make some minor change and see what happens. In fact, the student can control the steam plant and can make any change that he could make in an actual plant and then watch what happens in the plant. In other words, the student can experiment as much as he wants. Because the student has the gauges in front of him, he can observe the gauges changing and imme-

diately check to see what is happening in the plant.

STEAMER does not represent an expert system that is directly involved in instruction. What it does represent is a very dramatic, and very effective, instructional system designed to handle a difficult problem and utilize in a particularly effective way a lot of the software techniques that have been developed by knowledge engineers.

DEBUGGY

As opposed to STEAMER, which is being actively developed in San Diego, DEBUGGY is a system developed by researchers at Xerox Palo Alto Research Center that is strictly for research at this time. The essence of DEBUGGY is the assumption that a student's errors in solving problems represent "bugs," in the computer sense of the word, and that a discrete modification to correct the bug in the student's procedures will result in improved behavior.

DEBUGGY, and a number of systems like it, represent a major effort on the part of knowledge engineers to develop instructional systems that can develop models of users. The idea of a *user model* is the key to developing intelligent user interface systems. If one can develop a system that can, in turn, develop a model of the student who uses the system, then the system can continually modify its instruction to be more effective.

DEBUGGY has been used with several thousand students to find systematic errors in the domain of place value subtraction. This approach requires an elaborate procedural analysis of the particular domain. In this case, it requires numerous subtraction problems where patterns of errors are looked for. Each error pattern or "bug" is given a name. The system then develops a collection of all the possible bugs that a student could exhibit in dealing with problems. This problem is somewhat complicated by the fact that the analysis of subtraction leads to a set of some 20 primitive bugs and about 110 compound bugs that result from the interaction of the simple bugs.

DEBUGGY begins by giving the student a number

of problems to determine if any of the 130 bugs can explain all of the student's errors. In the language of AI, this is a classic problem in search. It is not practical to have the system consider all the possible ways that a student could have reached the particular wrong answers that he or she produced. Thus, the

Figure 15.3 *Photo of STEAMER being used.*

system must have heuristics that limit the search. The nature of the heuristics in this case takes the form of knowing a common way that students combine bugs to reach compound bug errors. The system systematically searches and attempts to explain the student's behavior by using these rules-of-thumb to focus on the most likely problems first. Once DEBUGGY determines a particular bug or set of bugs that will explain the student's behavior, the system then generates problems that it assumes will lead the student into particular errors if he or she is, in fact, using a particular bug. If the student makes the predicted mistakes, the system then knows what kind of bugs the student is dealing with and goes on to provide specific corrective information. Then DEBUGGY proceeds to ask the student to practice on a very particular set of problems—for example, how to carry zeros, or how to handle borrowing in certain types of subtraction situations.

The heuristic analysis of student errors depends at least in part on a skill hierarchy, an analysis of what bugs relate to or depend on other bugs; thus, if a particular bug can be definitely identified, then subsequent errors in the system, bugs in the repertoire, can be predicted, since one student bug typically results in other bugs that also need to be corrected. The system starts by correcting a particular bug and then works forward to be sure that the student understands how to handle the additional manifestations of the bug when it occurs in various compound situations.

DEBUGGY is currently being researched in classroom situations. It is a significant effort to bring intelligence to bear on programs that would otherwise be handled by means of drill and practice. The program depends on a detailed cognitive analysis of the types of errors that students can make. This analysis takes quite a bit of thought and effort, but once it is done, it makes it possible to develop a program that can interact with any particular student to figure out exactly what problems that student is having. Then the system offers the student only the remedial information and drill that is necessary to eliminate the specific bugs the student has.

DEBUGGY is clearly an effort to teach students to handle memorized approaches to problems. It is easy to imagine that this approach will become popular in educational situations. Hopefully it will replace drill and practice exercises that are only individualized in a trivial way.

This same approach will probably also be useful in various corporate training situations where individuals need to memorize complex procedures. If it is worth the time and effort to analyze those procedures to the level of detail that a cognitive model requires in order to allow the system to predetermine exactly what problems the trainee is having, this approach offers a significant improvement over traditional approaches.

GUIDON

GUIDON is a program developed by William Clancey at the Computer Science Department at Stanford University to follow up on the initial work with MYCIN. In fact, in certain ways GUIDON is simply MYCIN rearranged for tutorial purposes. MYCIN, as we have already seen, is a highly specialized medical diagnosis and prescription system designed to help doctors with meningitis and bacteremia infections.

GUIDON is designed to be used in medical schools to train physicians to conduct MYCIN-like consultations. GUIDON has the advantage of having the entire knowledge base of MYCIN, plus all of the actual case experiences that MYCIN has accumulated. The latter is particularly significant when one considers that generating good examples is often a very tricky part of any instructional training task. Typical training systems often rely on one to three examples. The GUIDON program has access to several hundred examples, since it can, in fact, retrieve any case that the MYCIN program has ever run.

When we talked about the origin of tools, we said that they derive from systems from which the knowledge base has been removed. In other words, tools are inference engines. With GUIDON it is almost the other way around. In this case the designers saved the knowledge base and the inference engine, but added an additional inference engine designed to manage the tutorial aspects of GUIDON's interaction with a user.

When a medical student sits down to use GUIDON, he or she begins by saying, in effect: "I would like to study a meningitis case." GUIDON offers a case selected at random from its files. In effect, GUIDON says: "O.K., here's patient 105; see if you think this patient has meningitis." GUIDON provides the student the same initial information that MYCIN was originally given about patient 105. When a physician turns MYCIN on, the physician identifies the patient and then the system asks for information about the patient. GUIDON reverses that process. The student is asked if he or she knows what is wrong with the patient, just as with MYCIN, the doctor would ask MYCIN what was wrong. MYCIN would consider rules and ask questions. With GUIDON, the student asks questions and GUIDON provides answers.

When GUIDON selects the initial patient for the student to consider, the system solves the patient problem in the way that MYCIN does. In the process, GUIDON creates a decision tree that indicates each of the considerations that MYCIN would go through to determine whether particular attributes did or did not apply to this particular patient. Thus, when a student asks GUIDON a question, GUIDON is, in effect, tracing the tree and seeing what route the student is following. If the student asks questions that GUIDON determines to be irrelevant because the student already has knowledge that should let the student know that branch is not appropriate, the system will ask the student why he or she wants that information. Depending on what the student says, the system will be more or less direct in telling the student that the information is irrelevant and why it is irrelevant.

When the student indicates that he or she knows what the patient's problem is, GUIDON will ask the student to make a diagnosis and a prescription. If MYCIN would have made that same diagnosis and prescription, GUIDON will simply ask polite checking questions to be sure that the student understands the diagnosis. If the student makes a diagnosis that MYCIN could not have made at that point in the

analysis, GUIDON will ask the student how he or she knew one or another fact or attribute that MYCIN would not have known. Depending on what the student says, GUIDON will be more or less assertive in pointing out that there is missing information that is necessary to be sure of the diagnosis in question.

Thus, in effect, GUIDON flips MYCIN inside out and puts the student in the position of trying to do the diagnosis that the MYCIN program was originally developed to do. GUIDON looks over the student's shoulder as he or she does that diagnosis, and if the student does it in the same way that MYCIN does, the student gets congratulated. If the student tries to reach conclusions without the data needed for those conclusions, GUIDON points it out.

GUIDON's major problem, as a tutorial system, is related directly to the problem of how knowledge is represented in MYCIN. GUIDON can easily tell the student if a rule is involved when certain preconditions of the rule have not been satisfied. Likewise, if one rule requires that some previous rule be considered before the later rule can be concluded, GUIDON is quick to point it out. If the student asks questions, the system can provide the student with information about why a particular path should be taken.

On the other hand, the tutorial system's weakness is the same as MYCIN's main weakness. Neither MYCIN nor GUIDON can define primitive terms for the student. In both cases they assume that the student knows a large amount of technical vocabulary as well as the meaning of a large number of chemical tests. Practicing physicians know such things, but a student may or may not know them.

The people who built GUIDON have become concerned with how knowledge is put into expert systems. They would like to see the knowledge in expert systems arranged in such a way that systems like GUIDON can be more effective. GUIDON is strictly a research effort at this point, and it will probably be several years before expert system building tools exist that will allow people not only to create expert systems, but also to flip those systems around into sophisticated tutorial systems. Thus, many of the stickier considerations of knowledge systems development concern representing the knowledge in a knowledge base in such a way that a tutorial program like GUIDON can use the same knowledge base. Although it will not happen in the next few years, in the early 1990s one can look to the possibility of using a knowledge system building tool to build an expert system and know that with a few changes one can adjust that system so that it can be used to teach new individuals to approach and solve the problem in the same way that the expert system does.

DELTA

We have already considered the DELTA system built by General Electric in Chapter 10. DELTA is an expert system that assists mechanics in diagnosing and repairing problems in diesel-electric locomotives. You will recall that DELTA not only provides expert advice but also presents information by means of a videoplayer to help the user locate items discussed in the dialogue. If appropriate, the system will even show the user laser disk instruction regarding specific repairs.

Thus, DELTA not only provides job aids that allow the student to determine whether a particular problem exists or not, it also offers specific training in how to make an actual repair. This adjunctive use of videotape with the expert system is a very useful combination and will undoubtedly be very popular in those situations where there is a preexisting video or film literature that can help users identify specific problems or explain the procedures to follow in correcting those problems.

PUFF

We have also discussed PUFF, the small pulmonary diagnosis system developed for the Pacific Medical Center in San Francisco. This system is discussed in detail in Chapter 9. At this point all we wish to do is point out that this type of small expert system, which is run as an adjunct to a piece of laboratory equipment and provides a quick analysis of the data produced by the instrument, constitutes a very effective performance aid. In effect, activity that would otherwise be done by a technician is done by a small knowledge system. The knowledge system is not replacing an expert. It is simply helping a technician to perform some difficult but well-understood procedure.

The incorporation of knowledge systems into instruments of various kinds will go a long way toward expanding the role of instruments so that they function not only as measuring devices, but also as performance aids. The instrument will not only make a determination; it will also make a recommendation. The power of performance aids has already proven itself in the training environment. It is almost always the case that if one can develop an effective paper performance aid—a checklist or worksheet—one can significantly reduce the cost of training and the number of errors. The ability to incorporate performance aids right into instruments will undoubtedly decrease the training time and the number of technical staff people required to perform numerous operations. It will certainly enhance the efficiency of many operations.

OTHER TRAINING APPLICATIONS

Since the 1960s, most training operations in large corporations have been dominated by behavioral psychology. Behavioral theories have inclined trainers to put a great deal of emphasis on the actual performance required of employees. This has been reinforced by government rulings that challenge the idea that employees may be hired on the basis of characteristics that cannot be shown to be related directly to the nature of the job. Thus, one area of training has focused on developing task analyses that describe the job requirements in ways that satisfy government regulations.

The behavioral approach to training began in manufacturing facilities where people have to learn production line jobs. Behavioral techniques are very good for analyzing exactly what a person on a production line does. A behavioral task analysis describes a sequence of actions to be performed. By the late

1960s and early 1970s, the people who had started out in the behavioral tradition had developed a number of generic training programs to help individuals learn how to do such things as sales and management. Other "behaviorally based" courses teach people how to analyze problems for computer programming.

The emphasis on actual performance is a very important one that trainers will not want to lose. On the other hand, when behaviorists try to tackle more complex types of performance, they have been forced to deal with questions about what particular experts know. Moreover, they have had to struggle with the problem of how to communicate the knowledge that an expert has to new performers. These are issues that classical behavioral techniques are not very well designed to handle.

To be a little simplistic, one might say that the behavioral psychology of the 1960s is the sort of analysis one does when one wants to determine how a robot will perform. When one seeks to build a knowledge system, one is, in effect, approaching problems that are better handled with the techniques that have been developed by cognitive psychologists and that underlie knowledge engineering.

People in training have followed the cognitive literature, and many have tried to incorporate cognitive ideas into training technology. Until recently, however, most cognitive concepts have been a little too vague or ill-defined to be applied to practical corporate training situations. This will change in the next few years. The practical techniques that have been developed by knowledge engineers are exactly the kind of specific techniques for which training technologists have been looking.

Figure 15.4 provides an analysis of sales training using a notation that one of us (Harmon, 1982) has suggested to training analysts. We propose that the analyst begin by developing an overview of the observable behaviors that make up the performance. Then we suggest that they determine the specific heuristics that underlie each specific behavior. In effect, we suggest that they act as if they are going to develop a small knowledge system to guide the performer in negotiating each step in the overall activity. Finally, we suggest that they look for the deep structures—the models and theories that master salespeople use—that underlie one or more sets of

Figure 15.4 Three levels of task analysis necessary for instructional design.

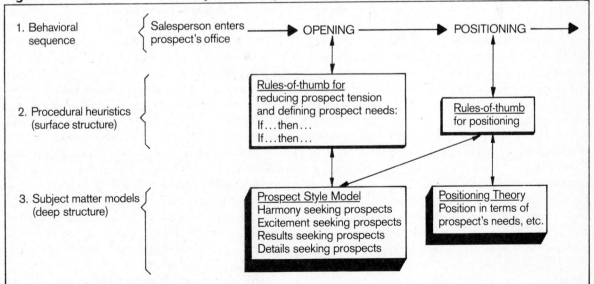

heuristics. This approach, which begins with a behavioral analysis and then proceeds to analyze the successively deeper layers of knowledge that guide the salesperson, is a practical extension of existing task analysis models. This approach, and others like it, will become increasingly popular in the coming decade and will lead to a much better understanding of how skilled performers actually approach problems. More important, it will lead to much more effective training programs.

Knowledge systems themselves, of course, will also play a major role in many training departments. Trainers will learn to analyze problems and to consider what sort of job aid would be most appropriate to help people perform their job. They might decide that the person has to memorize information. In some cases a paper checklist will be quite adequate. There is a distinct class of problems, however, where the most effective way to help an employee perform a job will be to provide a small knowledge system. The "automated procedures manual" we spoke of earlier is one example of the way knowledge systems will have a major impact on training.

In many cases, however, the concepts that trainers will learn from knowledge engineers will be applied to training problems without any need to use the computer. Thus, people analyzing all kinds of jobs will find it useful to think in terms of consultation paradigms: What is the nature of a particular specialist's expertise? Is it essentially a diagnosis/prescription problem? Or is it a planning problem? The conceptual categories that have been developed and operationalized in the process of developing knowledge systems will prove useful to anyone trying to develop a detailed job description.

Techniques now exist for quantifying the amount of knowledge a person has, the number of rules it would take to develop a system, the number of objects in the expert's world, and the number of chunks of information that someone needs to deal with a particular problem. These various measures that knowledge engineers use when they set about constructing knowledge systems will prove equally useful to people working in training analysis and design.

TRAINING MANAGERS AND SALESPEOPLE

One of the training problems that will face all large companies in the next few years is how to increase productivity by reducing the number of levels in the organization hierarchy. This will involve training managers in managing a larger number of diverse operations. It will also require training people to interact with customers to provide a much broader range of services to those customers.

Consider, for example, a branch bank operation. Until recently, the branch manager managed the branch. Loan officers specialized in various types of loans. One loan officer dealt with small individual loans, such as car loans. Another officer dealt with commercial loans for small business. An operations officer was available to help customers with particular problems about where checks might have been lost, or how money orders or telegraph money transfers might be accomplished. With the introduction of automatic teller machines and the rapidly increasing complexity of the financial marketplace, most banks want to change the people who staff their branches. They want their branch officers to be generalists rather than specialists. At the same time, they want to be sure that these people can offer high-quality service to customers. Thus, the branch officer of the future will function more like a financial counselor. The same individual may help a customer set up a checking account, offer the customer a loan, offer trust services, and provide advice about the vast array of financial services offered by the bank. Existing branch officers will require significant training to be able to fulfill this new role. If banks approach this training problem in traditional ways, they will try to get employees to memorize the vast amount of new information that their new jobs will require. Or they will ask employees to use elaborate manuals that will detail what they need to know about all the new products and services. If, instead, branch officers are provided with workstations that have a number of knowledge systems available, they will be in a position to handle their new, more complex jobs much more efficiently and effectively.

The way training is done, even in conventional

settings, will be significantly changed by the knowledge we are now acquiring of how people store information, how people manipulate knowledge, and how people make inferences. Knowledge engineers have determined that most experts are guided by relatively simple inference structures. The real power of experts lies in their large bank of knowledge. This insight can be transferred to training programs. Most sales training programs, for example, are currently organized around the idea that one ought to teach a new salesperson a general procedure for selling. Thus, sales training programs teach salespeople to "open the call," to "contact customers," to "probe for a customer's need," to "prescribe products the customer might want to buy," and then to "close" the sale. This kind of approach to sales is akin to teaching salespeople to be general problem solvers. In the 1960s, AI researchers struggled with the idea that a general problem solver could be built. They finally dropped the idea and concluded that expertise lies primarily in specific knowledge, not in general techniques.

When one examines the best salespeople in large organizations, one finds just what the knowledge engineers have found out about other experts. Good salespeople do have some general knowledge about opening, probing, presenting, and so forth. What they really have, however, is a great deal of very specific knowledge. They know just the right kinds of questions to ask particular types of customers to elicit the kinds of responses they can use to continue to develop their sales presentation. They know very specific ways to contact customers. They know very detailed things about their products that are important to certain types of customers. In other words, the good salespeople are good for exactly the same reason that other experts are proficient in any area: They have worked with a particular problem over an extended period of time, and they have acquired a large number of practical heuristics.

When one asks what kind of skills training one would develop to train such individuals, one realizes that the current crop of "generic" or "behavioral" sales programs are probably useful for beginners, but they are not very useful for advanced salespeople. With techniques borrowed from knowledge engi-

neers, training specialists will now be able to analyze exactly what sophisticated salespeople do. And they will be able to design programs to pass that information on to new salespeople.

In fact, it may not require very detailed cognitive analysis. It may be sufficient to know that heuristics are being used. In many cases it will be sufficient to interview the best salespeople and simply identify their 10 or 15 most powerful heuristics. Those heuristics can be printed up and passed along to other members of the sales force.

It is easy to imagine that training courses of the future will rely on a detailed analysis of heuristics. The purposes of the training will be to teach individuals to apply specific heuristics to particular problems.

One training company has already developed a problem-solving workshop based on concepts derived from knowledge engineering, AI, and cognitive psychology. Participants begin by learning about human problem solving. Then they do a number of exercises to determine what heuristics they typically use to reduce their search when they approach problems. The course essentially involves helping participants discover what heuristics tend to dominate their approach to problem solving and then helping the participants learn the use of alternative heuristics that would make them more effective in dealing with certain types of problems. This course is just one early example of the type of programs that will undoubtedly become more prevalent during the late 1980s.

Here is a scenario that suggests still another way that knowledge systems will be used in training. Imagine that a facilitator is standing in front of a small group of personnel managers who are attending an advanced personnel policy training seminar. The facilitator has a computer keyboard in front of him, and a 4 × 5 foot computer screen is mounted on one wall of the classroom.

"So how would you tell your subordinates to handle this issue?" the facilitator concludes. Five hands shoot up, and the facilitator calls on Ms. Thaigarigana, the junior personnel manager from the Asian division. Ms. Thaigarigana suggests two policy guidelines or rules that she believes would handle the case study the seminar is considering. "Let's try them," the facilitator responds cheerfully, and quickly types them on his keyboard. After checking the way the Personnel Policy System renders the rules into formal syntax, the facilitator merges the two rules with the 1,200 regular rules comprising the company's Personnel Policy System. Then he instructs the system to run a well-known case study. In an instant three absurd recommendations appear on the screen. Ms. Thaigarigana shifts uneasily in her chair, a couple of other participants laugh, and the facilitator wonders aloud what could be wrong. By asking WHY and HOW as he backtracks into the Personnel Policy System's rule base, the facilitator identifies several interactions that everyone realizes are causing problems. The facilitator finally summarizes by saying: "This illustrates that we must be careful not to write new rules that are so broad and heavily weighted that they override some of our narrow rules designed for special cases. Ms. Thaigarigana, how could you revise your first policy statement to assure that it would not override all those special rules on minority appeals and the calculation of European holidays?"

As the seminar continues to experiment with the problems of setting personnel guidelines and seeing what they mean, we slip through the classroom door and return to the present.

This scenario is set in the future because it will take time for the technologies we have described in this book to gain acceptance in boardrooms and classrooms. The techniques we have described, however, are already in existence; they are simply waiting for innovators to use them.

16.
Preparing for the Knowledge Systems Revolution

In this final chapter, we return to the practical problem of how to prepare for the knowledge systems revolution that will occur in the next few years. We hope that we have convinced you of the tremendous promise that knowledge systems offer to the business community.

Small knowledge systems, knowledge systems embedded in instruments, and some of the large, narrow expert systems are going to have a big impact during the next four to five years. Businesses that move quickly are going to be able to use these technologies to gain increases in productivity and significant competitive advantages. The more complex hybrid systems, the integration of natural language, and the development of intelligent workstations that incorporate a large number of different knowledge systems in a personal computer will begin to have a major impact around 1990. The transformation of American business by computers has already begun. It will culminate in the late 1990s as computer-based intelligence moves into every nook and cranny of our businesses.

A large number of Fortune 500 companies have already started developing AI centers to try to determine how knowledge systems can be used in their operations and their products. In addition, major national and military projects are underway that will revolutionize computer technology during the next five to ten years. The rate of change will continue to increase.

The important question, if you are in middle or upper management in a corporation, or the owner of a small business, for that matter, is how best to position yourself and your company to take advantage of the changes that are going to take place.

Depending on your responsibilities, you may wish to learn more about knowledge engineering, to acquire tools and experiment with the development of an expert system, or to set up a knowledge engineering department within your company. This chapter offers you some suggestions to guide you in any or all of these endeavors.

ACQUIRING MORE KNOWLEDGE

We have provided a broad, general overview of the field. We encourage you to think of the book in just those terms—an overview that establishes terminology, provides examples, and maps the landscape in bold strokes. Entire books have been written describing knowledge systems that we have described in a few pages. Each topic we discussed briefly, such as frames and methods of search, has an extensive literature.

To guide your reading, we have included an extensive, annotated bibliography. In it we have listed many books and articles that you might want to consider reading. We recommend that you skim the reference section and select additional reading material on the topics you would like to consider in more detail.

Keep in mind that knowledge engineering is still a new field. The literature reflects the youth of the field in two ways. First, there is an annoying tendency for two authors to use entirely different terms for the same construct, or for two authors to use the same term in different ways. You may have to track down terms and meaning by inspecting examples or consulting more than one source. The second indicator of the field's youth is that many experts disagree about various aspects of the technology. Thus, one article may assert that frame representations are superior, whereas the next may say exactly the opposite.

We have tried to avoid academic disputes in this book. Where there seemed to be good arguments on both sides, we have tried to take a middle path. As you venture into other literature, you will find considerable disagreement. As with all emerging technologies, you must read several different perspectives to gain an overall feeling for the issues and arguments. Knowing where the contested issues lie is quite useful. Many debates may not be related to the applications you have in mind, and you can set them aside.

We have found it particularly useful to monitor journals and magazines in the field. The best general overview is provided by *AI Magazine*, which is the official journal of the American Association for Artificial Intelligence (AAAI). The magazine is a benefit of membership in AAAI. *AI Magazine* is a blend of general-interest and technical articles that can generally be read by technicians and nontechnicians alike. The magazine also provides information about various meetings and conventions. The annual convention of the AAAI is a very good place to go if you want to see the latest hardware and software systems demonstrated. Tutorials given in conjunction with the AAAI convention offer an excellent way to learn more about the field, often directly from its creators. Membership information can be obtained by writing to: The American Association for Artificial Intelligence, 445 Burgess Drive, Menlo Park, CA 94025, (415) 328-3123. With membership in AAAI you are also offered the opportunity to subscribe to *Artificial Intelligence, An International Journal*. This is more academic than *AI Magazine*, but worthwhile if your interests are serious. The journal is available from Elsevier Science Publishers B.V., (North-Holland),

P. O. Box 1991, 1000 BZ Amsterdam, The Netherlands.

If your interests are general, another publication from North-Holland is a journal called *FGCS, Future Generations Computer Systems*. This journal provides a very readable survey of the international efforts to develop "fifth-generation" computing hardware and software.

If your interests are in data processing, the Association for Computing Machinery (ACM) has a special-interest group (SIGART) on AI that is worth joining. Likewise, the IEEE has a special-interest group on AI and has been holding conferences built around AI subjects.

If your interests are in training or in designing man-machine interfaces, the *International Journal of Man-Machine Studies* and *Cognitive Science* each publish important articles on human problem solving and on computer interface problems. Both journals are available from the Academic Press, Inc., 111 Fifth Avenue, New York, NY 10003.

The publisher, William Kaufmann, Inc., not only publishes books on AI but sells the conference proceedings of the last several years of both the AAAI and the IJCAI (the International Joint Conference on Artificial Intelligence). If your company is setting up an AI group, these proceedings might be useful. They can be obtained by writing William Kaufmann, Inc., Dept. AI 24, 95 First Street, Los Altos, CA 94022.

If you are setting up an AI group, you might also consider subscribing to a report service offered by Scientific DataLink, 805 Third Avenue, New York, NY 10022. This company reproduces the reports of the major AI research labs, including Stanford, Carnegie-Mellon, etc.

As knowledge system building tools emerge for the personal computer market, we expect that one or more of the personal computer magazines will support interest in this area with a regular column or even a special-interest publication.

Similarly, a number of newsletters that monitor the AI industry have appeared recently, although none has yet emerged as the standard.

SEMINARS AND CONSULTANTS

Several knowledge engineering consulting firms provide training services in various areas related to knowledge systems and knowledge engineering (see Appendix B). Some of these firms offer a schedule of seminars and courses. By following the journals and reviewing articles and books in the bibliography, you can find out about the seminars. We recommend attending a seminar focused on the topics in which you are most interested.

At the moment, seminars and consultants can be very expensive, but the price will fall rapidly as these systems become more popular and there is more demand for information about the field. Here are several pieces of advice:

- If you are interested in small knowledge systems, be sure that any seminar you attend will provide an opportunity to work with a knowledge engineering tool and try your hand at building your own small knowledge system.
- Pay careful attention to the prerequisites of the courses. Some of the companies that manufacture tools expect their tools to be used by programmers to build large systems, whereas others expect that users will use the tools to solve practical problems.
- Be sure you know what philosophy guides the company conducting the seminar you consider attending. You will be able to choose training that broadens your understanding by exploring new issues. You may also choose to deepen your understanding of one particular aspect of the field.

EXPERIMENTING WITH SMALL SYSTEMS

Probably the most promising strategy for an individual exploring applications is to purchase and experiment with one of the small knowledge system tools that are now in the marketplace. There are many reasonably small problems for which knowledge systems offer cost-effective solutions. And in the end

there is no substitute for the experience gained from building a prototype. With a small investment in software and training and a properly focused project, you can develop a useful prototype. This approach will allow you to investigate the field and develop interest within your company without making a major commitment.

HIRING OUTSIDE CONSULTANTS

Another way to bring knowledge engineering expertise into your company is to purchase the services from an outside consultant. We have listed a number of companies that build knowledge systems in Appendix B. No doubt several more will emerge in the next few years. Many of these same companies also sell expert system building tools. In most cases they will be happy to demonstrate their tools and discuss possibilities of developing an expert system for you.

Until the field gains maturity, we advise caution in approaching these new companies. First, because of the sudden popularity of knowledge engineering, there will certainly be companies that lack the ability to field quality systems. Software that is "intelligent" will be as hard to evaluate as software that purports to be "user-friendly" or "easily maintained."

Many people are already promoting systems and approaches that will not be practical. All kinds of software will be labeled "expert systems" by entrepreneurs eager to get in on the latest fad. Observers agree that there is and will continue to be a lot of hype. Some consumers will waste their money on absurd application efforts. The market is very exciting, and it will continue to change very quickly. Thus, as always, the buyer will need to be cautious.

The best evidence that a company can deliver a product that fits your needs is a track record of proven systems. Probe for evidence that knowledge systems have actually been placed in service. As you probe you are liable to encounter a problem we confronted several times as we explored companies: Their most interesting applications may be confidential. Expertise or knowledge about how to solve hard problems is often proprietary. Thus, knowledge engineering companies are often unable to display their most interesting projects because of confidentiality agreements. This problem is a real one, in our opinion, and is not unique to knowledge engineering. In choosing a lawyer or a doctor, we often find the information in which we are most interested is confidential. However, it ought not to cloak all applications that a company has fielded. We encourage sensitivity, but also a firm demand for information about fielded systems.

When you contact knowledge engineering firms, they are often eager to show you demonstration systems. This is perfectly reasonable behavior, but demonstrations can be difficult to place in context. If you find yourself dazzled by graphics displays, remember to ask yourself (and the vendor) the following questions:

1. What resources were expended to develop the system? Be sure to focus on the elapsed time, the human resources, and the computational resources. (MYCIN, for example, was developed over a five-year period, with an estimated 50 person-years of effort, and with the computation resources of a major research computing laboratory.)

2. How typical is the demonstration system of other systems the company has fielded? This applies to the scope of the knowledge system's competency as well as its speed, its packaging, etc.

3. Does the domain of the demonstration system match the application domains you have in mind? Be especially wary of very small systems or systems that behave well in domains where information is complete and relationships are certain. The ability of a knowledge system to represent and utilize a well-refined zoological hierarchy, for example, may not be relevant to your interests if your problem domain has no accepted taxonomy. Similarly, systems that fail to account for uncertainty may succeed in domains where complete information is available, but may not be useful to you in your domain.

Some companies demonstrate simple systems to show you the inner workings of a knowledge system in a domain that is commonly understood. This is a reasonable strategy, but is not equivalent to a demonstration of "power."

DEVELOPING AN IN-HOUSE KNOWLEDGE ENGINEERING GROUP

Many companies are already developing their own in-house knowledge engineering groups. The problems of developing an internal capacity at this time are rather formidable, however. The small number of AI professionals, coupled with major demands for that expertise, guarantees that knowledge engineers are going to demand high salaries, if you can find any willing to move to your site.

Most knowledge engineers are just out of the universities. They are not accustomed to business environments and are used to working with esoteric equipment, on episodic, research-oriented projects. It will require a very sophisticated manager to keep these individuals happy. Unless your company is located near a major center or university, you may have to make a strenuous effort to develop an AI shop that can hold onto talented people.

One strategy, of course, is to focus on a very narrow problem and acquire a very specialized AI group to help with that problem. The difficulties with this strategy are (1) finding a problem that will really give you a payoff, and (2) hiring people capable of solving that particular problem. All this is not to suggest that it cannot be done. Fifty large corporations are already developing AI groups, and many others are going to follow suit. But it isn't going to be easy, especially in the next few years, and a number of companies are going to experience a lot of grief and frustration as they attempt it.

A large corporation is probably very well advised to work with an expert system building company to develop their first expert system while they explore various possibilities. Several of the vendors of expert systems are quite willing to work with clients to help them develop an in-house capacity. This is one way to get around the lack of available knowledge engineers that ought to be given very serious consideration.

No matter how you decide to begin, give careful consideration to the in-house individuals you decide to train. Knowledge engineers are not just programmers or software engineers who know one or two additional languages. They have to work with experts in a way that most conventional programmers have never had to do. Moreover, their focus is much more psychological and performance-oriented than that of conventional programming personnel. If you plan to build large systems, you are certainly going to need some individuals who know a great deal about programming. If you are going to begin with small systems, however, you need analytic individuals who can be a little less concerned with programming than traditional programmers but more focused on human interactions. There are several well-recognized disciplines whose members are likely to emerge as the (nonprogrammer) knowledge engineers of the future. You should at least consider including one or more of the following individuals on your expert systems project team:

- *Instructional designers* spend a good deal of their time engineering knowledge. Teaching others requires the careful dissection of a body of information. Components are modularized and lessons are prepared. Students are often told: "As a rule-of-thumb, if you see these stimuli, then here is what to do." The results of an instructional design effort is a refined, coherent, and inspectable "knowledge base."
- *Technical writers* face very similar goals when, for example, they are handed the technical specifications for a computer language and asked for a useful reference guide. Technical writers must identify the "objects" that constitute the language, uncover the "attributes," and consider all permutations of "values." The resulting document is very much like a "knowledge base."
- *Managers* are constantly faced with the task of sorting out and transmitting policy decisions. One way to communicate a policy decision is in the form of a memorandum. Policies often turn out to be contingencies in a familiar form: "If you encounter situation X, then behave in manner Y." Of course, these rules of organizational behavior can be very complex. The conditions under which a loan is to be granted, a part replaced under warranty, or an appointment canceled or postponed can be very complex. Knowledge systems offer a way for managers to develop consistent policy, transmit it to employees far and wide, and maintain the policies as necessary.

We expect that in a very few years knowledge engineering tools will be as common as VisiCalc. Software packages that integrate word processing, data base management, graphics tools, and spreadsheets together will soon include a fifth component— a reasoning engine for maintaining and distributing advice-giving systems. When that day comes, you will be the knowledge engineer!

There will still be a place for knowledge engineers, of course, just as there remains a niche for programmers. When a large or unusual computing application is planned, programmers are employed to build it. Similarly, when very large or very difficult knowledge systems projects are planned, knowledge engineers will be needed. But the success of knowledge systems depends in large measure on their ability to permeate the work environment and become convenient tools that managers and technicians can use in their daily work.

A FINAL WORD

A more complex issue that will face all managers in the coming years will be the general issue of automation. Problem solving and decision making will be automated just as surely as production lines will. In a sense, expert systems will be the "robots" of middle management. Increasingly, tasks that we thought were impossible to computerize will become amenable to computer solutions. Jobs will disappear or be changed radically, and individuals will have to adapt.

The wise manager will want to anticipate these

changes and plan for them. If your work, or the work of those who report to you, depends on knowledge and decision making that can be captured in an expert system, you should begin to consider some alternatives. You might decide to position yourself to be one of the people who will develop and maintain knowledge systems. Or you may decide that you want to acquire a broader base of knowledge and emphasize more humane and intuitive skills.

In spite of the problems, however, we are convinced that the years ahead will be very exciting. We shall be forced to reconceptualize what we really know and how we do the things we do. We shall acquire many new insights into how our businesses work and how we can make them more efficient and more productive. At the same time, being human, we shall have to decide how to implement the new technologies in ways that will encourage employees to support them and enjoy using them. These are challenges that managers will have to face. As with past technologies, those individuals that can blend the power of these new technologies with the necessities and the constraints of their organizations will be the winners.

APPENDIXES

Appendix A

Glossary

Active Values. A special kind of value that can be changed in the course of a consultation. Active values are often used with graphic images to allow the user to change the values in a system by simply altering an image on the computer screen.

Agenda. An ordered list of actions. Some knowledge systems store and reason about possible actions; for example, whether to pursue a particular line of reasoning. HEARSAY uses agenda-based control.

Algorithm. A systematic procedure that, if followed, guarantees a correct outcome. In developing a conventional program, the programmer must specify the algorithm that the program will follow.

Artificial Intelligence. "A subfield of computer science concerned with the concepts and methods of symbolic inference by a computer and the symbolic representation of the knowledge to be used in making inferences. A field aimed at pursuing the possibility that a computer can be made to behave in ways that humans recognize as 'intelligent' behavior in each other." (Feigenbaum and McCorduck, 1983)

Attribute. A property of an object. For example, *net worth* is an attribute of a loan applicant. Attributes are associated with values in specific cases; thus, A. Smith's net worth is $34,000.

Automatic Programming. Several projects are underway to develop computer programs that will, in turn, write other computer programs. If successful, such "higher level" programs will be used to "automate" major portions of computer programming.

Backtracking. The process of backing up through a sequence of inferences, usually in preparation for trying a different path. Planning problems typically require backtracking strategies that allow a system to try one plan after another as unacceptable outcomes are identified.

Backward Chaining. (*Back-chaining.*) One of several control strategies that regulate the order in which inferences are drawn. In a rule-based system, backward chaining is initiated by a goal rule. The system attempts to determine if the goal rule is correct. It backs up to the *if* clauses of the rule and tries to determine if they are correct. This, in turn, leads the system to consider other rules that would confirm the *if* clauses. In this way the system backs into its rules. Eventually, the back-chaining sequence ends when a question is asked or a previously stored result is found.

Blackboard Architecture. (HEARSAY Architecture.) An expert system design in which several independent knowledge bases each examine a common working memory, called a "blackboard." An agenda-based control system continually examines all of the possible pending actions and chooses the one to try next.

Breadth-first Search. In a hierarchy of rules or objects, breadth-first search refers to a strategy in which all of the rules or objects on the same level of the hierarchy are examined before any of the rules or objects on the next lower level are checked.

CAI, or **Computer Aided Instruction.** Refers to conventional uses of computers to present instruction. Instruction presented in this manner may simply be in the form of statements followed by questions and answers, or it may involve simulations or games in which the student must learn to anticipate a pattern. The presentation may branch, depending upon the student's answers. The programs are not intelligent, however, in the sense that they cannot develop a model of how the student conceptualizes the subject matter and cannot modify the presentation to accommodate a particular student.

Certainty. The degree of confidence one has in a fact or relationship. As used in AI, this contrasts with probability, which is the likelihood that an event will occur.

Certainty Factor. *(Confidence Factors.)* A numerical weight given to a fact or relationship to indicate the confidence one has in the fact or relationship. These numbers behave differently than probability coefficients. In general, methods for manipulating certainty factors are more informal than approaches to combining probabilities. Most rule-based systems use certainty factors rather than probabilities.

Chunk. A collection of facts stored and retrieved as a single unit. The limitations of working memory are usually defined in terms of the number of chunks that can be handled simultaneously.

Common LISP. A dialect of LISP that is intended to serve as a standard version of LISP that will run on a number of different machines. The first efforts to develop such dialect have already met with some difficulties. LISP is such an easy language to tailor that people implementing it can hardly resist customizing it for the particular computer they are using.

Compiled Knowledge. As a person acquires and organizes knowledge into chunks and networks, the knowledge becomes compiled. Some individuals compile knowledge into more and more abstract and theoretical patterns (deep knowledge). Others compile knowledge as a result of practical experience (surface knowledge). Most people begin by acquiring theoretical knowledge and then, when they finish their schooling, they recompile what they have learned into practical heuristics. Expertise consists of large amounts of compiled knowledge.

Consultation Paradigm. Consultation paradigms describe generic types of problem-solving scenarios.

Particular system building tools are typically good for one or a few consultation paradigms and not for others. Most commercial tools are designed to facilitate rapid development of expert systems that can deal with the diagnostic/prescriptive paradigm.

Context Tree. *(Object Tree.)* In EMYCIN the context tree forms the backbone of the consultant program. It is a structured arrangement of the objects (contexts) or conceptual entities that constitute the consultation domain. There may be one or more contexts. A static context tree is an arrangement of context types (e.g., a *patient* for whom *cultures* have been prepared). A dynamic context tree is an arrangement of context instances (e.g., *John Smith* with a *morning culture* and an *afternoon culture*).

Context–Parameter–Value Triplets. *(Object–Attribute–Value Triplets.)* One method of representing factual knowledge; it is the method used in EMYCIN. A context is an actual or conceptual entity in the domain of the consultant (e.g., a patient, an aircraft, or an oil well). Parameters are properties associated with each context (e.g., age and sex of a patient or location and depth of an oil well). Each parameter (or attribute) can take on values: the parameter, age, could take the value "13 years."

Control (of a knowledge system). The method used by the inference engine to regulate the order in which reasoning occurs. Backward chaining, forward chaining, and blackboard agendas are all examples of control methods.

Deep Knowledge. Knowledge of basic theories, first principles, axioms, and facts about a domain. This contrasts with surface knowledge.

Default, or **Default Values.** Computer programs often have prespecified values that they use unless they are given alternative values. These assumed values are called default values. Knowledge systems often store default values that are used in lieu of facts. For example, a medical program may assume that a patient has been exposed to some common organism unless the user asserts that such exposure can be ruled out.

Depth-first Search. In a hierarchy of rules or objects, depth-first search refers to a strategy in which one rule or object on the highest level is examined and then the rules or objects immediately below that one are examined. Proceeding in this manner, the system will search down a single branch of the hierarchy tree until it ends. This contrasts with breadth-first search.

Diagnostic/Prescriptive Consultation Paradigm. Consultation paradigms refer to generic approaches to common types of problems. The diagnostic/prescriptive paradigm is used for problems that require the user to identify symptoms or characteristics of a situation in order to determine which of several alternative solutions may be appropriate. Most expert systems and tools are designed to handle this paradigm.

Domain. A topical area or region of knowledge. Medicine, engineering, and management science are very broad domains. Existing knowledge systems only provide competent advice within very narrowly defined domains.

Dual Semantics. The idea that a computer program can be viewed from either of two equally valid perspectives: procedural semantics (what happens when the program is run) and declarative semantics (what knowledge the program contains).

Dynamic Knowledge Base. See *Working Memory.*

EMYCIN. The first expert system building tool. EMYCIN was derived from the expert system MYCIN. After the developers of MYCIN completed that system they decided that they could remove the specific medical knowledge from MYCIN (hence *Essential MYCIN*). The resulting shell consisted of a back-chaining inference engine, a consultation driver, and several knowledge acquisition aids. This shell, or tool, could then be combined with another knowledge base to create a new expert system.

Environment. See *Programming Environment.*

Example-driven System. See *Induction System.*

Exhaustive Search. A search is exhaustive if every possible path through a decision tree or network is examined. Exhaustive search is costly or impossible for many problems. Knowledge systems often search exhaustively through their knowledge bases.

Experiential Knowledge. Knowledge gained from hands-on experience. This typically consists of specific facts and rules-of-thumb (surface knowledge). This is in contrast with deep knowledge of formal principles or theories.

Expert System. As originally used, the term referred to a computer system that could perform at, or near, the level of a human expert. Evaluations of MYCIN place its competence at or near that of highly specialized physicians. Configuration systems like XCON (R1) may well exceed human competence. As the term is currently being used, it refers to any computer system that was developed by means of a loose collection of techniques associated with AI research. Thus, any computer system developed by means of an expert system building tool would qualify as an expert system even if the system was so narrowly constrained that it could never be said to rival a human expert. Some practitioners would prefer to reserve "expert system" for systems that truly rival human experts and use "knowledge system" when speaking of small systems developed by means of AI techniques. The popular press and various software entrepreneurs have already used the term "expert system" in so many ways, however, that it now lacks any precise meaning.

Expertise. The skill and knowledge possessed by some humans that result in performance far above the norm. Expertise often consists of massive amounts of information combined with rules-of-thumb, simplifications, rare facts, and wise procedures in such a way that one can analyze specific types of problems in an efficient manner.

Explanation. Broadly, this refers to information that is presented to justify a particular course of reasoning or action. In knowledge systems this typically refers to a number of techniques that help a user understand what a system is doing. Many knowledge systems allow a user to ask "Why," "How," or "Explain." In each case the system responds by revealing something about its assumptions or its inner reasoning.

Fact. Broadly, a statement whose validity is accepted. In most knowledge systems a fact consists of an attribute and a specific associated value.

Fifth-Generation Computers. The next generation of computing machines. It is assumed that they will be larger and faster and will incorporate fundamentally new designs. Parallel processing, the ability of a computer to process several different programs simultaneously, is expected to result in a massive increment in computational power. Since expert systems tend to be very large and involve a large amount of processing, it is assumed that expert systems will not reach maturity until these more powerful machines are available.

Forward Chaining. One of several control strategies that regulate the order in which inferences are drawn. In a rule-based system, forward chaining begins by asserting all of the rules whose *if* clauses are true. It then checks to determine what additional rules might be true, given the facts it has already established. This process is repeated until the program reaches a goal or runs out of new possibilities.

Frame. (*Object* or *Unit.*) A knowledge representation scheme that associates an object with a collection of features (e.g., facts, rules, defaults, and active values). Each feature is stored in a slot. A frame is the set of slots related to a specific object. A frame is similar to a property list, schema, or record, as these terms are used on conventional programming.

Heuristic. A rule-of-thumb or other device or simplification that reduces or limits search in large problem spaces. Unlike algorithms, heuristics do not guarantee correct solutions.

Heuristic Rules. Rules written to capture the heuristics an expert uses to solve a problem. The expert's original heuristics may not have taken the form of *if–then* rules, and one of the problems involved in building a knowledge system is converting an expert's heuristic knowledge into rules. The power of a knowledge system reflects the heuristic rules in the knowledge base.

Hierarchy. An ordered network of concepts or objects in which some are subordinate to others. Hierarchies occur in biological taxonomies and corporate organizational charts. Hierarchies ordinarily imply inheritance; and, thus, objects or concepts higher in the organization "contain" the objects or concepts that were beneath them. "Tangled hierarchies" occur when more than one higher-level entity inherits characteristics from a single lower-level entity.

High-Level Languages. Computer languages lie on a spectrum that ranges from machine instructions through intermediate languages like FORTRAN and COBOL to high-level languages like Ada and C. High-level languages incorporate more complex constructs than the simpler languages.

Horn Clause. In logic programming, Horn clauses are expressions connected by "or " with at most one positive proposition. Thus, a Horn clause takes the form: "Not A or Not B or . . . or Not C or D." Logical programming is made more efficient by restricting the type of logical assertions to Horn clauses in much the same way that production systems insist on having knowledge stated in terms of *if–then* rules.

Human Information Processing. A perspective on how humans think that is influenced by how computers work. This approach to psychology begins by focusing on the information that a person uses to reach some conclusion and then asks how one could design a computer program that would begin with that same information and reach that same conclusion. Espoused by Herbert Simon and Allan Newell, this perspective currently dominates cognitive psychology and has influenced the design of both computer languages and programs.

ICAI, or **Intelligent Computer Aided Instruction.** (*Intelligent Tutoring Systems.*) Instructional software that incorporates AI techniques. At the moment, most "intelligent" instructional software is still in the research stage. The key to intelligent instructional software is the development of techniques that allow the system to monitor an individual student's responses and develop a model of how the student conceptualizes the situation. Then, based on such a "user model," the system would vary its presentation to systematically develop the size and accuracy of the student's cognitive model of the subject.

If–Then Rule. A statement of a relationship among a set of facts. The relationships may be definitional (e.g., If female and married, then wife), or heuristic (e.g., If cloudy, then take umbrella).

Implementation. *(Implementation Environment.)* In the context of this book, implementation refers to the overall environment in which an expert system will function. The implementation environment includes the hardware the system will run on, the operating system that will support the expert system, any higher-level languages that the system will depend upon, and any interfaces that the system will have with other computer systems or sensors. A small knowledge system, for example, might run on an IBM personal computer with 256K of RAM. The system would assume an MS-DOS 2.0 operating system and need to have a PC LISP program installed before the knowledge system would work. So far, most expert systems and tools have been developed to run in very specific implementation environments and you must consider the implementation requirements very carefully before deciding if you could use a system.

Induction System. *(Example-driven System.)* A knowledge system that has a knowledge base consisting of examples. An induction algorithm builds a decision tree from the examples, and the system goes on to deliver advice. Induction systems do not facilitate the development of hierarchies of rules.

Inference. The process by which new facts are derived from known facts. A rule (e.g., If the sky is black, then the time is night), combined with a rule of inference (e.g., *modus ponens*) and a known fact (e.g., The sky is black) results in a new fact (e.g., The time is night).

Inference, data-directed. Inferences that are driven by events rather than goals. See *Forward Chaining*.

Inference, goal-directed. Inferences that are driven by goals rather than data. See *Backward Chaining*.

Inference Engine. That portion of a knowledge system that contains the inference and control strategies. More broadly, the inference engine also includes various knowledge acquisition, explanation, and user interface subsystems. Inference engines are characterized by the inference and control strategies they use. Thus, for example, the inference engine of MYCIN uses *modus ponens* and backward chaining.

Inheritance. A process by which characteristics of one object are assumed to be characteristics of another. If we determine that an animal is a bird, for example, then we automatically assume that the animal has all of the characteristics of birds.

Inheritance Hierarchies. When knowledge is represented in a hierarchy, the characteristics of superordinate objects are inherited by subordinate objects. Thus, if we determine that an auto loan is a type of loan then we know that the credit check procedures that apply to all loans apply to auto loans.

Instantiation. The specification of particular values. A specific person with a particular sex and temperature is an instantiation of the generic object "patient."

Instructional Software. Computer software that is used either for instruction or to aid in the actual performance of a task. This definition is broader than the typical use of the term because it reflects the importance of job aids in business environments. Some instructional software help students memorize conceptual subject matter (i.e., educational software). Some help students practice tasks they will later perform on the job (i.e., training software), and some instructional software help individuals when they are actually performing the job. Small expert systems will be widely used as intelligent job aids.

Interface. The link between a computer program and the outside world. A single program may have several interfaces. Knowledge systems typically have interfaces for development (the knowledge acquisition interface) and for users (the user interface). In addition, some systems have interfaces that pass information to and from other programs, data bases, display devices, or sensors.

INTERLISP. A dialect of LISP. A programming environment that provides a programmer with many aids to facilitate the development and maintenance of large LISP programs.

Job Aids. *(Performance Aids.)* Job aids are devices that help individuals when they perform tasks. Well-constructed job aids allow the performer to avoid memorization. Thus, they allow individuals to perform jobs more quickly and more accurately than they would if they had been trained in any conventional manner. Moreover, since performers memorize frequently-used responses while using job aids, these aids serve as structured on-the-job training. Whenever they are appropriate, job aids are the current medium of choice among instructional designers. Small knowledge systems are ideal job aids for a wide variety of tasks and will rapidly replace most of the checklists, procedures manuals, and other common job aids currently in use.

Knowledge. An integrated collection of facts and relationships which, when exercised, produces competent performance. The quantity and quality of knowledge possessed by a person or a computer can be judged by the variety of situations in which the person or program can obtain successful results.

Knowledge Acquisition. The process of locating, collecting, and refining knowledge. This may require interviews with experts, research in a library, or introspection. The person undertaking the knowledge acquisition must convert the acquired knowledge into a form that can be used by a computer program.

Knowledge Base. The portion of a knowledge system that consists of the facts and heuristics about a domain.

Knowledge Engineer. *(Knowledge Engineering.)* An individual whose specialty is assessing problems, acquiring knowledge, and building knowledge systems. Ordinarily this implies training in cognitive science, computer science, and artificial intelligence. It also suggests experience in the actual development of one or more expert systems.

Knowledge Representation. The method used to encode and store facts and relationships in a knowledge base. Semantic networks, object–attribute–value triplets, production rules, frames, and logical expressions are all ways to represent knowledge.

Knowledge System. A computer program that uses knowledge and inference procedures to solve difficult problems. The knowledge necessary to perform at such a level, plus the inference procedures used, can be thought of as a model of the expertise of skilled practitioners. In contrast to expert systems, knowledge systems are often designed to solve small, difficult problems rather than large problems requiring true human expertise. In many cases, small knowledge systems derive their utility from their user-friendly nature rather than from their ability to capture knowledge that would be difficult to represent in a conventional program.

Language–Tool Spectrum. A continuum along which various software products can be placed. At one extreme are narrowly defined tools that are optimized to perform specific tasks. At the other extreme are general purpose languages that can be used for many different applications.

Large, Hybrid System Building Tools. A class of knowledge engineering tools that emphasizes flexibility. The systems are designed for building large knowledge bases. They usually include a hybrid collection of different inference and control strategies. Most commercial hybrid tools incorporate frames and facilitate object-oriented programming.

Large, Narrow System Building Tools. A class of knowledge engineering tools that sacrifices flexibility to facilitate the efficient development of more narrowly defined expert systems. At the moment, most large, narrow tools emphasize production rules.

LISP. A programming language based on List Processing. LISP is the language of choice for American AI researchers.

Logic. A system that prescribes rules for manipulating symbols. Common systems of logic powerful enough to deal with knowledge structures include propositional calculus and predicate calculus.

Long-term Memory. A portion of human memory that is exceedingly large and contains all of the information that is not currently being processed.

Machine Language. A low-level language consisting of primitive instructions. High-level languages are built in machine language.

Machine Learning. A research effort that seeks to create computer programs that can learn from experience. Such programs, when they become available, will remove a major barrier to the development of very large expert systems.

MacLISP. A dialect of LISP that is tuned for efficiency, but less friendly as a developmental environment.

Maintenance of an Expert System. Unlike conventional computer software that is only infrequently updated, expert systems by their nature are very easy to modify. Most expert systems that are currently in use are constantly being improved by the addition of new rules. In most applications, the user organization will want to establish a regular routine to capture and incorporate new knowledge into the system. It's a good idea to make one person responsible for entering new rules whenever data or procedures change or whenever questions arise that the current system could not answer.

Mental Models (of human experts). The symbolic networks and patterns of relationships that experts use when they are trying to understand a problem. Mental models often take the form of simplified analogies or metaphors that experts use when first examining a problem. Mental models can sometimes be converted into production rules, but in many cases they still defy AI techniques and are the object of considerable research in cognitive psychology.

Meta-. A prefix indicating that a term is being used to refer to itself. Thus, a meta-rule is a rule about other rules.

Mid-run Explanation. The ability of a computer program to stop upon request and explain where it currently is, what it is doing, and what it will seek to accomplish next. Expert systems tend to have features that facilitate mid-run explanation while conventional programs do not.

Modus ponens. A basic rule of logic that asserts that if we know that A implies B and we know for a fact that A is the case, we can assume B.

Monotonic Reasoning. A reasoning system based on the assumption that once a fact is determined it cannot be altered during the course of the reasoning process. MYCIN is a monotonic system; and, thus, once the user has answered a question, the system assumes that the answer will remain the same throughout the session. Given the brief duration of most MYCIN sessions, this is a reasonable assumption.

Multivalued Attribute. An attribute that can have more than one value. If, for example, a system seeks values for the attribute *restaurant,* and if *restaurant* is multivalued, then two or more restaurants may be identified.

MYCIN. An expert system developed at Stanford University in the mid-1970s. The system is a research system designed to aid physicians in the diagnosis and treatment of meningitis and bacteremia infections. MYCIN is often spoken of as the first expert system. There were other systems that used many of the AI techniques associated with expert systems, but MYCIN was the first to combine all of the major features with the clear separation of the knowledge base and the inference engine. This separation, in turn, led to the subsequent development of the first expert system building tool, EMYCIN.

Natural Language. The branch of AI research that studies techniques that allow computer systems to accept inputs and produce outputs in a conventional language like English. At the moment, systems can be built that will accept typed input in narrowly constrained domains (e.g., data base inquiries). Several expert systems incorporate some primitive form of natural language in their user interface to facilitate rapid development of new knowledge bases.

Nonmonotonic Reasoning. Reasoning that can be revised if some value changes during a session. In other words, nonmonotonic reasoning can deal with problems that involve rapid changes in values in short periods of time. If one were developing an on-line expert system that monitored the stock market and recommended stocks to purchase, one would want a system that used nonmonotonic reasoning and was thus able to revise its recommendations continually as the prices and volumes of stock changed.

Object. *(Context, Frame.)* Broadly, this refers to physical or conceptual entities that have many attributes. When a collection of attributes or rules are divided into groups, each of the groups is organized around an object. In MYCIN, following medical practice, the basic groups of attributes (parameters) were clustered into contexts, but most recent systems have preferred the term "object." When a knowledge base is divided into objects, it is often represented by an object tree that shows how the different objects relate to each other. When one uses object-oriented programming, each object is called a frame or unit and the attributes and values associated with it are stored in slots. An object is said to be "static" if it simply describes the generic relationship of a collection of attributes and possible values. It is said to be "dynamic" when an expert system consultation is being run and particular values have been associated with a specific example of the object.

Object–Attribute–Value Triplets. *(O–A–V Triplets.)* One method of representing factual knowledge. This is the more general and common set of terms used to describe the relationships referred to as Context–Parameter–Value Triplets in EMYCIN. An object is an actual or conceptual entity in the domain of the consultant (e.g., an oil well). Attributes are properties associated with objects (e.g., location, depth, productivity). Each attribute can take different values (e.g., the attribute depth could take on any numerical value from 0 to 60,000 feet).

Operating System. The computer software system that does the "housekeeping" and communication chores for the more specialized systems. Most conventional computers have standard operating systems that software is designed to utilize. Thus, for example, the IBM personal computer uses a version of MS-DOS. AI languages are often used to write operating systems so that the expert system and the operating system are written in the same language. LISP workstations, like the Xerox 1100 series and the Symbolics machines, are computers that use a LISP operating system to improve their efficiency and flexibility when running expert systems written in LISP.

Paradigm. See *Consultation Paradigm.*

Parallel Processing. A proposed architecture for computer machinery that would allow a computer to run several programs simultaneously. It would mean that a computer would have several central processors simultaneously processing information.

Performance Aids. See *Job Aids.*

Predicate Calculus. An extension of propositional calculus. Each elementary unit in predicate calculus is called an object. Statements about objects are called predicates.

Probability. Various approaches to statistical inference that can be used to determine the likelihood of a particular relationship. Expert systems have generally avoided probability and used confidence factors instead. Some systems, however, use a modified version of Bayesian probability theory to calculate the likelihood of various outcomes.

Problem Solving. Problem solving is a process in which one starts from an initial state and proceeds to search through a problem space in order to identify the sequence of operations or actions that will lead to a desired goal. Successful problem solving depends upon knowing the initial state, knowing what an acceptable outcome would be, and knowing the elements and operators that define the problem space. If the elements or operators are very large in number or if they are poorly defined, one is faced with a huge or unbounded problem space and an exhaustive search can become impossible.

Problem Space. A conceptual or formal area defined by all of the possible states that could occur as a result of interactions between the elements and operators that are considered when a particular problem is being studied.

Procedural versus Declarative. Two complementary views of a computer program. Procedures tell a system what to do (e.g., multiply A times B and then add C). Declarations tell a system what to know (e.g., V = IR).

Production. (*Production Rule.*) The term used by cognitive psychologists to describe an *if–then* rule.

Production System. A production system is a human or computer system that has a data base of production rules and some control mechanism that selects applicable production rules in an effort to reach some goal state. OPS5 is an expert system building tool that is normally referred to as a production system; it was initially developed in an effort to model supposed human mental operations.

Programming Environment. (*Environment.*) A programming environment is about halfway between a language and a tool. A language allows the user complete flexibility. A tool constrains the user in many ways. A programming environment, like INTERLISP, provides a number of established routines that can facilitate the quick development of certain types of programs.

PROLOG. A symbolic or AI programming language based on predicate calculus. PROLOG is the most popular language for AI research outside of North America.

Prototype. In expert systems development, a prototype is an initial version of an expert system, usually a system with from 25 to 200 rules, that is developed to test effectiveness of the overall knowledge representation and inference strategies being employed to solve a particular problem.

Pruning. In expert systems, this refers to the process whereby one or more branches of a decision tree are "cut off" or ignored. In effect, when an expert system consultation is underway, heuristic rules reduce the search space by determining that certain branches (or subsets of rules) can be ignored.

Reasoning. The process of drawing inferences or conclusions.

Recognize–Act Cycle. The cycle of events in a production or forward-chaining system. During the recognize phase, rules are examined to see if their *if* clauses are true based on information currently stored in memory. During the act phase, one of the rules is selected and executed and its conclusion is stored in memory.

Representation. The way in which a system stores knowledge about a domain. Knowledge consists of facts and the relationships between facts.

Resolution. (*Resolution Theorem Proving.*) The inference strategy used in logical systems to determine the truth of an assertion. This complex, but highly effective, method establishes the truth of an assertion by determining that a contradiction is encountered when one attempts to resolve clauses, one of which is a negation of the thesis one seeks to assert.

Robotics. The branch of AI research that is concerned with enabling computers to "see" and "manipulate" objects in their surrounding environment. AI is not concerned with robotics, as such, but it is concerned with developing the techniques necessary to develop robots that can use heuristics to function in a highly flexible manner while interacting with a constantly changing environment.

Rule. (If–then *Rule, Production.*) A conditional statement of two parts. The first part, comprised of one or more *if* clauses, establishes conditions that must apply if a second part, comprised of one or more *then* clauses, is to be acted upon. The clauses of rules are usually A–V pairs or O–A–V triplets.

Rule-based Program. (*Production System.*) A computer program that represents knowledge by means of rules.

Runtime Version or **System.** Knowledge system building tools allow the user to create and run various knowledge bases. Using a single tool, a user might create a dozen knowledge bases. Depending on the problem the user was facing, he or she would load an appropriate knowledge base and undertake a consultation. With such a tool the user can easily modify a knowledge base. Some companies will want to develop a specific knowledge base and then produce copies of the tool and that specific knowledge base. Under these circumstances the organization will not want the user to have to "load" the knowledge base, nor will they want the user to be able to modify the knowledge base. When an expert system building tool is modified to incorporate a specific knowledge base and to deactivate certain programming features, the resulting system is called a runtime system or a runtime version.

Satisfice. A process during which one seeks a solution that will satisfy a set of constraints. In contrast to optimization, which seeks the best possible solution, when one satisfices, one simply seeks a solution that will work. Most managers, when they seek to solve practical problems, are satisfied with a solution and do not proceed to search for the best possible solution.

Search and **Search Space.** See *Problem Solving* and *Problem Space.*

Semantic. Refers to the meaning of an expression. It is often contrasted with syntactic, which refers to the formal pattern of the expression. Computers are good at establishing that the correct syntax is being used; they have a great deal of trouble establishing the semantic content of an expression. For example, look at the sentence, "Mary had a little lamb." It is a grammatically correct sentence; its syntax is in order. But its semantic content—its meaning—is very ambiguous. As we alter the context in which the sentence occurs, the meaning will change.

Semantic Networks. A type of knowledge representation that formalizes objects and values as nodes and connects the nodes with arcs or links that indicate the relationships between the various nodes.

Short-term Memory. (*Working Memory.*) That portion of human memory that is actively used when we think about a problem. By analogy to a computer, short-term memory is like RAM; it contains all the data that is instantly available to the system. The content of human short-term memory is usually conceptualized in terms of chunks. Most cognitive theories hold that human short-term memory can contain and manipulate about four chunks at one time.

Slot. A component of an object in a frame system. Slots can contain intrinsic features such as the object's name, attributes and values, attributes with default values, rules to determine values, pointers to related frames, and information about the frame's creator, etc.

Small Knowledge Systems. In general, small knowledge systems contain under 500 rules. They are designed to help individuals solve difficult analysis and decision-making tasks without aspiring to being the equivalent of any human expert.

Small Knowledge System Building Tools. As used in this book, tools that can run on personal computers.

Software, levels of. A continuum that begins at the lowest level with machine language and extends up through low-level languages, high-level languages, tools, and then finally to systems that users can use to actually solve problems.

Software Engineer. An individual who designs conventional computer software. This individual serves a role similar to a knowledge engineer in the development of a conventional software program.

Surface Knowledge. (*Experiential* or *heuristic knowledge.*) Knowledge that is acquired from experience and is used to solve practical problems. Surface knowledge usually involves specific facts and theories about a particular domain or task and a large number of rules-of-thumb.

Symbol. An arbitrary sign used to represent objects, concepts, operations, relationships, or qualities.

Symbolic versus Numeric Programming. A contrast between the two primary uses of computers. Data reduction, data-base management, and word processing are examples of conventional or numerical programming. Knowledge systems depend on symbolic programming to manipulate strings of symbols with logical rather than numerical operators.

Syntactic. Refers to the formal pattern of an expression. (Contrast *Semantic.*)

Technology Transfer. In the context of expert systems, this is the process by which knowledge engineers turn over an expert system to a user group. Since expert systems need to be continually updated, the knowledge engineers need to train the users to maintain a system before it arrives in the user environment. In effect, some users must learn how to do some knowledge engineering.

Tools. As used in this book, tools are computer software packages that simplify the effort involved in building an expert system. Most tools contain an inference engine and various user interface and knowledge acquisition aids and lack a knowledge base. Expert system building tools tend to incorporate restrictions that make them easy to use for certain purposes and hard to impossible to use for other purposes. In acquiring a tool, one must be careful to select a tool that is appropriate for the type of expert system one wishes to build. More broadly, a tool is a shell that allows the user to rapidly develop a system that contains specific data. In this sense, an electronic spreadsheet program is a tool. When the user enters financial data, he or she creates a system that will do specific financial projections just as the knowledge engineer uses a tool to create an expert system that will offer advice about a specific type of problem.

Uncertainty. In the context of expert systems, uncertainty refers to a value that cannot be determined during a consultation. Most expert systems can accommodate uncertainty. That is, they allow the user to indicate if he or she does not know the answer. In this case, the system either uses its other rules to try to establish the value by other means or relies on default values.

User Interface. See *Interface*.

Value. A quantity or quality that can be used to describe an attribute. If we are considering the attribute "color," then the possible values of color are all of the names of colors that we might use. If we are considering a particular object, we observe it and assign a specific value to the attribute by saying, for example, "That paint is colored bright red."

VLSI. Acronym for Very Large Scale Integration. VLSI design is concerned with the layout and construction of extremely dense and powerful electronic circuits that can be put on small chips. VLSI technologies are the key to designing large computers that fit in small containers. Several companies are working on expert systems that can assist in VLSI design efforts.

Windows. Conventional computer terminals use the entire screen to present information drawn from one data base. Computer terminals that can utilize window software can divide the screen into several different sections (or windows). Information drawn from different data bases can be displayed in different windows. Thus, for example, with a Macintosh computer one can have a word processing program going on in one window and a graphics program going on simultaneously in a second window. Most current expert systems research is being conducted on computers that allow the user to display different views of the systems activity simultaneously. Windows are an example of a technique originally developed by AI researchers that has now become part of conventional programming technology.

Working Memory. *(Short-term Memory; Dynamic Knowledge Base.)* In expert systems, working memory is comprised of all of the attribute–value relationships that are established while the consultation is in progress. Since the system is constantly checking rules and seeking values, all values that are established must be kept immediately available until all the rules have been examined.

Workstation. *(Professional Workstation; Intelligent Workstation.)* Workstations refer to computer systems that help a performer do his or her job. Large financial institutions currently have trading rooms where individuals constantly monitor currency or stock prices and conduct trades by means of computers arranged in front of them. In the near future, most managers will have computers on their desks, and as knowledge systems are developed, these computers will be replaced by more powerful computers that will evolve into workstations to help the manager monitor and conduct business.

Appendix B

Companies Active in Expert Systems and AI-Related Research

The following is a short list of companies involved in commercial expert systems research and development. This list is certainly not complete, as new companies are being formed every day. The Fortune 500 companies on this list are mostly focused on internal projects at the moment, but many have plans to offer products for sale once the market develops.

Advanced Information & Decision Systems (AI & DS)
201 San Antonio Circle, Suite 286
Mountain View, CA 94040-1270
(415) 941-3912
Contact: Mary Margaret Morton

AI research and development

Apollo Computer
330 Billerica Rd., Dept. A1
Chelmsford, MA 01824
(617) 256-6600, ext. 4497

AI hardware

Applied Expert Systems, Inc. (APEX)
Five Cambridge Center
Cambridge, MA 02142
(617) 492-7322
Contact: Fred L. Luconi

Custom expert systems for financial service companies

ARCO Oil and Gas Company
P. O. Box 2819
Dallas, TX 75221

AI research and development

Arthur D. Little, Inc.
Acorn Park
Cambridge, MA 02140
(617) 864-5770

Consulting and research for businesses interested in AI

Artificial Intelligence Corporation
100 Fifth Ave.
Waltham, MA 02254
(617) 890-8400
Contact: Larry R. Harris

Natural language systems

Artificial Intelligence Publications
95 First Street
Los Altos, CA 94022
(415) 949-2324
Contact: Louis Robinson

Periodic reports on the state of AI for business interests

AT&T Bell Laboratories
2C278
Murray Hill, NJ 07974

AI research and development and internal expert systems development

Battelle Memorial Institute
505 King Ave.
Columbus, OH 43201

Workshops on AI and expert systems

Boeing Company
Boeing Computer Services Company
Artificial Intelligence Center
Advanced Technology Application Div.
P. O. Box 24346
Seattle, WA 98124
(206) 763-5404

Extensive AI research and development program and several internal expert systems projects

Bolt, Beranek & Newman, Inc.
10 Moulton St.
Cambridge, MA 02338
(617) 497-3367
Contact: Walter Reitman

Research and development contracts

Brattle Research Corp.
Cambridge, MA
(617) 720-0051
Contact: John Clippinger

Custom development of expert systems for the financial community

Carnegie Group
4616 Henry Street
Pittsburgh, PA 15213
(412) 578-3450
Contact: Larry Geisel

Expert system building tools, consulting, and training

Cognitive Systems, Inc.
234 Church Street
New Haven, CT 06510
(203) 773-7997
Contact: Roger Schank

Custom development of software

Data General
4400 Computer Drive
Westboro, MA 01580
(617) 366-8911, ext. 4738
Contact: Charles Piper

Hardware and software for AI

Digital Equipment Corp.
200 Baker Ave. (CFO 1-1/M 18)
Concord, MA 01742
(617) 493-2775
Contact: Jeffry R. Gibson

Hardware, software, and internal expert systems applications

DM Data Inc.
6900 Camelback Road, Suite 1000
Scottsdale, AZ 85215

Publishes an annual report on the AI market

ExperTelligence
559 San Ysidro Rd.
Santa Barbara, CA 93108
(805) 969-7874
Contact: Denison Bollay

LISP and expert systems development for the Macintosh

Expert Software International, Ltd.
Jeffrey Perrone & Associates, Inc.
3685 17th Street
San Francisco, CA 94114
(415) 431-9562
Contact: Jeffrey Perrone

Expert system building tool

Expert Systems, Ltd.
Expert Systems International
1150 First Avenue
King of Prussia, PA 19406
(215) 337-2300
Contact: Angelos T. Kolokouris

Expert system building tool and PROLOG

Fairchild Camera & Instrument Corp.
Lab for Artificial Intelligence Research
4001 Miranda Ave.
Palo Alto, CA 94304
(415) 858-4273
Contact: Ron Brachman

Internal expert systems development

FMC Corp.
Artificial Intelligence Center
Central Engineering Lab.
1185 Coleman Ave.
Santa Clara, CA 95052

AI research and development

Franz Inc.
6321 Thornhill Drive
Oakland, CA 94611
(415) 339-1481

Sell FranzLISP for a variety of machines

General Electric Company
Research and Development Center
P. O. Box 8
Schenectady, NY 12301

Extensive research in AI and in expert systems

General Motors Research Labs
Computer Science Department
Warren, MI 48090
Contact: Carole Hafner

Expanding AI group includes natural language, expert systems, robot planning systems, and intelligent CAI

General Research Corp.
Artificial Intelligence Lab
5383 Hollister Ave.
P. O. Box 6770
Santa Barbara, CA 93160-6770

Sales and Marketing

7655 Old Springhouse Road
McLean, VA 22102
(703) 893-5900
Contact: Wanda Rappaport

Expert system building tools

Gold Hill Computers, Inc.
163 Harvard Street
Cambridge, MA 02139
(617) 492-2071

LISP software and training for the IBM PC

GTE Laboratories Inc.
Box A, 40 Sylvan Road
Waltham, MA 02254
Contact: Cynthia Farrar

Expanding AI group includes expert systems, natural language, machine learning, and advanced prototype system development

Harmon Associates
3752 Sixteenth Street
San Francisco, CA 94114
(415) 861-1660
Contact: Paul Harmon

Training and consulting regarding the use of small expert systems in business environments

Hewlett-Packard
3000 Hanover Street
Palo Alto, CA 94304
(415) 857-5069

Expert systems for internal use

Honeywell
MN17-2349
2600 Ridgway Parkway
Minneapolis, MN 55413
(612) 378-5502

Hardware and expert systems for internal use

IBM
Old Orchard Road
Armonk, NY 10504
(914) 945-3067
Contact: Jim Griesmer

Hardware, software (LISP and PROLOG), and systems for internal use

IBM
Expert Systems Project
Palo Alto Scientific Center
1530 Page Mill Road
Palo Alto, CA 94304
(415) 855-3117
Contact: Peter M. Hirsch

Expert systems research

Inference Corp
5300 W. Century Blvd., Suite 501
Los Angeles, CA 90045
(213) 417-7997

Expert system building tools and consulting

Integral Quality
P.O. Box 31970
Seattle, WA 98103
(206) 527-2918

LISP software for the IBM PC

IntelliCorp
707 Laurel Street
Menlo Park, CA 94025-3445
(415) 323-8300
Contact: Sara Hedberg

Expert system building tools, consulting, generic software, and specialized workstations for medical applications

Intelligent Computer Systems Research Institute (ICS)
Applied Artificial Intelligence Reporter
P. O. Box 248235
Coral Gables, FL 33124

Periodic reports on the state of AI for business interests

Kestrel Institute
1801 Page Mill Road
Palo Alto, CA 94304
(415) 494-2233
Contact: Cordell Green

Natural language systems and consulting

Level 5 Research
4980 S A 1 A
Melbourne Beach, FL 32951
(305) 729-9046
Contact: Henry Seiler

Expert system building tools and consulting

LISP Machine Inc.
6033 W. Century Blvd., Suite 900
Los Angeles, CA 90045
(213) 642-1116

LISP machines and related software

Logicware Inc.
1000 Finch Ave. West
Toronto, Ontario M3J 2V5
CANADA
(416) 665-0022
Contact: R. von Konigslow

PROLOG language and environment and expert systems consulting

Martin Marietta Denver Aerospace
P. O. Box 179
Denver, CO 80201
Contact: Jim Lowrie

Expert systems research for internal projects

PERQ Systems Corp.
2600 Liberty Ave.
P. O. Box 2600
Pittsburgh, PA 15230
(412) 355-0900

AI hardware

Quintus Computer Systems, Inc.
2345 Yale
Palo Alto, CA 94306

PROLOG software

Radian Corp.
8501 Mo-Pac Blvd.
P. O. Box 9948
Austin, TX 78766
(512) 454-4797

Expert system building tool

RAND Corp.
1700 Main Street
Santa Monica, CA 90406
(213) 393-0411

Expert systems and expert systems building tool research

Rohm and Haas Co.
Computer Application Research
727 Norristown Road
Spring House, PA 19477
(215) 641-7000
Contact: Bruce Hohne or Thomas Pierce

Expert systems for chemical formulations and natural language interfaces for those systems

Schlumberger
Schlumerger-Doll Research
P. O. Box 307
Old Quarry Road
Ridgefield, CT 06877
(203) 438-2631

Extensive research in AI, including the development of expert systems for internal use

Scientific DataLink
850 Third Ave.
New York, NY 10022
(212) 838-7200
Contact: Chia Reinhard

Microfiche sets of AI technical reports from the major AI research centers

Smart Systems Technology
Suite 421 North
7700 Leesburg Pike
Falls Church, VA 22043
(703) 448-8562
Contact: Eamon Barrett

Training programs, expert systems software, and consulting

Software Architecture & Engineering
1500 Wilson Blvd., Suite 800
Arlington, VA 22209
(703) 276-7910
Contact: Andrew Ferrentino

Expert system building tools and consulting

SRI International
333 Ravenswood Ave.
Menlo Park, CA 94025
(415) 859-2464
Contact: Luis Fried

AI research and consulting, expert system building tools and systems

Standard Oil Company (SOHIO)
1424 Midland Building, 640 AI
Cleveland, OH 44115

AI research and development

Symbolics, Inc.
4 Cambridge Center
Cambridge, MA 02142
(617) 576-1043
Contact: Robert D. Stone

LISP machines and associated software

Syntelligence
1000 Hamlin Court
P. O. Box 3620
Sunnyvale, CA 94088
(408) 745-6666
Contact: Steve Weyl

Consulting and custom expert systems development
for financial institutions

Teknowledge Inc.
525 University Ave.
Palo Alto, CA 94301
(415) 327-6600
Contact: Kurt Joerger

Contracting, expert system building tools, and packaged training programs

Tektronix
Knowledge-Based Systems Group
P. O. Box 1000
Delivery Station 63-393
Wilsonville, OR 97070
(503) 685-3670
Contact: Mike Taylor

Hardware, software, and expert systems development
for internal use

Texas Instruments
12501 Research Blvd., MS 2223
Austin, TX 78769
(512) 250-7533
Contact: Daryl Robertson

P. O. Box 809063
Dallas, TX 75380
1-800-527-3500

LISP machines and other hardware, expert systems
building tools, expert systems research for internal
use

3M
3M Center (Building 224-IW)
St. Paul, MN 55144

AI research and development

United Technologies Research Center
Silver Lane
East Hartford, CT 06108
Contact: M. C. Marcin

AI research and development

Verac Inc.
P. O. Box 26669, Dept. 418
San Diego, CA 92126-0669

AI research and expert system building environments

Xerox Corp.
PARC (Palo Alto Research Center)
3333 Coyote Hill Road
Palo Alto, CA 94304
(415) 494-4000

Marketing: Xerox SIS

250 North Halstead Street
P. O. Box 7018
Pasadena, CA 91109
(818) 351-2351

LISP machines and software, expert systems building
tools, and research in expert systems

Appendix C

References

This annotated list of references is not intended to be comprehensive. Instead, we have tried to indicate the most important and most readily available sources that you should consider if you wish to learn more about the topics discussed in any chapter of this book. In most cases we have cited books because, even though they tend to be less current than magazine articles, they tend to be more readily available. Except in rare cases we have avoided journal articles and monographs. Articles cited in the text are included in this list of references.

Chapter 1. Introduction

Davis, R. "Amplifying Expertise with Expert Systems." In *The AI Business: The Commercial Uses of Artificial Intelligence,* edited by P. H. Winston and K. A. Prendergast. Cambridge, MA: The MIT Press, 1984.

Hayes-Roth, F. "Knowledge-Based Expert Systems: The Technological and Commercial State of the Art." *Computer,* Aug. 1984.

Hodges, Andrew. *Turing, The Enigma.* New York: Simon and Schuster, 1983.

Kolbus, David L. and Mazzetti, Claudia C. *Artificial Intelligence Emerges,* Research Report 673. Menlo Park, CA: SRI International, Nov. 1982.

McCorduck, P. *Machines Who Think.* San Francisco: Freeman, 1979.

Reitman, Walter, ed. *Artificial Intelligence Applications for Business.* Norwood, NJ: Ablex Publishing Corp., 1984.

Chapter 2. MYCIN and Chapter 6. MYCIN Revisited

Buchanan, B. G., and Shortliffe, E. H. *Rule-Based Expert Systems: The MYCIN Experiments of the Stanford Heuristic Programming Project.* Reading, MA: Addison-Wesley Publishing Company, 1984.

This is the summary monograph describing the MYCIN system and its derivatives. It presents the MYCIN system and explains why each element was designed. This is the place to look for a thorough presentation of confidence factors, for example, or for a complete presentation of the MYCIN evaluation.

Read this book for a deeper understanding of MYCIN and MYCIN-inspired systems.

Clancey, B. C., and Shortliffe, E. H., eds. *Readings in Medical Artificial Intelligence: The First Decade.* Reading, MA: Addison-Wesley Publishing Company, 1984.

This book places the MYCIN experiments in context by providing reports on other major medical knowledge systems.

Read this book for insight into knowledge system applications in medicine.

Davis, R. and Lenat, D. B. *Knowledge-Based Systems in Artificial Intelligence,* New York: McGraw-Hill, 1982.

This book is divided into two parts, one by each of the two authors. The second part by Randall Davis is on "Teiresias: Applications of Meta-Level Knowledge" and describes Davis's doctoral research during which he modified MYCIN to incorporate the explanation and knowledge acquisition facilities that he termed "Teiresias."

Read this book to obtain a detailed understanding of the problems involved in developing MYCIN-type user interfaces.

Chapter 3. Human Problem Solving

Boden, M. *Artificial Intelligence and Natural Man.* New York: Basic Books, 1977.

Boden's view of artificial intelligence is from the perspective of a philosopher. She is more concerned than most with the psychological and philosophical underpinnings of AI and less concerned with implementations.

Read this book for perspective.

Card, S. K., Moran, T. P., and Newell, A. *The Psychology of Human-Computer Interaction.* Hillsdale, NJ: Lawrence Erlbaum Associates, Inc., 1981.

This book provides the reader with a detailed discussion of the characteristics of the human information processing system that a designer should consider when designing a human-computer interface. The same analysis is applied to several human-computer interaction problems to show how errors can be predicted and eliminated.

Collins, A., and Quillian, M. R. "Retrieval Time from Semantic Memory." *Journal of Verbal Learning & Verbal Behavior* 8 (1969): 240–247.

Hofstadter, D. R. *Godel, Escher, Bach: An Eternal Golden Braid.* New York: Basic Books, 1979.

Godel, Escher, Bach is a Pulitzer Prize-winning book due to its excellent and novel explorations of number theory fundamentals. Along the way a good amount of computer science topics are covered, always in an amusing manner.

Read this book for the joy of it. You will gain an appreciation of computers as symbol processors, see examples of recursive programs (and music and drawings), and encounter delightful dialogues between Achilles and the Tortoise.

Lindsay, Peter H., and Norman, Donald A. *Human Information Processing: An Introduction to Psychology.* New York: Academic Press, 1972.

This is an excellent basic introduction to all of the important concepts involved in human information processing.

Newell, A., and Simon, H. *Human Problem Solving.* Englewood Cliffs, NJ: Prentice-Hall, 1972.

This is the classic book on human problem solving. It was this book that advanced the idea that production systems could be used to model human problem-solving activities.

Polya, G. *How to Solve It: A New Aspect of Mathematical Method.* Princeton, NJ: Princeton University Press, 1957.

———. *Mathematics and Plausible Reasoning.* 2 vols. Princeton, NJ: Princeton University Press, 1954.

It was George Polya who, when studying the behavior of his fellow mathematicians, noted that the use of heuristics was the key to discovery. Mathematicians ordinarily discover a new relationship by trying out an idea that seems plausible. Later they provide formal proofs that the idea is correct. The proofs, however, conceal the methods that were used for discovery.

Read these books to gain a deeper understanding of human problem-solving behavior.

Schon, Donald A. *The Reflective Practitioner: How Professionals Think in Action.* New York: Basic Books, 1983.

Simon, H. A. *The Sciences of the Artificial.* Cambridge, MA: The MIT Press, 1969.

Simon's collection of essays traces the emergence of several key themes pertaining to human problem solving. One theme is that humans satisfice rather than optimize. They do so by employing rules-of-thumb that provide acceptable solutions to problems.

Read this book to trace the emergence of heuristics as the source of human's cognitive abilities.

Sternberg, R. J., ed. *Handbook of Human Intelligence.* New York: Cambridge University Press, 1982.

Sternberg's book is an excellent collection of research and theory about human abilities. This volume is a rich index to research on all facets of intelligence—its development, measurement, and evolution. One chapter, "Artificial and Human Intelligence" by Natalie Dehn and Roger Schank, is particularly relevant.

Read this book to explore human information processing.

Chapter 4. Representing Knowledge and Chapter 5. Drawing Inferences

Barr, A., Cohen, P. R., and Feigenbaum, E. A., eds. *The Handbook of Artificial Intelligence,* volumes 1 and 2, and Cohen, P. R., and Feigenbaum, E. A., volume 3. Los Altos, CA: William Kaufmann, Inc., 1981.

The *Handbook* is currently the most authoritative overview of the history and present status of artificial intelligence research. The volumes reflect the many perspectives of the numerous collaborating authors.

The *Handbook* is an excellent encyclopedia of the field but is difficult to use as a textbook. You are cautioned to read lightly and selectively. The outline provided on the endpapers of the volumes provides an excellent map to the contents within.

Read this book when you need to locate details about one of the early systems, a technique, the usage of a term, or research identified by investigator.

Nilsson, N. J. *Principles of Artificial Intelligence.* Palo Alto, CA: Tioga Press, 1980.

Reddy, D. R., Erman, L. D., Fennell, R. D., and Neely, R. B. "The HEARSAY Speech Understanding System: An Example of the Recognition Process." *IJCAI-3,* 185–193.

The BLACKBOARD architecture originated with the HEARSAY project.

Rich, E. *Artificial Intelligence.* New York: McGraw-Hill, 1983.

Rich's text is a well-rounded view of artificial intelligence techniques and accomplishments. Rich handles each of the representation and inference topics we have introduced in greater depth. In addition, her book covers AI generally; our goal is to center on techniques for building knowledge systems.

Read this book to make a second pass through the basics of knowledge systems, and to broaden your understanding of artificial intelligence.

Weizenbaum, J. *Computer Power and Human Reason: From Judgment to Calculation.* San Francisco, CA: W. H. Freeman and Company, 1976.

Weizenbaum's book is a cynical response to the early claims made by researchers in artificial intelligence. He is convinced that the claims are exaggerated and unreachable.

Read this book to temper your enthusiasm and to challenge and test the enthusiasm of other authors.

Winston, P. H. *Artificial Intelligence.* 2d ed. Reading, MA: Addison-Wesley Publishing Company, 1984.

Winston's book is a classic introduction to the field of artificial intelligence. In its second edition, Winston's text emphasizes representational strategies, especially those developed to encode information about spatial relationships.

Chapter 7. Languages and Tools

Charniak, E., Riesbeck, C. K., and McDermott, D. V. *Artificial Intelligence Programming.* Hillsdale, NJ: Lawrence Erlbaum Associates, Inc., 1980.

This book focuses on the new languages and programming styles that have emerged to support symbolic programming. The focal language is LISP.

Clocksin, W. F., and Mellish, C. S. *Programming in Prolog.* Berlin, West Germany: Springer-Verlag, 1981.

de Kleer, Johan. "Book Review: E. A. Feigenbaum and P. McCorduck, *The Fifth Generation.*" *Artificial Intelligence: An International Journal* 22(1984):225.

Friedman, Daniel P. *The Little Lisper.* Chicago: Science Research Associates, Inc., 1974.

Goldberg, A., and Robson, D. *Smalltalk-80: The Language and Its Implementation.* Reading, MA: Addison-Wesley Publishing Company, 1983.

Kowalski, R. *Logic for Problem Solving.* New York: North-Holland, 1979.

Kunz, J. C., Kehler, T. P., and Williams, M. D. "Applications Development Using a Hybrid AI Development System." *AI Magazine,* 5 (3), (1984).

McCarthy, J. "History of LISP." *SIGPLAN Notices,* 13: 217–223. Reprinted in *The Handbook of Artificial Intelligence,* vol. 2, p. 15.

O'Shea, Tim, and Eisenstadt, Marc, eds. *Artificial Intelligence.* New York: Harper & Row, Publishers, 1984.

Teitelman, W. *INTERLISP Reference Manual.* Palo Alto, CA: Xerox Palo Alto Research Center, 1978.

Winston, P. H., and Horn, B.K.P. *LISP.* Reading, MA: Addison-Wesley Publishing Company, Inc., 1981.

Chapter 8. Commercial Tools

Forgy, C., and McDermott, J. "OPS: A Domain-Independent Production System Language." *IJCAI-5,* 933–939.

Hayes-Roth, F., Lenat, D. B., and Waterman, D. A., eds. *Building Expert Systems.* Reading, MA: Addison-Wesley Publishing Company, 1983.

Kunz, J. C., Kehler, T. P., and Williams, M. D. "Applications Development Using a Hybrid AI Development System." *AI Magazine,* 5 (3), 1984.

This article describes applications of the hybrid tool called KEE.

Stefik, M., Bobrow, D. G., Mittal, S., and Conway, L. "Knowledge Programming in LOOPS: Report on an Experimental Course." *AI Magazine,* 4 (3), 1983.

This article discusses the LOOPS programming environment and a particularly interesting teaching program called TRUCKIN'.

Weiss, S., and Kulikowski, C. *A Practical Guide to Designing Expert Systems.* Totowa, NJ: Rowman & Allanheld, Publishers, 1984.

The tool called EXPERT is discussed in this excellent book on knowledge system building.

Chapter 9. Early Systems

Aikins, J. S., Kunz, J. C., Shortliffe, E. H., and Fallat, R. J. "PUFF: An Expert System for Interpretation of Pulmonary Function Data." In *Readings in Medical Artificial Intelligence: The First Decade,* edited by B. C. Clancey and E. H. Shortliffe. Reading, MA: Addison-Wesley Publishing Company, 1984.

Barr, A., Cohen, P. R., and Feigenbaum, E. A., eds. *The Handbook of Artificial Intelligence,* volumes 1 and 2, and Cohen, P. R., and Feigenbaum, E. A., volume 3. Los Altos, CA: William Kaufmann, Inc., 1981.

Duda, Richard O., and Reboh, Rene. "AI and Decision Making: The PROSPECTOR Experience." In *Artificial Intelligence Applications for Business,* edited by Walter Reitman. Norwood, NJ: Ablex Publishing Corp., 1984.

Lindsay, R. K., Buchanan, B. G., Feigenbaum, E. A., and Lederberg, J. *Applications of Artificial Intelligence for Chemical Inference: The DENDRAL Project.* New York: McGraw-Hill, 1980.

Pople, Harry E., Jr. "Heuristic Methods for Imposing Structure on Ill-Structured Problems: The Structuring of Medical Diagnostics," (Chapter 5) in *Artificial Intelligence in Medicine* (AAAS Selected Symposium 51), edited by Peter Szolovits. Boulder, CO: Westview Press, 1982.

Chapter 10. Recent Systems

Bachant, J., and McDermott, J. "R1 Revisited: Four Years in the Trenches." *AI Magazine* 5 (3), 1984.

Kraft, A. "XCON: An Expert Configuration System at Digital Equipment Corporation." In *The AI Business: The Commercial Uses of Artificial Intelligence,* edited by P. H. Winston and K. A. Prendergast. Cambridge, MA: The MIT Press, 1984.

McDermott, J. "R1: The Formative Years." *AI Magazine* 2 (2), 1981.

Weiss, S., and Kulikowski, C. *A Practical Guide to Designing Expert Systems.* Totowa, NJ: Rowman & Allanheld, Publishers, 1984.

The Microprocessor-Based Electrophoresis Interpreter is discussed in this book.

Chapter 11. Building a Small Knowledge System

Tosti, Donald T., and Ball, John R. "A Behavioral Approach to Instructional Design and Media Selection," *AV Communication Review* 17, no. 1 (Spring 1969): 5–25.

Chapter 12. How Large Knowledge Systems Are Developed

Hayes-Roth, F., Lenat, D. B., and Waterman, D. A., eds. *Building Expert Systems.* Reading, MA: Addison-Wesley Publishing Company, 1983.

In a field where discussions of methodology are difficult to locate, *Building Expert Systems* is a rare find. The book grew from a conference where the developers of several knowledge tools met to discuss how systems are built. A common problem was posed, and teams sketched the approach taken by each tool. The resulting descriptions help readers to understand how difficult and tentative the task of building a system is.

Read this book for insight into how systems are planned and prototyped. In addition, some cross-tool comparisons are possible.

Weiss, S., and Kulikowski, C. *A Practical Guide to Designing Expert Systems.* Totowa, NJ: Rowman & Allanheld, Publishers, 1984.

The tool called EXPERT is discussed in this excellent book on knowledge system building.

Chapter 13. The Market for Knowledge Engineering

Austin, Howard. "Market Trends in Artificial Intelligence." In *Artificial Intelligence Applications for Business,* edited by Walter Reitman. Norwood, NJ: Ablex Publishing Corp., 1984.

Feigenbaum, E. A., and McCorduck, P. *The Fifth Generation.* Reading, MA: Addison-Wesley Publishing Company, 1983.

This provocative book describes the international competition to dominate applied artificial intelligence. Feigenbaum, a senior scientist, and McCorduck, a science writer, teamed up to communicate concern that Americans were not paying sufficient attention to the potential of the Fifth Generation, nor were sufficient funds dedicated to maintaining America's lead in the field.

Read this book to learn about one view of the near future.

Hayes, J. E., and Michie, D., eds. *Intelligent Systems: The Unprecedented Opportunity.* New York: Halsted Press, 1983.

O'Connor, Dennis E. "Using Expert Systems to Manage Change and Complexity in Manufacturing." In *Artificial Intelligence Applications for Business,* edited by Walter Reitman. Norwood, NJ: Ablex Publishing Corp., 1984.

Simons, G. L. *Toward Fifth-Generation Computers.* Manchester, England: NCC Publications, 1983.

An excellent overview of the Japanese efforts to construct super computers and some information on the responses of the other industrial nations.

Winston, P. H., and Prendergast, K. A., eds. *The AI Business: The Commercial Uses of Artificial Intelligence.* Cambridge, MA: The MIT Press, 1984.

Chapter 14. Knowledge Systems in the Next Five Years

Davis, R. "Expert Systems: Where are We? And Where Do We Go from Here?" *AI Magazine* 2, 1982.

Michalski, R. S., Carbonell, J., and Mitchell, T. M., eds. *Machine Learning: An Artificial Intelligence Approach.* Palo Alto, CA: Tioga Press, 1983.

Winston, P. H. and Prendergast, K. A., eds. *The AI*

Business: The Commercial Uses of Artificial Intelligence, Cambridge, MA: The MIT Press, 1984.

Chapter 15. Expert Systems for Training

Aikins, J. S., Kunz, J. C., Shortliffe, E. H., and Fallat, R. J. "PUFF: An Expert System for Interpretation of Pulmonary Function Data." In *Readings in Medical Artificial Intelligence: The First Decade,* edited by B. C. Clancey and E. H. Shortliffe. Reading, MA: Addison-Wesley Publishing Company, 1984.

Arons, A. B. "Computer-based Instructional Dialogues in Science Courses." *Science,* vol. 224, no. 4653, 8 June 1984.

Bailey, Robert W. *Human Performance Engineering: A Guide for System Designers.* Englewood Cliffs, NJ, 1982.

Brown, J. S. "The Low Road, the Middle Road, and the High Road." In *The AI Business: The Commercial Uses of Artificial Intelligence,* edited by P. H. Winston and K. A. Prendergast. Cambridge, MA: The MIT Press, 1984.

Clancey, W. J. "The Use of MYCIN's Rules for Tutoring." In *Rule-Based Expert Systems: The MYCIN Experiments of the Stanford Heuristic Programming Project,* edited by B. G. Buchanan and E. H. Shortliffe. Reading, MA: Addison-Wesley Publishing Company, 1984.

Gilbert, Thomas F. *Human Competence.* New York: McGraw-Hill, 1978.

Harmon, Paul. "The Design of Instructional Materials: A Top-Down Approach." *Journal of Instructional Development* 6, no. 1, Fall 1982.

Hollan, James D., Hutchins, Edwin L., and Weitzman, Louis. "Steamer: An Interactive Inspectable Simulation-Based Training System." *The AI Magazine,* Summer 1984.

Sheil, B. "Power Tools for Programmers." *Datamation,* February 1983.

Sleeman, D., and Brown, J. S., eds. *Intelligent Tutoring Systems.* New York: Academic Press, 1982.
    This volume is a collection spanning virtually all the work in Intelligent Tutoring Systems and Intelligence Computer Assisted Instruction (ICAI) prior to 1981. It gathers together research reports which otherwise can be difficult to assemble. Included are chapters on GUIDON (Clancey on a teaching system for MYCIN), BUGGY (Burton and Brown on a system for detecting consistent arithmetic errors), SOPHIE (Brown, Burton, and de Kleer on a tutor for electronic troubleshooting), and LMS (Sleeman on a system for modelling errors in performing algebraic tasks).

Index

Page references in boldface type indicate the location of key definitions or examples.

Page references in italic indicate the location of a figure or table that illustrates the concept or the relation of the concept to other concepts.